THE PROBLEM
OF A CHINESE
AESTHETIC

M E R I D I A N

Crossing Aesthetics

Werner Hamacher

& David E. Wellbery

Editors

*Stanford
University
Press*

———————

*Stanford
California
1993*

THE PROBLEM
OF A CHINESE
AESTHETIC

Haun Saussy

Stanford University Press
Stanford, California

© 1993 by the Board of Trustees
of the Leland Stanford Junior University

Printed in the United States of America

CIP data are at the end of the book

To J.F.N.H.C.,
who did not get to see it finished,

to Y.W.S.,
who already knows it by heart,

and to J.L.N.S.,
who has not yet learned to read,

this book is fondly dedicated.

My children, why do you not study the *Book of Poetry*? The *Odes* serve to stimulate the mind. They may be used for purposes of self-contemplation. They teach the art of sociability. They show how to regulate feelings of resentment. From them you learn the more immediate duty of serving one's father, and the remoter one of serving one's prince. From them we become largely acquainted with the names of birds, beasts and plants.

—Confucius, *Analects* 17.9 (trans. Legge)

Knowledge is defined more broadly still, inasmuch as we find it already in the Ideas or Terms before we come to Propositions or Truths. And we may hold that one who has examined more images of plants and animals than another, seen more figures of machines, more descriptions or representations of houses or fortresses, who has read a greater number of ingenious romances and heard more curious tales—such a one, I say, will have more knowledge than another, even supposing that there is not a word of truth in anything he has heard or seen depicted.

—Leibniz, *Nouveaux essais* IV.i

Acknowledgments

Part of this book was submitted as a doctoral dissertation to the Department of Comparative Literature at Yale University. In all its forms it has owed much to the advice and patience of my advisors, Professors Kang-i Sun Chang and Geoffrey Hartman. I am also indebted to Susan Willey Blood, Roger Blood, Hung-hsiang Chou, John Delogu, Charles Egan, Lothar von Falkenhausen, Paul Farmer, David Ferris, Debra Keates, Pauline Lin, William Nienhauser, Stephen Owen, Leslie Pincus, Suzanne Roos, Brian Roots, Michael Shae, Justine Stillings, James B. Swenson, Jr., and Deborah White for reading or hearing parts of the manuscript and making helpful comments along the way. I am grateful to have been exposed, however briefly, to the late Paul de Man's teaching. The members of my dissertation committee, Cathy Caruth, Marston Anderson, and Michael Holquist, made many valuable suggestions, as did an anonymous reader for Stanford University Press. Helen Tartar, as editor, supplied encouragement and skepticism as either was needed. I am also grateful to John Ziemer, whose zeal for accuracy, consistency, and clarity greatly improved the manuscript. For the mistakes I have only myself to thank.

Patricia de Man has graciously consented to let me quote from unpublished writings of her husband. Professor Hans Frankel lent me books and made possible various personal contacts. Professor Benson Mates supplied a copy of an exceedingly scarce piece of

Leibnitiana. Professors Kurt Rainer Meist of the Hegel-Archiv in Bochum and Zhang Longxi of the University of California at Riverside answered questions and are permitting me to quote from their letters here. Professors Arnold Band and Peter Lee gave me a chance to talk to the departments of Comparative Literature and East Asian Languages and Literatures, respectively, of the University of California at Los Angeles. It has been a privilege to have them as colleagues and department chairs. Charles Hartman (of the State University of New York at Albany) kindly encouraged me to present part of my argument as an informal lecture to the East Coast Chinese Poetry Group, and Ronald Egan of the University of California at Santa Barbara invited me to discuss another part with the nascent West Coast Chinese Poetry Group. The late Professor Dr. Albert Heinekamp, Director of the Leibniz-Archiv at the Niedersächsische Landesbibliothek, Hannover, kindly showed me how to make the most of the Archive's collections. Dr. Helmut Schneider of the Bochum Hegel-Archiv helped me locate the existing sources for Hegel's early lectures on history. I thank the manuscripts department of the Preussischer Kulturbesitz in Berlin for allowing me to examine rare Hegel materials, and the Academic Senate of the University of California for travel and research funds. Thanks are also due to the Center for Chinese Studies at UCLA, for providing a grant in aid.

Years ago, a piece of polite counsel from André Martinet helped to establish the necessary conditions for this book ("If it's compound words that interest you, maybe you should study Chinese"). Julia Fay Chalfant gave sagely advice and kept after me to finish it. Wang Yü-lin gracefully endured three years of more or less constant variations around one subject, for which she has, as always, my admiration.

H.S.

Contents

Note on Transcription
and Abbreviations

The Wade-Giles transliteration system for Chinese words is used here (and quoted text silently revised in keeping with it) except in the case of names of authors who publish in English and have their own preferred spelling. Unless otherwise noted, all translations are my own.

Works for which a chapter-and-verse or paragraphing reference is generally accepted (e.g., the *Analects* of Confucius or Plato's dialogues) are noted in that form, and specific editions are cited only when necessary. The following abbreviations are used in the Notes and Bibliography:

BIHP	*Bulletin of the Institute of History and Philology* (Academia Sinica, Nankang, Taiwan)
BMFEA	*Bulletin of the Museum of Far Eastern Antiquities* (Stockholm)
ch.	*chüan* ("volume" of a Chinese book)
CLEAR	*Chinese Literature: Essays, Articles, Reviews*
HJAS	*Harvard Journal of Asiatic Studies*
LH	Leibniz mss held in the Niedersächsische Landesbibliothek, Hannover; as catalogued by Eduard Bodemann
Li	*Li chi chu-shu* (*SSCCS* ed.)
LSJ	Henry G. Liddell, Robert Scott, and Henry S. Jones, *A Greek-English Lexicon*

MEGA	Karl Marx and Friedrich Engels, *Marx-Engels Gesamtausgabe*
OED	*Oxford English Dictionary*
Shih	*Mao Shih chu-shu* (*SSCCS* ed.)
Shu	*Shang Shu chu-shu* (*SSCCS* ed.)
SKCS	Ssu-k'u ch'üan-shu
SPPY	Ssu-pu pei-yao
SPTK	Ssu-pu ts'ung-k'an
SMSCS	Ch'en Huan, ed., *Shih Mao shih chuan shu*
SSCCS	Juan Yüan, ed., *Shih-san ching chu-shu*
Tso	*Ch'un-ch'iu Tso chuan chu-shu* (*SSCCS* ed.)
W	Hegel, *Werke in zwanzig Bänden*

THE PROBLEM
OF A CHINESE
AESTHETIC

Introduction

Kant's assistant, a theology student who was at a
loss as to how to unite philosophy with theology,
once asked Kant what books he should consult.
KANT: Read travel descriptions!
ASSISTANT: There are sections of Dogmatics that
I don't understand . . .
KANT: Read travel descriptions!
—Walter Benjamin

The book that follows is a hybrid, and not just in its choice of
subjects. It started as a study of a few definite questions in Chinese
poetics and could not be kept from spreading into the territory of
big general problems. I hope it may be a telescope useful to people
who come to it from either end.

The key word, if there can be only one, in this book's title should
be "problem." Why so? The book presents the results of several
years' experiments with translation, and translation is nothing but
problems.[1] Sometimes in the course of this book I translate texts;
elsewhere I try to translate (or to weigh the possibility of translating) implicit systems of concepts; and here and there, faced with a
dilemma, I have to admit impediment. We who translate tend to
talk less about successes and more about trade-offs, and our modesty is usually justified. If a translation is a trading post, it is one in
which "the most precious and the lowliest wares do not always lie
far apart from one another—they mingle in our eyes, and often,
too, we catch sight of the bottles, boxes, and sacks in which they
were transported."[2] The piling-up of disposable externals (synonyms, glosses, footnotes, parenthetical remarks) marks a translator who is honest or confused, or both, for although it is good to
know what is essential and what is incidental, the translator who is
also a diligent reader may be of several minds about that question
and prefer, when possible, to save the original wrappings.

I

What of the essentials of my book and the translating it tries to do can be called new? Some old methods are taken to new lengths, and some familiar texts are juxtaposed in new ways. The book's continuous argument, as it appears here and there in the studies composing it, pits the analytic methods of rhetoric against, first, the synoptic unity of a definite culture; second, a set of historical narratives forming the basis of the synoptic view; and finally, a categorical, that is, a philosophical, formulation of historical problems. If rhetoric outlives these many tests and trudges on toward the finish, the story brings about, not just rhetoric's triumph, but its education: surviving the tests means learning new rules at every stage.

To emphasize the discontinuous and the topical, the book consists of chapters on the theory of allegory today as compared to the practice of translation by seventeenth-century Jesuit missionaries to China and by one of their correspondents, Leibniz; on the history of the Chinese *Book of Odes* and its interpretative tradition (sometimes called allegorical); on the allegorical program of the *Odes* as I reconstruct it, half historically and half through rhetorical analyses; and on the place of China (no small place, but that needs showing) in Hegel's efforts to write and teach world history.

I offer new conclusions, or new arrangements of old hypotheses, on the nature of figures of speech in ancient Chinese poetry and on the relation of aesthetic thinking and practice to other kinds of action to which the aesthetic realm is sometimes, in certain moods of certain traditions at certain moments, contrasted. My colleagues in Chinese literature may be alarmed at my determination to make literary theory out of historical documents or wish I had spread some of those documents out for a period-by-period analysis instead of bunching them together as alternative positions; those whose main engagements are with literary theory may wonder at my failure to declare a theory of my own and feed it on a good diet of Chinese texts. I have no good answer to these objections. The choice of a comparative subject is always debatable. One penny flipped fifty times gives the same results as fifty pennies flipped once; would that comparative literature were so simple a field that the extension of its problems made up a variation, and not a check, on their depth!

Since I prize the business of getting to conclusions more highly than I do most conclusions, I try to let the how-questions take precedence over the what-questions. As a rule, I try to resolve problems of literary history and comparative literature by what is called (always unattainably) close reading. Not that my reading is closer than anybody else's, or that I use the method with exceptional purity; but I try to give reading the last word, especially where the problems I face would seem to lend themselves to other styles of interpretation. The comparative side of the job has been made easier, if that is the right word, by the fact that the Chinese corpus I start with has always been seen as a thicket of interpretative puzzles.

∼

At one end of the scale, then, the book handles philological problems in the reception of a lyric anthology; at the other, it heads toward the horizon of a universal human history (that discredited project), how it is to be written and understood. It is therefore about—it is a sample of—cultural relations that are apt to seem strained in some readers' eyes. "The Western image of China," as a questioner at an early presentation of part of this work put it, seems to be a subject entirely different from the present-day researcher's good-faith effort to understand the Chinese themselves. The contemporary use of the word "image" supposes this. What Hegel *knew* about China is not much more than Plato knew about Egypt or, some might insinuate, Atlantis. Is not the project, then, built around a coincidence, the occurrence in unrelated texts of a handful of proper names, or better yet a noncoincidence, a mistaken identity? To call on Goethe the translator again, "just as a metaphor, carried too far, begins to stumble, so a comparative judgment becomes less acceptable, the farther it is carried."[3] What if the trick of calling Hegel's China and the China of his contemporary Ch'en Huan "China" were just one of those metaphors, less acceptable the more sense we try to wring from it?

This book's various chapters have their common object not in a real but in an ideal or scriptural context, the China constructed (and then interpreted) by those various witnesses. This sounds agnostic, but the antiquity of one of the book's main subjects permits "construction" to be read in a sense more literal than modish. The compilers of the *Book of Odes*, the authors of the *Book of Documents*, and so forth created, in the same measure as Homer and Hesiod, the nation they celebrated, and in that sense they are not at all unlike Hegel trying to derive the concept of China from a speculative world-historical logic or Leibniz hoping to establish, through a kind of pun, the mutual tolerance of Catholic theology and Chinese physics. In Chapters 3 and 4 I push the idea of "construction" a little harder and find reasons for believing that the invention of China and the invention of Chinese poetic language are not only roughly contemporary but also related events.

China has always been, is always still, in the process of being invented; but does one invent it in whatever way one pleases? "China" names a country, of course, but it more accurately names an international culture; and "culture" is the identity-tag of a question having, these days in North America at least, a moral as well as an epistemological side. Cultures are—to paraphrase a received wisdom—spheres independent of one another, systems of standards that are not to be judged by other systems of standards, all such systems being, in any case, endowed with equal rights to existence (and rights no more than equal: to privilege one over the others is to risk being accused of cultural tunnel vision, a form of moral blindness). Knowing about cultures is a virtue and a way to virtue. For the crusading arm of the academy—and I am hardly in a position to count myself out of it—this way of putting things is now part of the all-purpose justification for the continued existence of the humanities, a stump speech it is unfortunately always necessary to go on making.

Accepting this definition of culture as the genus to which China belongs shapes one's own work and the public's probable response to it. Thanks to the intercession of other cultures, says Tzvetan Todorov, "I read myself between quotation marks."[4] In classrooms, courtrooms, and myriad places in between, what Emile Durkheim said some eighty years ago of religions (as spokesman for a new university discipline in a newly secular Third Republic) has become applicable to cultures: "Fundamentally, then, there is no such thing as a false religion. Every religion is true in its own way. . . . A religion is a consistent system of beliefs and practices concerned with sacred things ('sacred' meaning separate, forbidden): beliefs and practices that unite in a single moral community, called a 'church,' all those who belong to it."[5] True religions (the only kind) are like unhappy families: each of them true in its own way. As prelude to getting the sociology of religion started, Durkheim's definition makes a clean break between the formal character of being a religion and the content-character of religions. What is automatically true of all religions *qua* examples of religion (the predicate of being true) is also true of none of them singly, or *qua* itself. The content of religious representations is no longer an object of investigation, except as that content is mediated by the new definition of religion. The individual religions' *façons* (manners) of being true then become the sole focus of attention. Indeed it is only as the epithet "true" has been reshaped by that definition that it will continue to have a meaning in the sociology of religion. The researcher who forgets that turns into an apologist, a purveyor of the mere inventory of the subject, for all religions, however eclectic and tolerant, are bound to have propositions they assert as true.

Is the split between religion and religions (or that between the concept of culture and the demands of any particular culture) anything more than a logical taboo, a rule observed by the church of the sociological method? The question is raised by the generic character of Durkheim's definition itself.[6] (An American analogue would be the "establishment of religion" clause of the First Amendment.)[7] Reasons for the taboo are not hard to supply. If the sociological method is just one "religion" among others, then the truth of its conclusions will only be the bracketed, automatic truth of its particular religious style; and if it is to be situated outside and above the religions, it will appear to have gained that status magically, by becoming "sacred, separate, forbidden." Either way, the method would become one of its own objects, one of its own examples.

The ethnology of ethnology is a growing field, and the relativity principle has come in for its share of attention. Just as the establishment clause of the First Amendment would lose its prescriptive power if it were taken as another instance of the behavior it is supposed to govern, so too ethnography, in order to record and preserve the variety of human societies, needs to be able to locate its evidence on an invariant yardstick, a supra-cultural principle hovering above the cultural fray—the definition of "culture" in flush times or "me and what I felt" in more nervous ones.[8] Is anthropology self-consistent? Can its methods maintain their separateness from the realm of examples, or are they fated to end up on the pile of ethnic curiosa too? Anthropology must, but can't, become an example unto itself; and so an empirical discipline becomes a philosophy of reflection. The inconsistency of the discipline is the proof (maybe Pyrrhic) of its will to be consistent.

Here the investigator of literary language finds work to do— more and more work, since we are all anthropologists nowadays. Tics are revealing. Awareness that there is more to world history than we heard about in school and a sense that one ought to do something about all those people, even just acknowledge their existence, leads writers of every persuasion and rank (professors in their *summae* and undergraduates in midterm essays) to say "Western civilization," "Western metaphysics," where a few years ago they might have put "culture" or "philosophy" with no geographic qualifiers. Let us call this a step toward self-knowledge (knowledge of oneself *as a self*) and go on to look at the ways in which this knowledge recognizes its newfound self. No gesture can long go uninterpreted. Is the modifier restrictive or nonrestrictive (as a grammarian might put it)? Are we talking about "civilization, that is, the Western kind," or about "civilization—this thing specific to the West"? The apparent modesty of such phrases (being no spokesman, I can only imagine using them modestly) comes quickly to seem to mean that the author knows something about other varieties of metaphysics, philosophy, and so forth, and wants

to underline a contrast; or knows enough about "Western civilization" to have seen around it and known its limits.[9] That shows
great confidence, at least if "Western civilization" is one's usual
haunt. Is the self the sort of thing that *oneself* can put quotation
marks around?

The question is worth asking, although the practical point of
view may lead to a different answer from the theoretical view. Jean
Seznec and Anthony Grafton have seen the habit of treating the
classical past as a bounded and, above all, foreign object as the
Renaissance scholar's properly epochal, and self-defining, break
with a more recent past.[10] The temptation to talk about self and
other as unambiguous categories neatly sealed off from one another
is especially strong, no doubt for historical reasons, among students
of China. A. C. Graham begins his article " 'Being' in Classical
Chinese" by saying: "The Chinese language is especially important
for *any* study of the relation between linguistic structure and the
formation of philosophical concepts. . . . It is one of the few pure
examples of an isolating language, without inflection or agglutina-
tion. . . . Chinese is also the one language in which there is an
important philosophical tradition *entirely* independent of philosophies developed in Indo-European languages" (my italics).[11] Such
independence is grounds for optimism: an object that has so little
in common with the Indo-European philosophical subject provides the opportunity (and the felt obligation) of verifying or
revising one's convictions from the ground up. China is not a
country or a language but a world—the kind of parallel world in
which Leibniz would have wanted to carry out experiments on
causality and Providence.

The relation between us (whoever we are) and China becomes,
then, a way of learning about the relations of necessity and con-
tingency, nature and culture, genus and example, sign and meaning. Speaking quite generally, comparison is precious because it
yields evidence. -*Vidence* means "sight, seeing, what may be seen,"
but what of the *e-*? "Out, outward" translates it, and the phenomenology of perception—the fact that what is seen stands out against a
background—explains it.[12] Evidence from as far out there as it is

possible to go stands out as no other evidence can. Exoticism contributes more than a backdrop to anthropology: it is tied up with the epistemological topics of reference and perception. *Ta exō* in Plato's *Theaetetus*, 198 c 2, means "things outside the mind"; in Thucydides 1.68 it means "foreign affairs."[13] For the philosophical reader, travel journals are romances of reference, a diet of evidence and exhibits. (One edition of the French novelist Victor Segalen's China notebooks is titled, tellingly, *Voyage au pays du Réel.*) For travelers as dissimilar as Roland Barthes and Clifford Geertz, the voyage out is a trip into an outside where the outside—the public, outer, side of the sign, for instance—can, at last, exist for itself, heedless of a corresponding "inside."[14]

And Chinese evidence is exotic enough to give empiricism a speculative twist. Graham has said that "the great interest in exploring alien conceptual schemes is in glimpsing how one's own looks from outside, in perceiving for example that the Being of Western ontology is culture-bound, not a universally valid concept."[15] That is quite a "for example." We are invited to *perceive*, as a piece of evidence (for example) is perceived, that there are only examples, and that an example, say Being, has only culture to be an example of. Do such examples leave philosophy (which does not often get to perceive and has a long-standing rivalry with culture) anything to do?

I am not hoping to save the institution of philosophy from empiricism; rather, my aim is to show some of the problems that arise when an empirical discipline sets out to inherit philosophy's mantle. Durkheim's formula for the sociology of religion gives us the truth-value without truth; a questionnaire theory of philosophy or literature does the same but does not try very hard to separate the predicate of being true from that of seeming true. (What seems true to everyone may have a crack at being true.) "Truth-value without truth" recalls, in more than just a punning way, I hope, Kant's famous description of aesthetic objects as exhibiting "purposiveness without a purpose." For the only judgment one can pass on such objects is an aesthetic one—disinterested, to be sure, since the "real existence of the thing represented" no longer plays a part.[16] This certainly makes much of philosophy unreadable—or makes it readable as a curious department of aesthetic experience. Imagine replacing the word "being" with some culturally bounded equivalent, say "the Greek folk-concept of Being," in passages such as this one: "There is a science which studies Being *qua* Being. . . . This science is not the same as any of the so-called particular sciences, for none of the others contemplates Being generally *qua* Being."[17] That gives one the "alien" feeling, all right.

Yet Graham's demonstration lives in a different fishbowl from his conclusions—and I would argue that the same holds true for any epistemology that would make "culture," as we understand it today, the court of last appeal. Graham goes to China looking to validate or invalidate certain theses about the meaning of the (Greek) verb "to be." His conclusion (that you can only say, and *a fortiori* mean, Being in Greek or in languages touched by the Greeks) derives from a specific kind of disappointment: the disappointment of someone who had expected Being or first philosophy to translate, to bear authority and reference beyond these terms' (supposedly) native languages.[18] For this test to take place, philosophical languages must be supposed to be, as a rule, mutually translatable, and only incidentally untranslatable, as in the present case of blockage. If, however, we do not allow that sort of reference to tempt us—if we restrict in advance the effectiveness of the signifier "Being" to this particular set of language-games—then Graham's counterevidence will have no shock value at all; the ability to translate a word into Chinese could never validate or invalidate a particular concept. For those won over to Graham's conclusions, his argument will have no meaning, since it is based on premises that they no longer subscribe to (namely, the premise that Being might or ought to have been translatable). In order to gain anything at all from it, they must find someone naïve enough to play the game with conviction; after a time even these will be hard to find.

Graham's demonstration is thus a classically skeptical (i.e., destructive) one. But it's not as if nobody is in charge. It may not have a name yet, there may not be any professorships or call numbers assigned to its development, but something has to be there to take Being out for its stroll, watch it fail to adjust to local conditions, and write up the report. Whatever that thing is—anthropology, linguistics, semantics, common sense, ethology, pure reason, biological man—it pronounces judgment, and to do that it has to speak from a vantage point that is all-seeing, at least relative to the cultures and languages whose products it compares and finds, each according to its kind, incomplete and "culturally bounded" rather than "universally valid." This something has to be all of the above-mentioned local disciplines and more, but with none of their limits. It has to put itself in the position of a meta-language in regard to the former languages (Greek, Chinese, "Western ontology," etc.) whose limitations it surveys.[19] It has to do the job of first philosophy (to use a now discredited and discrediting term).

So appalling a use of words may, however, bring out the necessary inconsistency in an epistemological relativism that has to overstep the authority it grants itself. Skepticism like this requires making even stronger epistemic claims than does naïveté. It requires that the naïve claims be testable, and that it itself be capable of doing the testing. The theme of the passage from Graham is not just the educational encounter with the strange, a dialogue between self and other, but the supersession of the old self and the old other by a new self with expanded judicial powers. Yet nothing is said about this new self or its abilities. It emerges as a necessary byproduct of the skeptical arguments, without ever having had to face them. The self-knowledge provided by the encounter is therefore the knowledge of the old, culturally-bound, self, one's ritual substitute, the very self one observes, as we saw, in an aesthetic, disinterested frame of mind; which is to say that the self it knows is out-of-date. (Would it not have been more accurate, typographically as well as morally, for Todorov to say, "I read 'myself' between quotation marks"?) Since the differences it sets forth are differences relative to that superseded self, nothing is really at risk in any ethical engagements deriving from that difference. That is one way of solving the constitutional problem alluded to earlier: one simply removes the faculty of judgment from the set of objects to be judged.

There should be a way of revealing what is blocked by this play of quotation marks. Todorov's and Graham's distancing gestures would benefit from a contrast with the quotation marks one cannot rub out (that is, the ones that mark the difference between oneself and one's degree of self-knowledge). The notion of cultural or historical boundedness, together with its various products (cultural studies, proposals to see "philosophy as a kind of writing,"[20] and so forth), is not necessarily the alternative to some blinkered universalism. Comparison is as much hegemony as it is Balkanization— indeed it may hegemonize more effectively the more it tries to Balkanize. (The reader of this book may watch the same process at work in ancient Chinese poetics, which integrated balky regional forms through, not despite, its own increasing sophistication.) Universalism inhabits philosophies of cultural difference as a necessary constitutive moment, as the means by which they consolidate their authority to say how the different is different.[21] And it is through their universalizing moment that they take over all the tasks of the less fortunate philosophies, the merely Greek, the merely Chinese, and so forth. I hasten to say that this does not amount to calling the relativist project hollow or hypocritical; I merely want to thematize, that is talk about, its constitutive relation to its seeming opposite. That relation, as it appears in the work of translators, commentators, historians, semioticians, and others, is one of the subjects of this book. It is also, inevitably, one of the book's constituents, and something of a wild card among them. Taking comparative philosophy (or comparative literature) by its risky, synthetic, truth-claim-making side, rather than by its safe, compartmentalizing, summarizing side, means trying to catch up with what one is doing in a comparison. No method I know of is equal to *that* problem.

What one is doing is usually several things at once, and some of them may happen faster or more directly than others. In the past coins and plagues traveled the roads, connecting Granada and Cambaluc in a matter of months, while historians, theatrical troupes, and manuscripts stayed at home. Maybe it is always the small change of civilization that moves most freely. My way of handling the great solid ingots of culture is to break them down into copper coin, approaching them as they are mediated by problems of reading. Getting the ingot back should be easy, once one has collected enough coppers. Or is this the point at which the comparison stumbles? The careful readers will decide.

§ 1 The Question of Chinese Allegory

Il est de forts parfums pour qui toute matière
Est poreuse.

—Baudelaire, "Le Flacon"

If an allegory "says one thing in words and another in meaning," to quote Quintilian, it is an open question whether the verbal analyst can avoid giving a one-sided view of it. But the one-sided view may, in and through its incompleteness, lead the reader to reimagine how much has been left out, and in translations and comparisons we can hardly ask for much more than that. A series of statements, culled from strict critics and broad readers, on the allegorical mode and the problem of its compatibility with the Chinese tradition can serve as the background for my interpretation of both topics. Perhaps, as I try to say what my examples mean, the examples will succeed in meaning (better than I can) what I say.

Midway through Pauline Yu's influential *Reading of Imagery in the Chinese Poetic Tradition* occurs a moment of great poetic daring.[1] The passage's subject is the attitude of ancient Chinese commentators to poetic language—the assumptions they brought to their "readings of imagery." Its text, the "Encountering Sorrow" (*Li sao*) of the fourth-century B.C. writer Ch'ü Yüan, voices the sorrows of a misunderstood "suitor," in whom critics ancient and modern have seen a rejected official. The narrator of "Encountering Sorrow" adds to "inward beauty" "fair outward adornment": "I dressed in selinea and shady angelica, / And twined autumn orchids to make a garland."[2] For the commentators, Ch'ü Yüan's lingering over the details of his "outward adornment" betrays regret that his

13

"inward beauty" is going unnoticed. Yu cites one such gloss: "The word 'fragrant' appears three times in the next five distichs as Ch'ü Yüan describes himself, and Wang I [fl. 110–20] observes that 'fragrance is the smell of virtue.' . . . In other words, the epithet is true both literally and metaphorically" (93).

Does virtue have a smell? For comparative poetics this is a real question, not an insinuating one. For to take "the smell of virtue" as a literal proposition is precisely what, given present-day English semantics, we cannot do. Not that we have no way of giving it a satisfactory interpretation: we might say that since fragrance is a term of praise for smells, it ought to be understood as an epithet for equally praiseworthy behavior; or we could associate the diffusion of fragrances through the air with the improving influence Chinese moralists attribute to the virtuous person; or we could reduce the meaning of the statement to its "gestural" component (as I. A. Richards might have called it)[3] and paraphrase "fragrant virtue" as virtue to which people with an accurate moral sense react in the same way people with good noses react to a fragrant smell. We could talk about surrealism and synaesthesia or (were we the scholars of a hundred years ago) the vivid imagination of "Oriental peoples." But in all such attempts to provide a "literal" basis for understanding (or perceiving) the fragrance of virtue, an element of metaphor, of transference, of association, or of connotation creeps in, which is to say that at every turn we fail to observe the letter of the formula "true both literally and metaphorically."

The "shock of mild surprise"[4] provoked by a phrase such as "the smell of virtue" should not blind us to the fact that we are talking about not actual smells and virtues but the uses of language to describe them—and what is more, that we do so here by way of translation, the contact of two or more languages. A single word in a particular language may very well apply with perfect literalness to objects that the speaker of another language would consider self-evidently distinct, a situation that may lead the speaker of the second language to impute a vivid metaphorical imagination to the speaker of the first. It does not, however, follow that the speaker of the first language has done anything out of the ordinary. There must be languages in which the same verb does not do to say "the house stands" and "the child stands" or "the weeds filled up the garden plot" and "my glass is full, thank you." A literal translation here would be excessive, or at least misleading, for it would render an originally inconspicuous associative meaning obtrusive; although we might insist that that is what the English *literally* says, the phrase—the "same phrase"—would have different ways of being literal in English and in the other language. The odd-sounding foreign phrase would correspond to the banal English statement neither in content or emphasis. If the "fragrance" of "fragrant virtue" is just such an effect of translation, it lends itself to explanation—to being explained away, alas—as a piece of "mythology" that, for all its color in our eyes, is only "white" to the Chinese reader.

Since no translation is perfect, maybe what we need is a translation that makes compromises in a different direction. Let us suppose that the literal surrealism of "the smell of virtue" is *our* problem—as English speakers—alone, a problem of relative emphasis in translation; that in Chinese (or in a certain poetic dialect of Chinese, if our theory will bear the additional complication) the good smell of virtue raises no more eyebrows than do, in English, houses standing on a corner lot. In that case, need things be made so difficult for the reader? Since the original word would not have excluded contexts (e.g., moral qualities) typically excluded by the English word "fragrant," might not the Chinese be rendered more smoothly, and thus (in this respect at least) more accurately, by an English word that applies without a hitch to smells and moral qualities alike: "agreeable," for instance, or "lovely" or "powerful"? If the Chinese phrase is to be read literally, a translation that makes no special appeals to metaphor will tell the English reader more exactly what is going on in the Chinese phrase. That would dispense with the uncomfortable alternative of reading literally or metaphorically by depriving us of both: with "agreeable" the power of imagery is distinctly at an ebb.

Perhaps the term "literal" is inherently incomplete and needs always to be accompanied by a technical note saying in what way, in what language, and for whom the literal is literal.[5] That would require an endless task of specification—specification of senses, of contexts, of associations, of speakers, of idiolects—and in the end serve only to emphasize, once again, a principle on which everyone already agrees anyway, that perfect translation is an impossibility. What this example does show us, however, is that the modes of meaning—literal, figurative, and so forth—are as apt to be lost in translation as the meanings themselves are.

So far we have discussed the passage only as an example of a problem that lies outside it (the problem, familiar to everyone who has ever tried to translate a joke, of linguistically specific meanings). Yet it is more to our purpose—and a better approach to the issues to which the passage calls us—to view the passage as a linguistic event of its own. For the translation and commentary create something that was not there before. Whatever it is that is "true both literally and metaphorically" about Ch'ü Yüan's use of the word "fragrant" is true in different ways in Chinese and English. Yu's comment that the phrase is to be taken both literally and metaphorically proposes a riddle to the English reader, for we can do that only by constructing a new idiolect in which smells have a moral sense, one in which "fragrant" and "virtue" may join in previously unheard of combinations. The new idiolect counts, of course, as an innovation equally from the Chinese point of view, inasmuch as the problem—the surrealism of "fragrant virtue"—does not, according to Yu, apply in Chinese.

We are thus forced to acknowledge, on several planes at once, the properly poetic character of comparative poetics. It has to make up its own language as it goes along. Not only does it lead, by means of adventurous translations, to collocations that are original in any of the languages to which it refers, but in taking stock of the effects of its own translation it is obliged to set new standards of literalness and metaphoricity, truth and fiction. Comparative poetics is doomed to originality.

Elaborating the poetics *of* comparative poetics is the task of what follows. The first part of this chapter is guided by Pauline Yu's research—the most systematic exploration and uncompromising analysis of the field so far. At the same time, the reach of this topic requires that we relate the work of currently active scholars such as Yu to that of other writers who, over the past few centuries, have touched on the same problems. If, in the process, I seem to speak of schools of thought, the aim is only convenience of exposition—an effect of translation, or of mistranslation, that should be laid to the nature of the project.

~

"Allegory" has recently been the subject of fundamental dis-agreements among writers on Chinese literature. For every reader wishing to propose an allegorical interpretation of a well-known text or to remind us of the persistence of figural interpretations in the Chinese tradition, another has been eager to show that talk of "Chinese allegory" rests on a misunderstanding and that the pre-suppositions of Chinese "allegorists" do not just differ from those of European writers but are incompatible with them. The task of defining allegory (a particularly volatile term)[6] in a flexible enough way that talk of its regional variants makes sense has become a touchstone for the issue of the cultural specificity of literary or rhetorical genres. "The [Western] allegorical method . . . is a particular, rather than universal, occurrence of the mode"; "like any other literary concept, metaphor is culture-specific and is always situated in a conceptual framework characteristic of a cul-ture."[7] But the question of Chinese allegory is not one literary history or comparative literature in the usual sense can solve: as the following exposition is meant to show, the problem persistently outstrips the terms in which it is posed, be they linguistic, exeget-ical, or cultural-historical. The very possibility of making such statements is at issue. Finding the proper theoretical level at which to situate the matter is the business of this chapter.

Why should it have fallen to allegory to stimulate such discus-sions? The appearance of books such as Andrew Plaks's *Archetype and Allegory in "Dream of the Red Chamber"* at an opportune moment in the history of the discipline is only part of the answer. There is also the loyalty of comparatists to the practice of singling out a familiar Western genre (e.g., epic, tragedy)[8] and, by declaring it absent in the Chinese tradition, probing for some clues to the value or coherence of that tradition. The more specific a definition, the more it excludes; the aim of such studies is to exploit the opportunities of a failed translation and calculate how much culturally specific meaning is lost on both sides. But these discussions have been lacking in theoretical follow-ups, and not entirely because of the vagueness of the genre terms involved.

The reasons for asking such questions are not always clear. Why indeed should we want to discover a Chinese epic or tragedy? Tropes and figures—irony, for example, or metaphor, or allegory—are quite a different matter, however. By asking whether China has an *Iliad* or an *Agamemnon*, one tries to learn something from an identification (even an imperfect one), a process in which the nature of identification itself is not obviously at stake.[9] But to ask whether, for example, Chinese metaphors "attribute to one thing the name of another"[10] engages one's whole manner of reading— for it may well be the case that to speak of "Chinese metaphors" *is* to "attribute to one thing the name of another." (At least, we cannot know in advance whether the transfer of "names" involved in calling certain Chinese tropes "metaphors" corresponds to an identity in the "things.") If figures of speech describe not only the constituent devices of literary texts but also decisions inherent to reading, then questions about whether tropes and figures translate turn back on our ability to interpret the texts that prompt such questions.

The question of "Chinese allegory" refers us, then, to the question of the translatability of figures in general; moreover, it is only within the framework of the second question that we can find a means of working toward an answer to the first. Or to put it somewhat differently: the issue of Chinese allegory and that of the possibility of a comparative literature involving Chinese are linked; the resolution of both depends on an answer to the question of how far the theory of rhetorical language may be extended.[11] In this, straightforward or naïve comparison (a "theōrein ti pros ti" or "looking at this next to that") is of little help. Since the question of allegory reflects immediately on our ability to read, no number of examples (each of which would have to be *read* before being introduced into the argument) would ever be sufficient to solving it. Until we know more about allegory, our discussion has to sidestep this difficulty by taking its examples from already theoretical, or theorized, contexts. Through a reading of critical texts that stress the irreducibility of certain Chinese modes of interpretation to Western "allegory," we may hope to isolate the rules by which the Chinese figural modes are to be known as *distinct*.

~

Having made clear what we can expect from examples at this stage—circumstantial evidence at best—I can now introduce the main object of the discussion. The fluent summary of Herbert Giles gives the traditional point of view while dissenting from it, and this without once using the word "allegory":

> The *Shih ching*, or *Book of Odes*, is another work for the preservation of which we are indebted to Confucius. It consists of a collection of rhymed ballads in various metres, usually four words to the line, composed between the reign of the Great Yü [trad. r. 2205–2198 B.C.] and the sixth century B.C. These, which now number 305, are popularly known as the "Three Hundred," and are said by some to have been selected by Confucius from no less than 3000 pieces. . . . Confucius himself attached the utmost importance to his labours in this direction. . . . [He] may indeed be said to have anticipated the apophthegm attributed by Fletcher of Saltoun to "a very wise man," namely, that he who should be allowed to make a nation's "ballads need care little who made its laws." And it was probably this appreciation by Confucius that gave rise to an extraordinary literary craze in reference to these Odes. Early commentators, incapable of seeing the simple natural beauties of the poems . . . and at the same time unable to ignore the deliberate judgment of the Master, set to work to read into countryside ditties deep moral and political significations. Every single one of the immortal Three Hundred has thus been forced to yield some hidden meaning and point an appropriate moral. If a maiden warns her lover not to be too rash . . . commentators promptly discover that the piece refers to a feudal noble whose brother had been plotting against him, and to the excuses of the former for not visiting the latter with swift and exemplary punishment. . . . Possibly the very

introduction of these absurdities may have helped to preserve to our day a work which would otherwise have been considered too trivial to merit the attention of scholars.[12]

Marcel Granet, writing a few years later with the aim of combating the "impossible political interpretations" with which the poems had, from antiquity on, been "saddled,"[13] laid down a body of rules for reading. Among them:

> 1. We will take no account of the standard interpretation, no more than of its surviving variants. The only reason for studying them would be to learn about the *derivative* ritual use of the *Book of Odes*; they should not be studied for the sake of discerning the original meaning of the songs;
>
> 2. We reject in no uncertain terms the distinction drawn [by the classical Prefaces] between songs evincing a good state of morals and songs attesting to perverted morality.
>
> . . . . .
>
> 4. All symbolic interpretations, and likewise any interpretation that supposes a refined technique on the part of the poets, will be discarded.[14]

Critical and historical judgments go hand in hand. The canonical interpretations are not only, for Granet and Giles, absurd in themselves but also a late addition that must be scraped away in order to "uncover the original meaning of the poems."[15] (For a more detailed look at the *Odes'* textual history, see Chapter 2.) Giles and Granet have been joined by almost all readers, in China and elsewhere. The skeptical tradition begun by Cheng Ch'iao in the twelfth century has triumphed.[16] One meaning of the use of "allegorical" to describe the old school of exegesis is simply to announce this fact: more than do "symbolic" or "moral," the word stresses the mismatch of text and commentary.[17]

As a consequence, the commentaries have been stripped of their authority as the "textbook of morality for a thousand ages"[18] and handed over to the secular arm. Historians find in them a collection of documents valuable for the light they cast on the learning of the Former and Latter Han dynasties (206 B.C.–A.D. 220), and students of poetics sometimes find themselves obliged to treat the influence of poems and commentary as two separate questions.[19]

The texts at issue are, then, many: 305 anonymous poems, each bearing a few lines of (usually contestable) explanation in a preface. Early on the prefaces acquired an explanatory literature of their own, in the form of commentaries, annotations, notes, and glosses (*chuan, shu, chu, ku*) copied down and discussed from edition to edition. A glance into Ch'en Huan's mid-nineteenth-century edition will show the amount of detail deemed valuable by one annotator for the understanding of one of the shortest of the *Odes*.

> [Preface:] *"Lang pa," "The Wolf Tramples"*
> Poem in praise of the Duke of Chou [Chou Kung; traditional dates, ?–1105 B.C.] When the Duke of Chou became regent [for the child-king Ch'eng (r. 1115–1079 B.C.) of the Chou], rumors [slandering the duke] ran throughout the Four Realms, and the king in his court still did not know [the duke's intentions]. [The Duke of Chou responded by exterminating the rebel lords of the Four Realms in his Eastern Campaign, which took him to Pin.] An official of Chou [composed this to] praise [the duke] for not abandoning his sagely conduct. [Note by Ch'en Huan:] Since it refers to the duke's return to court, this poem must have been composed after the fourth year of the regency.
> [Text:] *The wolf tramples on his dewlap, he trips on his tail.*
> [*Chuan* commentary:] An evocation. *Pa* is to step on something; *chih* is to be hindered. An old wolf has a "beard." If he steps forward, he stumbles on the beard; if he steps backward, he trips on his tail. Advance and retreat are both difficult,[20] yet this does not affect his fierceness.
> [Text:] *The prince's grandson is great and beautiful; his red slippers,* chi-chi [*stud-adorned?*].
> [*Chuan* commentary:] "The prince's grandson" is Ch'eng, grandson of the dukes of Pin. [The poem is set in the "Airs of Pin" section; the ruling house of Chou originated from Pin.] *Shuo* means great; *fu* means beautiful. Red slippers are the full-dress shoes of nobles. *Chi-chi* here means "stud-like."
> [Ch'en Huan's note:] . . . As to the Commentary's statements that "the old wolf tramples on his dewlap, he stumbles on his beard,

advance and retreat are both difficult: a comparison to the Duke of
Chou's situation when the Four Realms were full of rumors and
King Ch'eng was unaware; far and near was danger," the commentary extends what is said in the Preface. But as to "yet this does not
affect his fierceness" applied to the Duke of Chou, this refers to the
latter part of the poem. "Princes" meaning the dukes of Pin, and
"grandson" meaning King Ch'eng: the Commentary treats King
Ch'eng as the "prince's grandson" and then reiterates this, calling
him "grandson of the dukes of Pin." . . . This poem is said to praise
the Duke of Chou. When the Duke of Chou returned to Chou,
King Ch'eng had reached his majority and was already resplendent
with sagely virtue. . . . To praise Ch'eng [as line 2 seems to do] is to
praise the Duke of Chou [as his tutor and chief minister]. . . .
Properly speaking, shoes worn on festive occasions are called *hsi.*
Ordinary shoes are called *chü. Chü* is the broader term. Hence the
commentary says that red *hsi* are the *chü* worn by nobles on festive
occasions. . . . [Ch'en next quotes a series of opinions on the
meaning of "the red slippers are *chi-chi.*"]

[Text:] *The wolf trips on his tail, he tramples on his dewlap; the prince's
grandson is great and beautiful, his reputation* [*te-yin;* lit. "the sound of
his virtue"] *has no flaw.*

[*Chuan* commentary:] "Flaw" means "fault."

[Ch'en's note:] The Commentary glosses "flaw" as "fault." This
simply means that one has done no wrong. [An obviously insuffi-
cient gloss, because] The "Ming t'ang wei" chapter in the *Record of
Ritual* [*Li chi*] says: "For six years [the Duke of Chou, as regent]
gave audience to the feudatories [of the Son of Heaven] in the Hall
of Light. He regulated ceremonies, composed music and established
common weights and measures, and all of the empire obeyed him."
And the "Record of Music" [chapter says]: "Once the empire had
been established, [the sages] rectified the six modes, harmonized the
five sounds, and sang to the accompaniment of strings the 'Laudes'
section of the *Odes.* This is what is called 'virtuous sound'; 'virtuous
sound' is music."[21]

The example is meant to show the necessity and the weakness of
traditional commentary on the *Book of Odes.* The poem needs
putting together. Its annotators forge a connection between the
parts provided, wolf-topic and prince-topic, by making the wolf's

predicament a "stimulus" (*hsing*) to the thought of a human one and by narrowing the meaning of "prince's grandson." The occasional inconsistencies Ch'en Huan notes are characteristic of the Commentary's explanatory style. Given the relevance of the Duke of Chou story to the poem—and its relevance is indeed given for the commentators, asserted but never tested against rival interpretations—it becomes important to explain how the portrait of a "prince's grandson" in the first stanza, which the Commentary applies to Ch'eng, can also redound to the praise of Ch'eng's uncle, the Duke of Chou. Bernhard Karlgren makes short work of all this. His note to the poem reads, "A young nobleman is likened to a fiercely springing wolf."[22] That may be all an immanentist reader like Karlgren can salvage from the traditional lore (and "salvage" is the word: an unadvised reader might see the dewlapped wolf not as fierce but as ridiculous).[23] Now certainly the commentators' linkage of the poem to the Duke of Chou is a leap out of whatever sense "Lang pa" makes by itself on the page; if that is suspicious, the way those suppositions dovetail with the commentators' tendency to read everything in the "Airs of the States" (*Kuo feng*), the first part of the *Book of Odes*, as testimonials to (and fruits of) the Chou monarchy's civilizing mission only makes it more so. But that too is a characteristic of the long-dominant school of *Odes* interpretation: the sense of the glosses to "Lang pa" depends on the glosses given to the preceding five poems, and those in turn rest on a sustained reference to another canonical work, the *Shang shu* or *Book of Documents*.[24] Everything in the old-style *Book of Odes* is cross-reference and mutual confirmation. By choosing not to read the classic as a chronicle of Chou, modern readers make it (again?) into the anthology of unrelated poems that, for centuries, it had not been.

～

> *Hippolyta.* It must be your imagination then, and not theirs.
> *Theseus.* If we imagine no worse of them than they of them-
> selves, they may pass for excellent men. Here come two noble
> beasts in, a man and a lion.
> —Shakespeare, *A Midsummer Night's Dream*, V.i.

Fortunately for the economy of this exposition, the past few years' debate over "Chinese allegory" has concerned not so much its actuality as its possibility. Even those willing to grant allegory a place in Chinese literature surround the term with reservations— reservations that, in another critic's hands, become reasons for rejecting it altogether. It is one measure of the intricacy of the problem that it presses critics as different, in other respects, as Stephen Owen, Andrew Plaks, and Pauline Yu into saying nearly the same things about the structure of the Chinese literary universe.

Discussing the eighteenth-century novel *Dream of the Red Chamber*, Andrew Plaks observes that for all its adumbrations of "another level of meaning" it "simply does not lend itself to the type of allegorical reading to which we have been redirected by twentieth-century medievalists."[25] Pauline Yu's objections are stronger: for her, the Chinese and Western cases cannot be seen as variants of a single "allegory" more broadly defined. The Chinese mode, "though superficially similar, was based on a fundamentally different set of assumptions from those of metaphor or allegory in the West" (116).

What characteristics distinguish European allegory from the Chinese genres we might mistake for it? For all these critics, the standard descriptions apply: allegory "indicates one thing in words and another in meaning"; it is a kind of "continuous metaphor."[26] Yu in particular takes this last phrase to heart; nothing is in allegory that was not first in metaphor. And as for the latter: "The most fundamental disjunction posited and bridged by Western metaphor is more than verbal—it is that existing between two ontologically distinct realms, one concrete and the other abstract, one sensible and the other inaccessible to the senses" (17).

The solidarity between ontology and literary theory, as Yu sees both being traditionally practiced in the West, is complete. Allegory "creates a hierarchical literary universe of two levels, each of which maintains its own coherence, but only one of which has ultimate primacy" (19).[27] Both metaphor and allegory are two instances of an omnipresent law, that of mimesis or fictionality: "Mimesis is . . . predicated on a fundamental ontological dualism—

the assumption that there is a truer reality transcendent to the concrete, historical realm in which we live, and that the relation between the two is replicated in the creative act and artifact" (5).[28]

Allegory is here described in such a way as to make it, not one Western genre among others, but the Western genre par excellence, the literary code that most perfectly expresses the "truth," as a Hegelian aesthetics would put it, of the Western "world."[29] Plaks also sees in allegory a mimetic expansion of metaphor, the literary "projection" of culturally structured habits of thought. "When we speak of allegory in the Western context we mean the creation of a two-level literary universe (in mimesis of an ontologically dual cosmos) by means of the projection into a hypothetical plane of structural patterns actually presented in the images and actions of narrative (the author's fiction)."[30]

Under the circumstances, to speak of a Chinese form of allegory would amount to erasing the differences between East and West. For in China the verbal work of art is understood differently. After quoting from the Great Preface to the *Book of Odes* a passage that has for centuries provided the charter for the political-didactic school of interpretation, Yu summarizes:

> What we have here is a classical statement of the expressive-affective conception of poetry prevalent in Asian literary theory. While certain assumptions resemble those in the West . . . the world-view on which these are based is a significantly different one. Indigenous Chinese philosophical traditions agree on a fundamentally monistic view of the universe. . . . True reality is not supernal but in the here and now, and this is a world, furthermore, in which fundamental correspondences exist between and among cosmic patterns (*wen*) and operations and those of human culture. Thus the Preface [to the *Book of Odes*] here can assume that what is internal (emotion) will naturally find some externally correlative form or action, and that poetry can spontaneously reflect, affect and effect political and cosmic order. In other words, the seamless connection between the individual and the world enables the poem simultaneously to reveal feelings, to provide an index of governmental stability, and serve as a didactic tool. (32–33)

Just as the diminished reality of the present sub specie aeternitatis conditions the possibility and the themes of Western literature, so the Chinese theory of poetry as documentary expression derives from the inconceivability of a supratemporal viewpoint.[31] The ideological base determines the forms of understanding. Historicism, Yu suggests, was "perhaps the only possible option for a tradition based on a stimulus-response method of poetic production rather than a mimetic one," "the only way" for a "non-dualistic cosmology" to assign value to its literary productions (82, 80). "Instead of the mimetic view that poetry is the imitation of an action, it is seen here as a *literal reaction* of the poet to the world around him and of which he is an integral part" (35). Even when anonymous, the poet is always (as he was for Wordsworth) "a man speaking to men." The seeming alternative between literal and allegorical readings of any of the ancient *Odes* is thus a false one. There are, rather, different kinds of "literal" sense. For Chinese readers, "the occasion *is* the meaning of a poem" and "there is always a concrete basis for an image" (82, 99). Thus Chinese reading can dispense with fiction altogether. All it needs is occasions. To cite Stephen Owen's remarks on the poetics of a different period, the Chinese reader came to poetry with a "faith" that poems were "authentic presentations of historical experience."[32]

If allegory and metaphor spring from a "fundamental distinction" between two realms of being, and if, as Plaks puts it, "the Chinese world-view simply does not utilize the two-level cosmology that we have found at the heart of Western allegory,"[33] the position to take about the *Odes* commentators and their moralizing interpretations follows almost syllogistically. The readings critics have called "allegorical" should be seen as something else. Yu proposes that they be put under the heading of

> *contextualization,* not allegorization. . . . The Confucian commentators on the [*Book of Odes*] were validating the anthology in the only way allowed by a non-dualistic cosmology—by attesting to its roots in history. Where Western allegorists attempted to prove that Greek myth possessed a deeper philosophical or religious meaning—an ab-

stract, metaphysical dimension—so the Chinese exegetes had to demonstrate the literal truth value of the songs: not a metaphysical truth,
however, but the truth of this world, an historical context.   (80–81)

Without "another world" to refer to, no Chinese writer can possibly produce allegories. There are only "contextualizations."

Are allegories, then, differentiated from other kinds of writing
only by the kinds of things they talk about (or seem to talk about,
to give the traditional definition all its weight)? In that case, it is
European literary history, rather than the attempt to repackage
exotic literatures into European terminology, that needs revising.
The passage from Horace (a version of the "ship of state" topos)
that provides Quintilian his first illustration of allegory offers no
resistance to historical "contextualization." Are the refugee shepherds of Vergil's first *Eclogue* on a different metaphysical footing
from the landowners they are traditionally understood as representing?[34] These passages have been cited as allegories for as long as
the word has been in circulation and have nearly acquired the force
of definitions; a theory of allegory that disregards them may well be
a theory of something else.

The stumbling block is nonetheless instructive. The description
of Western allegory has been based on an ideal or typical example
of allegory all along—Bunyan's *Pilgrim's Progress* or Spenser's *Faerie
Queen*, say. Now that counterexamples to that type of allegory have
surfaced on the Western side, the point of contrasting Western and
Chinese types of allegory has diminished. But something has been
gained: whereas the doctrinal definition of Western allegory ("creation of a two-level literary universe in mimesis of an ontologically
dual cosmos") led us to seek a Chinese case that contrasted with
it thematically (monism versus dualism, "response" versus "creation"), now we find that allegory—Western classical allegory—is
by no means dependent on the theme of the transcendent. A poem
that depicts senators as sailors passed Quintilian's muster. Can the
negative outcome of the search for Chinese allegories be attributed
to the way the question was framed? Is it a consequence of taking as
the representative case of allegory the "allegory of the theologians,"

which does not travel well, and not the "allegory of the grammarians," which should have a chance wherever there is grammar?[35]

The ancient grammarians defined allegory as a manner of speaking, not a set of things (however vast or implicit) to express.
Quintilian's formula *Aliud verbis, aliud sensu ostendit* ("it indicates
one thing with the words, another with the sense") might be
interpreted to imply a "hierarchical relation" between two "ontologically distinct realms." The phrase neglects, however, to tell us
which is which: both kinds of referent are simply other or *aliud*,
different from one another in an unspecified way—perhaps only by
being the objects of different means of reference. (Compare, for
nuance, the Christianizing version of Suidas's tenth-century encyclopedia: "Allegory, a metaphor [in which] the letter says one thing
and the thought another."[36] The grammar is significant. For Quintilian the allegory shows one thing *in* or *with* its words, another *in*
or *with* the sense; in Suidas the "letter" and the "thought" have
become verb-subjects and taken control of their respective par-
ticipial phrases.) Allegory in the technicist and—*sit venia verbo*—
pagan sense of the ancient rhetors says one thing and means
another, whatever the thing said and the thing meant may be.[37]

This adjustment makes things easier on the Chinese side too, for
"contextualization" is a potentially misleading word. How much
are we to read into it? Is it simply that the commentaries are true
and that their reading succeeds in the way a footnote clarifies a
matter of fact? Not exactly: ancient commentators (amply cited by
Yu in her discussion) disagree on the historical situations the poems
were meant to "reflect."[38] For the theory of contextualization, however, the difference in kind between a historical inaccuracy and a
"metaphysical truth" matters more than the difference between historical truth and historical error. The first difference is absolute; the
second, only relative. And in Yu's presentation an allegorical difference—the difference, in a proper allegory, between its expressed
aliud and its other *aliud*—has to be an absolute difference. One sees
this confirmed by the counterexample. The historical style of commentary to the *Book of Odes* cannot be called allegorical because it
was not, "from the Chinese point of view, a process of attributing
true otherness of reference at all" (65). Rather, Chinese com-

parisons occur in a medium of identity (for example, the identical character of historical pretension common to history and pseudo-history), and that identity, rather than pointing up the local differences, drowns them out.

In a passage that can be read as a structural description of the Chinese novel or as an optimal strategy for reading it, Plaks seems to describe this very economy of meaning.

> Since all reality, in the Chinese view, exists on one plane . . . the trope by which individual symbols in a Chinese allegorical structure refer to the invisible configurations of truth must be identified not as the similarity-difference relation of metaphor, but if anything as the horizontal extension of synecdoche. Each isolated element of the Chinese allegory, by virtue of the existential process of ebb and flow in which it is caught up, "stands for" or "partakes of" the sum total of all existence that remains invisible only in its extent, and not in its essence.[39]

Chinese comparisons, brief or extended, occur within a generalized metonymy or synecdoche, the boundless synecdoche of the Chinese cosmos: Yu and Plaks agree on this, differing only on the question of whether a series of synecdoches constitutes an allegory.[40]

Cosmologies vary. But what if there were simply no way for the Chinese poet or reader to "say one thing and mean another"? The study of Chinese poetics certainly raises this question. Traditional criticism speaks as if the poetic image

> provides a means of placing the situation at hand within a larger, more general context—of linking it with other members of the category to which it belongs. . . . As with the *Classic of Changes*, natural object and human situation were believed literally to belong to the same class of events (*lei*): it was not the poet who was creating or manufacturing links between them. They were linked by correspondence, but not—as in the Western case of allegory—one between two distinct orders; the critic's task lay simply in identifying the general category to which both belonged.[41]

Once again—and by a necessity implicit in thematic definition—we have left the territory of thematics, of descriptions of the world, for that of semantics, of the conditions on descriptions of the

world. A moment ago it was possible to counter a thematic description of allegorical "difference" with a more narrowly tropological
and semiotic one (once we found the use of different *names*, e.g.,
"sailor" and "statesman," an adequate hallmark of the genre, the
conceit of different *worlds* lost its definitional force). Now the
object of the discussion is meaning itself, rhetoric's necessary raw
material. The impossibility of a Chinese allegory becomes situated
not in some feature of general ideology but in the very logic of
sameness and difference that provides the means of telling a metaphor from a synecdoche, the figurative sense in which all flesh is
grass from the literal sense in which all bluegrass is grass.

This is not to say that appealing to the criteria of sameness and
difference must produce an answer: disagreements on this score can
go on indefinitely, meanwhile crossing the invisible line between
words and things.[42] The paramount linguist Ferdinand de Saussure, as is well known, found no deductive way of saying what
makes two instances of the "same" word or sign the "same." In the
Course in General Linguistics, he spoke categorically from a most
uncooperative example. "Consider the two phrase-members 'the
force of the wind' and 'at the end of one's forces.' In both, *the same
concept* coincides with the same phonetic series: it [the word 'force']
is therefore a single linguistic unit" (my italics).[43] But one need
press matters only a little further for "the same" to begin sounding
different. "The wind was at the end of its forces": "force" now
begins to seem a bit forced itself, a personifying fiction applied to
the inanimate wind.[44]

The move from thematics to semantics has the look of a move to
a logically prior level of investigation. But not even meaning, it
seems, can furnish a starting point primitive enough, unaccultur-
ated enough, to bridge the differences between European and
Chinese poetics or formulate them in a common language. According to Yu, for the sympathetic reader of Chinese texts,

> meaning is not attached externally and arbitrarily to an image but
> follows logically from the fact that objects and situations were believed
> traditionally to belong to one or more non-mutually exclusive, a

priori, and natural classes. . . . One cannot overemphasize the conviction of these early thinkers that [ethical] norms were not only "reflected" but in fact embodied in the images, by virtue of categorical correlations between different situations.   (42–43)

[For Chinese readers and writers the] links between things were always already there, grounded by shared membership in an a priori category (*lei*) antecedent to any individual artifice.   (116)[45]

Chinese semantics, in this view, is cut on the same pattern as Chinese tropes. The "category" is a "context" (65). This is the situation that leads to the challenging thesis of a "virtue" that is "fragrant," and literally so. The secret of Chinese rhetoric is that there is no rhetoric. The seeming allegories, metaphors, and tropes of Chinese poets do no more than report on features of the Chinese universe. The virtue of flowers and the virtue of the official—or the fragrance of each—are not akin but the same thing.[46] In the absence of "individual artifice," however, they can be judged the same thing only if there is, in the strong sense of the word "is," a preexisting category of goodness to which good scent and good behavior equally belong—that is, only if there are substantial Forms.

If the thesis of generalized synecdoche leads directly to a hypercategorical[47]—the Form of the Good—then the exercise has not come out as planned. It says one thing and means another and speaks in precisely the cultural code it was meant to supersede. Metaphor and fiction, instead of being dismissed or bracketed as constructs of Western ontology, have now been promoted (as categories) to the status of realities. It is an astonishing conclusion. And yet to read a plot twist on this scale as a mere inconsistency would be to underrate the critic's skill and the complexity of the problem. How might we better account for it? Is the deformation systematic? If so, what are the elements of its system?

We reached this crossroads at the moment in which synecdoche, or metonymy, in the guise of "contextualization," was about to take over all the functions of metaphor, in name at least. Is there something about metonymy that provokes such reversals?

The metonymy thesis needs to be formulated more generally

than it has been up to now. Metonymy may be founded on a logic of shared natures, but the roster of substances circulates in many versions, and short of a revised and improved *Categories,* rhetoric (or interpretation) has no way to tell us what things are the same as, or different from, what other things. The decision to identify a figure as a metaphor or a metonymy is therefore a kind of speech act, sometimes in constative dress: it gives notice of the critic's (or the poet's) decision to consider objects as organized in a certain way.[48] Since metonymy passes for the most nearly "literal," the least tropical of the tropes, the trope anchored in some relation of fact,[49] and since what counts as a fact is, in some sense, for theories of the world to decide, the appeal to metonymy has no particular content. One has only to give classes substantive existence, and all metaphors become synecdoches.[50] Believers in the Forms will see goodness as producing all good things; organicists will see brides and peach trees as simultaneous eruptions of spring.[51] The difference between metaphor and synecdoche may come down to a difference of beliefs, but not in the determinate sense offered by Yu and Plaks of a contrast between this set of beliefs (inherently metonymic beliefs) and that set (metaphoric beliefs).[52] What kind of a difference is it, then?

~

Answering the question about allegory involves stating the difference between East and West—proof, at least, that the problem deserves the attention it has received. The "category" is a "context" in China because objects of different species "were believed literally to belong to the same class of events." Far from stabilizing the matter or giving it a foothold in intellectual history, the category of belief brings in a divisiveness of its own; for if the anthropological fact of belief decides the literary character of a text, then no distinction between truth and fiction, literal and figurative, metaphor and metonymy, and so forth, will hold for enough codes for reading to occur across differences in belief. Yet that is exactly the kind of reading that, together with these critics, we are trying to persuade ourselves we can do. Comparative rhetoric, which a moment ago seemed likely to become a matter of belief or a branch of national psychology, now risks becoming an impossibility.

"Literal," "synecdoche" and the rest are used deictically, relatively to a world; but what world is it? "Western allegory looks upward, while Chinese allegory looks outward."[53] This seems overconfident: for the contrast to function both would have to be situated in a common space, an absolute space,[54] and something like an absolute space in which we could situate our different objects of study is exactly what we cannot yet say we have.[55]

Underneath the "fundamental differences" adduced by a culturally relative poetics, we find questions and relativities even more fundamental. How far down does difference go? Leibniz, in a preface designed to minimize the strangeness of his *Newest Tracts on the Chinese Question,* quotes Harlequin in the popular farce *Emperor of the Moon*: in China, despite differences in language and customs, *c'est tout comme ici,* "it's all just the way it is here."[56] That is, to consult another authority on the subject, "that the moon is a world just like this one, a world to which our world is a moon. . . . And so, it may be, someone in the moon is laughing tonight at another who holds that this globe of ours is a world." Cosmologies have it in common to be self-sufficient. The traveler to the moon finds the words "moon" and "world" becoming strange, each of them divided between proper noun and deictic, between utter specificity and utter generality, in a way that makes sense-certainty the guarantor of conflict. "Now the priests, on learning that I had dared to say that the moon I came from was a world and their world was nothing but a moon, decided that this gave them pretext enough to have me condemned."[57]

No less baffling are the deictics and prepositions of cross-cultural literary studies. To quote Yu, the "true reality" of the "indigenous Chinese philosophical traditions . . . is not supernal but in the here and now" (32); but where and when is that? Chinese poetry speaks "the truth of this world," in distinction to the Western kind of poetry, which seeks to express "a metaphysical truth" (81). By hypothesis, however, since the "other world" of metaphysics should become an object of thought for us only after we have agreed to entertain a "Western" worldview, this characterization of the distinctiveness of Chinese poetry is unavailable to those Chinese of whom the theory speaks. Yet to look at the two worlds in a "Chinese" manner would be, according to one of these critics, to see them as "just one more of the many complementary pairs included within a single, total frame of reference"[58]—that is, to do away with the antithesis between worldviews with which we began. (How might that happen? What would *that* "single, total frame of reference" be?) Either way, it seems that comparing nullifies comparison, the part swallows up the whole. Such are the difficulties of cultural contrast. One can only share these readers' wish for a firm standing place, *hic et nunc,* to which the Archimedean project could be anchored—while hesitating to grant it.

The juxtaposition of Eastern and Western poetics outlined by these critics seems to involve hypotheses inimical to their conclusions. Relativism is all very well, but relativism relative to what? The very category of relation (renamed, by Leibniz, *concogitabilitas*) proves elusive.[59] A moment ago our wish was to discover the traits by which Chinese and Western figurality could be distinguished; now, thanks to our efforts to distinguish the two, we no longer know whether or how to tell them apart. In this dialogue, and from *both* sides, "the language of the conversation constantly destroys the possibility of saying that which is under discussion."[60]

This difficulty takes many forms and is not limited to literary criticism. If the Chinese imagination is literal and the Western one figurative, their relation cannot be symmetrical; comparing the two will only reduce one to the other, make it the other's moon. The asymmetry is not just in the objects; it is first of all an asymmetry in the way the objects are reasoned about. The figurative has a place for the literal (as tenor or vehicle), but the literal cannot account for the figurative except by abandoning the literal position. For a theory that asserts the naturalness and self-sufficiency of a literal poetics, figure can only be an excess that has to be explained, an outgrowth on the literal sense. But whence comes this excess? The explanations commonly offered merely rename the difference or single out one type of difference as the cause of difference in general: for example, a theology of transcendence (the pattern of Western poetics for Yu, Owen, and Plaks),[61] "abstract or mental objects . . . a one–many paradigm for stating philosophical issues,"[62] the verb "to be,"[63] the Oedipus complex,[64] or poetic metaphor. These are perhaps best seen as brave attempts to localize a problem that is everywhere simultaneously.

Our attention is thus necessarily redirected to the act whereby, with some unavoidable violence, the reader of both "worlds" yokes them together. With so many worlds to choose from, the decision to prefer one interpretation of a figure over another is not a matter of bald perception, nor is it enough to call it a judgment. It may be best to call it, as I did a moment ago, an act. The critics perform their own speech act, commit themselves to an ontology (since they do, after all, distinguish a "dualistic" world from a monistic one, there must be more to dualism than a misunderstanding of monistic reality), and ask the Chinese about their commitment in return. To know whether the Chinese could write in an allegorical mode, or, as another part of the problem, to know whether our rhetoric can translate into theirs, we must know if they "recognize, or have ever recognized, spiritual substances."[65] Chinese silence on this matter is not, however, equivalent to consent; unbelief is synonymous with disbelief. The things we are asking the Chinese for an opinion on are "marked," in Jakobson's sense.[66] But having or not having allegory or metaphor, says common sense, is not as simple a matter as having or not having the wheel or the zero. The former are examples of things that exist, if at all, in the mind and are part of the interpretative work that goes into our attempting to answer our own question. "Are you acquainted with allegory?" The people who lacked allegory or metaphor would be unlikely to know how to answer the question with a yes or a no; either alternative would be equally mysterious. The questioner is obliged to name a substitute for the invisible evidence that we are really after—some adequate symbol of assent to the interpretation of those Chinese utterances as metaphors or non-metaphors.

"The pattern is not far-off"; or rather, "religions are the one interesting thing on earth."[67] The debates about Chinese "allegory" are a new version, a translation into literary-critical language, of a quarrel as old as the missionary beginnings of European sinology. The problem of allegory is both trivially and essentially one of translation, made to stumble here by our doubts that there are, for the Chinese, concepts or entities corresponding to those taken for granted by our "allegory." Translation, shorn of its "habitual equivalences" anyway,[68] is metaphor: it occurs because someone has "seen the sameness" in the uses of unrelated signs. That is the optimistic theory, at any rate; readers with a different view of Chinese semantics may argue that "allegory" broadly used betokens not metaphor but catachresis or "abuse."[69] In that case the substitute evidence—or the filler we have to call a "substitute"—would substitute for nothing at all. The purported reading or translation of Chinese figures as allegories would be an imposition, and by accepting it we would show ourselves to be easily satisfied. The issue of cultural specificity, so often a matter of description and dosage, here sharpens into a choice.

Metaphor or catachresis, "seeing the sameness" or the imposition of displaced names: the career of the Jesuit missionary and translator Matteo Ricci (1552–1610) can be read as an "allégorie réelle" of the problem.[70] Ricci's plan for the conversion of the Chinese involved appropriating the language of the canonical books and official Confucianism to give Catholicism the vocabulary, and incidentally the prestige, it lacked. Converting the Chinese required, as a first step, converting the Classics: Ricci therefore set himself up as a private scholar and occasional lecturer, holding receptions in an "academy" under the patronage of Confucius.[71] Ricci's works in Chinese mixed commentary on the Classics with a modestly presented "Western learning," combining outlandish phrasing (nonce equivalents of terms like "substance" and "accident") with familiar allusions (e.g., in the presentation of substance and accident, a reference to Kung-sun Lung's ancient paradox of the White Horse).[72] The Chinese philosophers referred to heaven as the source of moral authority, as did Ricci; to one Chinese it was evident that "the doctrine of a heavenly ruler is no creation of Mr. Ricci's. . . . Since antiquity [the Europeans] have been cut off from China and have never heard of the teachings of [the culture-heroes] Fu Hsi, King Wen, the Duke of Chou, and Confucius. At first Ricci's explanations could not be made to harmonize with those of this country, but his maxims concerning 'knowing heaven' and 'man's duties to heaven' fit like a tally with what is written in our Classics and commentaries." If there was any "opportunism" to Ricci's "empathy,"[73] it escaped his Chinese colleagues' notice. Ricci's appreciative reader continues: "On the shores of the Eastern or the Western sea, the mind is the same and reason [*li*] is the same. What most differs is a matter of language and script"[74]—differences that a mere technique of translation (*ya-hua,* "repolishing") could be counted on to overcome.

The more adventurously Ricci reappropriated the signs of Chinese culture, the more his technique veered from translation into punning; the controversies over Ricci's method have always centered on the dubious good taste of this play on languages. (Much of Gernet's *Chine et christianisme* deals with the responses of Chinese scholars to Ricci's "abusive" interpretations. One index of how well Ricci's strategy worked is the fact that many of his opponents attack his *scholarship*—as if his object had been to seek the meaning, and not just to acquire the audience, of the Classics.) Against him, and chiefly after his death, a group of doctrinal purists tried to assert the impossibility of translation, contending that the Catholic theology could be communicated to the Chinese only in a language free of Chinese associations, which is to say without being translated. It is to both sides' obligation to offer some idea of what those Chinese associations were that we owe Leibniz's "Letter on the Natural Theology of the Chinese."

The immediate pretext of Leibniz's letter was Nicolas Malebranche's (1638–1715) *Conversation Between a Christian Philosopher and a Chinese Philosopher on the Existence and the Nature of God,* itself directed less at the Chinese and their Jesuit interpreters than at Spinoza. ("You have only to read 'Japanese' or 'Siamese' in place of 'Chinese.' Or better yet, read 'Frenchman'—for the impious

Spinoza's system makes havoc here, and I find Spinoza's impieties have much in common with those of our Chinese Philosopher.")[75] Leibniz's letter refrains from mentioning the recently dead Malebranche, concentrating its defense of the Chinese (and Spinoza) on a critique of Malebranche's main source of information about Chinese philosophy, an anti-accommodationist tract by Ricci's successor in the China mission, Niccolò Longobardi (1559–1654).[76]

Longobardi's piece blames Ricci and his early associates in the mission for a curious predicament of translation and crosstranslation in which the Jesuits found themselves by 1615. The Society's Visitor to Japan, Francesco Passio, had forwarded Longobardi a complaint: books composed in Chinese by Ricci and others and full of "errors similar to those of the gentiles [i.e., pagans]" had got into the hands of converts there. The price of assimilationism was beginning to make itself felt. "While [the missionaries in Japan] have been fighting against these errors, the pagans found support for them in the books written by our own Fathers." Worse yet, the Chinese literati so delicately courted by Ricci were adopting his reading methods and failing to distinguish the Thirteen Classics and the Jesuits' catechisms. As analogy gave way to identity, Longobardi saw syncretism looming: "For the [Chinese] Christian literati [now] habitually ascribe the meaning of our scriptures to their own"—fine testimony to Ricci's scholarly powers!—"and fancy"—again in Ricci's footsteps—"that they can find in Chinese books reasonings that mesh with our own holy law, without considering the importance of pursuing nothing but the truth and of saying nothing that may be compromised by deceit and untruth."[77]

The literati had become translators of their own books, all within the Chinese language. They had fallen into the snares of allegory, but were doing so (as the critics mentioned earlier might put it) as *monists*: instead of seeing ontological splits where none were intended, they took Ricci's borrowed Confucian language as the unequivocal content of his doctrine. Since (Longobardi suggests) they had misunderstood the nature of the things they were being asked to believe in, they became, *qua* converts, automata reporting on inner states that they could not possibly have had. "Where they *seem* to speak of our God and his angels, they are mere apes of the truth."[78]

Longobardi's reason for writing was to stop translation at its source.[79] His intent was to prove that nothing in the Chinese canonical books lends itself to such a reading and "that the Chinese, on the principles of their philosophy, have never known of any spiritual substance distinct, as we conceive it, from matter; and that consequently they have known neither God nor angels nor the rational soul."[80] Making evident the Chinese converts' failure to distinguish between spirit and matter would prove the necessity and justice of distinguishing what Ricci, the unreliable commentator, had conjoined. By arguing that the Chinese Classics could not possibly have meant what Ricci represented them as meaning, Longobardi anticipated the terms of the literary discussion we had before us a moment ago: Ricci's version of Confucian Catholicism was to be excluded for the very reasons that, for some twentieth-century literary scholars, make "Chinese allegory" an impossibility.

The main exhibit in Longobardi's digest of Chinese philosophy, the concept about which Malebranche's Chinese and Christian interlocutors argued and therefore the main object of Leibniz's disagreement with both authors, is the word *li*. The first issue is (of course) how to translate it.

> The first principle of the Chinese is called the *li, Reason* or basis of all nature, a most universal reason and substance; nothing is greater or better than this *li*. This great and universal cause is pure, unmoved, subtle, having neither body nor shape; it can be known only by the understanding. From the *li* (as *li*) emanate the five virtues of Piety, Justice, Religion, Prudence, and Faith,

as Leibniz puts it, footnoting Longobardi at every comma.[81] A discussion of Reason in Chinese could, it seems, take advantage of the happy coincidence of meaning (and indeed the word here is exactly that used by Li Chih-tsao in his 1628 preface to Ricci's catechism, quoted above); no need to invent a new word for this content, at least. But does the Logos translate? Can it be replaced with ready-made pagan signifiers? "Beware lest you be taken in by those false attributes beneath which venom lurks," warns Longobardi; "penetrate to the root of the question and you will see that the *li* is nothing other than prime matter," or, according to Longobardi's understanding of Chinese physics, a kind of air. "This air is regarded by the [Chinese] philosophers as the sole principle of things, or indeed as [identical to] being." "Whatever *seems* spiritual [in Chinese philosophy] is called *ch'i*, that is, air or some quality of air."[82] If *li* is prime matter and its "emanation," *ch'i* or "being," simply a kind of all-pervading gas, then a missionary who used them to name attributes of the deity would be preaching, unknown to himself, a kind of pantheistic materialism.[83] Translating the Logos betrays it, in Longobardi's view. The passages of the Chinese Classics on which this critique particularly rests state that the *li* (like *T'ien,* Heaven, or, to give a translation that would satisfy Longobardi, "the sky") is "inanimate, lifeless, without foresight or intelligence."

Leibniz's response comes from his reading in eccentric theology. The epithets are perhaps to be taken figuratively, and the negatives as negations of figure: "If the classical authors of the Chinese deny life, knowledge, and authority to the *li* or first principle, they doubtless mean all these things *anthropopathically,* as applied to human beings. . . . While giving the *li* all the greatest perfections, they will give it something yet grander than all that." When the Chinese refuse the predicate of "consciousness" to the *li,* what they mean to negate is consciousness in the narrowly human sense, consciousness that worries about the future and is unsure how to choose the best means for the best ends. Their scruple respecting this necessarily inadequate likeness of the divine mind is "similar to that of certain mystics, among them Dionysios the Pseudo-Areopagite, who denied that God was a being (*ens, ōn*), while saying at the same time that he was more-than-being (*super-ens, hyperousia*)."[84]

Even Leibniz's defenders express dismay at this way of talking. What on earth can negative theology tell us about this very positive discussion? "Any ploy, any argument, relevant or not, is good enough in his eyes if it will bring the *li* of the Chinese philosophers closer to his God."[85] Theological bravado and a talent for hijacking the question sum up the interest of the *hyperousia* argument, and its pertinence goes unlooked for.

Two strands of pertinence concern us here. First, Leibniz does answer an argument with an argument and a reading with a reading, as we are expected to do in these situations, but he also answers Longobardi's thesis with a trope and reveals the necessarily rhetorical underpinnings of this translation from the Chinese. To reformulate their disagreement: Longobardi denies the *li*, and thereby the Chinese who speak of it as a "first principle," a metaphysical dimension and justifies this by reading his Chinese sources *literally*, that is, as if what they said (about what there is) were no more or less than what they meant. Leibniz counters with a reading based on a trope—call it allegory, irony, antiphrasis, catachresis, or litotes—that makes the relation between what is said and what is meant, or in this case between Being and Logos, rather less easy to determine. (Leibniz's reading is both an allegorism as regards the words on the page and a reading of those words *as* allegory: as the philosopher said of the enjoyment of pictures, allegory causes us to risk a "double error.") Longobardi draws up a list of the things the religious vocabulary of the Chinese refers to, a different list, to his mind, from that of the missionaries; Leibniz asks if religious language refers at all, or to anything at all.[86] (Reference in spite of, or in the absence of, its referents—that would be one way of putting allegory's relation to the rest of language.) Whatever else the discussion is about—intellectual history, theology, anthropology, or comparative literature—it is rhetorical through and through; for central to its other issues is the very possibility of reading, in particular of identifying statements as literal or figurative.

Second, it is no mean accomplishment—particularly for a logician—to turn the verb "to be" into a metaphor or even an antiphrasis of its own meaning, as Leibniz does when he equates "nonbeing" and "more-than-being."[87] Certainly the kind of being we are able to conceive of is anthropopathic being, being "à la manière humaine"; attributing it to beings that, like the *li*, are not human is

an abuse of terms, however unavoidable. "Being," like "life, knowledge, and authority," is a misnomer—but one with more drastic
consequences. For Being takes all naming—all nouns—with it.[88]
When we say that the difference between being and non-being may
be bridged or neutralized by a figure of speech (that is, by taking
the terms and their opposition as incidental, *merely* figurative),
figure gains immensely in power—all ontology now falls under the
sway of rhetorical reading—but loses in quality or application.
"Non-meaning" (or the "absent" signifier replaced by a catachresis)
takes on the proportions of "more-than-meaning." Making the
copula ("is"), rather than the terms (subject and predicate), the site
of metaphoricity makes every possible sentence about divinity part
of an extended metaphor and rather nicely (though heretically)
cuts the ground from under Longobardi's feet: in point of "spiritual
substances," we are no better informed than the Chinese, and the
purists' theology turns out to have for its real subject a displaced
anthropology. Translation in the everyday sense, or the assumption
of semantic correspondence between languages, breaks down at
exactly the same points as the assumption of literalness, or reference, does. It is not, as the objections to the notion of "Chinese
allegory" would have it, that the "other worlds" imagined by the
Chinese are just an extension of "this world," whereas the Euro-
peans' "other worlds" are truly "other." *C'est tout comme ici.*

Does Leibniz's critique of Longobardi end in a Pyrrhic victory
for both teams, with no conclusions surviving? If we accept Leibniz's objections—that no necessity attaches to the literal reading as
such, that it is just one trope among others, to wit, that of literaliza-
tion—the distance between textual body and semantic ghost may
no longer be constant or calculable. What can be pinned down,
however, is the effect of a tropological reading on the thing it claims
to read. Reading Chinese texts in an immanentist way, Longobardi
detects their immanentism; reading them as if their rhetoric had to
transcend their grammar, Leibniz sees evidence of transcendence—
a hyper-transcendence in fact, one that differs from the standard
version of theological transcendence by just as far as allegory differs
from metaphor. No "shared property," "transferred designation,"

"common meaning-class," or "system of associations" seems likely to rationalize this figure, since it is a translation (or catachresis?) based on a word use that erases the difference between similarity and difference.[89] It cannot be interpreted, at any rate, by reference to knowledge of existents. Is this how the possibility of translation, seemingly "destroyed" a few pages ago, is to be restored? Heidegger again: "But where it is a matter of bringing to language something that has not yet been spoken, everything lies in the question of whether language gives the appropriate word or refuses it. The latter case is the poet's."[90]

~

An Analogical Table: concerning incorporeal things that may be depicted through some resemblance to corporeals, including virtues, vices, divinity (here: Hieroglyphs). Characters of the Chinese. Moral Sphere. Syllogismometer. La carte du Tendre. Devises choisies. Choice of Emblems.

—Leibniz, "Atlas universalis"[91]

We began with a translation problem that could not be solved in either of the languages in which it was posed, and we came just now to a solution of a translation problem in which knowledge, or language's power of referring to objects, had to be sacrificed for the work of translation to be carried out. Does the last example answer to the first? How far does it carry? Is it a model to follow?

The thing to keep in mind here is that this solution is a choice—a recognizably Leibnizian solution, one aimed at ensuring the existence of the biggest, and therefore the best, set of compossible worlds.[92] Something has to go, however, and so Leibniz, acting as Solomon, chooses to preserve the translatability of human languages into one another by denying all of them access to the divine dialect. In an allegorical painting, this might be Faith's submission to Charity. We may call it an Enlightenment gesture (if a few years ahead of schedule), one after which talk about cultures and religions in the plural becomes possible. The coexistence of so many incompatible versions of what there is to refer to becomes tolerable by deriving reference itself from a figural logic.[93] Translation over-

leaps itself and passes into tropology. Or to put it in a slightly different language: when Leibniz finds a number of national under-
standings vying for the same piece of ontological *territory*, he makes
shift to reorganize that territory—every inch of it—into several
independent *realms*.[94]

Thus figural mediation (with its expansion into a new rhetorical
or aesthetic "space of representation") is called into being for the
sake of a cultural project both pluralistic and cosmopolitan, and it
is in the light of a lingering cosmopolitan ideal that we need to
consider the problems of aesthetic pluralism.[95] In what measure
does the nature of aesthetic reflection neutralize, by frictionlessly
integrating them, national themes and ontologies?

The agitation over allegory provides a splendid test case and a
curious revision of the cosmopolitan ideal. Strict culturalists would
sacrifice the linguistic or aesthetic buffer zone provided by a gesture
like Leibniz's, so that the cultures can contrast more starkly. But
contrast is a mode of relation and can be expressed only by invoking relations. There is therefore paradox, but also inevitability, in
the way the critics who propose alternatives to a "Western," metaphysical reading of Chinese figurative language resort to a language
of Christian connotations ("upward" versus "outward," etc.) to
provide the meta-language in which the relation of Christianity to
its "other" is to be stated. For the practical purposes of their
description, then, Christianity has no "other." The theory of difference runs ahead of its practice (and for good reason, too: there may
be no such thing as a single "practice of difference"). Can the differences between cultures be instances of such *determinate* negation?
If there is to be relativism, it should be thoroughgoing enough to
raise the critical question of how, and in relation to what, differences and relativities are to be discovered and formulated.

Leibniz's answer to Longobardi addresses this question too.
However Longobardi phrases the difference between the Chinese
and European mental universes, Leibniz is able to retranslate that
difference into a difference within European thinking. Far from
excluding or silencing the "other," this strategy makes Chinese
thinking right at home in Europe, or reminds European thinking

of its own unacknowledged strangeness. If the Chinese *t'ien* receives an exclusively physical interpretation, can the reader in good conscience grant automatic transcendence to such signifiers as "spiritual substance," "God," "angels," and "the rational soul" (to quote Longobardi's list of test cases)? The opposition of China to Europe, an opposition constructed on the model of the difference between signs ("apes") and their meaning ("truth"), cannot long survive the demonstration of an equally irreconcilable opposition between sign and meaning within Europe. Thus the paradox of linguistically mediated difference becoming partial and identical—a paradox that cannot but occur—is reformulated and, in some respects, reversed. In place of inter-linguistic difference guaranteed by an assumed inter-linguistic identity (i.e., the difference between European spiritualism and Chinese physicalism, which presupposes a generally applicable standard of discrimination between spirit and matter), Leibniz's formulation leaves us with inter-linguistic identities founded on intra-linguistic differences. The line Leibniz draws between being and reference erases the line Longobardi drew between spirit and matter.

The drawing of that second line introduces new ground rules for comparative reading. The conclusion of this chapter is that the Leibnizian rules are the only ones adequate to the game in which we (along with Longobardi, Yu, Plaks, and Owen, just to name a few) are already players. What are categories but sets of allowable moves with the verb "is"? And how are the many different categorical maps (maps not, by the way, coterminous with cultures or languages) to be reconciled except by allowing that verb to mean more than one thing at the same time? "Is" becomes figural for the same reasons that "literally," in the example of "fragrant" virtue, came laden with too many alternative literalities for us to hope it would keep to one literal sense. And the purpose of Leibniz's remarks on the word "pneuma" (breath/spirit) is not only to guarantee the equation *ch'i = pneuma* but also to remind us that the categories that permit us to detect allegory, literalness, and metaphor may themselves be unrecognized allegories. Behind the translator's problem (*ch'i = pneuma?*) lies the philosopher's and the philologist's problem (*pneuma* [breath] = *pneuma* [spirit]?). The allegory of the theologians *is* the allegory of the grammarians.

The question about the translatability of figures receives, there-fore, a mixed answer. It depends on what you think there is to translate—and on what you expect it to be translated into. For one group of readers, rhetorical language takes place under document-able cultural or ideological conditions, and reading that does not recover those conditions is just so much lost data. Translation, for those readers, is a matter of reconstructing the possibility of refer-ence in a new context. For a second type of reader—for Leibniz, that is—the way in which the social ontology is put forth only announces a further problem of knowledge and reference, one to which there can be no adequate "background," social or other. If allegory is not a mode of meaning or reference but a name for what happens when modes of meaning and reference are revealed to be incompatible, might allegory not then "translate absolutely"?[96] Allegory—unlike interpretation—would have nothing to lose.

Our task as readers of the *Book of Odes* leads back over this ground: first, then, toward the reconstruction of the possibility of reference.

§ 2 The Other Side of Allegory

> [There are] things . . . in which one sees a purpo-
> sive form, without being able to assign them any
> purpose: for example, those stone implements occa-
> sionally dug out of old grave mounds, with a hole
> in them, as if for a handle. Although their shape
> clearly does indicate a purposiveness, without any-
> one's knowing what the purpose is, they are none-
> theless not for that reason considered beautiful.
>
> —Kant, *Critique of Judgment*

How did there come to be a problem of "Chinese allegory"? If
there are Chinese allegories—for nothing has yet been proved
beyond their *possibility*—what do they allegorize and why? What
repercussions have they had on the Chinese literary tradition?

An exact answer will have to be a long one. The literary traditions best acquainted with the theory of allegory are, after all, those
of peoples long "cut off," as Ricci's friend Li Chih-tsao put it, "from
the teachings of Fu Hsi, King Wen, the Duke of Chou, and
Confucius." The Western reader has some catching up to do.

Fortunately, the *Book of Odes* has generated its own tradition,
even outside China. The theoretical wing of Chinese literary studies owes much to the tradition of *Odes* explication—as much,
perhaps, as it does to any other easily singled out period, author, or
topic. That the *Odes* can so readily become the testing ground for
the most wide-ranging hypotheses about the nature of the Chinese
literary imagination already tells us something about the frame of
mind in which readers still approach the collection. In this chapter
I argue that it is not only the text that is ageless. The question about
allegory in relation to the *Book of Odes*, though a recent introduction to discussions of Chinese literature and one, moreover, inspired by comparatist considerations, comes as a familiar guest.
Under its new vocabulary are outlines of some of the longest-lived

problems in Chinese literary history. A survey of those venerable puzzles may help us reframe and even solve some of the new ones.

~

The great mass of traditional *Odes* scholarship admits of few generalizations, but it is surely safe to say that working out a theory of literary allegory has not been one of its main concerns. Not the least reason for this is generic constraint, if the Chinese equivalent of "allegory" is to be *yü-yen*.[1] Closer to the heart of the problem, but a label for a style of commentary only, is *fu-hui*: "addition [of sense] from outside." In any case "allegorical," if the word had had much of a career in *Odes* exegesis, would have been no term of praise. It can hardly be a coincidence that the Prefaces, long canonical, disappeared from new editions of the *Odes* at about the same time as they began to be called "allegorical." Both events derive from a re-evaluation of the classical tradition whose after-effects are still with us. The epithet was first applied to the Confucian interpretations of the *Odes* by nineteenth-century translators impressed mainly by their absurdity;[2] a native strain of skepticism simply calls them inauthentic and contorted. Talk of the Prefaces as "allegorical" combines, in a possibly fortuitous way, documentary and hermeneutical suspicions that all is not as it seems.

How did this come about? Most historians of the subject point to the philosopher and erudite Chu Hsi (1130–1200), whose edition of the *Odes* often distances itself, on grounds of verisimilitude, from the moralizing maneuvers of the ancient Prefaces. As Chu Hsi tells it, "When I began to write my *Annotations to the Odes*, I used the Little Prefaces as my guides to the literal meaning, and where their glosses would not work, I twisted the sense in their favor. Afterwards, I felt uneasy, and when I redid the annotations, I kept the Little Prefaces but took issue with them here and there. Still, the poets' meaning could not come forth clearly. Finally I understood what I was doing: as soon as I had removed all the Prefaces, the meaning came through. When you've discarded all the old explanations, then the meaning of the *Odes* comes alive again." A generation later Chu Hsi's follower Wang Po (1197–1274) not only rejected the orthodox interpretations but on rereading the poems shorn of commentary denounced many of them as "poems of lust and elopement."[3] Twentieth-century critics may take a more nuanced view of lust and elopement, but they still claim to know the difference between what a poem does and does not say. In the 1920's Cheng Chen-to, for example, proclaimed:

> The greatest flaw of the Prefaces lies in their *distortion of the poems' meaning, their forced and incorrect interpretations.* . . . Not one of their interpretations is acceptable. If we are to pull the *Book of Odes* out from under this kitchen midden of accumulated notes and commentaries and do new work on it, the first order of business will be to overturn the Prefaces to the *Odes.*[4]

For Cheng as much as for Chu Hsi, the Prefaces were an obstacle worth trying to overturn. But to the reading public for Chinese poetry today all this sounds rather like a dead question, or like a debate decisively resolved in the past and recent enough not to need bringing up again. Not many people (without special scholarly provocation) read the Prefaces any more, and those who do read them know better than to swallow them whole. Their authority did not—could not, it may be—long survive the imperial examination system with its requirement of orthodoxy in the interpretation and application of the *Odes* and other Classics. And the qualities modern readers find to praise in the *Odes* need prefacing of a different kind: most admirers of the poems get along quite well without a prose accompaniment of "moral effusions" and "political significations." Presentations of the classic in schoolbooks, anthologies, and editions for the nonspecialist reader, not to mention translations like Waley's, usually relegate these matters to a few bemused paragraphs in a postface.

For centuries it has been a scholarly sport to hunt out errors and inconsistencies in the Prefaces. But in the critical lineage that runs from Chu Hsi to Cheng Chen-to, verisimilitude, and not mere factual accuracy, has been the best yardstick for measuring the Prefaces' failings. For readers like Chu and Cheng, just showing that the commentary deviates from the poems is enough to make it disappear. Marcel Granet speaks one language with centuries of

Chinese scholars when he contends that the Prefaces tell us about only the "derivative ritual use" of the classic and must therefore be ignored in a reading that aims to recover its "original sense." And Pauline Yu's defense of the Prefaces is closely tied to a claim that their meaning (when read rightly) is quite unallegorical. As if in answer to Chu Hsi, her defense stresses the substantial reality of the *lei* or "categorical correspondences" that unite image and meaning, poem and commentary.[5] Only recently have the old explanations regained a lesser textual respectability as documents typical of that strand of early Han thought deriving from Hsün-tzu (ca. 310–ca. 215).[6] But for a text that used to be honored as authoritative, this is a pale kind of afterlife.

Allegory, then, or "saying one thing and meaning another," is clearly not what Chinese readers want, or have wanted for some time, from a set of prefaces to the *Odes*. The matter is therefore somewhat different from the exegetical tradition of the *Song of Songs*, in which the sheer suspension of disbelief demanded by the moralizing approach proves as fertile literarily as anything it particularly says.[7] To take a positive interest in the Prefaces' allegorical character—in the ways they depart from the letter of the text—cuts across the grain of nearly all *Odes* research, for it amounts to devoting oneself to writings that everyone agrees are neither solid history nor interesting fiction. No wonder they find so few partisans. What do the readers want? Where did the Prefaces go wrong?

To ask these questions is to enter into the problem of the origin and meaning (and even, for reasons to be explained shortly, the purpose) of the *Odes*. The blame is variously placed. Maybe Confucius (551–479 B.C.) is at fault; that would make twenty-five centuries of *Odes* studies a case of his killing the thing he loved. To be convinced of that love one has only to look at the value Confucius placed on the *Odes* as a guide to manners and morals, a record of antiquity, and a storehouse of elegance in language. Confucius said: "It is inspired by the *Odes*. It comes to stand with the *Ritual*. It is perfected by the *Music*."[8] And again: "Study the 'Chou-nan' and the 'Shao-nan' [sections of the *Odes*]. One who has not studied the 'Chou-nan' and the 'Shao-nan' is like someone standing with his face to the wall."[9] Starting from the Master, then, around the *Odes* condense all the expectations a classic is supposed to fulfill. The *Odes* are the young person's initiation into culture (*hsing*, "be inspired," can also mean "begin"): there could hardly be a stronger way of putting their canonical standing.

Confucius referred to "the *Odes*" (*fu Shih*: *Lun yü* 17.9), but what has been passed down to posterity is not the genus but the species, that is, various competing schools of *Odes* learning, each with its own variant text and style of commentary. The *Odes'* position is indisputable, but can as much be said for their one surviving complete recension? This edition, technically known as the *Mao Shih* (The *Odes* as edited by Master Mao), may take its name from Mao Ch'ang, an otherwise little-known figure who taught his version of the *Odes* at a provincial court around 140 B.C., or from Mao Ch'ang's forebear Mao Heng, who is said to have studied under the philosopher Hsün-tzu. It first gained official recognition some generations after the other main schools of *Odes* learning and differs from each of them (as far as the fragmentary evidence permits judging) in ways great and small. How well does the Mao edition approximate the *Odes* Confucius knew or merit his extravagant praise?

There is much to separate them. Three times in the *Lun yü* appear lines or stanzas in the standard *Odes* meter and incorporating *Odes* phrases but otherwise unknown. Such fragments are known as "lost odes," poems that might have belonged to the corpus of some 3,000 poems from which Confucius is supposed to have made the anthology.[10] The identity of the lost odes probably matters less than the fact, which other sources confirm, that poems now in the canon were still being composed in Confucius' lifetime. The titles of other lost odes have been preserved in a prose fragment attached to the preface to Ode 177, "Liu yüeh," in the "Lesser Elegantiae" (*Hsiao ya*) section.[11] That fragment lists twenty-two titles within a thematic framework of the kind emulated by part of the Mao edition's Great Preface. Of the twenty-two, six are lost. If the passage survives from an earlier version of the *Book of Odes* and if it is a fair statistical sample, its rate of loss suggests that a hundred poems may have vanished from the collection between the date of that passage and the promulgation of the present text.

Although some of the poems are occasionally dated to the eleventh century B.C., and one, perhaps the last to join the set, alludes to events of the period 520–514,[12] the Mao commentary is first mentioned as attracting the attention of the bibliophile Prince Hsien of Ho-chien (r. 155–129 B.C.).[13] Several centuries, then, separate the probable date of an Ode's composition and the earliest date from which the Mao edition's textual history can be followed. Furthermore, the intervening years—namely, the Warring States and Ch'in periods—brought drastic changes to the cultural landscape in which the *Odes* had been produced. The reader of the Mao edition of the *Odes* needs to be informed about such latter-day events as the dwindling and collapse of the Chou empire (whose institutions the *Book of Odes* often mentions); Confucius, who made the *Odes* part of his teaching and influenced their transmission in incalculable ways; the rise of antagonistic philosophical schools; and the rise of two new dynasties, the Ch'in (whose first emperor ordered the destruction of all the old humanistic learning including that of the *Odes*) and the Han (whose policy of cultural reconstruction, veering between rival schools of interpretation, led at the very least to the rewriting of many pre-Ch'in texts under the guise of preserving them). All these developments postdate the composition of the *Odes*, but are very much part of the consciousness of their annotators.

It would be unusual if the Mao annotations were not a product of their times. The Prefaces are marked, to take the simplest kind of case, by eclectic and sometimes inaccurate historical information, complicated by well-meaning attempts to account for the poems' allusions to a vanished society. All these are easily attributed to belatedness and to the reconstructive character, following the Ch'in dynasty's destruction of the old classical schools, of the Mao editors' enterprise.

A more specific critique links whatever is wrong with the Mao Prefaces to the Mao text's role (a minor one) in the scholarly politics of the middle Han dynasty. When the *Mao Odes* first appeared, it was received into the canon of Old Text scholarship, as against the then predominant Three Schools of *Odes* learning,[14] not because it had any claims to Old Text authority, but because it drew for its historical and interpretative material on the classical texts favored by the Old Text school. Whereas the Three Schools took their background information from the *Kung-yang* and *Ku-liang* commentaries to the *Spring and Autumn Annals*, the Mao school referred to the *Tso Commentary*, the *Conversations of the States* (*Kuo yü*),[15] the *Rituals of Chou* (*Chou li*), and versions of the treatises compounded at about that time into the *Record of Ritual* (particularly the "Record of Music" or "Yüeh chi"; New Text counterparts to these texts survive as fragments in collections of Han apocrypha or *wei-shu*).[16]

Despite its implications, the "old" in "Old Text school" is a sign of belatedness. In the late third century B.C., the short-lived Ch'in dynasty tried to ban all writings except those on technology, agriculture, and divination. All other books were to be handed over to a central library, and citizens were forbidden to keep or teach them. Books were burned, and scholars buried alive; at the end, in the course of the dynasty's fall, the palace library in which all the old literature had been deposited burned too. (It is often forgotten that the First Emperor of Ch'in also instituted an imperial academy with chairs for "doctors" [*po-shih*] in various classics, a system continued by the Han.) This left the literati at the beginning of the Han dynasty with two ways of recovering the past. One was to make a new text from whatever remained in the memories of scholars (hence "New Text," i.e., written in the characters current after 200 B.C.). The other was to search for buried or hidden texts: these could be copied directly from the ancient script (hence "Old Text," from the form of the characters). Antagonism between Old and New Text scholars—who could be counted on to consider each other impostors—ran deep.[17]

In any case, the Mao edition's rise was pinned to that of the Old Text classics. While Prince Hsien of Ho-chien was encouraging Mao Ch'ang's researches into the *Odes*, the Han emperors Wen (r.

179–157 B.C.) and Ching (156–141) appointed doctors in each of the Three Schools. These chairs continued to be endowed, with occasional vacancies. It was not until the reign of P'ing-ti (A.D. 1–6) that an academic chair for the *Mao Odes* was established, as was one for the "Record of Music."[18] This victory came under inauspicious patronage. The great sponsor of Old Text scholarship in those days was Wang Mang, P'ing-ti's chief minister and later regent for the infant thirteenth Han emperor. Within three years of his assuming the regency, Wang Mang usurped the throne, justifying his action with phrases culled from the Old Text version of the *Book of Documents* and spurious writings of his own invention.[19] Upon the re-establishment of the Han seventeen years later, the Old Text school was seen as compromised. Only after another half century, through the energetic advocacy of Chia K'uei, was a doctor reappointed for the *Tso Commentary* to the *Spring and Autumn Annals*. In A.D. 83 the Old Text works as a group finally regained imperial support: an edict of Chang-ti (r. 76–88) enjoined scholars throughout the land to receive the *Tso Commentary*, the Old Text *Book of Documents*, and the Mao text of the *Odes*.

Thus, the Mao text and its version of ancient history embody one avenue, but only one and a disputed one at that, to the Han dynasty's goal of recovering, resystematizing, and laying claim to the literature of antiquity. Recent authors like K'ang Yu-wei and Ku Chieh-kang, inclined to New Text attitudes and opposed to the orthodoxy in force since the Han, see the Mao redaction's success as the reward of political agility, not of scholarship.[20] Since the political concerns are, in any case, those of the Han, not of the Chou, the "forced" and "derivative" interpretations of the Mao Prefaces are a matter of revisionism with its eye on the main chance.[21]

All these are ways of putting the responsibility for the Mao Prefaces on the editors and champions of the *Mao Odes*. What is wrong with the Mao Prefaces is, for the writers just mentioned, simply that they get in the way, that they hide the light of antiquity under a bushel of Han dynasty concerns. Interpretations of the Mao tradition always imply or require an interpretation of ancient history, and of intellectual history in particular; and interpretation, in such a case, seems fatally to involve choosing sides. Authors who trace the deviant character of the Prefaces to the Han tend to represent higher antiquity (the Chou, Spring and Autumn, and Warring States periods) rather differently than do advocates of the orthodox tradition formed on the basis of the (largely Old Text) Thirteen Classics. Critique carried out in this manner cannot but be sweeping. If the Han established the interpretative horizon within which subsequent readers have worked, then any text and any interpretation touched by the industrious commentators of the Han becomes suspect. The problems of the Classics' textual history then become very nearly identical to the problems of Chinese civilization as a whole.

A pattern of argument emerges: if the Mao Prefaces are the symptom of an ancient misunderstanding, then the historical critique that attempts to account for them must (like the epic muse) say where the first lapse occurred. The "forced explanations" encountered in the Prefaces are not of the kind that begin with a local mistake and spread along a chain of transmissions and reinterpretations; they result from definite presuppositions methodically applied. So consistent an error must originate in some basic misunderstanding, and to have gone on so long without being dispelled, that misunderstanding must have been common to the whole literate public. In the case of the *Odes*, the differences among schools shrink almost to nothing in comparison with what later generations have seen as the discrepancies between the classical texts and their post-classical commentaries (of whatever school). The problem is not really one of Old Text versus New Text, but rather one of the Han-era conflict of Old and New Texts versus the truly classical, but lost, pre-Han traditions.[22] The Old Text scholars were powerless to offer alternatives to *that* problem.

Perhaps, then (to paraphrase the logic of what has now become the received explanation of the *Mao Odes'* eccentricities), the flaw lies much farther down. All the theories discussed above treat the *Odes* as a defined corpus, different versions and interpretations of which could become matters of academic debate—a clerical theory of the *Odes* suited to the interests of those who wrote histories, collated editions, and advised emperors in ancient China. But that is to inquire into the transmission of the *Book of Odes*, not its origins. Where did the *Odes* come from before they fell into the hands of the scholars?

For the Mao school, that is not even a question, since most of the Prefaces refer the meaning of a poem back to the (supposed) circumstances of its composition, circumstances the brush-and-ink men were always happy to supply. To accept the Mao version of the meaning of a poem is to accept the Mao story of its origin. The formula "This poem was composed by such a one in order to satirize (or praise) so-and-so" stamps a reading with just that kind of authority, and the reader willing to explore the fine print of successive commentaries finds that later skeptics usually do the historical anecdote the honor of engaging with it briefly before rejecting the interpretation it is supposed to ground. The anecdote is, however, the weakest link in the chain, and the Mao school weakens it even more by accepting another theory, one found in many ancient texts, on the rise of the *shih* genre.

> From the princes down, each has fathers and elder brothers, sons and younger brothers, to guide and examine his administration. [In the case of the Son of Heaven,] the grand historians compose books, the blind musicians make poems [*shih*], the music masters chant admonitions, the officers rectify, and functionaries transmit [toward the court] what is said [by the common people]. . . . So the [lost work] *Documents of the Hsia Dynasty* says: "Heralds take up wooden clappers and go up and down the roads" [sc. in search of folk songs].

So runs a well-known passage in the *Tso Commentary*; the T'ang commentator K'ung Ying-ta (574–648) clarifies that the heralds' booty is "*shih* composed by the people. After a selection of folk chants had been made, blind musicians [at court] turned them into satirical and cautionary songs. But the blind musicians did not themselves compose the lyrics."[23]

Is this the origin of the *Book of Odes*? Chinese utopias tend to be set in the remote past, but the texts that describe them often prove more recent than claimed; true to type, the poetry-collecting bureau's activities are referred back (in this Han revision of a Warring States text) to an even earlier and less well documented dynasty, the Hsia. (Not even Confucius could speak with much confidence about the Hsia, according to *Analects* 3.9.) For strict historians, the poetry-collecting network—whose connections to the *Book of Odes* are in any case mainly inferential—may have to remain in the province of folklore about folklore.[24] But it is a tradition to which the Mao school often alludes, somewhat to the detriment of its penchant for interpreting through incident, background, and context: for in ancient China as elsewhere, indefinite origin and wide circulation rank high among the defining characteristics of folk song.

Modern readers have been quick to seize on this seeming incongruity. No one knows exactly where the *Book of Odes* comes from, yet the idea that part of it might derive from folk songs underscores in many readers' minds the absurdity of the old commentaries. Ku Chieh-kang argues that "because the literati of former ages had so little experience of popular songs, they were unable to understand their meaning. Not understanding them, they nonetheless forced interpretations on them and inevitably gave rise to irrelevant theories."[25] Granet, too, explains the uneasy fit of text and commentary as an effect of social discrepancies. For the reader willing to reject the allegorical interpretation, the *Odes* are by and large a faithful record of customs predating the Chou expansion through the central China plains. Under a new system of government and education, the immorality (in metropolitan eyes) of many of the songs required that a new reading be superimposed on the literal meaning, just as new and more restrictive customs had been imposed on the carefree villagers; "a preoccupation with moral orthodoxy hindered [the interpreters] from understanding the ancient peasant customs." Reading the poems in their "original sense" will restore the original autonomy of the village customs.[26]

The Mao interpretations therefore appear as an excess, an outgrowth on already self-sufficient works of folk art. The fact that here literati culture becomes the obstacle and folk tradition the lost truth of antiquity no doubt accounts for the popularity of this conception among what may be called the May Fourth generation of writers on literature, the revisionary critics and historians who, after 1919, came forward to propose new versions of the Chinese past.[27] With popularity goes some distortion: the "Airs of the States" (*Kuo feng*) section of the *Odes*, that in which the greatest number of folk songs has been detected, becomes synecdochic of the whole of the *Odes* as battle lines are drawn to oppose text and commentary. Witness Ch'en P'an: "The 'Erh nan' [i.e., the first twenty-five poems of the 'Airs of the States' section] originated as popular songs . . . but even these have been spoiled by those Han explainers with their footnote-trailing latter-day notions about the 'virtue of King Wen' and the like!"[28] The methods of the old scholars who could turn a trysting song into a cento of praise for some wise administrator symbolized the skittish hypocrisy of what Hu Shih called "Confucius & Sons."

Given the eternally politicized nature of literary studies in China, it is hard to see how scholars of Hu Shih's generation, still groping for their position in the new republican order, could resist taking up cudgels for the people (as opposed to their rulers), poetry (as against tartuffery in prose) and the free and easy mores described in many poems of the "Airs of the States" (as against the Han commentators' puritanism). The campaign to overturn the Mao Prefaces is May Fourth in a nutshell.[29] (It is also a remarkable gesture of devotion to what seemed worth saving in the Confucian canon, despite all that the canon had been made to say.) Yet in their eagerness to locate the first misunderstanding in the moment of the songs' passing from the mouths of the multitude to the repertoire of court musicians and the literary bureaucracy, opponents of the Mao Prefaces often pass over the dynastic hymns of the collection's second half and disregard the fact that the various odes were not composed in a day: indeed, the folk songs compose a late stratum of the work and most likely show in their composition the influence of temple and court music.[30] The pure folk element recedes the more ardently we look for it. The ever-skeptical Ku Chieh-kang leaves the reader of his essays on the *Odes* torn between iconoclastic alternatives: true, the Mao commentaries betray a courtier's distance from peasant life, but so, on a closer examination, do the songs.[31]

The *Odes* may not be pure folk songs, but calling them folk songs
has its advantages. It is an economical move. If a folk song seems to
be about poverty or elopement, it must be about poverty or elopement—or at least that is how the scholars view folk song. "When
the common people broke into song, it was purely a release of
emotions, and they gave no thought to any other purpose; but
nobles who composed songs had various applications in mind."[32]
The commentators' and pedagogues' taste for "applications" is by
now well known to us. Here it has been pushed back several
centuries and given a place in Warring States society. When poems
that are not originally noble are read as noble or erudite works, a
figurative sense is imposed on them from outside. And so the long-
standing issue of the Mao Prefaces' historical reliability is lined
with a distinction between literal meaning and figurative meaning.
With this, the *Book of Odes* takes its place at the center of comparative discussions of allegory, and a whole theory of Chinese figurality
develops around it. But the fact that calling the Prefaces allegorical
is still a criticism suggests that the opposition of allegorical sense to
literal sense is, for Chinese readers anyway, derivative of the major
premise of the Prefaces' inauthenticity and secondary to it.

Built into criticism of the Prefaces as ideologically weighted,
unnatural, and hypocritical is the supposition, both as a matter of
history and of interpretation, of an uncorrupted state in which the
poems might be able to speak for themselves. Here the figural
approach joins that of the history of scholarship: literalness is as
much a necessity of the rhetorical argument as a pre-Han, pre-
commentary *Book of Odes* is of the anti-Confucian one. The theory
of Chinese allegory as a subsection of *Odes* scholarship has not only
adopted this position but also reinforced it by deriving from it
further distinctions and definitions. Donald Holzman, going back
long before the Han in search of the Prefaces' intellectual background, calls Confucius' quotations from the *Odes* examples of
"ruthless misinterpretation," "condoning the deliberate misinterpretation of the poem so that it can be *used* as a moral tag."[33] If the
error is deliberate and the poem no willing party to it, then the two
moments—what the text says and what the reader makes it say—
ought to be easily separable. For Zhang Longxi, discussing a related

topic, "there is a crucial difference between allegorical reading of a non-allegorical work and allegorical writing consciously applying the mode of allegorization in weaving the text,"[34] and Pauline Yu advises that "critics would be wise to specify which of the two processes they are concerned with."[35] Zhang explains further:

> The love songs in the *Shih ching*, particularly in the *Kuo feng* section, are not conscious allegories, but they were read allegorically by Confucian commentators who imposed an ethico-political interpretation on the texts in spite of what the texts literally mean. It is beyond question for me that Confucian exegesis of the *Shih ching* is ideologically motivated allegoresis . . . [which] arose as a means to justify the canonicity of the *Shih ching*.[36]

In this reconstruction, the scandalous contents of many poems (if taken literally) account for the allegorizers' need to misread them. That should be overwhelming evidence of the secondariness and derivative character of the figurative readings. But this reconstruction, however convincing in itself, can, like the others, be turned around and shown to generate its own premises. It is important to distinguish allegory from allegoresis, lest the poems be seen as conniving in their own misuse (and allegorical and pre-allegorical meaning then collapse into one). But before we can distinguish literal and figurative meaning, or allegory and allegoresis, we have to have already made that distinction. That is, we have to be sure of knowing "what the texts literally mean" apart from their allegorical interpretation. And the difficulty of knowing that (other than by intimate conviction) may be what gives *Odes* scholarship its special charm.

A "first meaning," however described, is the logical precondition for theories about how the poems came to acquire their allegorical Prefaces—allegorical tending to mean, in this context, secondary, excessive, and ideologically fraught. The past hundred years of scholarship has tended to identify the disputed poems' "literal" meaning—what they say to an unbiased modern reader without footnotes, or what, in the folklorists' view, the simple singer looking for "emotional release" must have meant—with that logically required first meaning. The oddity is that the documents to support this schematic narrative are wanting. In countless texts from Confucius' day and before—the *Tso Commentary* being particularly rife with examples—the poems are never allowed to speak for themselves. "The *Shih ching* was used, in ancient diplomatic meetings, as an important *instrument of exchange*: by quoting appropriate verses, out of context and with tendentious interpretations . . . the diplomats could, guardedly and politely, put forth their respective positions" (my italics).[37] Again and again the exchange-value of the poems is shown as essential, and their intrinsic value is passed over in silence. Of course, there is a meaning to the silence. Wang Chin-ling's formulation of the problem is admirably concise:

> When the great officers of the feudal states "chanted poems to suggest their thoughts," they were *using* the *Odes*, and because they were using them, their only concern was to communicate their views through the poems; they were not about to analyze the thought processes that had led to their chanting, or to explain all the reasons why this or that poem fit the occasion. In a word: while the public recitation of poetry was based on [an associative pattern reminiscent of] metaphors and similes, all that concerned the reciter was his purpose; he had no reason to be interested in his own metaphors and similes.[38]

If we knew the historical sources but had lost the text of the *Odes*, the secondary and acquired meanings bandied about in conversation would simply become, for us, *the* meaning of the *Odes*. Perhaps our present scale of values, with the texts at the top and the ancient interpretations toward the bottom, would have defied the understanding of the literate classes of Confucius' time. Could it be that the self-explanatory meanings had to wait until the twentieth century (or the twelfth) to become an object of discussion? How did the bottom fall out of the poetic exchange market?

~

The matter of "use" and "meaning" (or "application") is pivotal here, for it not only provides the occasion of referring the question of the poems' original meaning to another inaccessible origin but also includes within itself an unsustainable, or at least delicate, difference. "Use" is the self-interested antitype to a scholarly, sympathetic, or reverent reading. Confucius, as Holzman puts it, "ruthlessly" turns his back on the passages he uses as teachings. Others, such as Granet, see the inveterate quoting of the *Odes* in diplomatic gatherings as inauthenticity's first inroad.[39] Such hypotheses have a hermeneutic side (the discrimination of the poem's meaning from, say, Confucius' meaning) and a historical one. Their common difficulty can be phrased historically: since "using" the *Odes* seems to have been a habit from time immemorial, the moment of meaning before use eludes historical scrutiny. And the emergence of allusive "use" from an understood or suppressed "meaning" is no less mysterious, and no easier to date, than that "meaning." How did antiquity conceive of poetry as "useful"? What part of its usefulness was attributable to circumstance and what part to the texts themselves?

The problem is the object of careful study by Chu Tzu-ch'ing. Confucius said (or is glossed as having said):

> My children, why do you not study the *Book of Poetry*? The *Odes* serve to stimulate the mind. They may be used for purposes of self-contemplation. They teach the art of sociability. They show how to regulate feelings of resentment. From them you learn the more immediate duty of serving one's father, and the remoter one of serving one's prince. From them we become largely acquainted with the names of birds, beasts and plants.[40]

Confucius' educational program is echoed by the mixture of moral and technical language in the *Rituals of Chou*: the Grand Music Master shall

> employ the virtues of music [*yüeh-te*] to instruct the sons of people of rank in uprightness, harmoniousness, respect, constancy, filial piety, and friendship; [he shall] use musical language [*yüeh-yü*] to teach them stimulus [*hsing*], exposition [*tao*], admonition [*feng*], praise [*yung*], utterance [*yen*], conversation [*yü*].[41]

Chu Tzu-ch'ing adds: "The differences between these six kinds of 'musical language' are lost to us now, but it must have been the words used in the songs that mattered most of all. *Hsing* and *tao* (for which read *tao*, 'lead') seem to have been orchestral passages, *feng* and *yung* solos, *yen* and *yü* the application of song lyrics to daily life."[42] *Hsing, feng,* and *yung* also appear in catalogues of the compositional devices used in various odes (notably that given in the first Mao Preface), but the concerns of the *Rituals of Chou* are not with analyzing texts: the allusion here must be to kinds of social occasions to which one is learning to respond in "musical language," not examples or models of correct diction to be found and studied in the classic. Hence Confucius' advice: "If you don't study the *Odes*, you will have nothing to say" (*Analects* 13.16).

"Poetry tells of intent" (*shih yen chih*): this formula has been at the center of Chinese criticism, both practical and theoretical, for more than two millennia. Every writer of poetry has had to appeal to it or circumvent it. James J. Y. Liu makes it the slogan of didactic criticism—which is only, for those familiar with the history of Chinese reading, to underscore its importance.[43] It appears in the "Yao tien" chapter of the *Book of Documents*: "The king said: 'K'uei! I appoint you overseer of music. . . . Poetry tells of intent; songs draw out [the sounds of] the words; we score them thus lengthened and harmonize them. When the Eight Notes cooperate without struggle, then men and spirits meet.' "[44]

The Mao Prefaces make this saying, or rather one interpretation of it, their motto. Given a poem, they supply the "intent" it is to be understood as "telling." But the social use of poetry makes this interpretation seem narrow: even, or especially, when it has been distorted, parodied, or macaronized, quoted poetry "tells of intent." The hard part is deciding whose intent counts. Chu Tzuch'ing speaks for most modern readers in holding that the "intents," whatever they were, original to the "Airs of the States" can hardly have been identical to those imagined by the Mao editors. And Chu corrects the assumptions of many readers of the *Odes* by pointing out that the passage in the *Documents* can hardly be as old as it is traditionally thought to be or mean quite what it is supposed to mean. It claims to report on the doings of the kings and sages who formed China, but it has been rehandled so many times as to have become a repository of the very literature for which it is supposed to provide a source. Indeed the phrase "poetry tells of intent," taken for the past twenty centuries as an assurance that poems can put their hearers in touch with their makers' thoughts, may derive from another formula echoed here and there in the *Tso Commentary*: *shih i yen chih,* or "using poems as a means of expressing intent," a condensed poetics of quotation.[45]

The *Book of Documents* passage gains from being read alongside a story from the *Conversations of the States*. On hearing of a ceremony in which a stanza of the *Odes* had been sung to raise, with all due indirection, the subject of marriage, the music master Shih Hai says: "Well done! . . . Done designedly but without overstepping, subtly yet in everyone's sight. The poetry is used to round out the meaning [*shih so i ho i*], and the songs are used for chanting the poetry."[46] There is every chance that Shih Hai's statement represents the earlier usage, from which the *Book of Documents'* derives. Chow Tse-tsung prefers to read the passages from the *Tso Commentary* and *Conversations of the States* as echoes of the *Documents,* but even if that is so Chu's point may be retained. Everything is in place, by the Spring and Autumn period, for a conscious and elaborate practice of poetic quotation.

That the "use" of poems could be distinguished, even at this early date, from their composition can be seen from the *Tso Commentary*: some recitals are introduced by the verbs *tso* or *hsien* ("make," "offer"), others by the verb *fu* ("present"). "The poems 'presented' in the course of a diplomatic meeting were never ones composed by their presenters, who simply borrowed existing poems to express their intent."[47] One passage of the *Tso Commentary* shows that the ancients were well aware of the difference between the texts as they were taught and the forms they took in social exchanges. Lu-p'u Kuei's wife had the same surname as he, which caused some scandal. His reply: "When quoting the *Odes* [it is normal to] take lines out of context [and why shouldn't it be normal to choose one's wife without regard to her family?]. I got what I wanted; who needs to know about ancestors?"[48] This is as close as the classical sources come to invoking a poem's "original" meaning, and it is telling that the reference should be dismissive. Lu-p'u Kuei says openly what Chao Meng, the advisors of Cheng, and even Confucius seem to have assumed: that the appropriate response to a poetry quotation was pragmatic rather than hermeneutic. The formula *shih yen chih*, "poetry tells of intent," applies in exactly the same degree to meaning and to use. It tells what the *Odes* are good for, not what they are.

That would make an interpretation no more binding than a quotation—a matter of audience and occasion. But it is plain that, by the time of the codification of the *Odes* in the various schools, the editors' sense of the *shih yen chih* formula had become stricter and more exclusive than this. *Yen chih*, "speaking of intent," no longer described what one *did* with a poem. (Such practices probably vanished with the educational system of the pre-Ch'in feudal gentry.) "Speaking" through poetry was now construed as a historical event that had occurred once for each poem. That event supplied the only context of performance adequate to determining the poem's meaning. Each poem now had to be supplemented with a story about how, by whom, and for whom it was composed. The interpreters' hunger for contextual minutiae pushes them, however, to overstate their case, or so it may seem to the reader who no longer knows if there was a single act of composition or if the first "intent" influenced the subsequent career of a poem. But the same medicine has to be served to the Prefaces' adversaries. If the poetics of the originary project is spun off from a practice of quotation,[49] then some of the arguments concerning the "secondariness" (in every sense) of the Mao Prefaces must be less compelling. What if quotation simply were the whole story? Conceivable as an extreme of ancient poetic literacy is a situation in which a poem, known to everybody and repeated in response to an open set of occasions, has become through repetition a linguistic unit like a proverb or a single long word.[50] In such a case it becomes pointless, or at least the mark of a stubborn essentialism in linguistics, to ask what the meaning is as opposed to the use.[51]

The tendency to see the origin of the Prefaces in a history of encroaching inauthenticity (i.e., of creeping allegoresis) has another immediate disadvantage: taking the folk songs of the "Airs of the States" as its type case, it ignores the prefaces to the oldest parts of the collection, the dynastic hymns ("Laudes," *sung*) of Shang and Chou. These prefaces break with the pattern of the Mao editors' notorious "allegories": instead of telling whom or what the poem was composed to praise or blame, they name the ceremonies in which the poem was sung. An unambiguous case is the preface to Ode 271, "Hao t'ien yu ch'eng ming," which reads in its entirety: "[For] the suburban sacrifices to heaven and earth."[52] The poem cannot possibly be said to be about the sacrifices, which it does not mention. Here at least there is no point in speaking of "use" as subsequent to composition.

Now if such prefaces are seen as the typical case, with the "allegorical" ones being an extension of their method, the theory of "use" and "meaning" must be revised. And so must the received teaching on the kind of assertion made by the "allegorical" prefaces. What do the prefaces mean in saying that a certain poem is "about" this or that ruler or situation? Saying that a poem is "for" a certain ritual seems to be a different kind of assertion from saying that it was composed "about" a certain singular event: for one thing, the ritual use implies repetition. To what degree can the specifics of historical contextualization be understood generally, that is, exemplarily, as a way of closing the gap between ritual and occasional "uses"? Or should the hermeneutics of ritual "use" be kept from impinging on those of categorical "use" and "meaning"? What distinguishes the speech contexts of diplomatic meetings and ritual observances, and what links them?

In sum, the historical hypothesis of a moment of pure folkish literalism in the transmission and interpretation of the *Odes* begs a few questions and leaves unclarified many others about the place of poetry in ancient society. It reduces to an always legitimate stance on the choice of interpretations; and yet there is much to be gained by seeing its virtues (like those of the Prefaces this view is meant to critique) as reconstructive rather than descriptive. Use and meaning, creation and quotation, literal and figurative, early and late, folk and court, feeling and edification, may now be seen as so many independent topics, not to be knitted together in a single rise-and-fall story.

If the *Odes* were composed over a span of several centuries, and if the chief style of poetry interpretation during those centuries was the appropriative citation ("using poetry to round out one's meaning"), then we can expect to find "use" not only as a para-literary practice subsequent to the text but programmatically inscribed within the texts themselves. These would be poems "meant for use," to adopt a saying of Ku Chieh-kang's,[53] and a categorical distinction between "use" and "meaning" would be misleading. "Chiung" (Ode 297), one of a group thought to contain the latest compositions in the *Book of Odes*, requires its reader to keep that distinction in mind, but only as a preliminary to overruling it. The poem reads:

> Sturdy, sturdy those stallions
> on the untended ranges.
> Now about those sturdy [stallions]:
> there are black ones with white haunches, there are white-
>   dappled yellow ones,
> there are black ones and yellow ones.
> They take the chariot and rumble off,
> yea, without limit.
> These horses are good.
>
> Sturdy, sturdy the stallions
> on the untended ranges.
> Now about those sturdy [stallions]:
> there are pale-gray hoary ones, there are yellow-and-white
>   hoary ones,
> there are roans, there are black-mottled ones.
> With the chariots they [go] mightily,
> yea, without ceasing.
> These horses are outstanding.
>
> Sturdy, sturdy the stallions
> on the untended ranges.
> Now about those sturdy [stallions]:

there are pied ones, there are black-maned white ones,
there are black-maned roans, there are white-maned black ones.
They take the chariot like born runners,
yea, without exhaustion.
These horses are spirited.

Sturdy, sturdy the stallions
on the untended ranges.
Now about those sturdy [stallions]:
there are shadowy-white ones, there are white-flecked chestnut
    ones,
there are hairy white-skinned ones, there are those with fish eyes.
They take the chariots [and go off] mightily,
yea, without swerving.
These horses are swift.[54]

The poem's main subject, according to the Mao Preface, is praise
of Duke Hsi of Lu (r. 659–626 B.C.).

> Duke Hsi was able to honor the laws of Po-ch'in [his ancestor, son of
> the Duke of Chou and founder of the dukedom of Lu]. He was frugal
> so as to have enough to meet his needs, but generous in his devotion to
> his people. He was attentive to agriculture and knew the importance
> of grain stocks; his herds were kept on the outer ranges. The people of
> Lu venerated him. Thereupon [Hsi's chief minister] Chi-sun Hsing-fu
> reported this to the Chou [sovereign], and the historian K'o made this
> song [or these songs] of praise.[55]

"This song" or "these songs," meaning all four of the "Laudes of
Lu"? The tradition passed down through the Mao editors and
Cheng Hsüan (d. A.D. 200) relates all four of the "Laudes of Lu" to
Duke Hsi. Hsi is supposed to have revived the ancient customs of
Lu (represented by the founding figure Po-ch'in) from nineteen
generations of neglect, reason enough, in the annotators' eyes, for
commemoration. But the *Tso Commentary* makes Hsi out to be
little better than his predecessors. His great deeds amount to the
following: he built a new Southern Gate,[56] he repaired the temple
dedicated to his ancestress Chiang Yüan (a feat not mentioned in
the *Tso Commentary* but supplied from the preface to the last of the

"Laudes of Lu," Ode 300, "Pi kung"), and he kept his horses on the outer ranges. Why should Hsi deserve this praise and the real hero of Lu, Po-ch'in, get none? In Po-ch'in's day "the world was at peace and the Four Seas were as one body; any songs of praise were assumed to refer to the Son of Heaven [i.e., the Chou monarch]. Since the feudal kingdoms [subservient to the Chou] had not yet fallen into decadence [of poetry or morals], there was no need for the people of Lu to compose praise poetry."[57] Hsi's good deeds are chiefly symbolic. The poem repays them in the same coin.

And there is no reason not to go another step further: Hsi and the rest are trimmings on a generic situation dictated by purpose. The "Laudes" were chanted in temples, providing the ruling lineage with occasions to praise itself through its ancestors, totem poles in verse. This one, ostensibly in honor of a herd of horses, is really in honor of their keeper, with the link to be made either causally (they are tireless, sturdy, unswerving, because the duke has been such a good trainer) or analogically (the duke is to his subjects as a good and careful horse breeder is to his animals). The analogy makes the ruler look like one of his subjects in their far humbler preoccupations. In K'ung Ying-ta's reading, the existence of these two kinds of link between immediate and principal topics becomes a praise-bearing rhetorical occasion of its own:

> It was because of his "attention to agriculture" that Duke Hsi caused his horses to be baited on the far-off ranges: thus they were kept away from people's dwellings and their good fields. . . . And of these horses kept on the outer ranges it is further said that they are fat and healthy. In this Duke Hsi's diligence may be seen. "Attention to agriculture" and "respect for Po-ch'in's laws" are not simply a matter of taking good care of horses. If he could devote so much thought to a lowly business like husbandry, surely he would let nothing go unthought of in the business of administering his subjects![58]

The *a fortiori* logic of this paraphrase, slipping distinctions of value between the "good husbandman" and "shepherd of men" topics, allows the poem to disown its metaphorical register in favor of its causal one. "Not simply a matter of taking good care of horses" can therefore be paraphrased as "not merely the vehicle of an allegorical fantasy"—the "simply" (*erh i*) of the sentence about the difference between horses and men acting to put both horse breeding and metaphorical pseudo-reference in their place.[59] The aim of K'ung's sentence, which surely captures an oscillation in the poem, is to confirm the import of the analogical reading while downgrading its importance next to the causal one.

"They take the chariot and rumble off, yea, without limit. / These horses are good." As a means of expressing the state's celebration of itself, the horses are well chosen. Had the animal metaphor called on cattle, sheep, chickens, or any other of the Six Domesticated Animals, doubts would have arisen whether "the shepherds and neatherds are considering the good of the sheep and cattle and fatten and tend them with anything else in view than the good of their masters and themselves."[60] And had the animal figure alluded to wild beasts, there would be no role for a keeper and hence no place for the relational argument discerned by K'ung. (What would be possible, of course, is a direct comparison between animal and person, as in "Lang pa.") Horses occur on the fringe of domestication, "tsai chiung chih yeh," literally "on the wild places of the uncultivated zone," where civilization and barbarism meet.[61] The size and placement of a local sovereign's territory indicated the nature of its ties to the imperial center; as a center itself, it radiated a semblance of imperial power to the surrounding settlements. One would be authorized by this model to see the relation of town and *yeh*, prince and horses, as being of the same kind as the relation (center and margin) of the Chou ruler to feudal lords such as Hsi, and also—since this model is meant to be extended indefinitely—as that of the Chou to their periodic allies among the nomadic peoples around them. One of the barbarian tribes mentioned in the Shang oracle texts is indeed named the To-ma Chiang, "the Horsey Chiang."

K'ung helpfully divides horses into four categories—"fine," "warhorses," "hunters," and "hacks." Those in "Chiung" are all stallions, *mu*.[62] So the herd is not expected to perpetuate itself as an ordinary horseman's might: it is less a herd than a collection kept for some aim other than reproduction and added to from outside.[63] When they "take the chariot," we are doubtless meant to think of a war chariot. But horses grazing in the wilds connote peacetime: after the decisive battle of Mu-yeh, the founder of the Chou dynasty freed his horses to graze on the south side of Mount Hua.[64] What these horses do for their keeper is what they are best at doing, something that reveals their native excellence (insisted on by the alliterative series *ts'ang, ts'ai, tso, ts'u* emphatically put at the end of the stanzas)[65]—something, the ode wants us to conclude, inherently profitable to herd and herdsman alike. And—here comes a cadenza of expert's terms that K'ung's science of horseflesh is at a loss to rationalize, much though he tries to correlate hide markings with breed and breed with aptitude for different tasks—the description of Duke Hsi's grassland utopia is rounded out with proof of how inclusively it welcomes good horses of every color and pattern (*liang-ma i-mao*).[66]

"Chiung," then, nicely fits William Empson's definition of "pastoral" as a form of literature that "was felt to imply a beautiful relation between rich and poor."[67] Or it seems to fit: a "beautiful relation" is doubtless intended, and on two planes, but if Duke Hsi is in one idiom the herdsman taking perfect care of his horses, who or what in the other register benefits from his attention? The horses of "Chiung" come in various kinds, but all are good for pulling the chariot. In the next of the "Laudes of Lu," Ode 298, "Yu pi," the stallions (again *mu*), by teams of chestnuts and grays, wait outside the palace for their riders, the court officials. Can the mounts of "Chiung" have turned into the horsemen of "Yu pi"? "The historian K'o" may be a fiction of the Prefaces' writers, but he can at least stand for the scholar-officials to whom this poem is due. The officials praise their ruler by praising themselves ("tireless, unswerving"). Their goodness evidences his goodness; his goodness explains theirs. The pastoral is (at least) double. The herdsman allegory has an upward direction, as a tribute from the courtiers to their prince, and a downward one, celebrating the regime for the edification of its subjects. The horse imagery with its implications has the virtue of being so unspecific that it can be applied equally to

any of the three vertical relations in question (horses are to herdsman as subjects to officials, as officials to prince, and as subjects to
officials-and-prince). And the Preface adds another row to the
quadrille. Whatever is said about the management of people and
affairs in Lu applies also to the standards of the Chou sovereign
who orders this poem of praise to be composed.[68] The emperor's
nod of approval to this poem is an act of caretaking of the same sort
as the acts for which Hsi is being commended.

The form of "Chiung" is virtually a quotation, a case of genre-
crossing. "Although it borrows the title of Laud, this is really a
poem in the 'Airs of the States' style; it is not the kind of poem one
chants to a spirit. That explains its stanzaic structure [*chang-chü*],"
with refrains and repetitions.[69] Aping the naïve is part of its strategy. Here the tropes of *yü-yen* ("attributed speech") and *chi-t'o*
("projection on an object"), which earlier we relegated to prose
fiction and the roll of poetic devices, find their place. The torrent of
horseman's language becomes a pledge of authenticity. "To start
from feeling is the nature of the common people," says the Preface
to Ode 1, "Kuan chü." Is the poem claiming a popular origin for
itself and a place in popular feeling for the prince it celebrates?
That is not even necessary for the point to be carried. Just as it was
the prince's pastoral to become a herdsman, so it can be the official's
pastoral to play the unlettered singer.

"Chiung" exemplifies the harnessing of meaning to use that is
the point of Confucius' *Odes* pedagogy. "The *Shih* will enable you
to make metaphorical allusions, to observe, to behave in society
and to express grievances. It helps in serving your father at home
and your sovereign abroad."[70] Most of the human relations to
which the sage applies the *Odes* with "enabling" effect turn out to
be vertical relations between unequal partners. It might be said that
the social usefulness of quoted poetry realizes the same goal as the
pastoral mode—that of bridging gaps that would otherwise remain
unbridgeable. "Music identifies; ritual distinguishes. Identification
makes for intimacy; distinction for respect."[71] Thus, if "Chiung"
begins its life, so to speak, as a quotation in search of an author, it is
for a good reason. The meaning presupposes a use; it is incomplete

without it. Here, at least, the conditions for allegoresis have not been fulfilled. What has just been said about "Chiung," a late poem, could be adapted to fit most of the pieces in the collection from the moment they were put into circulation as "instruments of exchange"—which may very well mean: from their conception.

§ 3 The Prefaces as Introduction to the *Book of Odes*

> In fact, fairyland constitutes a stable and well-
> determined domain of consciousness, that which
> the adult and the child have most in common. . . .
> About fairyland, the child only knows as much as
> he or she has been told by the adult. Fairyland thus
> becomes an area of understanding, a perfect center
> of reference, the home ground of exemplarity.
> —Michel Butor, "La Balance des fées"

Some version of the history of the *Odes* is always implicit in the reading of them, and certain Odes have every reason to want to stage a flattering account of their creation. The reading of "Chiung" as a type case leads to the recognition that there are no unshakable reasons why the use of a poem should always be subsequent and incidental to its meaning. To the ancients, the Odes may have been for all practical purposes—and what other purposes interested them?—"poems for use," messages that never needed to be unwrapped as long as they were kept in circulation. Is the quoting or use of an Ode, then, always a case of "saying one thing and meaning another," with the proviso that what one says is, in the manner of proverbs and pronouns, nothing much in itself?[1] On this minimal definition, the Odes in their oldest attested reception (quite apart from the Prefaces) qualify for the title of allegories instead of that of victims of allegoresis.

Such a conclusion would, of course, run counter to the venerable traditions of *Odes* scholarship, both pro and contra Mao, and as a critique of those traditions it makes somewhat too short work of their founding hypotheses. More may be learned about the nature of "Chinese allegory"—that excluded term—by observing the Prefaces' efforts to keep it at a distance. If there is little explicit theory of allegory in the older writings on the *Odes*, the term's negative imprint is easily found. The theory of poetry is in many respects

74

the converse of the theory of allegory (as misunderstanding). But that formulation makes it sound as if allegory had claims on the traditional critic's attention that we suspect it never had. Indeed, if allegory is almost never discussed in its own right, that may be because the tradition conceives of it not as a theoretical concern but only as a foil to a theory.

To pursue Chinese allegory, we must approach it through its opposite or antidote. How is misunderstanding kept at bay and the correct understanding of the poems affirmed? In the Mao edition of the *Odes*, the text that has elicited the most commentary of this sort is easily the few dozen lines in the first Preface that have been understood from antiquity to speak of "the general principles of poetry" (*shih chih ta-kang*).[2] The frequent disputes over the authorship of this Great Preface, said since middle Han times to be the work of a direct disciple of Confucius, have never affected its position as an obligatory reference for critics and poets. (Typically, the great sixth-century anthology *Wen hsüan* first pillages the Great Preface for its own preface and then includes the whole text as a model of the "preface" genre.) It is both canonical and prescriptive of what a canon should be, both a reworking of the most influential ancient texts on poetry and the chief influence on the later reading of those older texts—the *shih yen chih* formula's own history, discussed earlier, being the main example of the Great Preface's overpowering authority.

Like all truly canonical texts, the Great Preface is usually read in splendid isolation. Here, however, I shall be surrounding its statements with discussions by its major commentators, chiefly Cheng Hsüan (d. A.D. 200) and K'ung Ying-ta (574–648). First-time readers may prefer to brave the commentaries after the main text.

The Great Preface (i.e., the preface to Ode 1, "Kuan chü") says:[3]

[1] "*Kuan chü*" [has as its subject] *the virtue of the queen-consort.*
[Lu Te-ming (early T'ang), *Ching-tien shih-wen:*] According to the older annotations, [Paragraphs 1 and 2 here] are the preface to the Ode "Kuan chü," otherwise known as the Little Preface; the rest is called the Great Preface.

[Shen Chung (sixth century):] Cheng Hsüan in his *Shih p'u*, suggests that [Confucius'] disciple] Tzu-hsia wrote the Great Preface[4] and that the Little Prefaces were composed by Tzu-hsia and the Elder Mao together.[5] [That is,] wherever Tzu-hsia left something unsaid, Mao completed his words [in the Little Prefaces].

[Juan Yüan (1764–1849):] Some say that the Little Prefaces [as distinct from the Great Preface] are the work of Wei Hung of Tunghai.[6] I consider this preface to be that of the ode "Kuan chü" only. It does discuss the great principles of poetry, but that is no reason to split it into Great and Little [Prefaces]. . . .

[K'ung Ying-ta, *Mao Shih cheng-i*:] Each preface gives the meaning of a single poem. But the meaning of the *Odes* is deep and broad. This being the first poem in the collection, to it is added a "presentation of the general principles of poetry." . . . The Airs of the "Chou-nan" and "Shao-nan" sections result from the transformations worked by King Wen [of the Chou].[7] To praise the virtue of the queen-consort is to speak of the proper bond between husband and wife and to display the importance of human relations. For if the relation of husband and wife is correct, then that of father and son will be one of affection; if father and son are affectionate, then the relation of prince and subjects will be one of respect.[8] So it is that this Ode sings of human nature and treats maleness and femaleness as important. Its taking its matter from the doings of boys and girls and not speaking directly in praise of the consort's virtue are all part of the poem's composition; it simply responds to [*kan*] the bounty of her goodness and sings of her nature and actions so as to proclaim far and wide this sagely transformation and bring it to the knowledge of those not yet aware of it. [The purpose of the "Kuan chü" is to do all this—]not to commend the queen-consort for her accomplishments [as a hasty reading of the Little Preface might lead one to believe].

[2] *It is the beginning of the "Airs* [of the States]" [feng], *used to transform* [feng] *the world*[9] *and regulate* [the relations of] *husband and wife; used among communities of people and among federations of states.*

[Juan Yüan:] "The beginning of the 'Airs' ": that is, of the fifteen sections of "Airs of the States" [first part of the *Odes*]. The "Airs" [record] the exemplary rule [*cheng-chiao*, literally the "teaching-through-ruling"] of the feudal princes. In the next sections the "Airs" are said to be "the means of transforming [*feng*] the world";

the sentence in the *Analects* "The ruler's virtue is the wind"[10] has the same meaning.

[K'ung Ying-ta:] . . . The consort's praiseworthy virtue is the beginning of King Wen's transforming influence. Wen's influence began with his wives; so this poem is rightly put at the beginning of his teaching and influence. It is intended to transform the world's people and to make them regulate their husbandly and wifely relations. The Duke of Chou[11] instituted rituals and composed music, using them in communities of people. He ordered the headmen of the villages to use ritual and music for the instruction of their people. And he used them among the federated states, by having the feudatories instruct their officers with ritual and music. His aim was that all, from the Son of Heaven down to the multitudes, be familiar with this poem. . . . [Introducing it in village banquets and court ceremonies] is the way of accomplishing transformation. The Son of Heaven teaches the feudal princes. The feudal princes teach their grand officers. The grand officers teach their people. Transformation begins with the people [of a certain state] and spreads abroad: that is why the Preface mentions "communities of people" first and "federations of states" afterward.

[3] *"Airs," that is, "wind,"[12] that is, "teaching." Wind is what sets in motion; teaching is what transforms* [hua].

[4] *Poetry is* [that to which intent arrives:] *the manifestation of intent. In the heart it is intent; sent forth as speech it is poetry.*

[K'ung Ying-ta:] The first part of the preface tells how poetry may be used to educate; here it says where poetry comes from. . . . The preface says that the maker of a poem wishes to ease the feelings of resentment in his heart, and these feelings issue in a song. The "Yü shu" [chapter of the *Book of Documents*] calls this "poetry telling of intent."[13]

[5] *Feeling is moved inwardly and takes form in speech.[14] It is not enough to speak, so one sighs* [the words]; *it is not enough to sigh, so one draws them out and sings them; it is not enough to draw them out and sing them, so without one's willing it, one's hands dance and one's feet stamp.*

[K'ung Ying-ta:] The above says: Expression in speech is poetry. That distinguishes poetry from intent. Plain speech is not poetry. . . . The "I-wen chih" [chapter of the *Han shu*] says: "They intoned the words and called it poetry; they chanted the notes and called it song."[15] Consequently: what is in the heart is intent, once out of the mouth it is speech; words intoned are poetry, notes chanted are song; and when these [notes] have been distributed among the eight [kinds of instrumental] sounds, we call the result music. The differences among these are merely a matter of sequence, [different stages being] differently named.

[6] *Feeling is sent forth in sound* [sheng]; *sounds that form a pattern* [wen] *are called* yin [notes, tone].

[Cheng Hsüan:] "Expressed" means the same as "manifested." "Sound" means *kung, shang, chüeh, chih, yü* [the five notes of the movable Chinese scale].[16] "Pattern" refers to the way *kung* and *shang*, upper and lower, answer to one another.

[K'ung Ying-ta:] "Feeling is expressed in sound" means that people's feelings of joy and sorrow are manifested in the sounds of speech. For the moment, although one speaks of joy and sorrow, there is no reference to a scale; [speech] is all the "sound" there is to speak of here. It is when one comes to make a poem that the sequence of clear and turbid sounds,[17] rhythm, and high and low notes constitute a song with the five notes [of the scale], just as the five colors are brought together in a pattern.

[7] *The tone of a well-governed era is joyous and thereby peaceful. Its government is harmonious. The tone of a disordered era is angry and thereby* [expresses] *resentment. Its government is perverse. The tone of a country on the brink of destruction is anxious and thereby mournful. Its citizens are helpless.*

[K'ung Ying-ta:] From the idea that feelings are manifested in sound, the preface goes on to say that this sound changes in keeping with the times. [There follows a paraphrase of the paragraph above in which the phrase *cheng-chiao* ("teaching-through-ruling") is throughout substituted for the text's "government." Examples of each kind of "music" are found in appropriate lyrics from the *Odes*.] . . . The music of Cheng and Wei, the sounds of the mulberry grove on the river P'u:[18] these are the music of states on the brink of destruction. . . .

[8] *Therefore for pinpointing success and failure, for stimulating heaven and earth, for moving ghosts and spirits, nothing is equal to poetry.*

[9] *The kings of old used it to regulate the relations of husband and wife; to perfect filial piety and respect; to deepen human ties; to beautify the transformation* [of their people] *by culture; and to modify customs.*

[K'ung Ying-ta:] This preface says that poetry can change customs: exactly what the *Classic of Filial Piety* [*Hsiao ching*] says of music.[19]

Poetry is the heart of music; music is the voice of poetry. So poetry and music have a common aim. They support one another: if there were no poetry, there would be no music. . . .

[10] *In poetry there are six arts. The first is* feng ["airs"]; *the second is* fu ["exposition"], *the third is* pi ["comparison"], *the fourth is* hsing ["allusion" or "evocation"], *the fifth is* ya ["elegantiae"], *the sixth is* sung ["laudes"].

[K'ung Ying-ta:] Cheng Hsüan's note reads: "The 'Airs' tell of the transformations brought about by the rule of sages and worthies. To expose is to set forth plainly: hence an *exposition* sets forth the good and bad of the present government's teaching. In a *comparison*, one sees a present failing, but, not daring to say so, one chooses a similar case and tells of it. In *evocation* one sees a present excellence but, not wanting to flatter, one chooses some fine topic and praises by analogy.[20] *Ya* means 'correct.' The 'Elegantiae' speak of present-day instances of correctness for the emulation of posterity. *Sung* means 'to praise' and [connotes] 'form, appearance'; the 'Laudes' praise and describe as beautiful a present virtue." . . . [These definitions, however, are too narrow, says K'ung: not all "comparisons" speak of failings, and not all "evocations" tell of virtues; Cheng has tried to define the Six Arts (genres and tropes) through their modes ("correct" and "decadent").] Poems of praise and blame may equally have in them "evocations" and "comparisons." . . . *Fu, pi,* and *hsing* (in that order) are ways of expressing a thing. Straightforward speaking is the standard case, so in the text of the *Odes* the *fu* usually come before the *pi* and the *hsing.* . . . [The genres] *feng, ya,* and *sung* are made up of [the tropes] *pi, fu,* and *hsing.* If we were to divide the *Odes* into chapters and sections on the basis of their comparisons, expositions, and evocations, then there would be no [poems left over to be called] "Airs," "Elegantiae," or "Laudes."

[11] *Those above used the "Airs" to transform* [hua] *those below; those below used the "Airs" to satirize* [tz'u] *those above. The speaker who emphasizes pattern* [wen] *and admonishes discreetly is guilty of no offense, and the hearer is sufficiently warned. That is why the "Airs" are called* feng.

[Cheng Hsüan:] "Transformation" and "satire" [feng-hua, feng-tz'u] occur through likenesses [pi-yü], not through direct speech. To "emphasize pattern" is to take pains that the poem shall answer to the musical notes *kung* and *shang.* . . .

[K'ung Ying-ta:] A subject uses poetry to admonish his ruler, and a

ruler uses it to transform his populace: thus both high and low use
poetry. For the superior, the use of the Six Arts is to influence, move,
teach, and transform; for the inferior, it is to persuade and admonish the superior. Now as to the composition of the *Odes*: when the
poet sets himself to harmonizing [the words] with the patterns of
kung and *shang* as they answer one another, so that the verses are set
to music, he can rely on indirect expression and so admonish
discreetly without calling the ruler's faults by name. In this way, the
speaker does not offend, and the ruler is not outraged. . . . The effect
on the ruler is a gentle movement like the wind's. And when the
faults have been declared and amended, it is like the wind blowing
and causing the grass to bend. That is why the first part of the *Odes*
is called *Feng* or "Airs." . . . All the Six Arts can be described as *feng*,
since *Feng* is the beginning of transformation-through-teaching. . . .
Therefore the *Feng* is first [among the Six Arts].

All the *Odes* were originally addressed by subjects to their rulers.
Only later did the rulers begin to use them as a means of teaching
the people. But here the "transformation of those below by those
above" is mentioned first. . . . Above and below, all use the *Odes*, and
the greater honor of being first is the only reason why the rulers are
mentioned before the ruled.

[12] *When, as a result of the perishing of the Kingly Way, ritual and
loyalty were neglected and governmental tutelage* [of the mass] *was
abandoned, states had differing governments and families had differing
customs. It was then that the altered* [or decadent] *"Airs" and "Elegantiae"
were composed.*

[K'ung Ying-ta:] The *Odes* include orthodox [*cheng*] and decadent
[*pien*] songs. This passage explains decadence. . . . Upon the perishing of the Kingly Way . . . each of the various feudal realms had its
own way of governing, and among the common people no two
families had the same customs. The poets, then, praised what they
saw as good and reviled what they saw as evil. And that is the origin
of the "decadent" "Airs" and "Elegantiae." . . . Those who have
never seen evil do not know what makes good good, and those who
have never seen anything but evil do not know why evil is evil. In a
time of great peace, nothing can be improved on, and when the
Way has been utterly lost there is no point in protesting. . . . The
beginning of a turn for the worse: that is what produces folk
songs. . . . As [the Han dynasty historian] Pan Ku says, "After the

deaths of [Kings] Ch'eng and K'ang, the voice of praise fell silent; after the grace of the former kings had been exhausted, poetry was no more."²¹ . . . When the Kingly Way is endangered and teaching-through-ruling has begun to fail, but something can still be saved, altered "Airs" and "Elegantiae" will arise. For their authors have ready at hand the old statutes whereby the depth of the new losses may be measured.

[13] *State historians, perceiving the traces of success and failure, distressed at the neglect of human relations, and lamenting the inequity of punishments and administration, sang of their feelings in order to persuade* [feng] *their superiors.*

[14] *They were conscious of changes in affairs and full of regret for the old customs. Thus the altered "Airs" arose from feeling and yet do not exceed the bounds of ritual and loyalty. To start from feeling is the nature of the mass of people* [min]; *to stop within the bounds of ritual and loyalty is the grace of the former kings.*

[K'ung Ying-ta:] As to the poets' "starting from feeling and stopping within the bounds," this means that although each of them started from his nature as a man of the people, they ended by adhering to ritual. . . . Each one spoke his own mind, but owing to the [common inheritance of] grace from the early kings, they all stopped together within the bounds of decorum. . . .

[15] *Hence* [a poem that] *ties the affairs of a kingdom to their origins in a single person is called an "Air";* [a poem that] *speaks of the affairs of the whole world and gives shape to the customs* [feng] *of the Four Quarters is called an "Elegantia."*

[16] Ya *means "correct": the "Elegantiae" speak of the causes of kingly government's rise and fall. In governing there is a difference of small and great; so there are the "Lesser Elegantiae" and the "Greater Elegantiae."*

[K'ung Ying-ta:] The forms of the *Odes* are derived from different types of music. The "Airs of the States" preserve the tunes of the different regions. . . . But the music for the "Elegantiae" and the "Laudes" was composed for the ancient kings as they traveled to inspect the world. The music for the "Elegantiae" and "Laudes" gathers together the music of the Four Quarters. . . .

[17] *The "Laudes" bring praise to the shape and form* [hsing-jung] *of flourishing virtue.* [The "Laudes" arose] *as* [the rulers of old] *announced their successes to the spirits and ancestors.*

[K'ung Ying-ta:] This section explains the name and character of the "Laudes." . . . It begins with a gloss, clarifying *sung* ["praise"] by means of *jung* ["form"]. . . . The *Book of Changes* says: "The Sages [were able to perceive the secrets of all things under heaven and] molded [their knowledge] into shapes [*hsing*] and forms [*jung*], wherewith the natures and congruities of all things might be depicted [*hsiang*]."[22] So *hsing-jung* means "to give shape and form." . . . To compose a "Laud" is to praise the shape and form of sagely virtue. From this we see that the Son of Heaven's exemplary rule has its own shape and form. . . .

[18] *These* [the "Airs," "Lesser Elegantiae," "Greater Elegantiae," and "Laudes"] *are known as the "Four Beginnings": in them is the accomplishment of the* Odes.

[19] *The transformations* [evidenced by the poems] *"Kuan chü" and "Lin-chih"* [result from] *the ruler's influence. Therefore these poems are attached to the Duke of Chou. "Nan"* [in the title of the first part of the "Airs of the States," "Chou-nan"], *meaning "south," indicates that this transformation was carried out from north to south. The virtue* [evidenced in the poems] *"Ch'üeh-ch'ao" and "Tsou-yü"* [results from] *the influence of the feudal lords. Through them the kings of old carried out their teaching, so* [these "Airs"] *are attached to the Duke of Shao.*

[K'ung Ying-ta:] . . . The kind of ruler spoken of here must be a sage; since the Duke of Chou was a sage, the "Chou-nan" poems are attached to him. The feudal lords spoken of here must have been worthies; since the Duke of Shao was a worthy, the Shao-nan poems are attached to him. . . .[23]

[20] *"Chou-nan" and "Shao-nan" show the way of correct beginning and the basis of kingly influence.*[24]

[21] *So the "Kuan chü" expresses* [the senior wife's] *joy in finding a pure girl to marry to* [her] *lord and her concern that the worthy be brought forward, but no abandon in* [describing] *her beauty.* [The senior wife] *grieves at her seclusion and bends her efforts to promoting worth and talent, all without harming* [her] *good intent.*[25]

[Cheng Hsüan:] The word *ai* ("grieving") is an error. It should be *chung* ("sincere," "truthful"). The meaning is: she effaces herself with utter sincerity. "Without harming her good intent": this means that she is eager to find good matches [for her lord].[26]

[K'ung Ying-ta:] Having spoken of the "Chou-nan" and "Shao-nan" in general, the preface now returns to the meaning of the "Kuan chü." . . . Since it has named the "Chou-nan" and the

"Shao-nan" as the "way of correct beginning," it now first gives praise to transforming influence [*hua*] as seen within the [royal] household, in the form of an explication of the single poem "Kuan chü."

This is the meaning of the "Kuan chü."[27]

~

Both readers who call the Mao version's interpretations "allegorical" and those who contend that true allegory is an impossibility within the Chinese tradition find support in the Great Preface. For that reason it is instructive to ask how the Great Preface itself has been received—seemingly on its own terms or as a false-bottomed text with unspoken motives (i.e., in the sense of most Chinese writing on the subject, nearly "allegorical").

The Great Preface has that special canonicity of texts that are often quoted but rarely at length. For most of its history, indeed, the Preface reduces to a few attention-getting statements such as

Emotion is born of intent, song takes shape in words. Therefore, when a person is pleased, his voice is happy, and when frustrated, his sighs are sad. He is able to set forth his feelings, to express his indignation. To move heaven and earth, to affect the gods and demons, to transform human relations or to harmonize husband and wife, there is nothing more suitable than Japanese verse,

lines Timothy Wixted finds "stated as simple fact" by Ki no Yoshimochi, prefacer of the *Kokinshū*.[28] And the "Tsung ching" (The Classics as models) and "Ming shih" (Elucidating poetry) chapters of Liu Hsieh's *Wen-hsin tiao-lung* imitate the Great Preface by melting down and recasting the same ancient references for the same conclusions:

The guiding purpose of the *Odes* is to express intent. . . .

Great Shun said: "Poetry expresses intent; singing prolongs the words": the sage's pronouncement is quite transparent in itself. Do not [the principles] "in the mind it is intent; once expressed in words, it is poetry" and that of the unfolding of literature as a record of authenticity lie herein? . . . Man possesses seven emotions, which reverberate in response to objects; one is quite spontaneously moved by objects to express one's intent.[29]

There is little room to doubt, then, that the Great Preface is "the classic formulation of linguistic adequacy" in Chinese poetics, the *locus major* of "the expressive-affective conception of poetry."[30] The Great Preface explains poetry as the outcome of a quasi-natural process of cause and effect (*tzu-jan*, Liu Hsieh's word for "spontaneous," translates also as "natural"), yet without making the degree of naturalness in a poem a criterion of its being true poetry or not, good or bad writing. (That would come later.) Here aesthetic judgment defers to political judgment: the poem is as good or bad as the society that produces it, with the added condition that a poet at odds with a bad society can pin his work to the good society he remembers. There is therefore poetic justice in the fact that the Great Preface has borne more assaults on its political flank than on its aesthetic one.

> [The Prefaces] advance the ideas on pre-Ch'in writers, particularly Confucius, Hsün-tzu, and the author(s) of the *Book of Ritual,* reflecting the ways in which the feudal class sought to press poetry and song into its own service, for the consolidation of the feudal order. These theories embody Confucian thought on improving government, but fundamentally they worked to the advantage of the feudal ruling classes; so in the long history of feudal rule in our country, the Prefaces represent one type of powerful ruling-class thought broadly directing people's literary creation and criticism. . . . With their forced and inaccurate explanations, too, they catered to the political and moral expectations of feudal society.[31]

Such criticism of the Prefaces, though raw, makes it obvious that the Great Preface's qualities are not best defended by quoting and paraphrasing from it. What does the Great Preface say, what is its logic, and what accounts for its overwhelming influence? (Even the Fu-tan University committee responsible for the preceding quotation allows the Prefaces the attribute of "power.")

In the space of a few lines, the Great Preface manages to put forth a psychological-expressive theory of art, a statement of the civilizing influence of art on the community, a plea for the special political status of the poet, a typology of genres and figural modes, an outline of literary history, a categorization of valid and decadent art, and a suggestion that doubtful poems must be interpreted ironically (or allegorically, when content and not tone is at issue): lapidary answers to most of the questions posed by literary criticism and aesthetic theory. Of all these theses, the expressive one is best known and most necessary to the development of the whole doctrine. Without that hypothesis to ground them, the typology, axiology, interpretative scheme, and literary-historical logic of the Great Preface become isolated remarks to be entertained or rejected singly. Since the very possibility of a strongly coherent reading of the Preface depends on it, we may begin with the sentences in which that thesis is put most plainly:

(a) In the heart it is intent; sent forth as speech it is poetry. Feeling is moved inwardly and takes form in speech.

(c) Feeling is sent forth in sound; sounds that form a pattern are called "musical tone." The tone of a well-governed era is joyous and thereby peaceful. Its government is harmonious. The tone of a disordered era is angry and thereby [expresses] resentment. Its government is perverse. The tone of a country on the brink of destruction is anxious and thereby mournful. Its citizens are helpless.

From the knitting together of these two passages comes the main lesson, as it has been paraphrased, of the Great Preface, the principle of the continuity of the aesthetic, the moral, and the political. (From that principle, in turn, derive the typology of genres and the basis of literary periodization.) That continuity is psychological before it is anything else, and the sentences that connect the two passages quoted immediately above give the inferences made there the character of necessity:

(b) It is not enough to speak, so one sighs [the words]; it is not enough to sigh, so one draws them out and sings them; it is not enough to draw them out and sing them, so without one's willing it, one's hands dance and one's feet stamp.

The sentence "In the heart it is intent" interprets the familiar "Poetry expresses intent" of the *Book of Documents* as a statement about poetic meaning, not about the uses to which poetry might be put; its assumptions are therefore different from those of the *Tso Commentary*'s nobles and diplomats. Unlike other texts of the classical era, the Preface goes on to foreground the term *yen* ("speak," "express") instead of its companions *shih* and *chih* ("poetry" and "intent").[32] This emphasis on *yen* is somewhat startling; the means used even more so. For everything in passages (a), (b), and (c) above except for the paraphrase of the *Documents* formula is borrowed—with small but significant changes—from the "Record of Music" section of the *Record of Ritual.* A passage near the beginning of the "Record" says:

> As to every kind of tone [*yin*]—it is something that arises from the human heart. Feeling is moved inwardly; thus[33] it takes shape in sound. Sound forms a pattern, and we call it "tone." For this reason the tone of a well-governed era is joyous and thereby peaceful. Its government is harmonious. The music of a disordered era is angry and thereby [expresses] resentment. Its government is perverse. The tone of a country on the brink of destruction is anxious and thereby mournful. Its citizens are helpless. The way of sounds [*sheng*] and tones is identical to that of government.[34]

The Great Preface makes this, on the first occasion of quoting the "Record of Music," into "feeling is moved inwardly and is expressed in *speech*" (my italics). On the second occasion the sentence has almost regained its original shape ("feeling is *sent forth* [a self-quotation by the Preface] in sound; sounds that form a pattern are called 'musical tone.' The tone of a well-governed era is joyous").[35] The point of substituting "speech" for "sound" is obvious: that is how the Preface, for all its quoting from musical lore, is to become a work of *poetics.* But "speech" disrupts the logic of the passage borrowed from the "Record of Music." A passage from a story told elsewhere in the "Record," one that does mention "speech," is stitched in to smooth over the transition. In the original:

[The music master Ssu said to Confucius' disciple Tzu-kung:] ". . . Therefore singing is a form of speech—one that prolongs [the sounds of] speech. When affected by joy, one expresses it in speech. It is not enough to speak, so one draws out the words; it is not enough to draw the words out, so one sighs and shouts [them]; it is not enough to sigh and shout, so without one's willing it, one's hands dance and one's feet stamp."[36]

The Preface inverts the order of "sighing" and "drawing out the words," again for the sake of a better connection with the interpolated word "speech." It then leads off with its second version of the sentence from the "Record" ("Feeling is sent forth as sound"). But this transition is no better than the last. The quoted passages have beginnings but no endings, leading edges but no trailing ones. *Yen* at the end of one development corresponds to *yen* at the beginning of another, but the second development's conclusion does not introduce anything directly. The Preface can defer the problem of its own continuity, but not for long.

Should that matter? Steven Van Zoeren offers a view of the Great Preface's architecture that makes looking for its continuities hardly less misguided than reading the telephone book for its plot. "Characterized by a choppy and allusive argument" and evidently "made up of a series of exegetical digressions unevenly yoked together," the Preface "foils and frustrates our expectation of a unitary exposition."[37] At stake in the Great Preface's often frustrating transitions is, however, the relation of that piece of writing to the text from which it borrows most, and that is an issue larger than expository well-formedness. It has to do, rather, with the sense of words and the possibility of founding or adapting a language for poetics. Accordingly I organize my own "unitary exposition," or my hunt for one, around it.

The "Record of Music" demands less of its readers. "Feeling is moved inwardly; thus it takes shape in sound [*sheng*]. Sound forms a pattern, and we call it 'tone' [*yin*]. For this reason the tone of a well-governed country is joyous." Compare the Preface: "Feeling is moved inwardly and takes form in speech [*yen*]. . . . Feeling is sent forth in sound [*sheng*]; sounds that compose a pattern are called 'musical tone' [*yin*]. The tone of a well-governed country is joyous." The Preface seems to require that we take "speech" and "sound," *yen* and *sheng*, as equivalent. But to do that is to dishonor its own precepts, for in adapting the theses of the "Record of Music," the Preface had, precisely, used *yen* to push out *sheng*. The Preface introduces a concern (words) that disturbs the progression of the argument of the "Record," and it suppresses distinctions vital to the "Record." For there was a reason, in the "Record," for the ordering of *sheng* and *yin*: it corresponded to a derivation and a hierarchy.

As much as it may seem to be the Preface's task to establish continuity between each pair of stages on the way from feeling to speaking, sighing, singing, and dancing, the "Record" aims at distinguishing them. Tone (*yin*) is one stage of complexity further along than mere emotive sound (*sheng*). "Sound forms a pattern, and we call it 'tone' "; or as another formulation has it: "Sounds answer to one another; this produces modulation [*pien*]. Modulations combine in modes [*fang*]; this we call 'tone.' We put the tones in order [*pi*] and perform [*yüeh*] them; with shields, battle-axes, plumes, and oxtail pennants added, we call this musical performance [also *yüeh*]."[38] The difference between *sheng*—"sound," the word displaced by "speech"—and *yin* or "tone" matters for another reason.

> All tone springs from the human heart; music is that which penetrates the principles of social relation. Therefore one who knows sound but does not know tone is like the birds and beasts; one who knows tone but not music is like the mass of people; only the gentleman [*chün-tzu*] is able to know music. So one investigates sounds in order to know the tone; investigates tones in order to know music; investigates music in order to know government.[39]

"Music," orthodox music, has aesthetic and educational functions unknown to mere "sounds" and "tones." (Lacking the technical language to voice this distinction, the speaker of the first part of the "Ta yüeh" chapter of the *Lü-shih ch'un-ch'iu* can only say: "Countries on the brink of destruction and peoples given up for lost are not without music, but their music is not music.")[40] After the maxim "the way of sounds and tones is identical to that of government" comes the application:

> *Kung* [the lowest note of the pentatonic scale, nonce equivalent F] represents the prince; *shang* [G] his ministers, *chüeh* [A] the populace, *chih* [C] duties, and *yü* [D] resources. . . . If *kung* is out of place, the sound is rough: the prince is arrogant. If *shang* is out of place, the sound is steep: his officials are corrupt. If *chüeh* is out of place, the sound is distressed: the populace is resentful. If *chih* is out of place, the sound is mournful: labors overcome [the populace]. If *yü* is out of place, the sound is brittle: resources are insufficient. If all five of them are out of place, they repeatedly attack one another: this is called contempt. . . . The tones of Cheng and Wei are those of a disordered era, the paragon of "contempt."[41]

Is this what is meant by the identity of "the way of sounds and tones and that of government"? Something seems to be missing from the odd marriage of formalism[42] and ethical language in this version of the "expressive" thesis about music—namely, the rule that might account for the translations or identities it establishes between ethical qualities and properties of music. Lacking such a rule, the correlation is only a willful, or willed, one.[43] Yet the "Record" does suggest a reply to this objection. It lists the tones of the pentatonic scale from lowest to highest (*kung, shang, chüeh, chih, yü*). This is not as self-evident as it seems.[44] Building a scale, in antiquity, involved applying the "Pythagorean" ratios. A string or pipe of a given length was known to produce a tone a fifth lower than a string or pipe two-thirds the length of the first. With this ratio, the tones will be generated, starting from *kung*, in the order: *chih, shang, yü, chüeh* (or C, G, D, A, assuming that *kung* = F). Some ancient texts list the pitches in that order, suggesting that their authors were acquainted with the theory of tuning by fifths.[45] But the "Record" has them in their scale-order, not their generating-order. Its authors, whose musical training we have no other way of judging, must have had in mind a set of pipes or tuning strings in which the lowest note (*kung* or the "prince") had the visible eminence of being produced by the longest object, the next lowest (*shang* or the "ministers") by the next longest, and so on. Only the "prince" occupies the same place in both mathematical and eye-measurement sequences.

Musical theories of government run a predictable course. Society, no less than the musical scale, is the sum of its parts; each component of society has its place in the system of intervals and its responsibilities toward the general harmony. Although the Great Preface is certainly engaged in following out some of the analogy's implications, it is questionable how much detail it can accommodate. The seemingly arbitrary pairings between the musical scale and the social scale depend for their sense on the physical properties of musical instruments, and those long ago ceased to have any immediate relation to the *Odes*. And the more musicological pressure is brought to bear on the words *sheng* and *yin*, the more tenuous their connection to the argument of the Preface becomes. Without a formalizable backing of scales, notes, and defining ratios against which to draw its diagnostic parallels, the Great Preface is obliged to make do with only half of the "Record of Music" passage's field of reference. It can only echo the "Record" in its least specific character. For poetics, the whole topic of music—in other words, the principle linking the Great Preface to its model—is a backward-looking one.

What the Preface offers as a poetics seems, so far, to be a theory of music shorn of several of its main consequences and justifications. The career of the word *sheng* typifies the relation between the two texts: the Preface finds it useful as a connector but not as a carrier of meaning. As much could be said of the words imported by the Preface into the logic of the "Record." "Speech" (*yen*) becomes, if we are to read the Preface as a revision of the "Record of Music," a detour in the domino-like derivation of music from feeling—a situation that can lead only to instability in a treatise on *poetics*.[46] But principles, unlike evidence, survive the transition from field to field. The only way the Preface can merge its concerns with those of the "Record" is by moving higher up the generic tree and adopting the moral position common to all aesthetic theories inspired by ancient ritualism. Different eras have a characteristic "tone" (ethical habitus, musical mode). Not only does an era give forth a harmonious "tone" because its government is mild, but the period is harmonious because its music is.

> [9] The kings of old used [the *Odes*] to regulate the relations of husband and wife; to perfect filial piety and respect; to deepen human ties; to beautify the transformation [of their people] by culture; and to modify customs.

> [11] Those above used the "Airs" to transform those below; those below used the "Airs" to satirize those above. . . . That is why the "Airs" are called *feng*.

The influence of music on manners and the forethought of the ancient kings in leaving behind standards of music for later generations to imitate are frequent topics in the "Record of Music."[47] But the theory of "praise and blame" is the Preface's own (patterned, it is true, on anecdotes from collections such as the *Tso Commentary* and the *Conversations of the States*). Its contribution to a poetics that is to be more than a cut-down philosophy of music is clear: it gives "speech" something to do.

Like the "Record," the Preface gives examples of the principle it proposes, examples meant to show that the road from poetry to ethos to government can be traveled in both directions. Criticism, always moralizing and historicizing, has both a descriptive face and a prescriptive one. Poetry manifests, in the manner of a symptom, the ethos of its makers and of the state that governs them, but the best kind of poetry, by regulating the passions, furnishes a pattern for the "royal way," the civilizing mission of government. But what is the "best kind" of poetry? In the ritual texts the state is seen, not as the repository of power, religious authority, or even of national identity, but as a vast *Gesamtkunstwerk* of ethical import.[48] If the state is already aesthetic through and through, then the goodness of works of art will have no special character outside their usefulness to governing—at least the Preface proposes none to replace the terms of art in the "Record." The "Record of Music" could point to the difference between the ancient modes and the deviant scales of Cheng and Wei; the Preface can only refer to a canon by instituting it together with an interpretation. The best kind of poetry is that which receives the best interpretation.

Poetry interpreted descriptively (as evidence of social tendencies) should be no better or worse, for the ritualists, than the society it reflects; so (moving into the prescriptive) the poetry of good rulers should be circulated and chanted everywhere: this much is to be found in the "Record" as well as in the Preface. The Preface innovates in making poetry a means whereby the classes educate each other. "Those above" use the *Odes* to "transform" (*feng, hua*) "those below"; "those below" in turn use poetry to "prod" (*feng, tz'u*) "those above."[49] The core of the innovation lies in allowing "those below" a measure of social initiative. It is, however, a limited initiative, one that ultimately derives from "above." "The kings of old used [the *Odes*] . . . to beautify the transformation [of their people] by culture and to modify customs" (Preface, 9). The very fact that "those below" have a standard against which to measure their superiors' behavior shows that their "prodding" is an effect of the broader "transformation" wrought by the ancient kings and renders the Preface's innovation explicable through the mechanics of the "Record of Music." The preface to Ode 23, "Yeh yu ssu chün," the first satirical ode in the Mao edition, says: "Those who had undergone the change wrought by King Wen [of the Chou] still despised breaches of ritual, although the time was out of joint." Some poems are instances of *tz'u*, "satire," but all are examples of *hua*, "influence."[50]

The interest of Kung Ying-ta's commentary for our investigation lies in his stubborn attempt to read the specificities of poetics, as the Great Preface articulates them, *back* into the musical theories from which the Preface emerged. The Preface's passage about satire (Paragraph 11) foregrounds what can only be questions of linguistic tact and decorum; its subject is speech, as the words italicized here make plain, and it thus belongs on the side of what is new in the Preface. In a literal translation, the passage reads, "Those below used [poetry] to satirize those above. They emphasized pattern [*wen*] and *admonished discreetly*. The *speaker* [of the poem] is without guilt; the hearer [of the poem understands] enough to desist. [That is] why [the 'Airs'] are called *feng*."

K'ung reads this occurrence of "pattern" as equivalent to that near the beginning of the Preface and, like that earlier occurrence, as a reference to musical aesthetics. "Sounds that join to form a pattern [*wen*] are called *yin*"—a statement with a familiar load of musical implications. How is the musical hierarchy of forms to be combined with language's potential for moral judgment? By a thoroughgoing musicalization of speech and of the speech situation, it seems: "When the poet sets himself to harmonizing [the words] with the patterns of *kung* and *shang* as they answer one another, so that the verses are set to music, he can rely on indirect expression and so admonish discreetly without calling the ruler's faults by name. In this way, the speaker does not offend, and the ruler is not outraged."[51]

Unless the musical vocabulary is taken in a strict technical sense, the relation between "pattern" and "indirect expression" in K'ung's commentary is still unclear. Surely "pattern" makes expression "indirect" only by accident: distraction in the hearer, recoding of the message to fit a rhyme scheme or tone pattern, and so forth. But (according to the "Record of Music") "*kung* represents the prince, *shang* his ministers." The "patterns of *kung* and *shang*," the formula for musical adornment, contain in themselves by definition the relations of "those above" and "those below." The admonishing official's emphasis on pattern is not, for K'ung, just a way of sweetening the pill but a transformation of the unequal relation between "high" and "low" into a harmonious and necessary one.[52] Once speech, even the kind of moral and satirical speech that occurs between distinct social classes, has become a special case of music, K'ung can override the difference of kind between *feng* (transformation from above) and *tz'u* (moral prodding from below). He does this by praising the official's rebukes to his sovereign with the very words Confucius had reserved for the superior man's effect on the commons: "When the [ruler's] faults have been declared and amended, it is like *the wind blowing and causing the grass to bend*."[53] K'ung's musicology seems to aim at recovering for aesthetics the territory that the Preface had ceded to politics and, through a strongly unified reading of the Preface's less unified moments, to make both poetics and politics obsolete. His interpretation can serve the present discussion by marking more clearly what the Preface does not quite do—what it needed K'ung Ying-ta to do for it.

A varying balance between the social poetics of "influence" and "satire" is also behind the Preface's other great innovation, the reading of the "altered Airs and Elegantiae,"[54] poems that appear to fall short of orthodoxy but really—when understood as a parody of vice—confirm it. In the practical criticism of the Little Prefaces, the theory of generic "alteration" proves to be a theory of irony in the Western medievals' favorite sense, an alternation of praise and blame.[55] When rulers fail to "transform" society adequately, the poets, speaking for society, "chastise" them by composing poems that recommend vice—and who, in a world that remembered virtue, could seriously recommend vice?

> [12–14] When, as a result of the perishing of the Kingly Way, ritual and loyalty were neglected and governmental tutelage [of the mass] was abandoned, states had differing governments and families had differing customs. Then the altered "Airs" and "Elegantiae" were composed. State historians . . . sang of their feelings in order to persuade their superiors. They were conscious of changes in affairs and full of regret for the old customs. Thus the altered [or decadent] "Airs" arose from feeling and yet do not exceed the bounds of ritual and loyalty. To start from feeling is the nature of the mass of people; to stop within the bounds of ritual and loyalty is the grace of the former kings.

That is the Great Preface's historical explanation for the presence of "altered" poems alongside the "correct" ones. The passage as it stands is unexceptional; parallels to it can be found throughout the surviving pre-Han literature. But it is as a trigger for interpretative decisions that the theory provokes controversy and seems to break away from the principles laid down in the first part of the Great

Preface. An example will clarify the issues. Ode 48, "Sang chung," begins straightforwardly enough:

> I pick the dodder
> In the village of Mei.
> Of whom do I think?
> Of the beautiful Eldest Daughter Chiang.
> She met me among the mulberry trees,
> Invited me to the Upper Palace,
> Accompanied me along the river Ch'i.

The lyrics do not say so, of course, but the Little Preface to the poem describes it as "a satire on debauchery. The ducal house of Wei was given to wantonness and disorder, and men and women met freely. Nobles and officials took every occasion to entice one another's wives and concubines to remote places." Cheng Hsüan is concerned that the reader know the difference between the poem's righteous author and its immoral fictive speaker. He paraphrases line 3: "That is, of whom do dissolute and abandoned persons think? Of Eldest Daughter Chiang."[56] In such a reading, indeed, "poetry expresses intent"—but it is an intent the speaker disavows and ascribes to someone else.

"For Brutus is an honorable man": irony, as developed here, is a means of guaranteeing the best interpretation for any poem. (This is, incidentally, an obstacle to the symmetrical opposition often drawn between Greek mimesis and Chinese ethical "expression": for the trick of echoing an opponent's words, while giving them an ironical sense, is called by Quintilian *ēthopoiia* or *mimēsis*.)[57] "Praise and blame" and the unidentified "state historians" have come to be mainstays of anti-Prefaces writing: they seem to have been invented for the transparent purpose of making immoral poems moral.[58] But the business of the "altered Airs and Elegantiae" goes beyond the interpretation of individual poems to the generic definition of the *Odes* and the reach of the theory of "kingly influence."[59] Now we begin to see that it reaches everywhere. Poems may have their unkingly concerns and even silences, but the commentary always finds what it is looking for.[60] A limitless thematization corresponds to the concern, in another critical vocabulary, for the work's unity. Thus a blow struck for decadence is a blow struck for orthodoxy. The Great Preface is the amethyst dropped into the prince's cup.[61] This brings us back, through the theory of poetry as expression, to poetry's opposite, namely, "saying one thing and meaning another."

Here the distances from the "Record of Music" are evident: apparently no one had ever had to suggest interpreting a piece of music against the grain of what it seemed to "say." Tenuous as its correlations between notes of the scale and political actors may seem, the "Record" shows no sign of needing to abandon explicitly its doctrine of artistic signs' being sufficient to their own interpretation. (The gentleman can "study the tones in order to know the music, study the music in order to know the kind of government"; every sign has its relation to a bigger frame of reference plotted out.) With the introduction of irony, properly linguistic meaning, or content, has finally found a place in the Preface's reasonings. The "Record of Music" never got this far, despite all the resources of *yüeh-yü*.[62]

With the theory of praise and blame, the linguistic side of the Great Preface gets the upper hand. But the Preface needs at the same time to advance the view that the praising and blaming are tacit, that their expression in language is not the whole story. With the introduction of irony—"discreet admonition"—the poem becomes effective, like an artillery piece or Widow Wadman's eye, not so much in itself as by its carriage.[63] The same poem can offer either praise or blame, depending on how you take it. Mencius, in a famous passage, reads as praise a certain poem that the Mao preface reads as satire, and the four schools of *Odes* learning often disagree whether a poem praises (so-and-so) or blames (someone else).[64] This is a problem that the theorists of irony have created for themselves. What the poem says is no brake on the indeterminacy of interpretation, since the indeterminacy arises from the assumption that the poem may say something quite other than what it means, *if* it is a "decadent" poem and *if* it blames while appearing to praise. (If either possibility applies, we should not expect to see evidence of it in the poem itself.) Thanks to the theory of irony, the texts of the *Book of Odes* no longer bear very heavily on the determination of their own ethical sense.

The immediate subject of the Great Preface and the first ode of the collection, "Kuan chü," demonstrates how small a step separates orthodox poems from decadent ones. The poem mentions the call of ospreys, and the Mao *chuan* commentary pursues the hint:

> Ospreys are passionate but observe separation [of the sexes]. . . . The consort delights in her lord's virtue, always seeking to fulfill his wishes, and yet does not lead him to become infatuated with her beauty. She is careful, constant, retiring, and pure, just as are the ospreys with their separation of the sexes. As a consequence, [the consort] is able to change [*feng-hua*] the world. When husband and wife keep apart, fathers and sons are close; when fathers and sons are close, the relation of ruler and subject is one of respect; when the relation of ruler and subject is respectful, all is proper at court, and when all is proper at court, the royal influence [*wang-hua*] is complete.[65]

In a word, when the royal house behaves itself as it should (and the poem shows it doing that), the whole kingdom is at peace. The cumulative logic of the commentary may be meant to recall the symptomatic inevitability of certain passages of the "Record of Music" (e.g., the passage rewritten to form Paragraph 5 of the Great Preface). The poem even begins in a near-musical mode: the nonsense syllables *kuan-kuan* evoke the ospreys (by imitating their cry), who in turn evoke the consort, whose osprey-like actions acknowledge and preserve the Kingly Way. Yet the Three Schools interpret the poem's wedding congratulations ironically, as a satire on a certain dissolute ruler who failed to observe "the virtue of the ospreys."[66] The same music—*kuan-kuan*—falls differently on different interpretative ears. In other words, what the ear hears is no longer music. Although the "Chou-nan" section of the "Airs of the States" shows "the way of correct beginning" (Great Preface, Paragraph 20), the beginning of the "Chou-nan" is itself in need of a "correct beginning." That is what the Preface is meant to provide.

Modern readers refuse to make the poem serve its footnotes.

(Maybe there is need of yet another "correct beginning," a preface to the Prefaces, to overcome this resistance.) Since Chu Hsi, cognitive dissonance has been the best argument against reading the poems through their Prefaces: "Approach the *Odes* with an open mind and read them to the point of utter familiarity"—advice that would be fatal to the Prefaces.[67] Yet the distinction between traditional and modern reading is not only that between a cluttered view of the text and a clear one. What separates the two styles is more like a religious schism—a disagreement about the reasons why one reads—than like a disagreement about what the texts say. The prefaces and commentaries do serve a purpose, but not what we would call an artistic purpose. They provide a remedy to the moral peril of an uncontextualized poem.

What leads modern readers to discard the Mao Prefaces is something like disappointment at the Prefaces' refusal to follow to the end the program of spontaneous expression found in parts of the "Record of Music." In this, at least, modernity is anything but progressive. To make the "Record of Music" the standard by which to judge the moralistic reading of the *Odes* would be to applaud the Great Preface for its least original moments; for wherever the Preface adds something to the tradition represented by the "Record," it begins to reverse the logic of that tradition. Music was, for the ancients, the model of adequacy and self-sufficiency in works of art, but it is in the nature of the linguistic sign not to be self-sufficient. The very fact that poems have a content separable (as the existence of so many competing frame-stories attests) from their form calls into question the validity of the analogy with music. The interpreter of poetry can no longer study the local system in order to know the larger system of which it was a part; the only way to reach a stable interpretation is to reverse the process and "study the government in order to know the music," as it were. With music, the progress from "sound" to "tone" to "music" combined an ascending order of complexity with an aesthetic hierarchy. Here there is no such opportunity for a demarcation of levels. The "bigger frame of reference" into which the content of poetry is to be integrated is simply more of the same thing, another piece of content.[68] Any ear can tell when music goes chromatic, but it takes special knowledge to tell a poem about vice apart from a poem of vice.

In the teeth of this last assertion about language, the theory of praise and blame offers the means of telling the levels apart and inserts a difference of kind between what the poem says and what the "state historians" of a decaying kingdom might have meant by composing or recording it.[69] In music, the fact of a note's being above or below its assigned pitch was symptomatic: now a moral tuning fork provides the same facilities for the judge of poetry. The "grace of the former kings," active in both the *feng* poetry of transformation and the *tz'u* poetry of censure, affords the means of telling whether an Ode is "on" or "off" the scale, *cheng* or *pien*. The Mao readings are perfectly exemplary, exemplifying the fact that an example can never be an example without being an example *of* something. And the moral standard-pitch is what these examples are given to be examples (and counterexamples) of.

The analogy between music and poetry, which broke down with the replacement of *sheng* by *yen* and of immediately expressive sound by linguistically mediated content, can now be at least partly recovered. "Transformation-through-teaching" (*chiao-hua*), with its near-synonyms *wang-hua, feng-hua, cheng-chiao*, is not only the content of the Mao version of the *Odes* but also the normative rule that determines what their possible content can be. This way of seeing the relation between the poems and the Prefaces may help to reorient the modern distaste for the traditional didactic "allegories." If the hallmark of the didactic commentaries is the imposition of alien sense from outside, that way of characterizing them need not change, but it can be given a new meaning. The theory of *chiao-hua* can solve the problems of a musical-moral style of reading *because* it is external and prior to the *Odes* corpus, not in spite of that fact.

> The man who pushes the boat while he is himself standing in the boat and fixing himself against it naturally does not move it, since it is necessary that that against which he fixes himself remain still. But in

his case the thing he tries to move and that against which he is fixing himself are the same. If, however, he pushes or pulls from outside he does move it. For the ground is no part of the boat.[70]

Music knows this too. The natural setting in which music originates is one of undifferentiated and continuous "sound," *sheng*; the specifically human discovery of "tone" (*yin*) organizes *sheng* into distinct "modes." What the gentleman or *chün-tzu* alone knows is how to "contrast the tones and perform them," that is, how to set up a scale by choosing a ground tone and deriving from it the four following notes proportionate to it. The first note of a scale determines the remaining notes without being determined by them; the technical term for this note is the "prince." The prince or *kung* note, once posited, is the hinge between the strictly relational sphere of the five-note scale and the merely differentiated sphere of mode-values that lies outside it. Within its sphere (the qualification is necessary, for any one of the twelve pitches or *lü* can serve as *kung*), it is the absolute to which the scale of five *yin* is relative.[71] The necessary fiction of *chiao-hua* is meant to play the same role.

Archaeology comments on the necessity and the arbitrariness (at bottom the same thing) of such a standard. The first note of the *lü* system—known as *huang-chung* or "the yellow [= imperial] bell"—was, according to the "Record of Music," the foundation of both the twelve-note (tuning) and five-note (performance) series. But by the time the musical treatises were written, the original "yellow bell" had disappeared, and the specifications given in the books were useless. The *huang-chung* might be defined as the note produced by a pitch pipe 8.1 inches long, but the definitions of foot and inch themselves derived from the length of the standard pitch pipes, and those could only be tested against the *huang-chung*. The elusive *huang-chung* thus, for the Confucians of the early Han, "became symbolic of what was lost from China's classical age."[72]

Chiao-hua, as the key to the correct reading of the *Odes*, reconciles the sometimes warring vocabularies of music and language in the Mao edition's program for criticism; it also speaks to the scholarly issues that mattered most to the traditionalists gathered at the Prince of Ho-chien's court. And it solves those problems in the abrupt way characteristic of the philosophy of Hsün-tzu.

Both the Mao Prefaces and the "Record of Music" descend from Hsün-tzu, the "Record" being a reworking of the philosopher's fragmentary utterances on the topic. Most early Han classicists owed Hsün-tzu one or more of their credentials. The Elder Mao, whose edition of the *Odes* was adopted by Prince Hsien, is said to have been a disciple of Hsün-tzu or at any rate attached to his school, as was Shen P'ei, founder of the Lu school. As for the Han school, Hsün-tzu is the favored source of its *External Commentary on the Odes*, and the Elder and the Younger Tai, who drew so much of their reconstruction of the *Record of Ritual* from Hsün-tzu, studied the *Odes* with a master of the Ch'i school, Hou Ts'ang.[73] By the latter Han dynasty, however, Hsün-tzu had lost his influence among the literati, and the classical texts that had been edited and commented on by Hsün-tzu's school were being interpreted on different principles.[74] One of these texts is, of course, the Old Text *Book of Odes* edited by Master Mao.

Hsün-tzu's thinking on ritual may guide us toward some of the motives of the Mao redaction, as well as provide a cover for the ways in which the reading of the Great Preface given above may seem to contradict tradition and common sense. Hsün-tzu's great theory—unfortunately for his later reputation—is that "human nature is evil; whatever is good in man is artifice."[75] As proof for this thesis, Hsün-tzu adduces an extensive psychology of appetites, all of which we share with other animals. We can speak and think about ourselves as different from the run of animals only because we have rituals, social organization, and various limits on our desires that enable us to take part in societies. And whereas his predecessor and antagonist Mencius is renowned for his anecdotes tending to prove that the springs of morality are in every untutored heart, Hsün-tzu derives all the human virtues from the beneficent action of the sages.

Man is born with desires. From desiring and not getting, demands must necessarily follow; demands unlimited in their extent and kind make for struggle. Struggle causes disorder; disorder poverty. The kings of old, abhorring disorder, established ritual and loyalty as a means of making distinctions [among people]. . . . This is the origin of the rites.

Heaven and earth are the beginning of life; ritual and loyalty are the beginning of rule; and the prince [*chün-tzu*] is the beginning of ritual and loyalty.[76]

Just as there is no transition between human nature and moral nature (except the early kings' "abhorrence"; but this would have to be explained somehow, since it does not seem consonant with the description of humanity in the state of nature), the beginning of culture, instead of being a gradual working out of inborn tendencies, is sudden and total, an irruption into the causal order. This has long been a stumbling block for Chinese philosophers. The Han historian and bibliographer Liu Hsiang is said to have objected: "If this is so . . . where would man ever get an opportunity to *begin* doing deeds of virtue?"[77] Liu Hsiang speaks here with what most historians recognize as *the* voice of Chinese philosophy: "integrative," "spontaneous," "organic and non-mechanical," a style of thinking antipathetic to beginnings ex nihilo.[78] Hsün-tzu's story about culture is, of course, absurd and inexplicable in the natural course of things, a deus ex machina solution to a legitimate sociological question. But if nature cannot be our ethical guide and yet we have to get our ethics from somewhere, the absurdity makes its own kind of sense as the representation of a difference that cannot be mediated.

In the beginning, then, there were the sages, who instituted the various ways of being human, particularly rites and music.[79] Rites and music, and indeed everything worth knowing, are incorporated in the Classics. Hence the importance of a literary education, which is the first item in Hsün-tzu's aesthetics.[80] But literature, even classical literature, cannot be allowed to interpret itself, any more than Hsün-tzu will concede "that the eye alone sees or the ear alone hears."[81] "To wish, without a basis in ritual, to do what is done in the *Odes* and *Documents*—one might as well sound rivers with one's fingers, pound grain with a spear's point, drink soup with an awl: it cannot be done."[82] Ritual is the court of last appeal, the meta-aesthetics of which aesthetics, music, politics, and so forth are partial realizations. The model given by the sages informs cultural life without being part of culture; strictly speaking, it is prior to it and stands apart from it, just as the rule for reading given in the Great Preface has to inform reading without itself being evident in any part of what is read. The sages' unprecedented invention of ritual is the pattern and necessary precondition of every other kind of artifice. Most notably, it reappears in the *kung* note, which gives a basis to the musical scale, and in the *chiao-hua* principle, which orients the *Book of Odes.*

It may be, then, that the "arbitrariness" so often ascribed to the Han dynasty's pedagogues lies not in the exegetes' hermeneutic obtuseness or lack of skill but in the relation of moral reading to literary reading. "Allegory" (whether we take the word in Quintilian's sense or make it synonymous with the story of misunderstanding told by Chinese critics) resides in that relation, or in the gap where that relation should be. Little textual justification can be given for most of the Mao readings; they are often as unbeautiful as allegory is said to be.[83] What backs them up is, at bottom, less poetry, history, or philology than a moral imperative (roughly: Thou shalt read in this way, and it will then become true). And once the principle of their poetics has been granted, the only result of their readings of individual poems seems to be to justify the aesthetic-ethical poetics they began with. Words to that effect are put in Confucius' mouth by the authors of the *Han Shih wai chuan.*

> Tzu-hsia asked, "Why is the 'Kuan-chü' made to begin the 'Kuo-feng' [section of the Odes]?" Confucius said, "The 'Kuan-chü' is perfection. . . . Now the writings of the Six Classics are devoted to exhaustive discussion, but they all derive [their matter] from the 'Kuan-chü.' The subject of the 'Kuan-chü' is great! Vast and soaring, 'from the east to the west, from the south to the north, there is not a thought but does it homage.' "[84]

To put it somewhat differently, the model articulating the aesthetic and the political in the Prefaces can never found itself, since every attempt to say on what the theory rests results in a restatement of the theory. (Whether one has any business asking it to show on what it rests is another question. The sage's institution of culture should be self-explanatory.) Whatever one may say about the disagreements between text and preface, the communication between principles and applications (between the theory of *chiao-hua* and the supposed examples of *chiao-hua*) is perfect, as only a closed system allows it to be.

Now we know why it is closed. It is impossible to get into the Mao Prefaces' reading-machine from outside, from an agnostic position on the questions of ethical mimesis and moral "transformation," and just as impossible to get out of it from inside, because the Prefaces' logic reproduces the utter difference, in the ritualists' theory, between a world with culture and a world without it.

The aesthetically and morally exemplary work of art cannot have a natural origin; nor, apparently, can the theory that discovers certain works of art to be exemplary. The logic of criticism recapitulates the history it wrote for the artwork. Since the Prefaces' license to thematize—to put poems in frames—derives from the historical argument about "kingly transformation," transformation is not only the plot of the story they tell but also the name for the purpose of their reading, a purpose determined previously to and independently of the work being read. (Everyone agrees that the moral readings of the poems are strongly underdetermined by the letter of the text.) The theory of *chiao-hua*, by making the poems of the *Book of Odes* into moral exempla, does to them what the reality of *chiao-hua*, if there is such a reality, ought to have done to the world the poems describe.

That makes the relation between the aesthetic and the political hinge not on a quasi-natural causality of mutual influence or expression but first of all on an ethical decision to read in a certain way; which is to say that the descriptive and prescriptive discourses of the Preface do not quite coincide. Rather, they differ by as far as a language of description differs from a language of performatives (promising, commanding, giving notice, etc.).[85] This should prompt us to rethink the principle of expressive continuity on which the Prefaces overtly stake their claims and which has so often been held up against their actual results. The expressive thesis *has* to take second place to the prescriptive thesis if the theory explaining them is Hsün-tzu's. What poetry "expresses" is human nature, in which case it is evil; or it expresses the second nature of the sages, in which case its cause is not natural but artificial, emanating from a prescriptive sagely decree. Only a Mencian line on human nature would find expression alone an adequate key to the *Odes.*

The meaning of the Great Preface (and of the whole Mao tradition) has always been clear, and I have not tried to overturn it. What is missing from all modern assessments, however, and what the past few pages of comment have tried to recover, is an appreciation of the *mode* or *tense* of that meaning. The ancient tradition speaks a historical language but takes for its subject something that, as we have seen, cannot easily be called history, because the Prefaces' historical examples come with a plea that we grant their necessary preconditions. It makes more sense (and better history) to say that the tradition reads the *Odes* as the description of a possible ethical world. It reads them in the performative mode, as narrating, in the form of history, the model actions that its own reading must second in order to make them actual.

And allegory in all this? "There is allegory in examples, if the examples are set down with no previous reason [*praedicta ratione*]" (Quintilian, *Institutio* VIII.6.52). The Prefaces are a sustained attempt to prefix "reasons" to the poems. How are those reasons to be distinguished from the secondary "uses" and "applications" of poetry that the moderns name allegoresis? Exemplary reading understands "previous" not as marking a point in a discursive or historical sequence, but as signaling the reversal of natural time by a claim of ethical priority. The sage's edict may break into an existing amoral order, but it is the first word spoken in the new history it founds. The *all-* of "allegory" denotes the split, gap, or line that separates two human histories—the history of China with, and without, the "Kuan chü."

§ 4 The *Odes* as Exemplary Readings

Devotion to princes is a second self-love.
— La Rochefoucauld, Maxim 518

A rereading of the Great Preface is like a note that cannot be cashed at any of Chinese literary history's usual places of business. The Great Preface of the tradition, the immensely influential theory of influence, the Mencian rhetoric and hermeneutic of literary forms, the indispensable whipping boy of cultural critique since 1919—*that* Great Preface is beyond our power to affect it. But reinterpretation results in a new object. In order to understand what kind of literary object the *Mao Odes* was in the period of its growing influence, we must talk about the commentators' *Book of Odes* as something other than a distortion of the poets' *Book of Odes*. This entails redefining the objects of which the Great Preface and Little Prefaces speak—the *Odes*—not to mention the manner of the Prefaces' response to them.

The "Chou-nan" and "Shao-nan" sections of the *Odes*, says the Great Preface as it is usually translated, show "the way of correct beginning" (*cheng-shih chih tao*). Just what sort of beginning is meant is hardly in doubt: it is (to paraphrase the "Record of Music") the setting forth of a fundamental tone around which the aesthetic or musical state will organize itself. But to talk of beginning in this way is deceptive. The "Elegantiae" and "Laudes" sections of the *Odes*, the collection's historical and interpretative center, tell the story of a colonization, and colonization, by definition, breaks in *in medias res*.

"Correct beginning," then, may be a coded way of referring to a reappropriation. Only a little grammatical pressure is needed to make the sentence read: "the way to putting straight the matter of beginnings"—or in social-science jargon, "how to establish priorities." Here, too, the Great Preface, under the guise of describing its texts, sets forth its own dilemmas. The Prefaces' defense of poetry is built around the overcoming of one model of priority—the model they inherit from the "Record of Music," that is, the theory of expressive ethos—by another. What are the stages of this overcoming (or reappropriation)?

Poetry tattles on society—a society formed (in part) by the canons of its poetry. The work of art, it seems, gets lost and found between its two functions of documenting mores and changing them. What would be the importance of an artwork that serves only as a medium for society's reflection on itself, an interval between two social acts? It can only be incidental: hence the serious, anti-rhetorical, or utilitarian (*wen i tsai tao*: literature as the vehicle of the Way) strain in Chinese poetics. But a poetry that merely mirrors society is in itself no vehicle of change; so to its mirroring function must be added a critical one: along with a representation, the poem must be understood as offering a commentary (in the form of "praise and blame"). This makes poetic language something more than a shadow. Poetry's critical power (in both the loose and the strict sense of the word "critical") now puts it on a par not with music but with musicology, and indeed with musicology's representative figure, the sage. Music imitates ethical states, as the "Record of Music" holds with Aristotle. The sage not only recognizes the ethical tenor of a performance but—like Confucius judging the music of Cheng and Wei "dissolute"—determines it as good or bad. "Altered" poetry does this too. With "altered" or ironic mimesis, poetry comes into its own by adding judgment to expression, second-order predicates to first-order ones. To pursue the argument of the emancipation of poetry from music to a paradoxical conclusion: the Prefaces are not the frustration of the *Odes* but their culmination.

Although poetry, according to the Great Preface, exists for society, it nonetheless does not reduce to an image of society. The musical theory of poetry ends in expression; the theory that supplants it ends in exemplarity. The difference is both logical and political, and it opens the way to a more adequate notion of the role of political terminology in the Prefaces' aesthetic. Politics (in the trivial form of national borders) is basic to Confucius' musicology, a musicology built on comparisons. Music mimics local conditions, but musicology is pan-Chinese. Cheng and Wei are independent as political units, comparable as aesthetic types, and interchangeable as (counter)examples of the same doctrine. This new model of interpretation both deepens and broadens the reader's task. If expression is necessarily the expression of state ethos, then the possibility of a poetic musicology—a means of making exemplary, as instances of "praise" or "blame," the "licentious" lyrics of the corpus as well as the "correct" ones—is, formally speaking, identical or coterminous with the possibility of China.[1] (That is, it is a faculty of judgment whose *field* is identical to its *realm*.)[2] Keeping open the place of the universal empire (by way of instantiating the "law of the realm") is not the least of the *Book of Odes'* good deeds.

~

Thematization is kingship, kingship thematization: the parallel bears working out in detail. The modern political historian Hsiao Kung-ch'üan observes that Hsün-tzu broke away from his predecessors Confucius and Mencius in "making the prince's standards of deportment the means of reforming defective human nature. . . . Before a proper government has been established, there can be no education in private virtue, and apart from political life there can be no room for private ethical life."[3] Readers who come to the *Book of Odes* through the orthodox tradition will feel themselves on familiar ground. The *Odes'* only subject in that tradition is the prince and his ability to inspire correct social institutions. If there were other possible subjects for poetry, they would fall outside the realm of "ritual and loyalty," and what is outside the law, to this way of thinking, can only be against the law; so the Four Schools' defense of poetry is wholly a matter of keeping the prince in the poems and the poems in front of the prince.

Are there no chances for the reader of the *Odes* of establishing an independent sphere of "private [aesthetic] life?" The desire to carve one out dates at least as far back as Chu Hsi. Marcel Granet's *Fêtes et chansons anciennes de la Chine* is an uncompromising and much-studied modern example. "The *Book of Odes* has been made into a school text and practically a handbook of morality. . . . Things might have turned out differently if the *Book of Odes* had been read privately and for pleasure."[4] For Granet, the standard explanation of the *Odes* exists to wash away the memory of ancient ("pagan") folk customs preserved in the poems. But even as he rejects the content of the Mao edition's allegories, Granet vindicates their principle: the political order he reconstructs for the early feudal era corresponds point for point with a hermeneutic structure. The inappropriate commentary is clapped onto the poems *just as* new marriage laws are clapped onto the old rustic habits, thereby proving the solidarity of the aesthetic and the political. What Granet describes as absurd and forced in the union of text and commentary is explained as the result of social divisions, mutual incomprehension between peasantry and officialdom: Is this not "investigating the music in order to know the government"?[5] The one standard to which the Great Preface's performance can be held is, apparently, that of the Great Preface and its source, the "Record of Music." Moreover Granet is Hsün-tzu's, and the Prefaces', best glossator, for what could Hsün-tzu have meant by a wayward human nature if not the people to whom transformation, in the shape of the Chou sovereign and his edicts, had not yet come? Granet has captured the structure of the argument but mistaken its direction. His only error is in trying to tell the Prefaces what they already know (and never stop proclaiming) about princely rule.

What do the Prefaces know? Or rather (since the wording of the Prefaces rarely does more than set the legions of classical scholarship in motion), how much is lost by supposing they know noth-

ing? What is the service they render their "prince"? Granet's per-
ceptive but contrary reading leads toward an answer. The example
is Ode 6, "T'ao-yao," singled out by Granet as "one of the songs
least spoiled by symbolic interpretation."

In Karlgren's translation "T'ao-yao" reads:

> How delicately beautiful is the peach-tree, brilliant are its flowers; this
> young lady goes to her new home, she will order well her chamber and
> house.
> How delicately beautiful is the peach-tree, well-set are its fruits; this
> young lady goes to her new home, she will order well her house and
> chamber.
> How delicately beautiful is the peach-tree, its leaves are luxuriant; this
> young lady goes to her new home, she will order well her house-
> people.[6]

Granet notes: "A wedding song. Theme of flourishing vegetation."[7]
In readings from those of the Four Schools to the present, the
peach tree of the opening lines of each stanza tends to impose itself
on the rest of the poem, which then becomes an expansion of its
initial kenning (*hsing*: "opening," "stimulus," "allusion"). Modern
readers seem to like to make an exposition piece of this poem
because it makes such good sense. Granet mentions that "flowering
peach" is an almanac term. Peach trees do flower in the spring;
people get married when they are young, and often in springtime;
the poem's way of alluding to these two facts side by side poses no
problem to understanding. Michelle Yeh notes that "according to
an ancient Chou custom, the proper time for wedding is [mid-
spring]. . . . Therefore, both the bride and the peach are associated
with spring, the time when mating takes place in nature as well as
in the human world. . . . The bride and the peach are two
exemplars of a general pattern."[8] The descriptive appropriateness
of the lines praising the peach tree would then seem to be total,
explicable by both analogy and contiguity. Now to add on the
Little Preface: " 'T'ao-yao' is evidence of the queen's widespread
influence. She was not jealous [of the sovereign in regard to his
other wives], and so the relations of men and women became

regular. Marriages took place at the appointed season. The country was without bachelors and old maids."

One sees how the preface deserves Granet's (faint) praise. At least it does not make a wedding story into another kind of poem. And the device whereby the preface links this poem to its larger plot of "kingly transformation" is easily dealt with. For a poem so adequate to its own explanation, the queen is an unnecessary hypothesis; to ignore it is to disprove it. In the twelfth century Chu Hsi expressed impatience with her obligatory presence here, and even the glossators of the Mao tradition were uneasy about her: they disagreed whether to put her in the poem (as the bride being celebrated) or above it (as the inspirer of countless weddings in her state).[9] If the queen is the only agency by which the "prince" peeps into "T'ao-yao," then the poem can easily declare its independence from the Kingly Way, the fable of "the wind and the grass" to which all the Mao interpretations sooner or later reduce.

But Granet goes one step too far in saving the poem (and with it poetry) from the clutches of Confucius. The verses translated by Karlgren as "she will order well her house," become "Il faut qu'on soit mari et femme!" ("Everyone must take a spouse!"). Granet's translation is certainly exorbitant from a philological point of view. *I* does mean "suitable, fitting, it is meet that," and *shih-chia*, glossed as "the husband's and wife's parts of the house," can mean "the state of being husband and wife," but the phrase "*i ch'i* . . ." appears nowhere in the Classics as the utterance of a command, much less a general one. Save for one example (in the "Great Learning" ["Ta hsüeh"] chapter of the *Record of Ritual*), the phrase always occurs in reported speech, introducing an outcome as predictable of or deserved by a certain person, as in the *Tso Commentary*, Huan, 15th year: "The duke said: 'He communicated his plan to his wife; so *it was meet that* he die' "; Hsüan, 2nd year: "He broke with ritual and went against orders; so *he deserved to be* taken captive."[10]

Moreover, Granet's imperative jars with his and Michelle Yeh's interpretation of the poem: if the poem does no more than announce a "general pattern" of natural change, then a command to fall into step with that change seems unnecessary, to say the least.

The reasons for translating the line imperatively must be of another order. Both as a piece of philology and as an exhibit of his interpretation, Granet's rendering of the line reaches out of this self-sufficient poem toward something that should not even be a concern of the interpreter who wishes to "explain the *Odes* by means of the *Odes*."[11]

Perhaps the imperative is meant to counter another imperative. If so, that first imperative is not far to seek. For behind the approving comment "she will order well her house" lurks the whole machinery of exemplarity and royal sagehood. The gloss on "*i chi . . .*" adopted by Karlgren's translation ("she will order well her chamber and house") has a prestigious ancient source in the "Great Learning," but it seems to have remained a dormant or peripheral reading until the nineteenth century. For a commentator such as Ch'en Huan (1786–1863), the reading "she will order . . ." justifies the preface and keeps the queen in the poem; it rebuts the skepticism of readers like Chu Hsi.[12] The original Mao commentary to lines three and four, however, only paraphrases *i chi shih-chia* as meaning "suited to having a household, [because of] not having missed the proper time [for being married]." We are meant to hear an echo of the preface in the word *i* ("suited," "apt," "fitting"), then—that will account for the poem's existence and give it the moral character of a reward. The bride is worth (*i*) commemorating because she has chosen to be married at the proper (*i*) time, in emulation of that virtuous queen and in obedience to the dictates of the former kings.

The authors of the *Chuan* commentary and early annotators such as Cheng Hsüan and K'ung Ying-ta disagree on whether "the proper time" is a time of the year (springtime) or a time of life (youth), but either way the interpretation of the poem follows the same logic. Indeed the difference between the oldest comments and the nineteenth-century ones is small.[13] Whatever construction is put on "*i chi . . . ,*" the Mao tradition reads it as marking a course of action that one ought to choose to follow: putting one's house in order, as in the stronger reading; or getting married at the right time, as in the weaker one. Granet's translation may be playing at a grammatical disadvantage, but it does call attention to the sensitive point of the moral readings, the element by which they stand or fall as moralities, that is, the active and programmatic sense of *i*. Standing on the frontier between "is" and "ought," *i* can refer to properties that are not obviously the stuff of moral exhortation and at the same time class them as the properties possessed by a good specimen of the species of which those properties are predicated.[14] That is why it can pass unobserved by readers who want to make the message of the poem the merely passive integration, as by a natural change, of human actors into their landscape, into categories or "general patterns."

Deciding what the word *i* means here determines every step of the logic of both poem and commentary. The question is not only whether the bride is "fit" to marry, or what makes her so, but also whether the poem is fit to use her to give lessons in fitness. Under either interpretation (Mao's, obviously; Granet's, unwillingly) the poem includes both descriptive ("is") and prescriptive ("ought") registers; the question is how they are articulated to one another. And here, too, the old-fashioned commentators make use of more of the poem. They point out that the second stanza invokes the tree's fruits (Mao: "She has not only the beauty of flowers but also the wifely virtues [symbolized by the fruit]"). Flowers and fruit do not come simultaneously; the tree sung here cannot be a tree seen in one moment of time. The tree's relation to the bride has to be mediated through more faculties than some interpreters are willing to reckon with.[15] K'ung Ying-ta even extends the point so far as to argue that a peach tree old enough to flower is no longer "young" (*yao*, or in its paraphrase, *shao-chuang*).[16]

Why should the commentators be so eager to destroy the analogy on which the poem's intelligibility (an exemplary intelligibility, for its modern readers) rests? Ch'en Huan goes a step further: he congratulates the bride on having chosen the royally sanctioned mid-spring festival of the Great Go-between for her wedding day, a festival at which those past marrying age were free to choose partners and dispense with the usual ceremonies.[17] A bride "with the beauty of flowers; *yao-yao* describes her as young and strong. . . .

She has not missed the proper time" (Mao commentary) has suddenly turned into a hurried old maid: one could hardly ask for a stronger proof of the incompatibility of moral and naturalizing readings.

What Ch'en does to the object of praise, the preface's explicators did to the language of praise. The moral reading triumphs by turning the tree and the bride from pictures into emblems or ciphers.[18] Critics have often remarked on the sexual puritanism of the Mao editors but not on its poetic concomitant, an iconoclastic tendency in the handling of poetic imagery.

What explains this way of reading? Perhaps praise poetry and description do not sit well together as genres. Among the Four Schools praise is always the counterpart of blame. A tincture of praise changes description into evaluation. If the concept (say that of being a bride, or being a peach tree) were identical to the image or to the extension of its denotation, there would be no possibility of falling short of the mark and so no opening for praise or blame. "The Ode says: 'Heaven gave birth to the multitudinous people; there are things and there are rules. . . .' Confucius said: 'How well the maker of that ode knew [what he was talking about]! For where there are things, there must [*pi*] be rules.'"[19] The "things" in "T'ao-yao" are reminders of the corresponding "rules." If the poem's statements were *simply* true, they would be morally meaningless. Here the commentators show their skill as readers: they notice that the praise poem is drawn into the future by the need to justify its own evaluative language. This happens, moreover, as injunction, not as prophecy: you are a peach tree (and ought to do whatever a peach tree ought to do). The image has to be spelled out like a rebus and divided up into qualities and potentialities, because an image that could be exhausted in one glance could not say all the things that praise poetry has to say.

If the theme of Granet's and Yeh's reading of "T'ao-yao" is nature, that of the commentators' is human action (a not quite symmetrical opposition). The point at which they diverge is the question of the poem's implicit linguistic mode: Is it declarative or imperative? Criticism, of course, speaks through the voice it imputes to its objects: what is really at issue is the function of reading, whether one reads for descriptions or prescriptions. Whether compared for their inventories of tropes, paraphrases of theme, programs for criticism or scales of value, the Mao school and the modern readers are at loggerheads—but not blindly so. Granet's leap into the imperative mode betrayed a wish to seal off the last door whereby the preface might creep back into the analysis of the poem, and a good part of the ancient editors' work went into anticipating and forestalling the currently dominant reading.

They interpret each other, then. Who wins? From the point of view of inclusiveness, it is surely the moral reader. Moral reading supposes the possibility of an amoral reading, and true enough, the Prefaces move to correct a first reading (i.e., the reading that modern critics have had to labor to recover). (The morally indifferent reading is "first" logically, which is not to say that it came first historically: we have here a "counterexample" internal to the moral reading, not another hypothesis about the original meaning of the *Odes*.) Granet reacts to the moral reading too, but his imperative ("il faut . . .") is exorbitant and unnecessary in terms of his own interpretation of the poem and the preface; it makes sense only as a relic of the reading he rejects. It is as if Granet's avowed goal of recovering the intrinsic meaning of the *Odes* could be attained only through the characteristic devices of the extrinsic, moralistic reading. Perhaps the "naturalizing" reading as a whole (together with its supposition of a Mencian standard for interpretation, the injunction to "climb upward from the meaning to the intent: that is how to attain it")[20] should be added to the list of things the Prefaces already know about.

~

An age that loved ingenuity and did not consider it inimical to truth would have treasured the Mao readings (some of them, anyway) as showpieces of dialectical skill. But when poets and pedagogues agree that commentaries should say over again in prose what the poems ought to be understood as saying, the very character of artifice—the difference between raw material and finished product on which the Prefaces deserve to pride themselves—becomes a badge of secondariness. The Mencian hypothesis about the natural origins of ethical consciousness must have contributed to making the Prefaces seem unnecessary and dangerous appendages to moral teaching. The solidarity of the empire, as a moral community, had to seem unforced, indebted to no prodigies of argument. (Alongside the sage-kings Yao and Shun, who "let their robes hang down to the ground [i.e., did nothing] and the world was well-administered,"[21] the Four Schools display too much sweat of the brow.) A variation on folk themes such as the Mao tradition's reading of Ode 9, "Han kuang," then, has nothing to gain but the exercise of its own wit, a form of sport that moral utilitarians fear may encourage the dish to run away with the spoon.

> In the south there are tall trees; one cannot rest under them. On the Han there are wandering girls; one cannot ask for them.
> The Han is so broad, you cannot wade it; the Chiang is so long, you cannot cross it by raft.
>
> The thick firewood grows tall; I cut thorn from among it. Here a bride is setting out to be married; I feed her pony.
> The Han is so broad, you cannot wade it; the Chiang is so long, you cannot cross it by raft.
>
> The thick firewood grows high: I cut the stalks of the *lü* plant. Here a bride is setting out to be married; I feed her colt.
> The Han is so broad, you cannot wade it; the Chiang is so long, you cannot cross it by raft.

The preface reads: " 'Han kuang' shows the spread of [royal] virtue. The way of King Wen covered the countries of the south; his civilizing influence ran throughout the basin of the Chiang and Han rivers. None thought of going against propriety; one might ask and not attain" (i.e., find no one to accept a rendezvous). This preface holds no surprises—few of them do. The commentary, which glosses the poem and the preface at once and tries to hold them together, is the thing to watch. (Throughout this chapter, to see how exactly the commentaries reshape the *Odes*, the reader is invited to keep handy a translation that deliberately shuns the influence of old interpretations. Karlgren's is dry but meticulously documented; Waley's is more persuasive and better crafted.)

"The southern trees," says the Mao commentary, "are beautiful and lofty" (with the associated meaning: awe-inspiring). Cheng Hsüan, the next commentator in historical order, considers that "the leaves and branches of the southern trees are high up, and so one can get no rest under them" (i.e., in their shade). "The girls on the Han," therefore (since the southern trees are supposed to have been brought in as a *hsing* or "evocation" of the main topic), "are not the sort one can think of pursuing" (Mao again). That, according to the nineteenth-century editor Ch'en Huan, is what the preface meant by saying "none thought of going against propriety."[22] And Cheng Hsüan insists on seeing the whole of the preface in that one line. " 'You cannot' means that one used to have the way" to cross the river or parley with the young women, but no longer does, an interpretation that, whatever it may do to the analogy of the southern trees, inspires K'ung Ying-ta to fit a little essay on women into his commentary.[23] The two rivers one cannot cross repeat the topic of unattainability.

What the commentators do next revises from top to bottom the poem as set forth up to now. The "I" who emerges in the lines about cutting firewood could just as well have been a "we" in the original. Nothing predisposes the poem to be given a singular speaker, or a masculine one: that is an unprompted innovation on Cheng Hsüan's part. (Karlgren, for example, paraphrases: "First the girls of the region are praised as desirable but not easily attained; then this girl, who is setting out on her marriage journey, is eagerly served by her comrades, who feed the horses for her.")[24] Cheng goes on to say: "The thorn is, amid the various kinds of thick firewood, the tallest" (or the most *ch'iao-ch'iao*, whatever that means for Cheng). "I want to cut it for my own: that is to say that in a crowd of girls who are all pure and virtuous, I want the remotest and purest of all."[25] Cheng invents the speaker for later generations—invents him out of the figures of *hsing*.

Ch'en Huan makes the firewood into an indicator of marriage

too, but connects the topics differently: "The thorn and *lü* plant in the thick firewood, plants that can be cut and used to tie wood into bundles, evoke the purity of this bride in a disordered time—one must fulfill all the conditions of ritual to get her. This is varying the words to explain the *hsing*," Ch'en adds, somewhat disingenuously—for what is being varied is the articulation of the various *hsing* to one another and to a main topic, a topic (witness Karlgren) by no means evident or necessary.

The bridegroom's entry into the poem happens quite inconspicuously, helped along by a commentatorial habit: wherever the poem speaks of menial labor, the commentators allegorize it. "Man and woman need ritual to become complete, just as firewood needs human labor [*jen shih*] to be bound up into bundles. The poem uses the binding of firewood as an expression for marrying according to the rites. . . . Concerning the horse, the speaker says 'feed' and not 'ride,' just as, when speaking of firewood, the speaker says 'cut' and not 'bind'—all these mean that he is abiding by the rules of ritual before acting. This is what is meant by 'asking and not getting.' "[26] " 'This girl'—the speaker does not dare to say directly that she is meant for him. 'I will feed her horse'—by carrying out the ritual, I let my wishes be known."[27] To take the poem's humble language literally would widen the gap between the speaker (or speakers) and the bride. Her pony, as it emerges from K'ung Ying-ta's research into the Chou sumptuary laws, is of the kind ridden by the lesser gentry, and it is being fed with grain, not grass or hay (as the poem says with a special verb). What might the rider of such an animal have to do with someone who goes out into the thicket collecting brushwood? The speaker is a servant, but the servant of ritual observances (*li*) is no longer a servant. The commentaries have made what might have been a poem of separation and longing into a marriage song.

~

"Just as firewood needs human labor"—the authors of the Prefaces and commentaries are not afraid to praise their *Book of Odes* as a made thing, a product of interpretation. Their subject is not "that is what the poem meant" but "this is what you should make the poem mean"—and the poem as read thus turns out to narrate the manufacture of a meaning. If Chu Hsi and other skeptical readers object to a commentary that seems to skew the meaning of the text, the Prefaces, for their part, look forward to a complete subsuming of examples under the rule of *hua* ("transforming influence"). Reading, in the two cases, takes on a different time-character. The model for reading toward a possible *Book of Odes* "tied in bundles" is work, the replacement of a given object by a made one. The work of the reader in moralizing the text is thus an indispensable sub-theme of the *Mao Odes*. (Even the most farfetched, ugly, and absurd readings gain in value, as conspicuous expenditures of labor.) "T'ao-yao" praises it; "Han kuang" holds out marriage as its reward. The anthology itself is only a concretion of that work. It has a weak form of coherence and announces a stronger. Thematiz-ation, as *feng* ("moral influence"), claims territory and examples for the profit of the empire (i.e., reshapes all the poems of the collec-tion in the likeness, positive or negative, of the "Elegantiae" and "Laudes"). Thematization is work, the reader's work that produces, through the anthology, the concept of empire. (As Confucius says: "Not a one but thought of submitting" to the "Kuan chü"; or as the Ode says: "Under the wide heaven, none but is the king's land; on to the edges of the earth, none but is the king's servant.")[28] If the description of nature was something of an embarrassment to the Mao exegetes—a wrong or doubtful beginning, a figure to be got through as quickly as possible—no such worries attach to the depiction of work.

In Ode 250 ("Kung Liu") the leader of an emigrant band took with him "bows and arrows, shields and dagger-axes, axes and battle-axes" and picked up "whetstones and hammering-stones" along the way.[29] The prince goes out armed for work. But what kind of work is it? The *Mao Odes* seems to apply a double scale of values. In "Han kuang" the allegorization of work as ritual was the pivot on which the reading's transformation of the poem turned. Work in poetry is only figurative work, then; the reader's work on the "work" depicted in the poem makes of "Han kuang" a finished product, a pastoral allegory like "Chiung." Kingship is thematization, and thematization is work; to say, however, that kingship is work collapses together the distinctions that ritual exists to maintain. Poetry and its interpretation second ritual and music.[30] The double entendre surrounding work (the interpretation of work as ritual and ritual as work) is a means for the *Odes* of making the classes transparent to one another and of turning life into art. "Work," then, is the name for a whole appropriative and figurative strategy. But as a self-designation of reading, the anthology's frequent allegorization of princely rule as work is not figurative at all. The redescription of work as ritual is, rather, an occasion for the ancient readers to "interpret the *Odes* by means of the *Odes*," to honor Granet's phrase.

ODE 157, "P'O FU"

Broken were our axes
And chipped our hatchets.
Then came Chou Kung to the East
And ordered the Four Realms.

[Commentary (Mao):] Axes and hatchets are what the common people use. Ritual and loyalty are what the great families use.[31]

Ode 158, "Fa k'o," which modern critics see as a wedding song, is taken by traditional readers to extend and interpret the axes of "P'o fu":

In hewing an axe haft, how does one do it?
Without an axe it doesn't happen.

[Commentary (Mao):] 'Haft' means 'handle.' Ritual and loyalty are the handle whereby one rules a country.

In marrying a wife, how does one do it?
Without a matchmaker one doesn't succeed.

[Commentary (Mao):] Through the matchmaker, the rites are observed [*mei, so i yung li yeh*]. A country ruled without ritual will have no peace.

In hewing an axe haft, in hewing an axe haft,
The pattern is not far-off.[32]

Ch'en Huan explains the piling up of figures in the most scholastic way, by stating what they have in common.

> In cutting an axe handle, one must already have the axe in hand, just as when one takes hold of the ruling of countries, one must first have a grasp of ritual and loyalty. . . . In taking a wife, one must have a matchmaker; a matchmaker is an observer of ritual. . . . The axe alludes to ritual and loyalty, the matchmaker alludes to the observance of ritual and loyalty: two allusions with one meaning.[33]

The axe is the agency for changing wood into an axe handle, the rites change a raw country into a civilized one, and the go-between, according to Cheng Hsüan, "causes the words of two different clans to come together." What they have in common is the character of being a way to do something.[34] "Still today, and even in distinguished circles of society, it is the women who act as go-betweens and arrange marriages. It is obligatory to have a female matchmaker, since everything having to do with marriages is dealt with by women. Nowadays, the matchmaker's activity is a trade."[35]

Axe and matchmaker are both emblems of work, and work is the common people's equivalent to the noble practice of the rites. The matchmaker's work is ritual work on a plebeian scale. (Noble marriages are contracted by the fathers.) The matchmaker is "a person who uses ritual," and to call on a matchmaker's services shows that one has enough ritual sense to use a person who uses ritual (and thus that one already has the axe necessary for cutting that axe handle). But the matchmaker, a means of obtaining another like herself (a younger woman for the perpetuation of the patrilineal clan), is an axe too. She is and has an axe, occupying two places in the circuit, acting as both tenor and vehicle for herself. As allegory, she stands for ritual; as category, she practices it. As user of ritual, she uses an axe; as bringer in of women, she is an axe. She uses herself to produce herself. This is hardly a mark of bad logic. The apparent clumsiness of the analogy only makes clear what is true of all axes. In the hand of the potential husband, the matchmaker is the handle of a handle. In the hand of the ruler, ritual—the handle—is the means to government by ritual. All axes, in effect, are handles of handles of handles—to stop the series, quite artificially, at that.[36] They bespeak a pure and theatrical instrumentality.

The matchmaker, says Cheng Hsüan, "alludes to King Ch'eng's desire to receive the Duke of Chou at court" as first minister, that is, Ch'eng's desire to be the bridegroom, the person who uses a person who uses ritual as the handle for governing. "Fa k'o" ends with:

> Now I see this person,
> And offering vessels are laid out in a row.
>
> [Commentary (Cheng Hsüan):] "This person" refers to the Duke of Chou. King Ch'eng wanted to receive [his uncle] the Duke of Chou [as prime minister] and therefore set out a ceremonial feast for him.[37]

Exactly when Ch'eng is supposed to have set out this feast is unclear. *Chih tzu,* "this person," is drawn from the formulaic lines of marrying poems like "T'ao-yao" and "Han kuang," where it named the bride on her setting out. Applying it to the Duke of Chou only extends the logic of the poem, *pace* readers allergic, like Waley, to every kind of political allegory; it shows exactly how reading generates its "prince." The matchmaker is an axe and the user of an axe: the lesson is that ritual practice is both performance (it changes things) and mimesis (it repeats things).[38] In her double role, the matchmaker may be (as Cheng Hsüan says) a type of the Duke of Chou. But by the end of the poem the Duke of Chou is the hoped for bride as well, which is to say axe handle, axe (several times over), and user of an axe. The Duke of Chou is, once the interpretation has finished with the poem, the answer to all the poem's "how to" questions, the thing figured by all its figures: means, object, and actor of work.

And so work produces its own "correct beginning." If the Duke of Chou is the ultimate "how to," the ruler is the corresponding "what for." The ruler is work emblematized, made autotelic, a multiplication of handles. The prince is the most serious thing there is, identical to every stage of work, but since there is nothing more serious than he to which he could be a means, his work is aesthetic through and through. Like the rites, he can have no finality outside himself and the indefinite exercise of the means he calls into play. The work of reading leads everything back to the ruler, which is to say that it works relentlessly to supersede itself as work.

Hence a difficulty in the representation of culture heroes at work. The time frame of princely work is double. Since it changes things, its characteristic time divides into a before and an after; and yet its changing does not admit of any intermediate stages of delay or effort, since the goal of work, the prince, is already at hand in the means of work. "Now I see this person, / and offering vessels are laid out in a row." The prince's function is to civilize, but whatever he looks on is already "no longer wild."[39] This causes an ode like "Kung Liu" (number 250) to break out of the syntax of historical narrative, to the great puzzlement of its readers.

> Thereupon [Kung Liu] opened his march.
>
> . . . . .
>
> He passed by those hundred springs,
> Viewed that wide plain,
> Then climbed the southern ridge
> To look on the *ching,*
> The wilds of the *ching-shih.*
> And there he settled settlements
> And there he lodged lodgings,
> There spoke his speeches
> And there talked his talks.

The deictics ("those," "that") show Kung Liu to be moving through known territory. The hearer is supposed to recognize it and, through recognition, to add present experience to the praise of this hero of the past. Foundation stories call for interpretation in the present perfect—they tell how things got to be the way they are. But it is pushing the lingering presence of the past right into anachronism to say that the founder "looked on the *ching.*" *Ching* means "capital," and the poem has not yet said how the capital was built. The oddity is only made stronger in the next line, which names the new territory "the wilds of the *ching-shih*" (*ching*, "capital," plus *shih*, "host," "multitude"; the compound means the same as *ching*). The Mao gloss tries to straighten out this jostle of tenses and actions: " 'Capital' here means a place suitable for the mass [of Kung Liu's followers] to live in," that is, a *future* capital.[40] When the ode says that the wilderness is a capital, the scholiasts intervene and say that what is meant is that the wilds are suitable (*i*, as Mao puts it) for being a city, a fit potential or future city. Later readers do the same for the continuation of the litany. (Wang Ching-chih: "In *yü-shih ch'u-ch'u*, the first *ch'u* ['settle'] is a verb, the second, a noun; the sentence means that they settled the places that were fit for them to settle.")[41]

But what is an obstacle for the scholiasts is none for Kung Liu. The end of the stanza with its series of parallel clauses announces the true model for the changes Kung Liu and his followers bring to the landscape. To speak is ipso facto to speak a speech; for Kung Liu the difference between calling something a settlement and settling it is no greater. Raw material is already the worked over product; "the wilds for the capital," as Mao calls them, are the capital. Description is performative. Its eschewing the obvious forms of command and wish only adds to its power: here is a performative that does not know a contrasting mode of factual speech. The appropriateness (*i*) of the natural setting is acknowledged and made inconsequential by the prince's action. It is as if the prince, *qua* prince, cannot possibly have anything to work *on*. As magic or miracle, Kung Liu's performative is the very negation of work and thus the opposite of edification.[42]

A similar unruliness surfaces in "P'o fu," by way of a pun. One must marry outside the clan, hence the need for a go-between. The "axe" (*fu*) that exemplifies the go-between's talents puns, however, on *fu* ("father"), as if to suggest that the patrilineal clan could, if words were truths, reproduce itself with no help from outside and without expenditure of ritual "work."

The Mao glosses skittishly turn Kung Liu's word back into work. That means translating it into the idiom of another social class and another way of reading. The commentators are so accustomed to using reading as a laboratory of "correct beginnings" and to reshaping ordinary work in the image of ritual work that when an efficacious beginning, not yet the example of anything, is mimed by a poem they are at a loss to know what to do. They fail to recognize the model of their own enterprise when it surfaces in categorical form. The prince is representable and citable—everything that is read represents or alludes to him sooner or later—but that whereby he is prince is not. The work that reading does hereby marks itself off from its model, the work that rulers do.

Cheng Hsüan comments on the third couplet of "Fa k'o": "'Pattern' means 'rule.' To hew an axe heft, you must use an axe heft; for size and length you can copy the one at hand."[43] Any axe is the pattern of an axe, any pattern is the pattern of pattern, work, imitating ritual, can signify ritual; so long as imitation and not princely beginning is before us, the work of reading and thematization can go on unhindered. Where the reading of "T'ao-yao" and "Han kuang" led to appropriative gestures meant to subjugate description to injunction, musical mimesis to musicology, and paraphrase to the exemplarity of moral influence (*feng*), "Fa k'o" shows that the performative is the mimetic: an instance of beginning (the problem: "in hewing an axe heft, how does one do it?") is referred to an already accomplished thing that doubtless began in the same way. Practice is mediated by example; without example, it doesn't happen. And examples are made—as are axes—by applying other examples. The reader's work on the text has before it the example of those uniquely powerful readers, the sages, who take hold of ritual as their instrument and refashion the given in the image of ritual.[44] Mimesis is the mimesis of performance. When the "Record of Music" speaks of *staged* mimesis (as opposed to inescapable ethical mimesis), it is to define musical performances as "the image of successful actions" (*hsiang ch'eng che*).[45] That is the one kind of mimesis to which the Prefaces can wholly give themselves—the nature poetry, so to speak, of a made nature.

All of the *Book of Odes'* exemplary figures are axes, products and operators of change, figures whose function is to carve out the possibility of figure.[46] And so they are not originally, or not purely, descriptive. A poem such as "Han kuang" leads us to recognize the difference between nature and the kind of "natural imagery" such poetry can deploy. The southern trees, tall and shorn of their lower branches, are as unaccommodating as the young women on the Han. Those young women must be won by strict adherence to ritual; now the speaker of the poem, a woodcutter, is to be understood as just such an observer of ritual. His work (or "work") results in a landscape of trees with their lower limbs trimmed off, trees under which it is as hard to find shade as it is to meet a complaisant girl on the banks of the Han, and so on. The poem's opening couplet, far from invoking a case of natural correspondence, is marked by the work (ritual or woodcutting) that it is the poem's goal to perform. The poem deduces itself from itself; it has no more description in it than it has a single absolute beginning. Nature tends to become a trunk on which relations between people are carved. This goes some way toward sharpening the relation, underdetermined at last sighting, between moral reading and literary, aesthetic, or "private" reading.

~

Ode 44, "Erh tzu ch'eng chou," takes a different tack. Its first stanza runs:

> You two gentlemen board the ship,
> And its reflected image spreads everywhere.
> When I think of you two gentlemen,
> My heart is aggrieved.

The "two gentlemen" went knowingly into the ambush their father, the tyrannical Duke Hsüan of Wei, had set for one of them—"stepping into danger," the Mao commentary says, "as one gets into an unanchored boat."[47] The translation of line 2, *fan-fan ch'i ching*, given here needs defending; it does not seem possible to steer a middle course between all the readings suggested by the commentators. On the second line, the Mao commentary says only: "*fan-fan* means 'swiftly and without anything to hold it back.'" The usual meaning of *fan*, however, seems to be "spreading" or "distant"; it has etymological links to a word meaning "all, every," and to other words related to seamanship. "Spreads everywhere" may not capture all those associations, but with the added explanation it may evoke some of them. *Ching* "can be pronounced as *ying*," a related word meaning "shadow" (Lu Te-ming's sound gloss). But Ode 218, "Chü-hsia," seems to give *ching* the meaning of *chiung*, "far away," and other well-known occurrences of *ching* in the *Odes* are traditionally paraphrased as "great." Wen I-to and Bernhard Karlgren adopt the sense of *chiung* for *ching* in this ode, reading thus: "floating on, it goes far away."[48] There are parallels for *ching* in the sense of *chiung* (notably Ode 299, "P'an shui"), but many more for *ching* in the sense of *ying*: *ching* and *ying* were not consistently differentiated until some time after the period of the Mao and Cheng edition of the *Odes*.

If *ching* here is to be read as "shadow" or "reflection," then the figure that opens "Erh tzu ch'eng chou" is a figure of figure, one that argues that nature is mimetic. K'ung Ying-ta reads irony into that mimesis, stressing the difference between shadow and substance. Just as the "unanchored boat" is an image for the two princes' decision to "step into danger and choose death," so "the 'shadow' means the shadow of the ship. Observing their departure, all one sees is the [ship's] shadow. This stands for the fact that once they have gone away, they will never return."[49] The shadow of the ship is a double marker of the princes' demise (as shadow of the *ship*, and as its *shadow*). It is the image of the inadequate image, and thereby pathetic.

For the Mao and K'ung commentaries, then, the shadow is ominous because everything that makes this trip up the river different can be read into it. But there is a further pathos in the way the ship rides on a medium suitable for propagating its image, an image that, like a good shadow or wave, "never moves of itself," to quote the Mohist axiom about shadows.[50] The *Lieh-tzu*, too, treats the shadow as the type of dependent imitation. "[The shadow's] bending and straightening follow [those of] the object, they do not inhere in the shadow itself."[51] Is poetry then no more than a shadow? With its division of the image into active and passive sides and its one-way causality—action from the top down—the natural mimesis invoked by the *hsing* of this ode corresponds at every point with the formula for *feng*, "kingly influence" or ethical mimesis. In Confucius' parable of the wind and the grass, the bending of the grass mattered as the cause-and-effect evidence of kingly power; here, along with producing a reaction, the source of mimesis prints its image on the mimetic medium. And as if to confirm the relation, the etymon of *feng*, "wind," is hidden in the term (*fan*) which describes the repeated image as "spreading," "floating," or "everywhere."[52]

The poem gains if we superimpose the two passages, for the two princes who are in the position of the moral and mimetic exemplar, the strongest position the theory of mimesis knows, are unable to avert their murder at the hands of a wicked ruler. A shadow is helpless. By boarding the boat, the princes have put themselves in the same plight. Put together, the two models of ethical mimesis here, the explicit one of "shadow" and the implicit one of "wind," result in an anomaly: power in one system corresponds to power-lessness in another. The princes' reduplicated image, which, in a good allegory, should be the "grass" obediently bending under their influence, leaves its mark on memory. Unable to do anything about the doomed princes, the person who watches the disappearing shadow vows to remember (*ssu*) them.[53]

As a short course in the poetics of the *Mao Odes*, "Erh tzu ch'eng chou" begins with dependent imitation and works its way around to the position of poetic and moral independence. It is no accident that "Erh tzu ch'eng chou" is placed under the heading "altered Airs," the songs of a time out of joint. The point of its images depends on their inadequacy, their reversal of the logic of "wind and grass" mimesis, just as, in the Great Preface, the sense of the ironic "Airs" depends on the clash of meaning and occasion in their distribution of praise and blame.

Its shadow then joins up with the more straightforwardly exemplary shadows of the narrative odes. There the word for the "image" or "shadow" (*ching/ying*) with no force of its own, that figure of a poetics for which imitation is enough, appears as a transitive verb. Duke Wen of Wei "shadow-measured [*ching*] mountains and hills" (Ode 50, "Ting chih fang chung"), and Kung Liu "surveyed [*ching*] that ridge and inspected its north and south" (Ode 250, "Kung Liu"). Because they are regular and mimetic, shadows guarantee measurement, and measurement, another skein of human facts spun from a beginning that no one would think of questioning, both repeats and frames the question of poetry as an ethical and kingly calibrator. The shadow wielded by the surveyor is another tool of kingship, another how-to. To read the shadows of "Erh tzu ch'eng chou" through those in the surveying poems is to make description once again a mimed performative—to make nature, in short, an axe for the reorganization of nature.[54] It is as if those shadows heading toward martyrdom wore the badge of the initiators of culture.

～

These reasonings are hard to fit with the usual teaching about the *Odes'* figural language. Ever since the first commentaries on the Great Preface, that theory has been worked out in a vocabulary anticipating the later "poetry-talk" language of correspondence and interplay between *ching*, "scene," and *ch'ing*, "feeling." At issue are the canonical three figures of the Great Preface, *hsing*, *pi*, and *fu* ("stimulus," "comparison," and "exposition"). Despite a number of recent studies, many questions about the three figures remain unanswered and, indeed, hard to frame clearly on the basis of the old texts.[55] Why should that set of tropes have caught the attention of the *Odes* commentators, to the point of being ranked with genres like the "Airs," "Elegantiae," and "Laudes," the other three of the Six Arts mentioned in the same passage? Were *fu*, *pi*, and *hsing* rules for poetic composition taught alongside the poems themselves, or were they always descriptive in nature, the familiar hermeneutic tools of commentators on the *Odes*? What is the semantic or logical structure of the three terms? Are they mutually exclusive or mutually interpenetrating? Are they jointly exhaustive of the field of poetic naming, or is there room for more tropes besides them?

Because the *hsing* is the figure that leaves the most unsaid, and perhaps because the meaning of so many well-known instances of *hsing* has always been obscure, it has always struck readers as the

figure most in need of a good definition. The critic Liu Hsieh (ca.
465–ca. 520) founds the *hsing* on "the stimulation of feeling" (*ch'i-
ch'ing*); some six centuries later Chu Hsi says: "A *hsing* first mentions some other thing [*t'a-wu*] by way of leading into the theme of
one's song."⁵⁶ What sort of "other thing" is it that can "stimulate
feeling"? Ch'en Huan clarifies: "Feigning in order to make clear
one's intent: this is *hsing*. . . . Whenever 'birds, beasts, plants, and
trees' are pressed into service [*t'o*] to complete a statement, these are
hsing."⁵⁷ "From the *Odes*," Confucius had said, "you may learn the
names of many birds, beasts, plants, and trees." Ch'en Huan claims
the "birds, beasts, plants, and trees" as the province of *hsing*, but the
passage could equally well be the charter for the interpretation of
every kind of figure as *fu*. Cheng Hsüan's discrimination of the
three tropes has long formed the basis of discussion. "*Fu* ['exposition'] is the same as *p'u*, 'to spread out': [in an 'exposition'] one sets
forth without reserve the good and evil of the present government's
teachings. *Pi* is a comparison modeled on an object. *Hsing* entrusts
[*t'o*] to an object a matter of concern."⁵⁸

The characterization of *fu* as description of good or bad *government* can be attributed to the preoccupations of Cheng and his
contemporaries. It has not left much trace in subsequent criticism,
where *fu* stands simply as the zero degree of figural language, the
kind of statement that makes sense just as it is. "*Fu, pi, hsing* (in
that order) are ways of telling about a thing, and straightforward
exposition is the normal case," as K'ung Ying-ta puts it. "*Fu* is
obvious, whereas *hsing* is hidden; *pi* is straightforward, whereas
hsing is twisty" (Ch'en Huan).⁵⁹ *Fu* describes; *pi* describes this and
then describes that; *hsing* describes this in lieu of describing that.
Interpretative practice confirms what this caricature of a summary
suggests: for the purposes of paraphrase, all three tropes dissolve
into their *fu* element. *Fu*, "the normal case," needs no explaining
(or rather, any explanation of a *fu* simply prolongs it in a more
explicit *fu*); the explanation of *pi* and *hsing* paraphrases them as
what they are not, that is, as *fu*. The transformation is never so
great as in the case of *hsing*, which loses in the process all the
characteristics by which Ch'en Huan, for instance, distinguished it

from the others. One sees this from the Mao commentary's first discussion of a trope.

ODE I, "KUAN CHÜ"

Kuan-kuan cry the ospreys
On the river-bound islet.
This retiring and pure girl—
She will make a good match for the lord.

[Commentary (Mao):] A *hsing*. . . . These birds are passionate yet observe the separation of the sexes. . . . The ["retiring and pure"] royal consort has the virtue [*te*] of the ospreys.[60]

The work of rhetoric (as we have been defining "work") is not much in favor, if this is what reading does. Interpreting tropes now looks no more complicated than locating the objects to which a *pi* or *hsing* refers, identifying the relevant properties, and testing for a match or mismatch (thus praise or blame, depending on the properties). The commentary to Ode 183, "Mien shui," shows the method's inherent virtues and vices.

Swollen is that fast-flowing river
As it rushes to pay tribute to the sea.
Swift that flying hawk
Now flying, now still.

[Commentary (Mao):] The current is laden, as if it had someone to pay court to.
[Commentary (Cheng):] A *hsing*. The water rushes into the sea: the small joins the great. An allusion to the feudal lords, who go to pay court to the Son of Heaven in just this way. . . . When the hawk needs to fly, it immediately starts flying; when it needs to stop, it stops right away. The allusion is to the feudal lords' pride and laziness. When they ought to attend audiences, they stay at home; they lack the sense of their own duty.[61]

In Cheng Hsüan's reading, the fiction (based on a pun, as it were "tribute"–"tributary") noticed by the Mao annotation has become a predicate to be applied to the courtiers as literally as the "virtue of the ospreys" was applied to the queen-consort. That destroys the pun, as only seriousness can, and it takes the invention with it too. Mao's "as if it had someone to pay court to" recognizes the line as having added something to nature, but Cheng's "the feudal lords pay court in just this way" takes the poem's invention and subordinates it to the piece of common knowledge the poem's language had departed from. Teachers the world over may do just that to literature, but the result can be given a definite name from within Cheng Hsüan's own work. The *fu*-content has taken over the poem and decided the direction of interpretation. *Pi* and *hsing* are applications of tacit *fu*, and Cheng Hsüan reads as if it were unimaginable that a successfully analyzed figure might be anything but *fu*.[62]

Call that law, then, a rival pattern of pattern, a rule that has as its root not work but description. The interpretation of poems becomes a subset of the interpretation of things. And the lore of things must be of the kind that discovers constant properties in things and their relations—a static ontology of kinds to contrast with the ontology of forms and reshapings that interested the readers of "Fa k'o" and "Han kuang." This model of interpretation leaves reading nothing to do but get the references wrong, should such originality be its lot. One result of centuries of *fu-pi-hsing* study is that the *Book of Odes* is, for many readers, identical to just this form of speech.

There are, of course, odes that appeal to the reader's knowledge of natural properties to ground an analogy or rather, as in the second example below, beg the reader to agree with the speaker that the analogy must be grounded. Ode 150, "Fu yu," explained by the Mao commentary as a satire on an extravagant ruler:

> The wings of the ephemeron—
> Brilliant clothing indeed!

Ode 52, "Hsiang shu":

> Observe the rat, it has its skin;
> A man without manners,
> A man without manners,
> Why doesn't he die right away?

An ephemeron is colorful, short-lived, and no rival in dignity to a true king; naming the naturally occurring object not only gets the properties across in a hurry but also suggests a connection between them (if you insist on being so colorful, you may not last long—so goes the Mao Preface's argument). The second example begs some questions of the jury, but makes its point with force, and force may be all it intends. Figures like these depend for their sense on nature as a source of regularities and definitions. It is the very nature of nature to collapse the singular example into the genus, to predicate of any peach tree or mayfly what is true of every peach tree or mayfly. Behind every figure, then, the reader of the *Book of Odes* should be able to infer a rule, and behind every rule a set of constant properties, if the strong version of a descriptive poetics holds out.

Ode 26, "Po chou," seems intent on frustrating this kind of interpretation. The troublesome lines are cast in one syntactic pattern, which ought to simplify interpretation but may only multiply the uncertainties.

> The pine boat lurches
> On the current's flow.
> I am wide awake
> As with a secret pain.
> Not that I lack wine
> To divert myself with.
> My mind is not a mirror:
> It does not *ju.*
> True, I have brothers,
> But I cannot rely on them . . . .
>
>   . . . . .
>
> My mind is not a stone:
> You cannot roll it about.
> My mind is not a mat:
> You cannot roll it up.
> My demeanor has been strict:
> You cannot take exception to it. . . .

The *Wen-hsin tiao-lung* cites "Po chou" as its main example of *pi*—doubtless on the intercession of its commentators. What room does "Po chou" leave for comparison?

"My mind is not a mirror: / It does not *ju*." Difficulties start with the word that every commentator takes as explaining what a mirror does and thus why a mirror cannot represent the speaker's mind. The Mao gloss gives the verb as "measure"; Karlgren suggests "scrutinize." (What would it mean to scrutinize a mirror? The mirror, as means of scrutiny, eludes it.) The word most commonly means "to swallow," "to contain." Wen I-to opines that "the ancients' mirror was a bowl of water, and water seems to contain images. . . . The mirror's capacity to contain images is here used to signify a mind willing to tolerate slander."[63] The word choice may have been dictated by pun or association, for *ju* is an elaboration of (and may substitute for) the graph for "like" or "as." The person addressed, obviously less of a moralist, will not find his face reflected in the speaker's mind, if ever he gets a look in. A translation just vague enough to cover all cases might be: "it does not assimilate."

"*Erh ya* and *Shih-wen* define 'mirror' as 'that which is used to observe shapes,'" says Ch'en Huan. Further, he notes, "'Not a mirror, / It does not *ju*,' is grammatically parallel to the subsequent passages 'Not a stone, you cannot roll it about' and 'Not a mat, you cannot roll it up.'" The parallelism is not perfect (*pu k'o i ju* versus *pu k'o chuan yeh* and *pu k'o chüan yeh*); it is more semantic than grammatical. Indeed, the "mirror" verse's departure from the other two verses is more significant than its similarities to them. By refusing to "mirror" the verses it resembles, it demands an interpretation for which no model is readily available. In that verse the speaker refuses to be assimilated to anything—negating every possible figure in the most economical way, by negating the figure that connotes all figures: "my mind not being a mirror, you cannot mirror (or figure) it." And the poem seems to carry out its threat: with the sense of *ju* open to so many possible readings, one does not even know with certainty why the speaker's mind is not a mirror.

To try to say why the mind is not a mirror is to make it into a mirror again, as Cheng Hsüan's explanation proves. "'The mirror is used to examine shapes,' [as the Mao note says]. But a mirror is limited to the knowledge of round and square, black and white; it cannot discriminate between [things'] truth and falsity. My mind is

not like that mirror. I am able to judge in my mind of men's good
and evil, inwardly and outwardly."[64]

Cheng's reading of the trope as a resemblance recalls the epistemological confidence of the early Han thinker Tung Chung-shu,
who wrote the following in the course of a discussion of the
reliability of the Classics: " 'Other men have their thoughts, / but I
am able to evaluate them' [a quotation from Ode 198, 'Ch'iao yen'].
This means: all objects are related to one another. On examining
their exteriors, one may perceive what lies inside them."[65]

"Not a mirror" therefore means "not just a mirror." Rather than
negate the whole figure—which would be to admit defeat—Cheng
negates its limitations, coincidentally inverting Leibniz's reading of
"Heaven is without mind." The mind judges of "good and evil, inwardly and outwardly": if it can still perform that particular assimi-
lation, it is still a mirror (a reflector of outward forms), only more so.

And in the same way "not a stone" is more stone than stone, "not
a mat" a mat beyond mats.

> The good man does not meet with favor; so he speaks of himself as a
> virtuous man deserving a position of trust. "My mind is not a mir-
> ror" . . . it is not passive as a mirror is. For examining things, nothing is
> brighter than a mirror, but my virtue surpasses it. . . . A stone is firm,
> but it can still be moved; my mind is too firm to be moved. . . . While a
> mat is even [= equitable], it can be rolled up; my mind is even and
> cannot be rolled up.[66]

This treatment of negation could have been taken from Pao Hsien's
notes on a maxim from the *Analects*: "The gentleman is not an
instrument" (2.12).

> [Pao Hsien:] Every instrument covers its own use. Now as for the
> gentleman, there is no use unsuited to him.
> [K'ung Ying-ta:] "Instrument" is here the name for every sort of
> thing: they are perfected by being made into instruments. "Each
> covers its own use," as a ship is used for crossing rivers and a carriage
> for moving across the land; put them in each other's place and neither
> is any good. The gentleman's ability is unlike instruments and objects,
> which have one use apiece.[67]

Cheng Hsüan is making the best of a technique of reading that asks of every object what it is like. But along with making the mind a mirror, Cheng surreptitiously makes the mirror a mind; that is, he forgets that it is a tool and turns its capacity to be used into an independent ability. The tool that might have helped in the work of reading is now the machine that reads all by itself, "able to discriminate between truth and falsity." Here, reading for the likenesses encounters a text that ought to be unreadable for it, and commits an unreading—a paraphrase that makes the text say what it tells us is not the case.

Ch'en Huan expresses reservations about this way of reading the negation. Was not the text categorical enough? "According to Cheng's explanation, a mirror cannot scrutinize, but my mind can scrutinize. But the text openly says: you can scrutinize a mirror, but you cannot scrutinize my mind."[68] For Ch'en, the line's obscurity is a willed effect, not an accident of understanding that asks to be explained away. Thus: " 'My mind is not like a mirror'; hence people cannot ascertain my intention. This continues the first stanza's speaking of 'a secret pain' and expresses anxiety over the fact that no one can understand [the speaker's] intent."

Ch'en resolves the deadlock between the figure and its own negation by taking the negation at its word, rejecting the figure just as the speaker had done: a feint unknown to the usual method of interpreting *pi* and *hsing*. "My mind is not a mirror" is thereby taken to mean that the mind and a mirror are not even comparable; the interpreter's task is referred to psychology, not optics.

To make sense of the "not a mirror" lines, the customary method of *pi* and *hsing* must ignore the negative and act as if the poem were in fact some other poem, a poem more in keeping with their theory of figures, a poem that would have announced: "My mind is a mirror, and it assimilates." "Po chou" supposes that such a poem could have been written but says what it has to say against that possible poem, as if it knew of and expected to meet with the interpretation Cheng gives it. A mirror "is like," it "assimilates," anything put before it, but it is most like the reader who asks of everything what it is like. And the speaker of "Po chou" refuses to be mirrored in such a reader.

Something similar happens in Cheng's note to "Mien shui." His reading agrees with that of the Mao commentators as to the sense of the poem and the purport of its images. The ingredients are the same but combined in a different order, and the order of operations affects the sum. Both Mao and Cheng understand "Mien shui" as the Little Preface directs them to.

> [Preface:] "Mien shui" was composed to compass [*kuei*] King Hsüan.
> [Commentary (Mao):] A compass is a tool for correcting roundness.

The analogies of "Mien shui," then, have the force of tools or models; they are instances of regularity against which irregularity may be measured. ("The rites are to ruling a state what the scales are to the measurement of heavy and light; what string and chalk are to crooked and straight; what compass and ruler are to round and square.")[69] Cheng applies this logic without a hitch, making the first two lines into a tacit rebuke. They could be paraphrased as "The rivers rush down to the sea laden with silt, but you feudal lords do nothing of the kind; if you were truly lords as the rivers are truly rivers, you would hurry to the Son of Heaven's court." This makes the poem's opening conceit a reasoning based on natural properties and situated logically downstream from them, just as the doctrine of the three figures we inherit from Cheng would lead us to predict. The particular natural object cited soon ceases to matter much for this reading, except as a representative of a general regularity ascribed to nature: the hawk of lines 3 and 4, for instance, puts across the identical point that the feudal lords are not truly feudal lords in the way that the hawk is truly a hawk. Cheng's explanation of the figure dissolves it into the general nature of nature, as the source of self-identical concepts. Compassing of this sort can be done by means of any thing that is whatever it is because it has certain defining properties. The reasoning that grounds the *hsing* in general reduces any particular *hsing* to a reflection or shadow of the rule of nature's regularity.

The far shorter Mao commentary, by acknowledging the poem's beginning in a pun, reverses this order of operations. There the natural image derives from the mark the pun makes on language.

The pun on *ch'ao-tsung* ("pays court/tribute to"), in fact, interprets the natural object, makes it pertinent to the business of compassing. That locates the poem's language upstream from its nature and gives its utterance the status of an event. A pun is nothing if not an event—a linguistic surprise—and if the *Odes'* exemplary figures are required, by their moral project, to inscribe themselves on nature rather than merely to echo it, then the mode of reading adequate to their project has to allow for surprise.[70] That is why Cheng's explanation seems to fumble just at the moment of rationalizing the figure. The error is one of priority in both its temporal and axiological senses, senses that, as we have seen, are intimately linked. If the poem cannot be an event, then reading it can never change anything; and in that case there will be no reactivating the "grace of the former kings."

The doctrine of figures has practical consequences. A theory of poetic language that makes no distinctions between before and after has nothing to say about work (which is not work unless it changes something). The reading of *pi* and *hsing* as likenesses grounded in nature can account for everything in the poem, but it cannot say much about the poem itself and what it does. Whenever the poem departs from the descriptive language of *fu*, it steps into a territory where this reading scheme is visibly not at home, as the notes to "Po chou" and "Mien shui" reveal. Cheng Hsüan's theory of the tropes is clearly not up to the task of reading everything a figure implies. If the center of our interest is the object constructed by the reception of the *Odes'* texts in late antiquity, definitions such as those formulated by Cheng are not even a reliable guide to Cheng's own techniques of reading. (In reading "Han kuang," for instance, Cheng could give labor its due.)

But the theory of *pi* and *hsing* is hardly the traditional *Odes'* sole center of command. The explanation of figures, in the *Mao Odes* and its sequels, almost always leads toward a reading of the poems for which historical authority is claimed. Some of the *Odes'* most diligent modern readers have concluded from this style of commentary that the mode of meaning most important to the *Odes* (and to Chinese poetry generally) is historical. This raises new questions, to which the ancient reception of the *Odes* may also supply answers. Since the notion of history is subject to historical pressures—each age determines what it considers "historical"—it, too, must be defined *ex datis*. In what sense of the word "historical" can the meaning of the *Odes* adequately be described as "historical"? Does the reading of figures have any bearing on the historical-anecdotal style of commentary, or is it merely a convenient means to ends that lie outside it? What do the *Odes* have to do with history?

The term *fu* provides an opening on this question, for alongside the meaning it has acquired in poetics as "description" or "exposition," it can also be used, as it often is in historical texts, to designate a type of event involving poetry. To *fu shih* is to present or chant a poem, typically for the edification of a sovereign or of the opposite party in a diplomatic negotiation; *fu* is simultaneously "exposition," a poetic technique, and "presentation," the means by which poetry comes before its audience.

Fu in its double sense expands to cover the whole field of the interaction of poetry with its readers, including those who know the *Odes* only through its presentation in the Mao edition. Just as the ancient diplomats turned well-known poems into reflections on a contemporary situation, so the later critics saw in historical background a short way of fixing the meaning of a poem that might otherwise have remained ambiguous.[71] All *pi* and *hsing*, all "comparisons" and "stimuli," by virtue of belonging to the *Odes* genre, are also, in this second sense, material for potential occasions of *fu*. Wherever *fu* is found, an implicit poetic and hermeneutic can be discovered.

Episodes of poetry quotation abound in narratives such as the *Tso Commentary* and the *Conversations of the States*.[72] None of them, however, can compare with the "Chin t'eng" (The metal-bound coffer) chapter of the *Book of Documents*. This chapter purports to give not the occasion of a recital but the circumstances in which a poem was composed. "The Duke of Chou dwelt in the east for two years, until the troublemakers had been brought to justice. And afterward he made a poem to give to the king. He called it 'Ch'ih-hsiao.' The king still did not dare to blame the Duke of Chou."[73] The Little Preface to "Ch'ih-hsiao," Ode 155, reads: "[The subject of] 'Ch'ih-hsiao' is the Duke of Chou's suppression of disorder. King Ch'eng did not yet know the Duke of Chou's intentions [*chih*]. Thereupon the duke made a poem to give to the king. He called it 'Ch'ih-hsiao.' "[74] The two texts' agreement is, of course, no proof that the passage in the *Book of Documents* gives the true story about the origins of the poem, although the language of the Mao preface, with its slightly awkward turn on the word "thereupon," shows that the Mao editors thought it did.

In both texts the composition of "Ch'ih-hsiao" is anchored in a particular moment, a moment designated by the words "afterward" (*yü-hou . . . nai*) and "thereupon" (*nai*). *Fu shih* is probably not the exact term for the Duke of Chou's action, if we accept Chu Tzu-ch'ing's opinion that to *fu* a poem usually implied that the poem already existed and one was only quoting from it.[75] But the *Documents'* narrative includes the poem (more precisely, its title) in the events of King Ch'eng's reign in exactly the way that the reciter of a familiar verse would quote it and bring it to bear on the situation. What the Duke of Chou did may have been, in the words of the text, *wei shih i i wang*, "making a poem to give to the king," but the writers of the "Chin t'eng" chapter and the Mao Little Preface *fu shih*, "displayed a poem," in the course of their narrations.

Is the historical character of the "Chin t'eng" and *Mao Odes* contexts adequate to answer all the interpretative questions raised by the poem, as we should expect it to do if the destiny of Chinese poetry is historical and if history is its adequate medium? The story of the "Chin t'eng" chapter is not, however, about poetry's remainderless integration into history. It bears telling—it captures the hearer's attention—as a reflection on the ways in which *hsing* and *pi* resist immediate understanding, even of the historical kind.

At the beginning of the chapter, King Wu, the Duke of Chou's elder brother and the future King Ch'eng's father, has fallen sick, and the Duke of Chou intercedes on Wu's behalf with the ancestors, offering his life in place of the king's. This offer is made in a secret ceremony, transcribed by some mute historians, and their document is locked away in a metal-bound coffer reserved for such things.

The document languishes in its hiding place, while the Duke of Chou's worth similarly goes unnoticed.

> After Wu's death, [the Duke of Chou's younger brother] Kuan Shu and his host of younger brothers spread rumors throughout the land, saying that the duke intended no good to the infant king [Ch'eng]. Then the Duke of Chou addressed the two dukes [of T'ai and Shao], saying: "If I fail to punish them, I shall have no [merits] to announce to our former kings." The Duke of Chou dwelt in the east for two years, until the troublemakers had been brought to justice. And afterward he made a poem to give to the king. He called it "Ch'ih-hsiao." The king still did not dare to blame the duke.[76]

If Ch'eng had doubts about the Duke of Chou, the duke's way of dealing with slanderers must not have put them to rest. The "Ch'ih-hsiao" poem does little to clarify things. As the Mao preface puts it, "the king," the poem's destined recipient, "did not yet know the Duke of Chou's intentions"; and the duke chose as the vehicle of his "intentions" (*chih*, a word whose history in Chinese poetics needs no more emphasizing) a poem in the *hsing* form, the "twisty and obscure" form best suited to concealing a *chih*.

> Owl, owl,
> You have already taken my young,
> Do not destroy my house!
> I have given them my bounty, I have labored for them,
> My innocent children: for them you should have pity.[77]

Having returned to the point at which the Mao preface rewrites its historical source, we can ask what makes them different. Does the context explain the poem, as the "historical" view would have it? It certainly explained nothing for the participants in that context, for whom the poem was just one more baffling element in an already baffling situation. To claim to know what the poem means by reference to its context, in this case, means that one claims to have understood the context itself, and that is a way of overlooking everything the poem does in its context.

Before a battle, the kings and heroes of the *Book of Documents* gather the troops and expound, point for point, the justice of their cause. At length this comes to seem so much the normal Chou procedure that the Duke of Chou's obscure little poem, delivered *after* his eastern expedition, puzzles all the more. The *hsing* mode disturbs the parallelism of act and deed that the earlier kings had sought to establish. And it blocks the mutual transparency of poetry and history—or so the various solutions that have been proposed over the centuries for this enigmatic poem seem to indicate. Most of the older commentators read it as the duke's address to the "owls" (slanderers) who have endangered the (Chou royal) house, in particular its young (Ch'eng); a minority, following Cheng Hsüan, imagine the Duke of Chou to be writing from the east to defend his "family" of officials against Ch'eng's desire to be rid of them.[78] Were it not for the explicit statement that "*afterward* the Duke of Chou *made* a poem to send to the king," it might seem best to read it as the slanderers' brief against the duke, suspected of planning to do away with the dynasty's "young" and seize its "house."[79] Fang Yü-jun replaces the Mao preface with a new one of his own making: in his view, "Ch'ih-hsiao" shows "the Duke of Chou expressing regret for his own past mistakes, in order to warn King Ch'eng."[80] These questions belong to the tradition of "Ch'ih-hsiao" more than they do to that of the "Chin t'eng" story, but they do go some way toward explaining the inconclusive hearing given the poem in the story. For the story, all that matters is that the duke offers the poem as a vehicle of self-justification and that it does not quite succeed. The king's acknowledgment of it goes only so far as "not yet daring to blame the duke."

The Duke of Chou's presentation of the poem ought to be readable as a commentary on the situation, a case of *fu shih*, but it can be made to say too many things, not all of which can be true at the same time. If to *fu shih* was to treat a poem as pretext for an "exposition," a declaration of intent, the *fu* component here seems to be losing ground to the obscurity of *hsing*. The king failed to understand the central conceit of the poem, so it did no good to present (*i*, a rough equivalent of *fu*) it to him. The poem only gave him one more thing to be undecided about. Or rather, it restated and mirrored the problem to which it was a response. It invited an answer, for the good reason that if the king had solved the poem's riddle he would have been on the way to resolving the historical situation. Deciding what to do about the Duke of Chou is like deciding what a *hsing* means. The duke's behavior (his secrecy, his withdrawal, his message in a borrowed voice) amounted to a series of narrative equivalents of *hsing*; he might as well be an incarnate *hsing*.

The Duke of Chou's behavior in and around the poem allows us to reopen the question, occluded by talk of likenesses, of the moral valence of literary figures. That is very much a live question for the Mao interpretation and its sources. The Mao edition makes the author of the "Kuan chü," that model poem, commend through analogies (that is, modestly and retiringly) a "modest and retiring" girl; and a similar embodied *hsing* (and *hsing* of *hsing*) occurs in the first lines of Ode 184, "Ho ming."

> The crane calls in the nine marshes;
> Its voice is heard all the way to the sky.
>
> [Mao *chuan* commentary:] A *hsing*. . . . This describes someone whose self is hidden, yet whose name [or reputation] is bright.[81]

The Duke of Chou's position as the hierarchical inferior of his hearers (the spirits of the former kings, the present king) may account for his repeated "hiding of the self" through *hsing* and its equivalents throughout the story. That position demands indirect speech.[82] The Duke's readiness to put himself in the position of a substitute (offering to take King Wu's place in death, acting as regent in King Ch'eng's name, re-enacting the military exploits of his own father King Wen) recalls other patterns of ritual substitution: for example, those of the ancestral sacrifices, in which a younger person (typically a grandson) impersonates a departed older one.[83] It is hardly an exaggeration to say that the Duke of

Chou of the "Chin t'eng" story *is* ritual. A Confucian cult of the Duke of Chou has often been noted in the *Mencius*, the *Tso Commentary*, the ritual books, and other works of the Warring States period: if the "Chin t'eng" chapter pictures that hero as a most scrupulous ritualist and as the savior of the dynastic enterprise, it only perfects a legend already in place.[84]

A ritual context is therefore ready to receive the oblique language of "Ch'ih-hsiao." But although *hsing* is the mode of language best suited to assuring communication between unequal partners, there is more to it than a handy device. The *Hsün-tzu* passage from which the Mao editors derived their interpretation of the *hsing* figure in "Ho ming" deserves to be quoted at greater length. "The noble man is hidden [*yin*] yet manifest [*hsien*], subtle yet obvious. He demurs and yields, yet conquers. As the Ode says: 'The crane calls in the nine marshes; its voice is heard all the way to the sky.' "[85] In a vocabulary both semiotic and ethical, Hsün-tzu defines the *hsing* in such a way as to make it the verbal portrait of the virtuous man. The Duke of Chou's power to affect the course of Chou history is inseparable from his evasiveness, and that in turn can hardly be distinguished from his choice of linguistic register.

The oblique reference of *hsing* delays understanding; it is to straightforward reference what the "noble man's" yielding is to the lesser man's grasping. And delay is essential to the effectiveness of "Ch'ih-hsiao" as an event tied up with other events (the expedition, the circumstances of the poem's presentation to Ch'eng, Ch'eng's wavering). The *hsing* with its several possible meanings mirrors the suspense of its historical moment. It underlines the necessity for the reader to decode the figure and the surrounding situation. Writing the poem is a historical act, but it is as such an action—in its immediate context—that it least makes sense. In the historical present of the king's indecision and ignorance, the poem means one thing (or rather has one set of possible but unverifiable meanings); for the historian, however, and for the readers of the historical narrative, it means something quite different. Historical omniscience makes a different poem of "Ch'ih-hsiao." It makes it a poem from which the specifics of the *hsing*, and thus of the virtuous historical actor, are absent. It privileges the history a poem reflects at the expense of the history it makes.

The purpose of a literary compilation like the *Mao Odes*, which constantly surrounds the song texts with historical narratives rather like this one (only much shorter), is to bring its readers to the final and adequate viewpoint, the viewpoint of history-as-document rather than that of history-as-event, the position from which all the riddles of *hsing* have settled into the kind of meaning appropriate to "exposition" or *fu*. The "historical mode of meaning" relevant to such an enterprise is historical in the sense of a history that is over with and definitively interpreted.[86] The Mao Prefaces and the readings of the Three Schools have little respect for ignorance. They usually present history as the best-known and most automatically understandable thing in the world. The "Chin t'eng" chapter, subtler on this account, spells out the process whereby history takes on a knowable meaning.

The king is not there yet. In the third part of the chapter, the year turns out badly, and omens follow hard on one another. The king, suspecting that a punishment is being visited on his house, orders the archives opened and finds there the secret record of the Duke of Chou's *chih* (intention), the one thing that had been missing from Ch'eng's previous and unsuccessful interpretations of the duke.

Everything turns on a reading. A look at the hidden documents acquaints Ch'eng with the facts of the situation, puts him in a position of greater rather than less knowledge, and persuades him to change his behavior toward his uncle. Not least, the "owl" poem now makes sense to the king, who forthwith translates it into the language of *fu*, "exposing without reserve the good and evil of government"—his own government. "Formerly," proclaims the king to his ministers, "the duke *exerted* himself for the royal *house*; only I in my childishness did not come to know it."[87] The underlined words are repeated from the poem. King Ch'eng's paraphrase, as it *fus* or cites the poem once more in a changed historical situation, now gives its motifs (and its maker's motives) their decisive interpretation.

From here on the tale undoes—it replays in reverse—events from its first part. The secrets buried in the opening scene are now brought to light; where earlier the Duke of Chou withdrew from the court, now the court goes out to meet him; and, most astonishing of all, the trees blown down and the grain flattened by an ominous wind are now restored to their original position by a "returning" or "reversing" wind (*fan-feng*). The reading of history works miracles, if we are to believe the *Book of Documents*; history is, apparently, both easier to understand and more effective in promoting change than poetry.

The fable about *hsing* ends by proclaiming the era of history, the victory of *fu* (or knowledge) over *hsing* (or ambiguity). *Hsing* is in this story, as in the *Mao Odes'* "decadent" mode, the language suited to a time out of joint, and its translation into the plain speech of *fu* makes the happiest possible ending. But the last touch of the story, the counter-entropic "reversing wind," is no prosaic weather. As King Ch'eng puts it, "Heaven has," exceptionally, unnaturally, "moved its power to magnify the virtue of the Duke of Chou." "Does heaven speak?"[88] If it chooses to speak, what language will it use? Like a visiting dignitary, the weather has made its intentions known by quoting from the *Book of Odes*. The flattened crops and trees are borrowed from the climactic stanza of Ode 255, "T'ang," which repeats a harangue by Ch'eng's grandfather:

> King Wen said:
> "Ah! You Shang-Yin!
> People have a saying:
> 'When the trunk is down and the roots are in the air,
> The branches and leaves have not yet come to harm';
> Indeed the trunk will be disposed of first.
> The mirror of Yin is not far:
> It is in the generations of Hsia!"[89]

This is the command to read history on which the whole story pivots. It is really a command to read poetry. When nature, intending to correct historical errors, cites (or *fu*s) back at humanity the very poems for which nature had already furnished vehicles of comparison (*hsing* and *pi*), the participation of poems in history has gone far beyond what we are used to thinking of as historical reference. Instead of alluding to history, they plot it out.

And the outcome of the recognition of truth, the reading of history that changes history, is a hyperbolic variant of the one critical text the *Odes* cannot forget. The wind that attests to the right reading of history is a "reversed wind," an "opposite *feng,*" that comes to straighten the crops it had previously "flattened" or "bent" (*yen*, the attitude of the grass in Confucius' parable).[90] The second gust of wind, reversing the laws of cause and effect, undoes the image of naturally occurring, but ethically indifferent, mimesis. The historical episode resolves itself by recalling the program of the *Mao Odes.* If the *Book of Odes* is a text to be interpreted historically, its history is so revisionary that its successful reading makes time flow backward.

Reading the preface to "Ch'ih-hsiao" and the "Chin t'eng" story side by side illuminates the ways in which the generic distinction between history and poetry is drawn. The ancient interpreters seem to base their reading of this Ode on historical documents. But the documents obliterate the distinction between history and poetry; indeed, they put poetry above history, allow it to dictate history's course. For the Great Preface, history took place under the eye of ritual, and the poets are simply historians "conscious of changes in affairs and full of regret for the old," and perfect, "customs." "Altered" poetry stabs (*tz'u*) at the unjust ruler by prodding his memory. It refers to history, but its real concern is with ritual standards. Here, however, the lesson of poetry is stronger. In the deeds of the founders, the Duke of Chou and King Ch'eng, exemplary history sets forth in choreographic form the principles of the *Odes'* poetics: the riddling *hsing*, the praise of virtue through *sung*, a mimetic and a counter-mimetic *feng*. Poetics has the last word on the Duke of Chou's "intent."[91] Not even the sage is more worthy of imitation than this theory of imitation.

∼

This reading of the *Book of Odes* has gone from asking about allegory to investigating exemplarity—a step that may seem to put the whole topic of allegory on the shelf. What do allegory and example have to do with each other? Precious little, it seems; allegory emerges as a technical term in the rhetorical analysis of texts, but whether something is an *example* of something else would seem to be a matter for cognition, not figurative language, to decide. A relation of fact is, like the famous smoking gun, "beyond the art" of rhetoric. Does not the shift from tropes to a language of reference and category inclusion amount to changing the subject entirely?

The argument of the preceding chapters is meant to show that the transition is negotiable and that the two domains can be made to communicate. It tries to clarify how the *Mao Odes* conceives of the example (the exemplary figure, the exemplary moment in poetry, even the exemplary pun) as linguistically posited. Exemplarity is a relation of fact, but one made in and by the poetry.

The commentaries to the *Odes* contain two interpretations of the relation of exemplarity: one that treats all examples as instances of (quasi-natural) kinds, and one that traces every example (in a chain of axes that begat axes) to a law-giving deed of the founders of culture. For the first or static model of exemplarity, all the history the reader needs to know has already happened, and the language of criticism has only a descriptive or constative function; for the second, history happens in the present as a repetition (and commemoration) of those founding acts and can be transmitted only in a performative reading, a reading that does something to the text. For this second mode of reading, no grounding could be both given and adequate. These two languages are closely related, if mutually antagonistic—indeed, the axes of the second are often sharpened on the tree trunks of the first—and the millennial effort to read the *Book of Odes* as an inventory of natural kinds only accentuates the points of contact and contrast.

Does the question about allegory in the *Book of Odes* tradition correspond in any way to this alternative? It certainly does: the choice of interpretations presented to the reader of the *Mao Odes* is also presented to the student of the *Odes'* poetics and hermeneutics.

The story the Great Preface tells, the tale of poetry "used" by the ancient kings "to beautify the transformation [of their people] by culture" and sung by state historians "conscious of changes in affairs and full of regret for the old customs," is one such two-sided interpretative test case. Its historical fable ("the poem recounts the process of moral transformation") has as its practical content a command ("read the poem as telling that story, and the story shall become true"). Its constative language (the language of fact) is a pretext for the performative message (the language of wishing and willing), and its talk of history refers to a future conditional. Thus, even if the Great Preface is unable to ground its interpretation in a prior history, it reorients interpretation toward an ongoing history, the history of exemplary reading.

Here the declared function of interpretation is to construct, for the examples, the thing they are to be examples of. Insofar as that thing is not given, but rather made through reading, the interpretations subject the texts to a qualitative change; they remake them according to their wish. But to the degree that the wish is realized, and culture is created by the will to read the poems as if they were (already) manifestos of the sage, the distance between wish and fact shrinks. It is the reader who adheres to the second, non-natural, model of exemplarity who most successfully counters the charge of "allegorization" leveled against the *Mao Odes*. But that reader has already "become a parable by following the parables," to borrow a phrase from Kafka.[97] Tropes read in that way obliterate themselves as tropes.

"Allegorical" enters the discussion on the *Book of Odes* as a term for the traditional readings' failure to achieve the solidity of history; the intent of calling these interpretations "unallegorical" is to make their relation to history, or to historical belief, unproblematic. Neither term represents the position we have been reconstructing for the *Mao Odes*. To read as if one could choose between the exemplary reading and another is to choose a world in which an irreversible history—the sages' history—did not happen. And to read as if there were no question of a choice, as if the normative readings were inevitable, is to take the history out of history.

The *Mao Odes'* interpretative tradition knows only one kind of history, and it is a poetic or allegorical history: *poetic* because it produces the events it narrates, and *allegorical* because its narration of events and its production of events occur in the same words, though in different linguistic modes. The task of determining the linguistic mode of the classical texts is here—as it was for seventeenth-century Jesuits or is for present-day scholars of comparative poetics—the central problem of a Chinese aesthetic. And since the readings advanced by such documents as the *Mao Odes* aspire to remake history in the image of poetic language, the scope of aesthetic problems exceeds, "in parable" and perhaps in ancient China too, that of a philosophy of beauty, perception, or works of art. "Chinese aesthetics" can no longer name one form aesthetics may have taken in its historical development, an instance of a generally discoverable problem; rather it now comes to name the common source, or goal, of history (Chinese history) and aesthetics. To reproduce this aesthetic is to reproduce the empire. The empire is a mimesis of mimesis. The specificity of the "transformations" necessary to the existence of both China and the aesthetic project of the *Odes* opens the way not only to comparative aesthetics but to comparative Chinas.

§ 5 Hegel's Chinese Imagination

RIEN

 N'AURA EU LIEU

  QUE LE LIEU

—Mallarmé, "Un coup de dès"

Often [Hegel's manuscripts for the *Lectures on the
Philosophy of History*] contained nothing but isolated words and names, with lines drawn to connect them—apparently as an aid to memory while
teaching.

 —Eduard Gans, "Vorrede"

Following out the consequences of the performative reading of
the *Book of Odes* puts the student of literary language in front of an
intimidating object: China, the artwork whose medium is history.[1]
The *Odes'* utopian aesthetic organizes history as a series of mimetic
acts: realizations of and failures to realize the concept of empire.
The empire is simultaneously a work of art and a program for the
interpretation of works of art. Produced by the actions of sages such
as the Duke of Chou—ritual-political actions patterned after the
strong mimesis of the *Odes'* poetics—China is poetry writ large, the
product of the mimesis of mimesis. The choice of a language in
which to interpret the figures of the *Odes* is an integral part,
possibly the decisive turn, of China's realization. China, in the
reader and elsewhere, is the reward of the right kind of reading—
which might be the moral of the story, told above, of Ricci,
Longobardi, and Leibniz: each got the China he deserved and to
which his understanding of figural language entitled him. The
"problem of a Chinese aesthetic" is thus a problem of the aesthetic
itself, of the relation of artistic production and interpretation to the
production and interpretation of historical events. The writing of
history—of Chinese history even—is a special case of this double
production. Indeed, since history writing is an enterprise both
interpretative and mimetic, any attempt to write Chinese history

will invite comparison with the poetic/historical project of the *Book of Odes*. How generally does the comparison apply? How specifically are its terms tied to the topics of China and poetic reading? Hegel's writing on Chinese history, since it explicitly draws its substance from aesthetic categories, provides a test case for both questions.

The first time Hegel taught his course on the philosophy of world history (in 1822)

> he spent a good third of his time on the Introduction and on China, which was covered in numbing breadth and detail. Even though in his later lectures he became somewhat less meticulous about this empire,

says Eduard Gans, the editor of Hegel's posthumous *Works*,

> nonetheless the editor's presentation of the Chinese part has had to be cut down to such size that it will not be encroaching and intrusive as regards the remainder of the exposition. . . . It was only in the school year 1830–31

—that is, on the last of five attempts to teach the course—

> that Hegel found a way to deal somewhat more fully with the Middle Ages and the modern era, and the presentation in this book [*Lectures on the Philosophy of World History*, 1st ed.] relies mainly on this last version.[2]

Despite Gans's recollection of a more inclusive syllabus, the last version of the course was still announced as "Philosophy of World History, Part I." One wonders: Was there ever a Part II? What kind of a Part I is the "first part" of world history? Is it a Part I to be classed with *Being and Time, Part I* or with Hegel's own *System of Science, Part I, The Phenomenology of Mind*? All those Part I books promise a Part II that never comes to second them, but the *Philosophy of World History, Part I* sounds, in light of Gans's remarks, less like a promise of more to come than a confession that the lecturer will never get to the end of his subject. Or perhaps, again, it shows a determination to seal off Part I as only a part, to bring it to a conclusion, and to keep it from intruding on and damaging the rest of the subject that Part I should only introduce.

On this surmise, there may be no contradiction between the modest claims made by the 1830 course title and Gans's memory of a fuller—more nearly "complete"—Philosophy of World History. The material of Part I, proliferating like a "bad infinity," has to be assigned a limit, made a part of something else, subsumed and superseded, for there to be anything to talk about but that part. "World history" is a matter of fragile definition. Establishing its Part I *as* Part I is a sign that it intends to make good its claim to be world history, a feat akin to Hercules' strangling the serpents invading his cradle.

The mythic parallel rings false, though, for the Hegel who shuts the door on Part I of the world's history is no heroic baby but a renowned professor setting up the topics for what will be almost his last course. Why is such a man unable to put Part I behind him? The better analogy may be with a story Hegel tells in the "Philosophy of Nature" section of the Berlin *Encyclopedia* about the intimate relation between the living and the dead, about bones and the resistance they put up to their rhyming partners, stones. "Plants allow their wood, their bark, to die and their leaves to drop off, but the animal is, itself, its own negativity."[3] Is Part I, the history of China and its neighbors, that impediment to world history? Is Part I, in its declared incompleteness, the "own negativity" of Hegelian history? What kind of "own" and what kind of "negativity" are at work here?

The bone model deserves to be expounded more fully before we begin attaching the "own" to the "negative." In Hegel's elucidation of nature, "shape" (*Gestalt*), the first subsystem of animal organism, divides into three sub-sub-systems: sensibility, irritability, and reproduction. Sensibility, the characteristic distinguishing animal from plant life, shows the animal as its "undivided identity with itself."[4] In its aspect of "sensibility"—as nerves and bone—the animal is, it might be said, a naïve participant in the physical world: all reaction, at the receiving end of sensations that are only its own and that are all the "own" it has yet. They are the "own" of a "self" that has as yet acquired no individuality beyond that of being identical to itself. What this animal feels is what this animal feels.

That is not much of an individuality—a stone, after all, is identical to itself—and until it can give itself a better definition, the animal suffers the logical fate of "a passing on into immediacy, into unorganic being and insensibility."[5] No well-constituted animal accepts this fate willingly, and the prospect of resistance emerges at one end of the theory of "sensibility," when the bone "extends itself outward in solid points of contact [*Anhaltspunkte*], such as horns, claws, etc." This brings us close to an argument about natural philosophy from the *Phenomenology*.

> Not only should signs [*Merkmale*] be essentially related to the activity of knowing, but they should also contain the essential determinations of the things [known]. The artificial system [of knowledge] should be apportioned to the system of nature itself. . . . The *distinguishing* signs of animals, for example, are their claws and teeth; for in actuality it is not only knowledge that distinguishes, through teeth and claws, this animal from that one, but also the animal itself that uses them to hold [the outer world] at a *distance*.[6]

Ex ungue leonem! The "own" now comes into its own. Teeth and claws are the model signs, the signs of an individuation to which both animals and the study of animals should aspire. These outgrowths of the "system of sensibility" seem to lie poles apart from the indistinct, "point for point," feeling of self with which the system began.[7] What happens in the middle? How is the theory of "sensibility" to get from indistinct passivity to combative activity, from the nerve end to the sharp end of the horn?

The middle stage is "the production of the *bone* system, which [presents itself] to the *inside* as a covering, but seen from the *outside* is the inside's [own] firm defense against the outside."[8] The bone is "the innermost part of the body's members, immediate and solid—but at another stage ceases to be the inside—as the wood is the inmost part of the tree . . . but reverses itself in the seed (there it is only the outer coating)—so the bones become an outer coating for the entrails."[9] The bone, for all that it can only belong to an animal, encapsulates the successive stages of plant life, so that it is the inside of the outside and the outside of the inside for both the individual animal and the category "animal." Whereas the plant can let its dead layers fall away, the animal is compelled to store them up inside it and carry them around with it. The question of what is alive and what is dead presents itself differently, and is solved differently, for the plant and animal kingdoms. Here the *Zusatz* (supplement) clarifies and literalizes the main *Encyclopedia* text, from the principle of "sensibility" onward.

> As the identity of sensation with itself, reduced to abstract identity, *sensibility* is insensibility—that which is motionless and dead, a dying off of itself that nevertheless still belongs to the sphere of live things; and that is the formation of the *bones*, through which the organism grants [*voraussetzt*] itself a ground to stand on. The bone is, like the wood of a plant, the simple and consequently dead force that is not yet process but [merely] abstract reflection-in-self. And so it is a dead thing reflected in itself.[10]

Bones look no lovelier here than they usually do, but Hegel takes care not to elide their necessity. "He climbs over corpses," as the proverb has it, could be said of any vertebrate; only the corpse one walks on so ruthlessly is one's own. The bone is "a dead thing." It restates in material form the "motionless and dead" tautology of the first level of the "system of sensibility," that wherein the animal was unable to define itself in any way other than the most general (and indefinite) way of all, as identical with itself. Hegel's presentation here, instead of resolving the tautological impasse, simply deposits it in the midst of the theory of animal life. Pure "sensibility" gave the animal no way to distinguish itself from inorganic matter, and now the bone is an internalized stone, as if it were the residue of the unaccomplished synthesis between particularity (*my* sensations) and generality (the sensations of every unspecified *me*). There is not much to do with this "dead thing reflected into itself" except build on it. Without bones, the animal, lacking an autonomous "ground," would sink into the ground and be indistinguishable from inorganic being and plant life. Without the bone to prop it up, it would *be* the bone. Having a skeleton is a way to gain "mechanical objectivity" vis-à-vis the earth and to postpone sensibility's headlong advance toward "abstract reflexion-in-self" (i.e., toward being a stone or skeleton).[11]

And having a Part I is a way for history to escape being identical to its Part I. The Part I Hegel had such trouble leaving behind, the section of his *Philosophy of World History* entitled "The Oriental World," has been held up as the model of a Eurocentric world history, a narrative that selfishly seizes every opportunity to crowd its protagonists out of the story, a book, in short, unsuited to being either a *world* history or a world *history*. Critique along these lines takes for its object—and rightly so, considering the uses to which the phrases have been put—Hegel's adaptation of the *translatio imperii* topos and the consequent characterization of the peoples of Asia as "still living fossils."[12] But what we can discover about bones, and indeed about the purported distinction between life and death, from other places in Hegel's work leads in the direction of quite another reading of Hegel's "Oriental World" *and* of the embarrassment it causes us. The ability to cast off one's "fossils," as some of Hegel's disciples would cast off the historical sedimentation of Asia and as some of Hegel's critics would cast off Hegel's *Philosophy of History*, belongs to plants and trees and can be called (without injury) symptomatic of a pre-vertebrate way of handling the question.[13] (That history needs to be performed by animals is confirmed, should any doubt subsist, by the *Philosophy of Nature*.)[14] Might the rest of history not owe to the first, "numbing," inert part of history its capacity for moving forward, just as the animal props up and propels itself on its stony framework? What is there in Hegel's Part I that makes it, in the fullest sense, a Part I? Does Hegel, even in 1830, ever find a way to Part II and to a degree of "mechanical objectivity" vis-à-vis the beginnings of history?

Geography

The rules of universal history writing are well known, all the more so since they mirror the rules of historical development outlined again and again in Hegel's oeuvre.

History is Spirit giving itself the form of event or of immediate natural actuality. The stages of its development are therefore presented as *immediate natural principles.* These [principles], because they are natural, are a plurality external to one another [*als eine Vielheit außereinander*], and they are present therefore in such a way that *each of them* is assigned to *one nation* as [the principle of] its *geographical* and *anthropological* existence.[15]

The "immediate natural principles" of the nations are discrete—on the model of the thing rather than that of the quality[16]—and positive. An enumeration that stays within the bounds of natural principle must leave them that way.[17] But world history has something else in mind. World history is cumulative. That is how the "principles" get to be "stages" in an ongoing story. "The stage [of development] reached thus far by spirit is present as the natural principle of a people, that is, as a nation. . . . A people cannot run through more than one stage [of development], nor can it have its day in world history more than once."[18]

"Time is the Negative in sensible form"[19] and an operative principle in world history far more than in national history. (It is not clear how much time can mean for a national history that merely relates the unfolding of this or that people's "immediately existing principle.") At first the "natural principles" excluded—negated—one another in the manner of objects in space; now they are a *series* of things. Subsumed into the course of world history, with their negations of one another duly negated, they become episodes of a longer story, the story of the development of spirit, a story that, if it is to be told according to the rules, should mention only one thing at a time and refuse to repeat itself.

What happens when a determinate "national spirit" fends off, negatively, the (second, temporal) negation of the (first, spatial) negation? History begins with a system or region—one does not know quite what to call it—that the philosophy of history has trouble incorporating. This is most simply because the peoples east of and older than the Greeks stand outside history. Supranational history (the development of spirit, the progressive realization of freedom) walks away from the East in much the same way as the East, being the dawn of civilization, had to distance itself from nature. Or as Michel Hulin elegantly puts it: "The Orient, as a historical formation, *has* no genesis. . . . The Orient prepares the rest of history without having been 'prepared for' in the same way. This asymmetrical structure makes of the Orient a 'hybrid reality' or *Mittelwesen* that can only with difficulty be brought into a constructive dialectic."[20]

China is the eminent case, an Orient within the Orient where "all change is excluded, and the stationary [*das Statarische*] . . . replaces what we could otherwise call the historical."[21] One sees immediately why Hegel's lectures on "world history" kept seizing up where they did. If China is the land of stasis ("Reich der Dauer"), then the telling of it could very well never come to an end. It becomes a matter of intense concern for the lecturer on world history to find a "break" somewhere within this unending moment, a break that justifies moving on to another moment, and eventually a break decisive enough to get history out of Asia and onto its proper course. At the European end of the continent, opportunities for announcing such a break abound, as the Israelites take leave of worldliness and the Persians encounter the Greeks.[22] But in neither of those cases does the break arise from within the Asian historical process. The Persians come to know the Greeks as combatants, and "the first act through which Abraham became the forefather of a nation is a separation," an epochal break with "the whole system of relations in which he had previously lived together with man and nature."[23] The *Philosophy of History* is hard put to give its rationality an appropriate expository form. There seems to be no way of producing history—Greece, Israel—out of the givens of non-history, which means that the necessary character of the movement from East to West is in doubt; Europe no longer presents itself as the answer to a problem posed by Asia.[24]

The absence of any bridge between Europe and Asia is mirrored in the description of Asia itself. It seems to fall into two parts: a vast hinterland without history and an edge rubbing up against history.

Mediating between Asia's two parts—its inside and its outside—is the shortcut to solving the problem of relating Europe to Asia. From one version of the lectures to the next, Hegel experiments with ways of transforming a two-part scheme that mirrors the (uncertain) relation of history to non-history into a scheme of three or more parts; that is, he has to differentiate the static Asiatic part of history into moments, agents, and mediations.

China (with Mongolia a cruder, but not essentially distinct, version of the Chinese theocratic principle) then remains the East of the East; India prepares the transition to Persia, West Asia (Phoenicia, Syria, Israel), and Egypt. Since these last three "sections," the outside edge of Asia, are already in contact with the historical process, China becomes Asia pure and simple and India the means of transition to West Asia and to history.[25] This requires taking a free hand with chronology so that it may be accommodated to geography and to the paradoxical condition of West Asia's entry onto the world stage—that is, the contact, which must and yet cannot be simultaneous and immediate, of both Egypt and Persia with Greece. The *Volksgeister* seemed (in the *Philosophy of Right* and the introduction to world history) to belong to a physics of discrete objecthood, but the "national spirits" of Persia, West Asia, and Egypt impinge on the succeeding moment, Greece, as a class and not as individuals (*Besonderheiten*). In its organization of topics, world history makes clear the difference between its imperatives and those of national history. If this handling of chapters is representative of the new discipline of *Weltgeschichte*, we cannot get to world history through a sum or sequence of different national histories. This makes it hard, too, to know exactly what kind of object Hegel's Asia is, for the ease with which these empires can be expanded, contracted, and moved backward or forward in time shows that for Hegel the problem of the East was not one of history or chronology—of reference generally—but one of logic.[26]

Physically (as a chapter of the book entitled *Philosophy of History*) the East has been sealed off from history. How can historical reason talk about it, if the usual historical categories (first among them change) do not apply? Hegel's introduction warns against the temptations of anachronism—or of seeing the products of history as interchangeable, as if they were terms possessing a meaning but no inherent syntax. It is pure "formalism and error" to translate the Chinese *Tao* as the Spinozan One or the Johannine Logos. Such assimilations are merely formal and analytic, mistake the isolated moment for the development of the idea, and so on.[27] It comes as a most peculiar vindication of historicism's strivings to leave formalism behind that what Hegel finds most objectionable in Chinese philosophy is its very formalism ("a logic you might compare to the old-fashioned logic of Wolff").[28] *Qua* fossils, the *Book of Changes* and Christian Wolff are contemporaries. Historicism sees no compelling need to distinguish their two kinds of ahistoricity. World history is constitutively—that is, it must be—a method at odds with its objects, or most clearly at odds with an object like this one. To study Chinese philosophy as something other than a fossil would be to become Chinese, formalistic, Wolffian.[29]

Looking back from within history toward something that stands outside it requires some demarcations of territory. One wants to guard against the "formalism and error" involved in likening the unlike, and yet history is a concept generated by the historical process, a concept with a definite beginning of its own. One of Asia's edges, Israel, performs "the reversal of the principle of the East" when

> the spiritual breaks free from what is natural, sensory, immediate. . . . Here . . . nature retreats and is treated as something external. This is properly the truth of nature. . . . The representation of nature as a created thing founds a new and different relation between divinity and nature, [i.e.,] the sublimity of God. . . .
>
> Thereby, and essentially for the first time, a genuinely *historical* view of things first presents itself.[30]

The beginning of history properly speaking is also the declaration of a difference between that history and whatever seemed to be history in the foregoing. The word "history" applies to this history's Part I in a derived, approximate, ambiguous, rhetorical, or in any case an ungenuine sense. Part I is at best an example, a trial run, on which nothing serious is to depend.[31]

If Part I is not history, what is it, then? The question can be re-stated with reference to the broadest outlines of Hegel's philosophi-cal project. If we recall the main divisions of Hegel's *Encyclopedia*—

I. Logic, science of the idea in and for itself;
II. Philosophy of Nature, science of the idea in its otherness [*in seinem Anderssein*];
III. Philosophy of Spirit, that is, of the idea returning to itself from its exteriorization[32]

—then the first problem that confronts the study of Asia is to decide whether it belongs to the study of Nature or of Spirit, *res extensa* or *res cogitans*. For a post-Mosaic, historical consciousness at any rate, Asia is a negative moment, a glimpse of what it itself is not, and the study of Asia one of the idea in its "exteriorization." To give it the name that applies to it only after the start of (genuine) history, Part I is Nature—"something external" when seen from within history, "de-divinified" (*entgötterte*).

What is this Nature, then, for us, the historians?

Nature presents itself as the Idea in the form of *otherness* [*Anderssein*]. Since the Idea is thus as it were the Negative of itself or *external to itself*, so Nature is not only external relative to this idea; rather, this exter-nality is the entire determination whereby Nature is Nature.
Supplement. The infinite divisibility of matter means nothing other than that matter is something external to itself. That immeasurability of Nature that instantly stuns the understanding is none other than this externality.   · · · · ·

In this externality the determinations of the concept [of nature] have the appearance of an *indifferent compoundedness* and mutual *isola-tion*. . . . Nature in its determinate being shows *necessity* and *chance*, but no freedom.   · · · · ·

Nature is divine—*implicitly*, in its Idea; but as it is, its being does not correspond to its concept. Rather nature is the *unresolved contradic-tion*. Its distinctive characteristic is its *positedness*, its negativity.[33]

"Nature" is "sun, moon, animals, plants, etc."[34]—but "Nature" is, first of all, a program of interpretation. Indeed there is little else to it if the category of spirit always predominates and if the end of the philosophy of nature (its recognition plot, its "change from ignorance to knowledge")[35] is to reveal nature to spirit as another form of spirit.[36] If "Nature" comes about through an imperative to consider it as (merely) Nature, then we are the authors of Nature.

"Nature" is, then, mainly a name for the mode of our relation to nature. If Part I is a version of Nature, that means it is Nature-for-us. Its being Nature is like its being-example—it was an example for the sake of history (without being history). The intermediate status of the example—or the logical intractability of the concept of the Orient—lay in its being made an example of, or for, what it was not. Metaphor is, of course, the pattern of this process, and Hegel's chapter "The Oriental World" lends itself all too easily to being read as allegory or sustained metaphor—for example, as an allegorically developed Aesopian critique of Leibniz, Spinoza, or Fichte.[37] But that is to take the Orient as an instance of metaphor instead of as a reconstruction of the model for metaphor. Hegel's Orient is "good to think with," to be sure, a logical model applicable to all sorts of content, but applying the model is quite different from reading it. Hegel's use of his own Orient is hardly more than an application.

Nature is subjected to time but has no history. "That universal, nature, has no history," only a manner of "bald happenings with nothing more to them than a difference in time."[38] What "the construction of the earth immediately shows" is, or should be, unreadable as history; Hegel ridicules the efforts of geologists to interpret the stratifications of the earth's crust as evidence of eras of change and overlay. Spirit refuses to recognize itself in "bald happenings" such as rocks coming to rest on one another. Histories of the earth are false histories. They make too much of mere natural dispositions of "externality." "Their whole method of explanation is nothing but a transformation of here-and-there into before-and-after" (*eine Verwandlung des Nebeneinander in Nacheinander*).

So the East is history in the manner of nature, a history reducible to nature, history that does not yet know itself as independent of nature: the correlation bears instant interpretative fruit. All relations in nature are substantive ones; natural events are matters of necessity and chance; the Oriental principle, likewise, is one of "substantiality of the ethical," with no distinctions yet available between habit, custom, law, force, conscience, and luck. The unchanging Chinese constitution rests on the family—"a substantial unity . . . of blood and naturality."[39] In China "moral determinations are expressed as laws. . . . The laws of the nation are in part judicial, in part moral, so that the inner law, the subject's knowledge of the content of his will as his own inwardness, is present as an external command of the law." "The unity of substantiality and of subjective freedom is so entirely without difference and antithesis on either side, that for this very reason substance is unable to achieve self-reflexivity or subjectivity."[40] The one subject exempt from the substantiality of relation is the ruler, whose freedom, since it acts on a background of sheer necessity, must take the shape of arbitrariness.[41] The concept of nature as seen from the vantage point of spirit reframes the familiar notion of Oriental despotism[42] (Nature is an Oriental despot), and the inert externality or collaterality of the parts of nature to one another (*Äußerlichkeit, Außereinandersein, gleichgültiges Bestehen, Vereinzelung*) provides the basis for what will later become the "Asiatic mode of production."[43]

But since Nature, like history, is a figure of interpretation written into (and out of) the story, it is not just anybody who can say that the East is history in the manner of nature. The concept of nature is inseparable from the concept of history, and for two reasons, both of which stem from the Jewish break. It is with the beginning of history that nature becomes properly nature; it there receives a determination and a negation. Second, nature has no history, not only because the sequences of events in nature would make no sense if we tried to make them into history but chiefly because, for the purposes of explaining nature to spirit, "the process has no content beyond its product."[44] Earth has no history in the *eigentlichen* sense of the word, and yet it is necessary to say "that the earth has had a *history*, that is, that its construction is the result of successive changes." How can the earth, as part of nature, have a history and yet no history? Its history is the history of the artifact (*ein Geschaffenes*),[45] a minimal one: once it was not, then it came to be. All the rest, "what the structure [*Beschaffenheit*] of the earth immediately shows," is just a naming of parts. The history of created nature is not *eigentliche* (genuine) history because it is not *eigen* (inherent) to nature: it belongs rather to theology, the language in which Spirit is trafficking at the time of its departure from nature. So the maxim about the process being empty apart from its product applies directly to nature as interpretative schema, or to its elaboration as the putative content of the middle third of the *Encyclopedia*.

The *Encyclopedia* provides (as it should) the context of contexts. Saying that the East is history in the guise of nature, or nature in the guise of history, is a peculiar kind of metaphor; its tenor and vehicle are separated not by differences in kind or attributes but by a gap in time.[46] The gesture of opposing the East to history, or history to nature, is yet another *Voraussetzung* ("groundwork," "presupposition"), another laying out of the props for a (double) recognition plot, with the denouement being the collapse of those two analogous metaphors (or examples of non-exemplarity), "the East" and "nature." The interpretation of Asia as nature—as the negative, natural moment in human history—receives a determinate meaning only when the lecturer reaches Israel and performs the separation of nature and history together with that determination of nature (nature as product) that enables nature—and Asia with it—to become part of history. The writing of Part I is facilitated by a figure or system of figures that the meaning of Part I, when we attain it, is supposed to annul (it wasn't history although we said it was: it was just nature) and verify (it was nature, but for that reason it was history all along). The dismantling of the figures is part of the recognition plot. History is necessarily cumulative because it is structured like a reading.

Whatever linguistic traffic connects East and West (including the writing of histories) is in principle one-way. That the West is supposed to come as the *Aufheben* ("sublation," "overcoming") of the East is no surprise at all; that it has to be, at the same time, the *Aufheben* of the difference between the East and the West is a little stranger, and a conclusion that the telling of the *Philosophy of History* only imperfectly vindicates. The first thing that must be overcome in the writing of universal history is history's tendency to turn into Chinese, a language that according to Hegel "has no way of indicating grammatical case [*Kasus*]. Rather, it simply leaves its words standing one next to the other [*nebeneinander*]."[47]

The moment of transition from East to West—the break—can therefore be seen as the central event in the story, the one that provides the interpretative formula for history before and after it. And its abruptness reflects the very nature of a break. The transition from Asia to Europe in its several forms (the command to stop deifying nature; Oedipus' answer to the Sphinx; the Persians' failure to annex Greece) is a reversal, too heavily thematized a discontinuity to count as discontinuous. It poses no insoluble problems from the point of view of history (properly speaking), because each version of the epochal event efficiently interprets the East away. The break is meant to be a clean one. (For this reason discussions of Hegel's inability to come to grips with "the Other," for example, Asia, fall right into step with Hegel's own sequence of mutually external moments as it is most commonly misunderstood.) The point of view that becomes possible after the break interprets the East as the inability to come to a break. But the break is its own interpretative law. Built into the formula for interpreting the East (as failure to come to a break) is a provision for the East's unreadability. By not making sense, the East makes sense as an object for interpretation. The East cannot be translated into history, only transcribed. Is the resistance it offers to being read a prop, crutch, or tool of the advancing dialectic and nothing more? Two instances are considered here.

DIFFERENCE: SPACE AND TIME

The contradictions of the East generate its history (or its pseudo-history). The East is nature; nature is not history; but nature is (seen as artifact) part of history; so the East is and is not nature, is and is not history. "Only in time can both of two contradictorily opposed determinations meet in one thing—they meet, that is, in succession."[48] The backwardness of the East is a correlate of epic retrograde motion.[49] The East is readable in the future perfect tense—prospectively and retrospectively—as what it is not (yet). The transition from East to West is necessary and rational from the point of view that is ours once we have made the break: its necessity and its truth are proleptic. The break is not just the central event of history, but, in a strong sense, its first event.

This means that the break will seem quite irrational, or indifferent, from within Asia (supposing that to be a possible point of view). The determination of Asia as nature accounts for that, however; it is not nature's business to interpret itself. More difficult by far—and a difficulty squarely in Hegel's hands—are the transitions from one moment to another of the Asian historical process. These can only be transitions without reversal or purpose, "bald happenings" neither explicable nor necessary because through them we attain no explanatory advantage. Getting out of Asia is one quandary, but that process at least has a goal and an ending; getting from part to part within Asia would seem to pose a Zenonian problem for historical reason.

In Hegel's organization of the first part of the march of history, the kingdoms of Asia elude periodization, but not classification. "On one side we see stasis, stability—empires of space, so to speak, an unhistorical history, as, for example, in China. . . . On the other side [i.e., in India] stands the form of time, in opposition to this spatial stasis."[50]

In the classroom, classification can stand in for the unavailable sequence of events. And Asia, like nature, lends itself to classificatory talk ("on the one hand," "on the other hand"). Its moments lie conveniently "outside one another"; their logic is not cumulative. Going from Asia to Europe was a passage from non-history into history proper; going from one of the static patriarchal states of Asia to a region in perpetual flux—for example, from China to India—is the same thing as going from space to time.

What can this possibly mean—that China and India, or any two realms representative of the division in Asia between stasis and chaos, are simply two different orders of things? That China is called unchanging and India a ceaseless flux is incidental to the argument. The real question is whether the lecturer can get from any starting point to any second place, whether he can make the transition from transitionlessness to the possibility of making transitions. In that case the difficulty of getting from point to point within Asia would seem to be a quite general one. Only in prehistory does the truth about the difficulty of history writing surface.

In Marx the double aspect of Hegel's Asia is called on to illuminate (as only a figure of non-relation can) the relation between ancient communalism and the money economy:

> Objects in themselves are external [*äußerlich*] to man, and consequently alienable [*veräußerlich*] by him. . . . But such a state of reciprocal independence has no existence in a primitive society based on property in common [*für die Glieder eines naturwüchsigen Gemeinwesens*], whether such a society takes the form of a patriarchal family, an ancient Indian community, or a Peruvian Inca state. The exchange of commodities, therefore, first begins on the boundaries of such communities [*wo die Gemeinwesen enden*]. . . . Nomad races are the first to develop the money-form, because all their worldly goods consist of movable objects and are therefore directly alienable; and because their mode of life, by continually bringing them into contact with foreign communities, solicits the exchange of products.[51]

The model is still that of the coexistence of antitheticals. The "naturally formed community" does not, cannot, evolve the nomads' system of money and exchange, nor can it even be a trading partner of those nomads so long as "reciprocal independence" of person and property remains in the future for it; presumably rapine, and not trade, is the first Asian form of the circulation of goods.[52] An Asia so constructed can hardly be more than (Metternich's phrase) a "geographical expression." Its parts can be related to one another—and also to Europe—only by their boundaries. And the comparison with space and time suggests that the task of rationalizing this transition might be better left to the philosophers of nature, of "exteriority." Evidently the model is the natural one, that of a taxonomy: we have China, or a chapter about China, and when the inventory of things to say about it is exhausted, we have India.

"Space and time, as imagined, lie far apart, so we have space, and then we have time *too*; philosophy resists this 'too.'"[53] Instead of calling space and time transcendental presuppositions of any possible experience, the Hegel of the *Encyclopedia* wants to derive one of them from the other and do away with their bare (natural) coexistence. How is this to be done? "The truth of space is time, so space turns into time; it is not we who subjectively cross over into time, rather space itself makes the transition."[54]

The production of the concept of time is a case of irreversible and self-reflecting translation, exactly the kind of translation at issue throughout this book. The interpretation of time as sublated space will make space, and the difference between space and time, readable as forms of time: that is what the anticipated constitution of Asiatic "history" (or temporalized space) out of European history would lead us to expect. The form of a book like the *Philosophy of History* or the *Encyclopedia* is a strong guarantee of its rationality, or so Heidegger seems to suppose when he says: "The transition from space to time does not signify that these are treated in adjoining paragraphs [which, of course, they are]; rather 'it is space itself that makes the transition.'"[55] Perhaps space deputizes a part of itself—the blank space between paragraphs 257 and 258 of the *Encyclopedia*—to do the job. Heidegger's dry joke on the formula "space itself makes the transition" reminds us that the sublating, since it is structured like a reading, requires a reader's help. Why refuse it? Under the guidance of a reader like Heidegger, we might solve two problems at once: make the logical transition from space into time, and also (but more than just "also") read or leap over the space that joins India and China, those two unconnected paragraphs; and all this within the bounds of "space itself."

The difficult passage in Hegel's analysis of time as the truth of space is paragraph 257 of the *Encyclopedia*:

> Negativity [first or immediately] relates itself to space as the point. It develops its determinations in space as line and plane. But in the

sphere of self-externality [*Außersichsein*], negativity is equally *for itself,* as are its determinations. Negativity, thereupon, appears to be indifferent to the inert side-by-sideness [*Nebeneinander*] of space. Negativity, thus posited for itself, is Time.[56]

That lines and planes "negate" space is easily understood, for both lines and planes are boundaries. If having a place "in space" means having a place of one's own, then negativity as applied to space, if it is *in* space (and we have just seen it at work delimiting lines and planes in space), must be granted some kind of address, however strange this seems. The line and the plane, however, only negate (or limit) portions of space, whereas negativity itself, if it is to be true to itself while taking up residence in the realm of "mutual externality," must be the negation of space as a whole. Heidegger's discussion concentrates on the series of transitions by negation.

> Space is "the unmediated difference of Nature's *Außersichsein*." This is a way of saying that space is the abstract multiplicity [*Vielheit*] of the points that are differentiable [*unterscheidbar*] in it. Space is not interrupted by these, but neither does it arise from them by way of joining them together. . . . Nevertheless the point, insofar as it differentiates anything in space, is the *negation* of space, although in such manner that, as this negation, it itself remains in space. . . . But it is not as if space were a point; space is rather, as Hegel says, "pointedness" [*Punktualität*]. This is the basis for the sentence in which Hegel thinks space in its truth—that is, as time.[57]

At this point Heidegger quotes the difficult paragraph 257 and then continues:

> If space is represented [*vorgestellt*]—that is, if it is intuited immediately in the indifferent subsistence of its differences—then the negations are, as it were, simply given. But by such a representation, space does not get grasped in its Being [*in seinem Sein*]. Only in thinking is it possible for this to be done. . . . Only if the negations do not simply remain subsisting in their indifference but get transmuted—that is, only if they themselves get negated—can space be *thought* and thus grasped in its Being. In the negation of the negation (that is, of pointedness) the point posits itself *for itself* and thus emerges from the indifference of

subsisting. As that which is posited for itself, it differentiates itself from this one and that one; it is *no longer* this and *not yet* that[—to refer to the existential-ontological interpretation Heidegger has given some pages earlier of Aristotle's definition of time]. In positing itself for itself, it posits the succession in which it stands. . . . According to Hegel, this negation of the negation as pointedness is time. If the discussion has any demonstrable meaning [*einen ausweisbaren Sinn*], it can mean nothing else than that the positing-of-itself-for-itself of every point is a "now-here," "now-here," and so on.[58]

Heidegger negates the negation by telling a story. The point used to be sunk in "the indifference of subsisting," but it *posits* itself and *thereupon* becomes a "now-here," measurable as a before-and-after relative to its fellows in what has become an order of successions.[59] The best preparation for making the transition from space to time is to have the concept of time already and to conceive of "positing" (in Hegel's text, negativity "posits" itself for itself in the sphere of self-externality and thus becomes time) as an event. "As represented," "as imagined" (*in der Vorstellung*), space and time are far apart; philosophy combats their far-apartness. The philosophical reader combats their far-apartness too, but does so by rationalizing the difference between space and time—carefully expressed by Hegel as space (*weit auseinander*)—as a difference between before and after, by putting them in the same time zone. *At first* there was only space, and *then* there was time.

It is as if the difference could be bridged only by a "transformation of 'here-and-there' into 'before-and-after.' " The means of sublation here, as with the sublation of the difference between East and West, remains in suspense. Does Heidegger's performance of the transition depend on thinking (*Denken*), as he says it must, or on mere representation (*Vorstellung*)? *Vorstellung* is to *Denken* as space is to time; the reader's ability to leave *Vorstellung* behind is correlative, maybe indispensable, to the possibility of philosophical thinking about time. But when it happens in Heidegger's text, the transition seems to come about not exactly through *Denken* but by an inability on *Vorstellung*'s part to depict the passage from un-differentiated space to the plurality of points except as a sequence or a story. Time enters the discussion of space as a recuperative device, functioning like the totalizing moment of the mathematical sublime.[60] The fall back into representative thinking takes us back to Kant who, in his aesthetics of the sublime, gives an outline of the process by which temporal sense is made out of a spatial sign.

> Measurement of a space (as apprehension) is at the same time a description of it, and so an objective movement in the imagination and a progression. On the other hand, the comprehension of the manifold in the unity, not of thought, but of intuition, and consequently in the comprehension of the successively apprehended parts at one glance, is a retrogression that removes the time-condition in the progression of the imagination, and renders *co-existence* intuitable. Therefore, since the time-series is a condition of the internal sense and of an intuition, it is a subjective movement of the imagination by which it does violence to the internal sense—a violence which must be proportionately more striking the greater the quantum which the imagination comprehends in one intuition. The effort, therefore, to receive in a single intuition a measure of magnitudes which it takes an appreciable time to apprehend is a mode of representation which, subjectively considered, is counter-purposive [*zweckwidrig*], but objectively is requisite for the estimation of magnitude, and is consequently purposive [*zweckmäßig*].[61]

If that is how the reader is to get out of China and into India (and on into world history), the reader must perform that transition from within China, by a necessary and final anticipation: so farewell to the difference between China and India. The last thing we should expect from this passage and its reading is an *a priori* proof of the possibility of moving historically about and out of the East; it would be truer to say that the relation between the means of transition offered here and its realization through reading is, as Kant puts it, an imaginative violence.[62]

"We cannot conceive of a literal sublime."[63] Maybe not, but inconceivability is precisely the chosen territory of the sublime. The seemingly self-sufficient pattern of reason represented by a figure of opposition (Nature) and its dismantling through reconciliation (Spirit) generates forms of resistance beyond that pattern's control. The transition from space to time is just such a form of resistance (violence). Either it is accomplished by smuggling temporal categories into the understanding of space, making the difference between the two unsustainable and eliminating the need for (or the possibility of) a transition, or else the transition never happens, and the act of measuring, carried out eternally on a boundless and indifferent space (China), remains decidedly counter-final. In either case Nature declines the honor of being nature, of being an other for spirit, and the recognition plot leaps to its conclusion before it has been quite set up. The history of the East as it is set up for dialectics is a little too strong for dialectics to handle. Perhaps nature is really nature after all—not just temporarily so. The consequences should be momentous. Whether we read it as history, logic, philosophy of nature, or psychology, the unity of the Hegelian *Encyclopedia* depends on spirit's being able to recognize that which is (*das Seiende*) as its own (*das Seinige*) or, to be more precise, as "its own other" (*das Andere seiner selbst*).[64] What happens if the recognition falters? A dozen contemporary philosophies of alterity are designed to answer that question. The construction of Hegel's China, however, leads us to ask: What if the recognition never fails? What if the philosophy of identity depended on recognition's seeming to fail?

REPETITION: "PROSA"

> The devil is . . . a most prosaic person.
> —Hegel, *Ästhetik*[65]

Another mystery of the East—artistic this time, not natural—is the word "prose."

To be exiled from history is to be exiled from beauty; that is the conclusion to which a joint reading of Hegel's *Aesthetics* and *Philosophy of History* leads. Just as the history of Oriental peoples is not really history, so their art is more precisely described as a *Vorkunst* ("pre-art"), a setting forth of the antinomies that the Greeks will one day reconcile in the form of classical art.[66] Hegel discusses almost no Chinese artifacts in the *Aesthetics* itself,[67] but in the

China chapter of the *Philosophy of History*, he uses one aesthetic category again and again to describe objects (moral codes, philosophies, family structures, modes of government) that are by no means self-evidently works of art. The Chinese "constitution, if one may speak of such a thing," makes for "an empire . . . that is moralistic and at the same time absolutely prosaic"; the Chinese state, that "prosaic empire," rests on "prosaic understanding," and so forth.[68] The "prosaic basis of their outlook" renders the Chinese historians incapable of writing epic and capable only of transcribing "a prosaically regulated historical reality."[69]

Hegel's use of "prosaic" as a qualifier for the Chinese way of life dates to his first cycle of lectures on world history, in 1822.[70] As far back as we have evidence, "prose" is part of Hegel's characterization of China. What explains the connivance of history and aesthetics that the word seems to suggest? A standard Hegelian answer is given in the introduction to the *Philosophy of History*, which puts forth religion, art, and philosophy as three forms of "the unification of subjective and objective in the spirit." Another way of saying this is that Professor Hegel of Berlin always wrote the same book (or rewrote it out of his Jena manuscripts) and the same story no matter what it was about. (Earlier, Hegel had assigned each of the three forms a period of optimum development in history; the present texts of the history lectures allude to this aim, but indistinctly.)[71]

In their broad outlines, Hegel's *Aesthetics* and *Philosophy of History* are comparable to the point of monotony. As an instance of the parallelism of Hegel's history and aesthetics, or of their mutual translatability, one thinks immediately of Egypt with its hieroglyphs, pyramids, and sphinxes doing double duty as symbols of the symbol and of prehistorical humanity's inability to grasp its own essence.[72] And he quite explicitly makes the passage from Egypt to Greece, in the *Aesthetics*, into the historical type of the passage from symbol to "free, self-sufficient meaning—not a meaning belonging to something else, but that which means and expresses itself."[73] The movement from symbolic to classical art, or from the inadequate symbol to the self-sufficient meaning, takes place (in this interdisciplinary chronology) at the same time as the transition from prehistory to history. But on the subject of China the communication between aesthetics and history becomes one-sided; the parallelism between the two books breaks off, and seemingly in the *Aesthetics'* favor. It is as if aesthetics had supplied the terms needed to describe what history—or the quasi history of the East—could not.

Good prose, said Coleridge, is "the proper words in their proper places."[74] By this definition Hegel's use of "prosaic" to qualify Chinese society is by no means good prose. It is the wrong word in the wrong place. For "prose," no less than "history," emerges from the historical process. Oddly and most unprosaically, it has (like history itself) two distinct birthplaces. It is with Israel's leave-taking from mere nature that "a genuinely *historical* outlook first presents itself—prose that can be understood as objective prose, and yet as poetry too."[75] An epoch in aesthetics no less than in history, the prose of Israel is the counterpart of the sublime, a negative moment to which Hegel gives much attention in the *Philosophy of History*, the *Aesthetics*, and the *Philosophy of Religion*.[76] Yet a Chinese sublime would seem unthinkable. A history that speaks of Chinese prose is going a little too fast.

The other prose, Greek prose, begins, for the *Aesthetics*, with Aesop, who saw men and animals "with prosaic eyes. . . . Prose begins in the slave, and this whole genre is therefore prosaic."[77] Inferior, hybrid art forms such as fable, proverb, and parable belong to the "pre-art [*Vorkunst*] of the symbolic, as they are generally imperfect and a mere searching after true art."[78] Greek prose is accordingly less a period or genre than a permanently open possibility of decline. Another Greek lapse into prose, this one more durable, occurs with the disintegration of the old gods and the failure of the Olympian "art-religion."[79] Greece echoes Israel's turn to prose, and that puts an end to classical art.

The prose of Israel negates and concludes the "symbolic" period of art history. Greek art, classical art, dissolves the symbolic too, but in another way: where symbolic art only "sought" its adequate expression, classical art "finds" and exemplifies it.[80] Greek art solves the aesthetic problem from within aesthetics; the Jewish sublime

ought by rights to have broken out of aesthetics and keeps its place
there only as the highest expression of "inexpressibility topoi."[81] As
two ways of departing from the symbolic, Greece and Israel together bar aesthetics from following a single historical path. The
order of topics followed in the *Aesthetics* shows the obstacle most
clearly: after the confused materiality of Indian and Egyptian art
comes the heading "Symbolics of Sublimity," which implies that
Hegel conceives of the Jewish sublime as a form of the symbol
(which it negates). The next chapter ("The Conscious Symbolism
of the Comparative Art Form") leads into Greek prose, without,
however, having discussed classical art, whose decadence that prose
represents. "Symbolic art," then, as a category, binds together
developments whose histories diverge and whose logical identities
depend on a relation to what is not symbolic. And "prose," which
enters the *Aesthetics* only as the counter to the properly symbolic
and the properly post-symbolic (classical) forms of art, inherits
something of those categories' patchwork construction.

Is this the intended gloss on China via the categories of the
aesthetic? If it is, it implies a thorough downgrading of the *Aesthetics*' historical scaffolding—no great loss in itself—and repeats, in
a slightly different register, the anachronism and imposition of
terms by which Hegel's Oriental history has to be written. The
Chinese may have produced no works of art, but we can interpret
them—the Chinese—as works of art. Critics of Hegelian history
often speak as if they were Kantian aestheticians, deploring the
teleological interest it takes in its objects: here they may catch him
poaching on the aesthetic's home ground.[82]

"Prose begins in the slave." With this cross-reference, the figure
of speech—"China has a *prosaic* constitution"—that purported to
clarify a social condition with words borrowed from aesthetics now
refers us to society again, but with a difference: it equates the whole
of Chinese society with one position in a single social relation. One
is not a slave per se, as a tree is a tree or a crystal a crystal; one is the
slave of somebody. (Aristotle, in *Categories* 7a31–b10, cites "master
and slave" as the type case of "relation.") Similarly, prose, in the
Aesthetics, appears only as an infirmity of other categories; it has no
existence or territory of its own, save, perhaps, that granted by

aberrant phrasings such as "prosaic empire." What is the relation that can explain prose? Of whom or what is prose the slave?

The enslaved condition of Israel's prose seems at first to differ in kind from that of Greece, and to be better accounted for. Jewish prose is the slave of the Jewish sublime. The sublime expresses inexpressibility: it divides the truly sublime from whatever else is considered great (nature, space, time, false gods, etc.) and casts the latter down as prose, "de-divinified and prosaic."[83] For this reason, prose has a constitutive function as regards the sublime. Lordliness, as readers of the *Phenomenology of Spirit* know, is largely a matter of the objects one has the privilege of negating.[84] Mastery, like slavery, has no per se.

It is in his Greek mode that Hegel speaks the language of the master.[85] His abuse of Greek prose is all the more violent because its prosiness has no truly sublime counterpart. It is the slave of the nobler artistic genres, of the Olympian "art-religion"; and that religion is doomed to become prosy too, identical with its slave. The Jews have a better economy of religious representation, greater foresight: they foretell and take upon themselves as theory what the Greeks find happening to them from outside as an event, the failure of any theology based on the model of relation. Prose is the best protection against the death of the gods.[86]

"Prose" is, then, a uniquely summarizing figure. It names the Chinese constitution as history and nature at once, not to mention non-history and non-nature. But the parallelism it suggests between history and aesthetics links both fields at their weakest points. If the thematics of nature put the East in a framework of ignorance overcome by knowledge, a victory for relation, that of prose does just the opposite: the relation it institutes is a balance of forces and a division that must be maintained at all costs—the waning of the Greek artistic spirit only prompts Hegel to shriller denunciations of prose. Hegel's *Aesthetics* does not coexist with its anti-aesthetic as cheerfully as does the *Aesthetics of Ugliness* of Hegel's student, Karl Rosenkranz.[87]

The sublime of Abraham, Jacob, and Moses issues in "das Gesetz" (the Law), and the *Aesthetics*, on a far less imposing scale, follows suit.[88] Prose, in the *Aesthetics*, is always subject to one or another form of the law (typically, the law of classical or of sublime art), without ever becoming a law unto itself. No section of the *Aesthetics* defines prose. As a symptom of the absence of true art, it leads the parasitical life of the adjective; if it were to attempt to set itself up as an independent category, a subject, it could aspire only to the shadowy and ultra-prosaic standing of the "allegorical being," that "grammatical subject."[89] So the aesthetic metaphor that enlivens the most "numbing" chapters of political history—China, the Empire of the Prosaic—leads straight into the most transparently politicized bits of aesthetic doctrine. It bounces back to its starting point, which makes for an exceptionally flat, or prosaic, metaphor. (Politics is—here a pause—political.) Aesthetics per se vanishes in and through the telling, both as a field of inquiry and as a system of value. The outcome of the allusion to "prose" only underlines the unlikelihood of political mediation's ever assuming a reconciliatory, relational, or (in Hegel's terms) symbolic character. A "prosaic constitution" is hardly exceptional, as constitutions go.

Measure

The doctrine of space and time ended with a perpetually suspended identification, and the doctrine of "prose" circles round on itself: we learn more each time about the process whereby the Hegelian Orient comes to expressible form, but always find the "Orient" itself turning hollow. It is as if our dictionary contained all the metaphorical meanings, but none of the literal ones—none of the truly prosaic ones—in Hegel's Oriental vocabulary. A direct approach through the letter may have better chances of success.

Chinese artworks seem to have had little effect on Hegel, but he has much to say about Chinese semiology: indeed Hegel's writings on the Chinese character in the *Encyclopedia* could do service as the China chapter missing from the *Aesthetics*.[90] Or, what is much the same thing: the second, historical part of the *Aesthetics* lets itself be read as an expanded version of the *Encyclopedia*'s paragraphs on "theoretical mind" (paras. 445–68). Greek art, since it "means itself and refers to itself," can be paired off with thinking, "das Denken," and so stands on the far side of the section on memory, language, and signs. The Egyptian chapters of the *Aesthetics* and *Philosophy of History* are condensed, in the *Encyclopedia*, into a few lines on the (traditional) distinction between sign and symbol, to which is added: "Once the intelligence has marked out something with a sign, it has thereby dispensed with the content of that intuition. . . . Intelligence that *designates* shows a greater freedom and mastery [*Willkür und Herrschaft*] in its use of intuition than does [intelligence] that symbolizes."[91]

If the sphinxes, burial practices, animal cult, riddles, and other hybrid expressions of the Egyptian spirit symbolize the inadequacy of the mind that expresses itself through the symbol, the freedom and mastery attained through the sign have their counterpart in the "symbolics of sublimity": "in the Jewish view of things and in their sacred poetry."[92] The step from the symbol to the sign and to the aesthetics of the sublime is also, perforce, a transition from hieroglyphics (Egyptian, but presumably Chinese as well) to alphabetic script. No other script is so purely script as the alphabet, and a script that, like the Egyptian, mixes signs with symbols cannot possibly convey the iconoclastic, antisymbolic character of the theological sublime. A hieroglyphic language requires a "previous analysis of mental representations [*Vorstellungen*]," whereas the sublime is predicated on the impossibility of adequate representing. (Translated into pictograms, "Thou shalt not make unto thee any graven images" must lose a great deal—unless it suddenly rebounds into an unheard-of sublimity.) Insofar as the Chinese language is, for Hegel, a pictorial language of representations, it can never be sublime or participate in the intelligence of the sign. Its prose, then, has to be of the Aesopian kind, repeating "only given, previously discovered materials," a "deficiency of form" inseparable from its "deficiency of content."[93] From Chinese writing the capacities of Chinese art can be deduced: a semiology in good working order can always stand in for an aesthetics.

Semiology restates some of the teachings of aesthetics, but not blindly or literally. One of the positions it repeats is that of the constitution of prose. The sign, like the sublime, is all about mastery (*Herrschaft*). It confers mastery over its contents for the simple reason that the institution of the sign is an example of mastery. The sign appropriates an external representation and "demotes" (*setzt herab*) it to the task of "serving" (*dienen*) that which is to be signified. If, in the religion of the sublime, the sign is the slave of the ineffable, within semiology the signifier is the slave of the sign. Among the advantages of alphabetic writing, not the least is the narrow margin of independence it gives to its letter.[94]

The fact that the Jewish poets were true *vates*, and that their aesthetic iconoclasm was not just aesthetic—indeed theirs is for Hegel nothing less than an iconoclasm *of* the aesthetic—makes it seem as if the relation among artistic forms, the capacity to make signs, and religious forms cannot be a loose and casual one.[95] And indeed at least the historical part of the *Lectures on the Philosophy of Religion* seems to have been constructed out of the same indispensable notebooks that produced the *Aesthetics* and *Philosophy of History*. India cultivates a fantastic mythology; Egypt is once again the bondage of spirit; Israel maintains the "religion of sublimity" and Greece the "religion of beauty," each heading subtended by the same examples as in the other two lecture volumes.[96] As for the decay of art, Roman religion is "prosaic," its principle that of "outer purposiveness," and a manuscript page that begins by noting the "negative circumstances" that account for such "prose" could almost have been a sketch for the China chapter of the *History*.[97]

China has its religion, or its religions, but Hegel's emphases and analyses of it change from year to year. What Hegel has to say about it at first is easy to harmonize with the evolutionary schemes—historical, aesthetic, and semiological—in which China always furnishes a beginning to be improved on. Chinese religion is sorcery: self-interested, superstitious, empirical, a means of acquiring power over nature, "the first, rawest, and simplest form of religion."[98] But from 1827 on (as a result of Hegel's contacts with the French sinologist Abel Rémusat, according to Hulin),[99] a new term creeps in. Now Taoism represents magic, and the state reli-

gion of Confucianism detaches itself to take on the title of the
"religion of measure."[100]

What kind of religion is this? In China, "Substance is known as
measure," a substance that the emperor, giver of measures, actual-
izes. Measure itself, law or Tao, is identified as "determinations,
figurations—not abstract being or abstract Substance, but figurations of Substance, all of which could have been expressed more
abstractly" if the Chinese had felt more of a philosophical vocation.
Just to list these "fixed, general determinations," "wholly simple
categories," suggests the shortcomings of a "religion of measure."
They are vehicles for the understanding that have somehow been
promoted to the status of "that which exists in and for itself."[101]
Confucianism overrates the means of cognition to the point of
letting the objects of cognition disappear. The big *Logic* of 1812 has
strong words for this kind of error.

> A measure [*Maß*], taken as a standard in the usual meaning of the
> word, is a quantum that is arbitrarily [*willkürlich*] assumed as the
> *intrinsically determinate* unit relative to an external number. . . . It is
> therefore foolish [*töricht*] to speak of a natural *measure* of things. . . .
> The interest and significance of an absolute measure is merely that of
> something *common* [*Gemeinschaftlich*, social]; and such a measure is a
> universal, not of itself but only by agreement.[102]

The measure is a sign, arbitrary in its origin, social in its currency,
and external to what it measures: it is "foolish" to think it natural.
Its only signifying property is that of having been posited. And like
a true sign, it is expressible only through another thing of the same
order—as a certain measure of another measure.[103]

The definitions of "measure" and of the "religion of measure"
reenact the very conditions that caused the breakdown of Hegel's
identification of the East with nature, pre-history or atemporal
space. A "religion of measure" is, on Hegel's account, foolish. By
glorifying the "figurations of substance" as if they were the substance itself, the measure-worshipper brings to a premature end the
work of the Hegelian encyclopedia, the identity of nature and
spirit. For the fool, recognition never has a chance of failing.

Hegel's historical narrative would situate the East in an aesthetics and semiology of the "symbolic" (to use the *Asthetics'* term), the controlling principle of which is the dominance of signifying form over signified content.[104] In the measure, however, no such disproportion or "unmeasuredness" (*Unangemessenheit*) can be discerned, simply because the measure, if it is a signifier, corresponds to no prior thing or signified. "No one can say or understand mentally what an inch is, or a foot," as Leibniz puts it. If it refuses translation, it is not because it has some content that no other form is adequate to express, but rather because with it the difference of form and content simply fails to occur. The measure does not translate because it itself is nothing but a (potential) figure of translation.

It remains to be shown that the Chinese understand the measure as "natural." Perhaps their folly goes in another direction. The worship of "measure," the religion of the signifier, would be a cult of some prose beyond prose—especially if one knows, as Hegel's Chinese must, that the existing measure can be "destroyed" (*zerstört*) at any time (by the emperor) and replaced by a new one. But it would also be a cult of the performative utterance. The choice of a measure is, if anything is, a pure performative interpretable only by reference to earlier performatives, a performative from which the constative aspects have dropped out. The definition of the foot refers to the inch, the inch to the grain, the grain to the dimensions of the *huang-chung* pitch pipe, and the *huang-chung*, in the end, to the positing power of the prince.[105] The cult of measure singles out for honor the signifier that is slave (or bone) to the sign; the sign, in turn, is slave to the spirit revealed in the sublime or the beautiful—a thrice-distilled residue of prose.

The semiology of religion would be hard put to fit this religion into its picture of regular progress from substance to symbol to sign. The "religion of measure" may look like a thin description of the categories of reason, but it certainly cannot belong where Hegel puts it, immediately after magic in the "Forms of Natural Religion." That would be "foolish." No one should have to spend time establishing, for the history of religions, that the Chinese are not the Jews; yet that is exactly the task that this new typology of religions of the sign sets before us, with no assurance as to how it will all turn out. The map (that convenient chart for laying out world history) refuses to stay open of itself. It curls up and can be read only in thin latitudinal segments.

Political history, too, finds in Hegel's last formulation of the Chinese problem a contribution to its own, rather too well-known central problem. "The Orient knew and knows only that *One* [namely the despot] is free; the Greek and Roman world, that *Some* are free; the Germanic world knows that *All* are free."[106] The freedom to choose measures is a total, if empty, freedom: any measure will do, just so long as there is a measure. What Saussure will later name "the immutability and the mutability of the sign" is written into the constitution of the Chinese national church. "The maintenance of the laws [e.g., those of the common measure] is the business of the emperor. . . . Only the emperor shows honor to the law: his subjects hold him in honor as the one who handles the laws."[107] If the emperor's rule is arbitrary, it is so only because there is no reasonable or natural way to posit the prosaic laws of common measure. The definitions of freedom, necessity, and arbitrariness that obtain for the Chinese constitution are, like those that apply to the sign, not historical but categorical. (Hegel's history of China is therefore the true ancestor of Barthes' *Empire of Signs*, that semiological Utopia where the sign is never opposed to its substance or the superficiality of form to the depth of meaning—the only difference being that Hegel is an unhappy tourist and Barthes a delighted one.)

History may not recognize itself in this formal freedom because the "religion of measure," in its utter self-adequacy, resembles nothing so much as the Hegelian-derived program for the posthistorical.[108] Could this account for the immobility of Chinese "unhistorical history"? The Chinese have a semiology of the symbol and a religion of the sign (thus a semiology far richer than anything it might want to express). This places them exactly opposite Hegel, who thought the sign "a great thing" (*etwas Großes*) but held out for Christianity to supersede in symbolic reconciliation the transcendence declared by Israel. The Chinese must be romantics of a sort, then, and probably ironists too. Theirs, after all, is the one religion that can never be demystified. The stage is set for a concert of recognitions and crossed signals like that in Act IV of Lessing's *Nathan der Weise*,[109] but we will delay it—so that world history may occur. A few more of these coincidences, and world history may find itself turning into space again, an "order of coexistences,"[110] the very "empire of space." Whether this empire is the same old China, or China all over again, is precisely what the spatiality of the empire makes it impossible to say.

Whatever happened to Hegelian "linearity"? The forward movement (*prorsa oratio*)[111] of history keeps leaping ahead of itself, saying two things at the same time, undoing its recognition plots by enacting them backward or all at once: making, in a prose medium, the turns and returns of verse. Hegel, as historian, ought to write in prose, but he succeeds no better at that than at being literal. The reason for both frustrations is the same, the lack of a language in which to name China, univocally, both as itself and as something that can be brought into relation with history. Hegel's China is a realm of indifference that has to be understood in its difference from non-indifference (a difference that history has to consolidate before it can pronounce on it).[112] (The difficulty Hegel faces is thus the same as that faced by the authors discussed in Chapter 1.) The historian of Asia speaks categorically, but the writing of Asiatic history shows, behind every category, an allegory. Content goes one way, language another.

The subplot of Hegelian world history could be summed up with the Formalist watchword: "thematization of the device."[113] And the devices of Hegel's history writing are (again in keeping with the Formalist program) no mere devices. "Prose," "space," "the slave," "the signifier," "China," even "the language of history writing," all have it in common to be the indispensable foundation—ground of possibility as well as principle of differentiation—of nobler, more expressive structures. The East is typical rather than exceptional in this. All of Hegel's determinations of the Orient are necessary figures, figures that establish, without participating in, the possibility of the writing of history. Yet the possibility they establish is the language in which Part I is simply the whole of history: "the formation of the *bones*, through which the organism grants itself a ground to stand on." To uncover this fact, however, is not to undo the edifice of speculative reason but rather to complete it: at the far end of a reading that takes the slave or the signifier for its guide, content, or other, resolves into method, or self. What appeared at first as an obstacle to the *theory* of history—the fact that the laws of historical development so closely resemble the rules of history writing—now comes to fruition as a (surely prosaic) parody of absolute spirit.

Read for its explicit themes and representations, the China of Hegel's *Philosophy of History* resembles Longobardi's. But read from its seamy side—namely, the side from which the work is done— Hegel's work narrates, as do the *Mao Odes*, the aesthetic production of a history. It shows a history occurring before history, where it should not, by definition, occur: it shows the Letter turning into the Law, and the Law imitating the Spirit. (Indeed, the verbs of this last sentence mislead, for it is part of the thematic reversal that these developments should not require unfolding in time. The Law and the Spirit are already there in the Letter, or in the religious form taken by the Letter, that is, the Measure.)

The flaw of hieroglyphic reading (the fact that the representations kept asking to be looked at for themselves, impeding the immediate progress through the sign to the idea) answers to a worry most germane to historical writing: that its understanding will necessarily take an aesthetic form. What need, then, to look ahead to history as the fulfillment of the figures?

§ 6 Conclusion:
Comparative Comparative Literature

The transfer—from the Empire of China to the
empire of oneself—is constant.
　　—Segalen

"You know the story about the man who thought
he held the princess of China in a bottle. Delusion,
of course. He was cured. But as soon as he was no
longer mad, he became stupid."
　　—Proust, *Le côté de Guermantes*
　　(Charlus speaking)

If what Hegel, Leibniz, Ricci, and the compilers of the *Book of Odes* did is comparative literature—and I would suggest that that is exactly what they did—then it looks as if comparative literature can only with difficulty unify its field. The unification of the field comes at a price—a remarkably constant price, considering the variety of the means employed.

Leibniz's peaceable solution to the conflict of Chinese philosophy and Catholic theology is symbolic of the sacrifices comparative reading demands. In Leibniz's "Letter on the Natural Theology of the Chinese," mutual translatability between the two idioms is assured, but only after the little word "is" has been stripped of its meaning. Once the being has been taken out of being, there is not much left for ontologists to disagree about.

Leibniz's gesture is a profligate one; elsewhere we see the same results achieved at less expense, simply because they are inherent to comparative reading. For example, the elegant and economical formula whereby the previously vague relations of the literatures of China and Europe crystallized around the familiar pairing metaphor-metonymy proved to repose on incomparables as soon as we looked into metonymy's defining characteristics. The reading of Chinese figurality that undeniably occurred through the invocation of metonymy did so at the expense of all comparison, since it necessitated presupposing a single language and a single set of categories common to the texts being compared, whereas the point of the comparison lay in forcing the reader to do without those assumptions. Comparative literature is not just a Noah's Ark; it is also a sinking raft whose passengers can never be sure what must be tossed overboard next.

The strategy of the Great Preface transferred to poetry the authority of a moral code: a situation in which poetry became a mere local department of ritual but gained, in the process, ritual's necessary independence from nature. Ritual is its own beginning and standard, and the poems, as read, repeatedly enact the qualitative difference between a social act or a poem without a base in ritual and the same act or poem interpreted through ritual. Thereupon the tool's relation to nature becomes the pattern for the artwork's (and also for the interpreter's relation to the text), and the sage comes forth as the final referent, as well as the best pupil, of the correctly interpreted poem. But for interpretation this means that no text explains itself and, likewise, that no moral reader reads without his or her reading being grounded in the "previous reasons" of the sages. Only the sage can be an autonomous reader.

The annotators of the classical *Book of Odes* managed to gather into the fold of their interpretative model all the poems of the collection, even the most wayward, but in the process they found themselves trading the expressive poetics of the earlier musical tradition for a new model that took irony as its starting point. The new model emerged out of a tension between interpretative principle and examples, one of the hallmarks of comparative reading. As I see it, comparison, in the reading of the *Odes* exemplified by the Great Preface, takes the form of a translation internal to aesthetic doctrine, the move from a weak form of mimesis to a strong or prescriptive one. In the end the strong form leaves nothing for the weak form to do—even the most reverential reading of the *Odes* has to be cast in the heroic moral mold. In their concern to make the *Odes* a true classic (*ching*), the annotators sacrificed the individual poems of the collection to their obsession, as more temperate readers since Chu Hsi have reminded us. The gain and loss are, I would hold, roughly comparable to Leibniz's disinvestment in the word "is." Each of the *Odes* loses its presumable prior horizon of meaning when it is inscribed within a new theory of mimesis, rather as the seemingly illimitable reference-field of the word "is" becomes, in Leibniz's argument, a merely provincial boundary.

The elevation of the work of art to exemplary status and the necessary reorganization of aesthetic attitudes that follows from it are tasks far too big for any single poem to complete, and one after another the *Odes* were put to use and used up. This has often been described as a denial of the autonomy of literature from politics, but the story can be told in more than one way. The independence of politics from literature, in the light of the legends about the Duke of Chou's use of poetic speech, seems no less precarious. There, too, the devices of comparison—of conceiving government *as* the prolongation of a poetic program—are no doubt ambitiously at work. In any case, this program derives, like the classic *Book of Odes* as a whole, from the decision to endow poetic language with performative force.

The artwork thus holds a peculiar position for the comparative readers we have been investigating. Each episode in the present history shows the work's value going up a step, and each promotion is a refiguring of the questions readers ask of literature. The questions asked by this book are no exception. "Can we speak of a Chinese form of allegory?" "Are tropes independent of themes?" "What does the Mao tradition tell us about the *Odes*?" "Is the interpretative tradition of the *Book of Odes* a reliable guide to Chinese poetics generally?" "What is the sense of bringing China into comparative studies?" The question comparative reading answers is never quite the same as the question asked.

For Hegel the comparative problem lay in the phrase "world history"; for although China is quite clearly part of the world, he was not prepared to give it a place in history. Still, history has to describe it, and in describing China with bits of figurative language whose proper sense is to be sought elsewhere, history finds itself describing itself as China. The perspective gained at that point seems to be one from which the initial subject, history, is absent. The artwork—the narrative devices of history writing or China itself—has taken its place. By what right does art answer the question asked of history? The question—"What is China for history"?—could be addressed only to art, on Hegel's own showing. Aesthetics is the limit-function of history just as allegory is that of category. History writing has only to take up the history of non-history—which is also, immediately, the history of the making of history—to find itself declaiming, like the Duke of Chou, a script drafted by the theorists of poetic language.

Of all the translations enumerated here, that one, the translation of the Chinese aesthetic into an aesthetic China, may be the most forced—but it is also, given the way "force" comes to inhabit the readings we pursue here, the most necessary. For comparative reading is a force: it cannot leave things as they are.

Ode 237, "Mien," narrates the construction of the Chou capital.

> They loaded the earth: *jeng-jeng*!
> They piled it up: *hung-hung*!
> They beat it hard: *teng-teng*!
> They scraped it even: *p'ing-p'ing*!
> A hundred walls rose together;
> The drummers fell behind.

The drums "fell behind" the pace of the work they were there to regulate—a hyperbolic figure for the Chou population's eagerness to have a "celestial city," to be sure, but also a model for the central problem of this book. In an aesthetics of exemplarity, the mimesis of nature and action by art matters less than the expectation that nature and action will come to imitate the patterns laid down for them by the artwork. Works like the classically interpreted *Odes* reverse the so often assumed priority of the thing represented (nature, being, the *Odes'* real meaning, what happened in history) over its representation (art, language, commentary, history writing). But, when, in the mimesis of mimesis, the thing represented takes on the qualities of the representation and even exceeds it in those qualities, aesthetic patterning supersedes its own work and takes up the secondary position once again, falling behind to minister to a reality now of an age to rule.

Reference Matter

Notes

For complete author names, titles, and publication data for the works cited here in short form, see the Bibliography, pp. 249–81. For the abbreviations used here, see the list on pp. xv–xvi.

Introduction

EPIGRAPH: Benjamin, "Unbekannte Anekdoten von Kant," *Gesammelte Schriften*, 4: 809.

1. I am happy to find that the word *problem*, at the same time as it translates the Latin *pro-ject*, has in Greek the connotation of a limit: "*problēma (pro-ballō)*, anything thrown forward or projecting: *pontou problēma halikyston* (Sophocles), 'sea-washed promontory' . . . 2. hindrance, obstacle . . . II. anything put before one as a defense, bulwark, barrier . . . IV. task, business . . . 2. problem in Geometry, etc." (LSJ, *s.v.*).

2. Goethe, "Allgemeines," *West-Östlicher Divan*, p. 154.

3. Ibid., "Warnung," p. 174. "Metaphor" translates *Gleichnis*, which can also be rendered as "parable."

4. Todorov, "Comprendre une culture," p. 10.

5. Durkheim, *Les Formes élémentaires*, pp. 3, 65.

6. I am grateful to Allan Stoekl for suggesting a family resemblance between the theory of "totem" as identity-marker of the group and the educational policies of the Third Republic.

7. Challenges to constitutional secularism have tried to establish just such a contradiction. The sponsor of Louisiana's Creationism Act argued that the Supreme Court had previously given "secular humanism" the

status—and thus, by implication, the legal disabilities—of a religion (quoted, Justice Scalia in *Edwards* v. *Aguillard,* 482 U.S. 578 [1987], p. 624).

8. For some recent views, see Geertz, "Anti Anti-Relativism"; Clifford and Marcus, *Writing Culture*; Marcus and Fischer, *Anthropology as Cultural Critique.* Inasmuch as one consequence of relativizing studies has been, precisely, to focus argument on the cultural specificity of the European "self," what Clifford, Marcus, and Fischer hail as a self-conscious, overtly autobiographical, and subjective turn in anthropological writing may represent the death of epistemological relativism as a workable "totem."

9. Gayatri Spivak ("Translator's Preface," p. lxxxii) points out an instance of this problem—particularizing statements that can be read as "almost a renewed ethnocentrism"—occurring in the very passages of *Of Grammatology* where Derrida is concerned to show the bounded nature of the European understanding of the "East." Chang Han-liang takes a more self-assured tack in "Te-hsi-ta, shu-hsieh yü Chung-wen" (Derrida, writing, and the Chinese language).

10. Seznec, *Survival of the Pagan Gods,* pp. 319–23; Grafton, "Renaissance Readers." For the sense of the gesture that declares a "break," see Chapter 5 below.

11. Graham, " 'Being' in Classical Chinese," p. 1. The substance of this 1967 article is drawn from Graham's " 'Being' in Western Philosophy Compared with *Shih/Fei* and *Yu/Wu* in Chinese Philosophy" (1959), written at roughly the same time as Benveniste's well-known "Catégories de pensée et catégories de langue" (*Problèmes,* I, pp. 63–74).

12. *Evideor,* a related verb meaning "to appear completely or plainly," stresses the visible thing's coming "out" into common view. For there to be *evidentia,* the thing observed must stand out, and there must be a public space to observe it in. Quintilian cites the Greek *enargeia* ("distinct perception," "vivid description") as an equivalent to *evidentia* (*Institutio* IV. 2. 63).

13. See LSJ, *exō, exōterikos,* and compounds.

14. Barthes, *L'Empire des signes,* pp. 43, 83, 106, 135; Geertz, *Interpretation of Cultures,* esp. pp. 83, 386, 400.

15. Graham, *Disputers of the Tao,* p. 428.

16. Kant, *Critique of Judgment,* paras. 2, 16.

17. Aristotle, *Metaphysics,* Book IV, opening (trans. Tredennick).

18. On this expectation, see Quine, *Word and Object,* pp. 73–79; and idem, "Two Dogmas of Empiricism," *Logical Point of View,* pp. 20–46.

19. On "meta-language" and "object-language," see Tarski, "Semantic Conception of Truth," esp. pp. 349–52.

20. Rorty, "Philosophy as a Kind of Writing," *Consequences of Pragmatism*, pp. 90–109. The word "kind" makes the most trouble for Rorty's proposal to "think of truth horizontally."

21. The comparative genus is thus irreducibly subject to what Uriel Weinreich calls, in another context, the law of "double interference." "When a lay unilingual hears his language spoken with a foreign 'accent,' his perception and interpretation *of the accent is itself* subject to the interference of his native phonic system" (*Languages in Contact*, p. 21; my italics).

Chapter 1

EPIGRAPH: "There are strong perfumes for which all matter / is porous." Baudelaire, *Oeuvres complètes*, 1: 47–48.

1. The following argument is greatly indebted to Pauline Yu's work, the fullest presentation in English to date of the important question signaled in its title. Subsequent references in this chapter to *Reading of Imagery* are given in the text.

2. Trans. David Hawkes, *Songs of the South*, p. 69; cited in Pauline Yu, *Reading of Imagery*, p. 89.

3. Richards, *Mencius on the Mind*, pp. 114–16.

4. Wordsworth, *The Prelude*, V. 407.

5. Compare William Empson's chapter on Lévy-Bruhl's theory that "savages" take their own figures of speech literally ("The Primitive Mind," *Structure of Complex Words*, pp. 375–90). Since "white mythology" was Anatole France's elegant rephrasing of "dead metaphor" (see Derrida, "La Mythologie blanche," *Marges*, p. 253), this may be the place to remind the reader that the story frequently told about "dead metaphors" exemplifies the relative meaning of "literal." To resurrect a dead metaphor is to call on an earlier literal sense in light of which the present and customary literal sense is shown to be derived or figurative.

6. Its volatility is due to the contestability of both its intension and its extension (its distinguishing characteristics and the range of its instances) a debate that echoes the uneasy relationship between allegorical technique and the argumentative structure of exemplarity. For two vividly contrasting approaches to the place of exempla in allegorical writings, see Benjamin, *Ursprung des deutschen Trauerspiels*, in *Gesammelte Schriften*, 1: 350, 368–69; and de Man, *Blindness and Insight*, p. 207. Discrepancies

such as these abound in accounts of allegory; the failure of critics to agree on what would be meant by "Chinese allegory," if it existed, is not wholly to be blamed on the difficulties of cultural mediation between East and West.

7. Plaks, *Archetype and Allegory*, p. 108; Yeh, "Metaphor and *Bi*," p. 252. Masao Miyoshi puts this more militantly: "The need to de-universalize and particularize the Western norm remains foremost on our new critical agenda" ("Against the Native Grain," p. 531).

8. "The Chinese possess no national epic" (Hegel, *Vorlesungen über die Ästhetik*, 3 [*W*, 8: 396]). See, as modern handlings of this question, Dembo, *Confucian Odes of Ezra Pound*, pp. 91–95; Tōkei, *Naissance de l'élégie chinoise*, pp. 15, 202–3; and C. H. Wang, *From Ritual to Allegory*, pp. 53–72.

9. On the nature of this identification, and for a hint about the hyperbolic element in comparative reading, see Aristotle, *Poetics* 1448b15–17 on pictures. "The observers [*theōrountas*] have an opportunity to learn and to make identifying statements [*syllogizesthai*] about every detail, as for instance by saying: 'this one is so-and-so.'" Compare 1459a7–8: "The way to make good metaphors is to observe [*theōrein*] the sameness [*to homoion*] [in things]." The meaning of *theōrein*, the verb common to these two passages, ranges from "perceive" to "speculate." "Theōrein ti pros ti" means "to compare one thing with another." Artemidoros (*Oneirokritika* 4.1) defines *theōrēmatikoi* dreams as dreams in which future events are seen for themselves, in contrast to *allēgorikoi* ones, those which show the future in a rebus (LSJ, *s.v. theōreion* and derivatives).

10. Compare Aristotle, *Poetics* 1457b7, definition of metaphor: "the reattribution of a name belonging to some other thing, whether it be [reattribution] from the genus to the species, from species to genus, from species to species, or in keeping with an analogy." Usually translated tautologously as "transfer," the *epiphora* used to explain the meaning of *metaphora* deserves better: hence, here, "attribute" and "reattribute." For a fuller picture, see LSJ, *s.v. epiphora*.

11. Prospects for a comparative rhetoric are not enhanced by the fact that Chinese rhetoricians largely did without a specialized vocabulary. Alvaro Semedo (1586–1658), in his *Histoire universelle de la Chine*, reports that although "rhetoric is in usage there" and "the conceits and figures used in their poetry are the same as in Europe," learning takes place "by imitation rather than by precepts, since they are content to point out

whatever they find good in the writings of others and to model themselves on these examples" (pp. 84, 76–77). Manuals such as Ch'en Wang-tao's *Hsiu-tz'u-hsüeh fa-fan* combine an inventory of tropes with quotations from model texts. See also Kao, "Rhetoric."

12. Giles, *History of Chinese Literature*, pp. 12–14.

13. Ibid.

14. Granet, *Fêtes et chansons*, p. 27.

15. Ibid., p. 17.

16. See Ku Chieh-kang's preface to the "Shih i" ("Doubts about the *Odes*") of Cheng Ch'iao, in idem et al., *Ku shih pien*, 3: 406–19.

17. Zhang Longxi sees "allegoresis" as inseparable from its "relations with ideology." "We resent traditional commentaries on the *Book of Poetry* . . . because they read poems in such a way as to make them nothing but disguised propaganda for ideologies we now reject" ("Letter or the Spirit," pp. 213, 215). This may, however, tell us more about the polemical use of the term "allegory" than about the thing. "It is significant that nineteenth-century critics' castigation of 'mere allegory' usually touches on *ideas* they thought were outmoded trumpery" (Tuve, *Allegorical Imagery*, p. 165, *n*14; italics in original).

18. Paraphrasing P'i Hsi-jui, *Ching-hsüeh li-shih*, p. 9.

19. Compare Karlgren, "Glosses on the *Kuo Feng* Odes," p. 71: "Most of this commentary literature is void of value and it may be disregarded, since 95 percent of it consists of homilectics and moralizing effusions." Yet Pauline Yu (*Reading of Imagery*, p. 117 and elsewhere) argues with great pertinence that the commentaries' influence on subsequent poetics and poetry writing far outstrips that of the poems. This should be sufficient reminder that the *Odes* shorn of their commentaries (the form in which they are usually taught today) make up a "classic" whose very presence in many centuries of Chinese literature is disputable.

20. The phrasing may derive from the *Book of Changes*: see the interpretation of the hexagram *hsün* for a rough parallel. For the possible mutual influence between the *Changes* and the *Odes*, see Pauline Yu, *Reading of Imagery*, pp. 37–43; and Waley, "*Book of Changes*."

21. *SMSCS*, 15.16a–b. The prose translation of the ode is adapted from Karlgren, *Book of Odes*, Ode 160. For the source of the remarks on music, see *Li*, 31.4a–b, 39.2a. The phrase *te-yin* ("virtuous sound" or "reputation") occurs in other odes (e.g., Ode 218; Ode 228, where it is again the attribute of a prince; and Ode 29) and at least one prose text older than the Mao Commentary, the anecdotal chronicle known as "Conversations

of the States" (there describing music; see "Chou yü," *Kuo yü*, 1: 130). Ch'en Huan chooses to exploit the ambiguity of *te-yin* rather than restrict it to one or the other of its senses.

22. Karlgren, *Book of Odes*, p. 104. See also Karlgren, "Glosses on the *Kuo Feng* Odes," p. 244: "There is, of course, no reason whatever to connect the ode with either Ch'eng Wang or Chou Kung."

23. How comparison to a wolf fits in with the aim of "praising the Duke of Chou" is no small lexical problem in itself. *Tso* (21.21a), Duke Hsüan, 4th year, cites "the wolf-cub's ambition," applied to a ruler bent on extending his territory, as proverbial and anything but favorable.

24. See the "Chin t'eng" chapter of the *Shang Shu* (*Shu*, 13.6a–14a); and *Shih*, 8:2, 1a–5b. On the origins and history of these canonical books, see Chapter 2. Creel calls this chapter of the *Documents* "China's first short story" (*Origins of Statecraft*, pp. 457–58). On the cross-references between *Shih ching* and *Shang shu*, see Chapter 4 below.

25. Plaks, *Archetype and Allegory*, p. 84.

26. For "words" versus "meaning," see Quintilian, *Institutio*, VIII.6.44: "But allegory, which in Latin we call *inversio*, either indicates one thing with the words and another thing with the sense or else indicates something quite the opposite [of what it seems to mean]." The formula parallels one found in the near-contemporary *Homērika problēmata* ascribed to Heraclides Ponticus (5.1): "[logos] alla men agoreuōn . . . hetera de hōn legei sēmainōn" (a speech that says one set of things openly, but means something different from what it says). A common source is likely but unknown. Buffière (*Les Mythes d'Homère*, p. 47) finds the word emerging into sudden popularity around 60 B.C. On allegory as "continued" or "extended" metaphor, see Cicero, *Orator ad M. Brutum* 27/94; and Quintilian, *Institutio*, VIII.6.14 ("the continued use [of a metaphor] leads to allegory and to riddles") and 44 ("the first type of allegory is produced by a series of metaphors"). Granted that allegory is a product, perhaps a limit-function, of repeated metaphor, does that bring it under the genus of metaphor? Michel Charles puts aside the pigeonhole attitude of most writers on rhetoric, calling allegory a case of redoubled metaphor, "discourse *as* figure" (*Rhétorique de la lecture*, p. 147, condensing a remark of Dumarsais; my italics).

27. Compare Owen, *Traditional Chinese Poetry*, pp. 96, 292–93.

28. See also Owen, *Traditional Chinese Poetry*, pp. 21, 55. The "replication," not only of existents, but of an already doubled ontology in works of art would seem to pose problems for the consistent "dualism" ascribed

here to European thinking. "Whenever a painting misleads us, there is a double error in our judgments . . . for all we see properly [*proprement*] is the image" (Leibniz, *Nouveaux Essais*, II.9). See also Derrida, *La Dissémination*, pp. 211–13, 217.

29. See Hegel, *Ästhetik* II.3 (*W*, 14: 136–41).

30. Plaks, *Archetype and Allegory*, p. 93. For an argument against the persistent metaphor of the "two levels," see Quilligan, *Language of Allegory*, pp. 25–26.

31. See also Pauline Yu, *Reading of Imagery*, pp. 18, 27, 60, 138, 218. In recent years Joseph Needham and Frederick W. Mote have strongly emphasized the need to draw the consequences of seeing the Chinese as an atheological people; the critics discussed here owe them a considerable debt. See, e.g., Mote's "The Arts," pp. 6–7: without revelation, "the past (*ku*) was proper (*cheng*) because something had to be, and nothing else could acquire competitive validity."

32. Owen, *Traditional Chinese Poetry*, p. 57.

33. Plaks, *Archetype and Allegory*, p. 109.

34. Quintilian, *Institutio* VIII.6.44, quoting Horace, *Odes* I.14, an imitation of several Greek poems (e.g., Archilochus 56; Alcaeus 6, 326); these occur as illustrations in the near-identical discussion in *Homērika problēmata* (5.1–8), showing that definitions and examples were alike traditional. Pauline Yu (*Reading of Imagery*, p. 21) gives the Western "world-view" precedence over the practice of political and historical allegory, which then seems to drop out of the genre.

35. On this distinction, see Tuve, *Allegorical Imagery*, p. 48. Dante acknowledges that "the theologians take this [allegorical or hidden] sense differently from the poets" (*Convivio*, II.1).

36. Suidas, *Lexicon*, *s.v. allēgoria*: "metaphora, allo legon to gramma kai allo to noēma." Read as a sequel to Saint Paul's "The letter killeth . . ." (2 Cor, 3.6), the Suidas definition is an early witness to the medieval split between "allegory of the grammarians" and "allegory of the theologians."

37. In dealing with blatantly political allegories such as Orwell's *Animal Farm*, Carolynn Van Dyke judiciously adapts the allegorical "dualism" to the individual case: "The allegorical text confounds *some polarity* . . . which its readers regard as fundamental" (*Fiction of Truth*, p. 41; my italics).

38. Compare the section on the *Odes* in the "I-wen-chih" (Record of arts and letters) of the *Hou Han shu*: "Those who embraced the various *Chronicles* [for their historical glosses] and collected arguments right and

left all missed the original meaning [of the *Odes*]. If you must choose one [school of interpretation], that of Lu is the closest" (Pan Ku, *Han shu* 30.10a–b). The Lu school vanished under the Western Chin, ca. A.D. 300.

39. Plaks, *Archetype and Allegory*, pp. 109–10; cf. Needham and Wang, *Science and Civilization in China*, 2: 281, 526–70, 582–83. For a similarly expressed thesis about modern Chinese literature, see Jameson, "Third-World Literature," pp. 69, 72, 78.

40. On metaphor and metonymy (similarity and contiguity) as symmetrical poles of verbal structure, see Jakobson, "Two Aspects of Language." The use of "metonymy" in recent literary criticism diverges from the classical sense; as in Jakobson's work, it comes to stand for any relation between parts and wholes, causes and effects, etc., which may be paraphrased without recourse to similarity. I follow the current usage. If allegory is a continued metaphor, "blason," a term retrieved from obscurity by Michael Riffaterre, may be the best candidate for an example of the logical possibility "continued synecdoche." As a series of "namings of parts"—usually body parts—the blason poem attains an always risky logical coherence while seeming to hover between the aims of praise and caricature. The apparent instability of theme and tone is, however, easily rethematized (see Riffaterre, *Semiotics of Poetry*, pp. 77–78, 128–29). In "A la recherche du corps perdu," Cathy Yandell interestingly describes a "blason du miroir" as an attempt to write "the final *blason*."

41. Pauline Yu, *Reading of Imagery*, p. 65. And see Owen, *Traditional Chinese Poetry*, pp. 18–21, 61–63 (for an "art of reading"), 294. This naturalizing model of *lei* may be counterposed to a story from the *Tso Commentary*. The marquis of Chin invited his allies' representatives to recite verses to him, "specifying: 'When you sing a poem, it must be appropriate [*lei*].' The poem of Kao-hou of Ch'i was not *lei*. Hsün Yen [first minister of Chin] was furious and said: 'The feudal lords have ambitions of their own [*i chih*]!'" (Hsiang, 16th year). The reciters, as poetry critics, have more freedom of action than some modern readers are willing to give the poets. On the semantics of recitation, see below. For a discussion of category or *lei* (with several apparently differing interpretations), see Hansen, *Language and Logic*, pp. 112–17. Hansen's general argument—that Chinese ontology is one of stuffs rather than of kinds—leans toward the views developed by Plaks, Owen, and Yu. For a memorable short discussion of *lei*, see the chapter "T'ung-lei hsiang-tung" ("Things of the same kind act on one another") in Tung Chung-shu's *Ch'un-ch'iu fan-lu*, translated and commented in Needham and Ho,

"Theories of Categories," pp. 188–90. There, however, the link between "things of the same kind" is a physical one, passing through the universal medium of *ch'i* (variously translated as "air," "fluid" or "ether"; see below). The "Ssu-shun" chapter of the *Lü-shih ch'un-ch'iu* includes many valuable paradoxes about categories and category inclusion.

42. Puns are good experimental samples of semantic sameness and difference. For a number of puns, near-puns, and non-puns, see Turbayne, *Myth of Metaphor*, pp. 15–17; see also Percy's memorable piece, "Metaphor as Mistake" (*Message in the Bottle*, pp. 64–82).

43. Saussure, *Cours de linguistique générale*, p. 147.

44. Saussure's example has a long history. On "force" as category and dissolver of categories, see Leibniz, "De primae philosophiae emendatione, et de notione substantiae," *Philosophischen Schriften*, 4: 468–70; on the literal-metaphorical force of "force," see Durkheim's work on *mana* (*Les Formes élémentaires*, pp. 290–303). On "force" as a pivotal moment of Hegel's *Phenomenology*, see Hegel, "Kraft und Verstand," *Phänomenologie des Geistes* (*W*, 3: 107–36); and Gadamer, "Hegel's 'Inverted World,'" *Hegel's Dialectic*, pp. 35–53.

45. See Pauline Yu, *Reading of Imagery*, pp. 33, 36, 60.

46. The critic's supposition here is that all figurative statements are of the logical form "*x* is *y*": the point of difference is to show that for the Chinese *x* really is *y*, hence that the figure is not a figure. But not all metaphors have that form. The simplest counterexample is negative metaphor, of which the *Odes* offers some famous cases: e.g., Ode 26, "Po chou": "My mind is not a mat, you cannot roll it up." The "self-evident and literally true" model of Chinese meaning would make it impossible for the speaker to say this without meaning at the same time that his or her mind was a mat, "by shared membership in an a priori category." (That later readers have understood the image in exactly that way is perhaps a pedagogical warning to us.) Transfers by analogy (in Aristotle's sense) are another instance: they refer, not to things, but to relations between things.

47. See Aristotle, *Nicomachean Ethics* I.4, 6 (1095a26–30, 1096a25–30). The choice of example is, of course, not indifferent. A world in which goodness and beauty "literally belonged" to the same category would be one in which aesthetics could take the place of ethics. See Schiller, "Tenth Letter," *On the Aesthetic Education of Man*, pp. 60–71.

48. The announcement of that decision is here termed a "speech act"

or "performative," following John Austin. "The idea of a performative utterance [is] that it [is] to be (or to be included as a part of) the performance of an action." Canonical examples are "I pronounce you man and wife," "I name this ship the . . . ," "I promise . . . ." Such utterances, according to Austin, "do not 'describe' or 'report' or constate anything, are not 'true or false.' " Sentences that do purport to describe or report on actions and states of affairs and can therefore be judged true or false are dubbed "constatives." A sentence such as "I liken x to y" both makes a constative claim—that x is like y—and performs an action, the verbal act of likening (*How to Do Things with Words*, pp. 60, 6, 90; and see pp. 3, 47, 54–55, 145–47).

49. Or, to put it more carefully, the trope that alludes to a relation unknowable except as a fact. Rulon Wells, in an article about reconstructing the stages in semantic change, suggests that "similarities between things are not themselves merely experienced, as contingent, but are known a priori, as necessities; whereas contiguities, in time or in space, between objects of experience are themselves merely experienced, i.e. are learned by experience"; hence interpreting a transfer of meaning as metonymy requires hypothesizing special connections among "extralinguistic data" ("Metonymy and Misunderstanding," pp. 196, 201, 210). See also one of Wells's principal sources, Emile Benveniste's "Problèmes sémantiques de la réconstruction," *Problèmes*, I, pp. 289–307.

50. The Groupe Mu's notorious analysis of metaphor as a joining of two synecdoches owes something to this view of classes. See Dubois et al., *Rhétorique générale*, p. 108.

51. For Carolynn Van Dyke, Christian allegory is based on just such a philosophical realism: to read Prudentius's allegory sympathetically, we must grant, for example, that "*Faith* [a character in the *Psychomachia*] *acts* in its embodiments" (*Fiction of Truth*, p. 39; my italics). For the example of the bride and the peach tree (from Ode 6, "T'ao-yao"), see Michelle Yeh, "Metaphor and *Bi*," pp. 250–52.

52. The contrast may have to be drawn differently for every set of beliefs. What might the difference between allegory and historical context have meant to the medievals, those rugged literalists? Rosemond Tuve centers medieval reading on "the relation, taught in the word 'type,' between history itself (actual persons, events) and revealed truth, so that the actual people and events pre-figure or shadow what later comes to pass, and thereby fulfill the figures. . . . In fact, the chief contribution of [allegory's] theological background may be not its didactic force (which it

shares with many types of figures) but the unrelaxed insistence on the importance of the literal sense. . . . Herein lies the main difference between [medieval allegory] and the grammarian's allegory, the allegory of late classical tradition" (*Allegorical Imagery*, pp. 46–48). Emile Durkheim makes a kindred point in speaking of ethnologists who derive religion from a sense of "the immaterial," "occult forces," or "the mysterious." "Mysterious" means mysterious *to* somebody, and the believer is unlikely to be that somebody. "To the primitive, these explanations, which astound us, are the simplest thing in the world. The powers he invokes by these various [magical] means are, to him, nothing specially mysterious. They are just forces [on which he can rely as we do on] gravity or electricity" (*Les Formes élémentaires*, pp. 35–36). Calling on history or physics resolves nothing; what answers our call is always *a* history or *a* physics, and the most they can tell us is what they are able to consider historical or physical.

53. Plaks, *Archetype and Allegory*, p. 109.

54. See Leibniz, "Third Letter to Clarke," *Philosophischen Schriften*, 7: 364.

55. Linguists have an example for this: Carl Abel's astonishment at the noncontradictory thought processes of the ancient Romans, who could designate with "altus" both "high" and "low." As soon as we paraphrase "altus" as "distant from the observer on a vertical axis," however, the problem disappears into the translation from which it emerged. See Freud, "Antithetical Meaning"; Benveniste, "Remarques sur la fonction du langage dans la découverte freudienne," *Problèmes*, I, pp. 75–87; and on translation as a source of misprision, Firth, "Linguistic Analysis and Translation," *Selected Papers*, pp. 75–76.

56. Leibniz, preface to *Novissima Sinica*, *Opera omnia*, 4: 80. The play survives in an English version of 1687 by Aphra Behn. The phrase "just as it is here" runs like a refrain through Leibniz's writings. In biology, for example, "one can always say about an animal, 'everything's just the way it is with us,' the difference is only one of degree" (letter to Rémond, 11 Feb. 1715; *Philosophischen Schriften*, 3: 635).

57. Cyrano de Bergerac, *L'Autre Monde*, pp. 1, 65.

58. Plaks, *Archetype and Allegory*, p. 109.

59. "A relation is an accident inhering in more than one subject; when several ideas are being contemplated together, [their relation] is their 'concogitability' [*concogitabilitas*]." Manuscript fragment "Illatio, veritas, probatio duplex: vel contingens vel necessaria" (LH IV.7.C, 74).

60. Heidegger, "Aus einem Gespräch von der Sprache," *Unterwegs zur Sprache*, p. 89.

61. See also, on the Greek "separation between the worlds of gods and men" and the habit of public dispute, Vernant and Gernet, "Histoire sociale et évolution des idées en Chine et en Grèce," p. 90.

62. Hansen, *Language and Logic*, p. vii.

63. Gernet, *Chine et christianisme*, pp. 323–25.

64. Hu, "Mao Tsé-toung."

65. Leibniz, "Lettre sur la philosophie chinoise, à M. de Rémond," *Opera omnia*, 4: 170.

66. Jakobson and Waugh, *Sound Shape of Language*, pp. 90–91.

67. Ode 158, "Fa k'o": "In hewing [sc. with an axe] an axe haft, in hewing an axe haft, / the pattern is not far-off"; Baudelaire, "Mon coeur mis à nu," *Oeuvres complètes*, 1: 696.

68. Quine, "Meaning and Translation," pp. 148–50.

69. Quintilian, *Institutio* VIII.6.34: "And hence the necessity of catachresis, which gives to those things that have no name the name belonging to the thing nearest at hand. . . . From [catachresis] the whole genus of metaphor must be distinguished, for catachresis takes place where there is no proper word, but metaphor, where a proper word already exists." The presence, in a theory of meaning, of a class of "things that have no name" is rather an embarrassment, and as if to forget it, Quintilian goes on to treat catachresis as identical to metaphor, twice demanding that metaphors justify themselves (their semantic cost) by replacing a worse or nonexistent literal term ("[locum] in quo . . . proprium *deest*," 6.5; "metaphora . . . *vacantem* locum occupare debet," 6.18, my italics). The theory of catachresis—like the theory of trope that follows it—is a catachresis too, for where in a language are there any "vacant spaces"? (But what else could one call them?) As if anticipating this difficulty, Aristotle's discussion of some celebrated catachreses in *Poetics* 1457b16–32 treats them as instances of syntactic analogy, that is, of relational propositions waiting to be filled out ($a : b :: c : x$). See also on this question Warminski, "Prefatory Postscript," *Readings in Interpretation*, pp. liv–lx.

70. Courbet subtitled his painting *The Atelier* "A Real Allegory of My Life as a Painter."

71. See Gernet, *Chine et christianisme*, pp. 27–29, for a description of these "academies" (*shu-yüan*).

72. Ibid., p. 329.

73. Terms lifted from Stephen Greenblatt's discussion of Iago as "improviser" (*Renaissance Self-fashioning*, p. 228).

74. Li Chih-tsao (1565–1629), preface to the 1628 reprinting of Ricci's *T'ien-chu shih-i* (The true doctrine of the Master of Heaven, 1604), in Li, *T'ien-hsüeh ch'u-han* 1: 351, 354, 356.

75. Malebranche, "Avis au lecteur, touchant l'entretien d'un philosophe chrétien avec un philosophe chinois," *Oeuvres complètes de Malebranche*, 15: 42. On this passage, see Etiemble, *L'Europe chinoise*, 1: 353–59; and Vernière, *Spinoza*, 2: 346–54. See Robinet, *Leibniz et Malebranche*, pp. 474–93, for a reprinting of Leibniz's marginalia to the *Entretien*, as well as letters of 1714–15 that throw light on the various topics addressed by Leibniz's letter to Rémond.

76. Longobardi's report was translated and published in 1701 amid the quarrel over the "Chinese rites" as *Traité sur quelques points de la religion des Chinois* (reprinted with Leibniz's notes, in Leibniz, *Opera omnia*, 4: 89–144). It must have been composed in the 1620's, since it mentions events of 1617, alludes to the author's two years at the Chinese court (perhaps a stay as military advisor that began in 1627), and builds on prior writings by another Jesuit in China, Sabatino de Ursis (author of "Copiosus tractatus," 1618). Louis Pfister (*Notices biographiques*, p. 136) describes Giulio Alieni's "Sententia circa nomina quibus appellari potest Deus in Sinis," 1633, as a response to Longobardi.

77. Longobardi, *Traité*, pp. 90–91.

78. Antonio Caballero [known as Antoine de Sainte-Marie], *Traité sur quelques points importants de la mission de la Chine* (Paris, 1701), cited in Gernet, *Chine et christianisme*, p. 50; my italics. The "apes of God" theme reappears in Longobardi's *Traité*, p. 96: in order to make sure his pronouncements carry without exception, Longobardi exaggerates the degree of agreement among Chinese philosophers. "Which may, incidentally," says Longobardi, "recall the uniformity among the holy interpreters of the Scriptures."

79. Another way of handling the difficulty, token of quite a different, indeed a magical, approach to language, appears in Longobardi's *Libellus precum cum officio funebri et sepulturae*, printed at Shao-chou in 1602. It rendered the formulas and responses of various Latin services into phonetic sequences of Chinese nonsense syllables. See Pfister, *Notices biographiques*, p. 65.

80. Longobardi, *Traité*, p. 93.

81. Leibniz, "Lettre . . . à M. de Rémond," *Opera omnia*, 4: 172.

82. Longobardi, *Traité*, pp. 133, 115, 116 (my italics). To the last passage, Leibniz adds: "*pneuma* signifie aussi Air" (" 'pneuma' means 'air' too": ibid.; cf. "Lettre . . . à M. de Rémond, *Opera omnia* 4: 176). Since *pneuma* in its two senses is the letter of Saint Paul's word for "spirit," the cross-reference could hardly be more pointed.

83. Which is what common knowledge of the time understood by Spinozism: Father Mathurin Veyssière de la Croze, writing on two different days to Sebastian Kortholt, lumps Confucius together with Spinoza and accuses the former successively of atheism and pantheism (reprinted in Leibniz, *Opera omnia* 4: 211–15).

84. Leibniz, "Lettre . . . à M. de Rémond," *Opera omnia*, 4: 178; and see the annotations to Longobardi's *Traité*, pp. 108, 110.

85. Etiemble, *L'Europe chinoise*, 1: 417. Henry Rosemont, Jr., and Daniel J. Cook footnote but otherwise scarcely mention the passage in their annotated translation of Leibniz's *Natural Theology of the Chinese* (pp. 49, 81–82); David Mungello ignores it (*Leibniz and Confucianism; Curious Land*), as does Needham (*Science and Civilization in China*, 2: 496–505).

86. The philosophical implications are doubtless directed at Malebranche's intuitionist use of Descartes's *Third Meditation*. "Thinking about nothing and not thinking, or perceiving nothing and not perceiving, are the same thing. So whatever the mind perceives immediately and directly is something that exists. . . . Suppose I think of infinity: I perceive infinity immediately and directly. So it exists. For if it did not exist, I could not perceive anything when I try to perceive it, and so I would not perceive at all" (*Entretien*), p. 5. See also Leibniz's marginalia, in Robinet, *Leibniz et Malebranche*, pp. 483–86.

87. The "primitive truths" of Leibniz's projected logical language are "those which are self-evident or those of which the opposite is self-contradictory. For example: 'A is A,' or 'A is not non-A.' " " 'A not A' is a self-contradiction. By 'possible utterance' is meant one which does not contain a self-contradiction, some [form of] 'A is not A.' " Nonetheless, "terms of the mysteries of revealed religion are not subject to this kind of analysis," as the common words there take on "a certain more eminent sense" (Leibniz, *Opuscules et fragments inédits*, pp. 518, 364, 285). A critic may say that Leibniz prejudges the question by allowing the predicates of *li* a *sensus eminentior*. And indeed the factoring out of specifically human meanings (*anthrōpopatheia*) is a reading technique associated with scriptural interpretation, used here by Leibniz on texts that are (for his

opponents) precisely *not* scriptures. Kant invokes the term in a passage of his *Conflict of the Faculties* where the demarcation of philosophical from theological territory is at issue (*Der Streit der Facultäten*, I.ii.1, *Werke*, 9: 306). In *Religion Within the Limits of Reason Alone*, Kant's objection to anthropomorphism is that it leads the reader to confuse the legitimate and unavoidable "schematism of analogy (as a means of illustration [*Erklärung*])" with the "schematism of objective determination (as a means of extending our knowledge)" (*Die Religion innerhalb der Grenzen der bloßen Vernunft*; Kant, *Werke*, 7: 718–19; on the sacrificial character attributed to symbolic analogy in this passage, see Caruth, *Empirical Truths*, pp. 79–82). Leibniz's reading of Chinese theology similarly puts illustration in the place of knowledge.

88. That verbs involve an implicit copula ("Socrates runs" equals "Socrates is running") has been part of logical theory since Aristotle. Leibniz's sketches for a rational language would redefine nouns too, so that "'a human' is the same as 'a human being,'" and "a stone" the same as "a stony being" (*Opuscules et fragments inédits*, p. 289). Now "every proposition is ultimately reducible to one which attributes a predicate to a subject," as Russell's condensation of the doctrine has it (*Critical Exposition*, p. 9); in the projected rational language, predicate, subject, and their link (*symplokē, vinculum*) will all be composites of the one verb. For the obstacles natural language presents to this project and Leibniz's efforts to get around them, see Ishiguro, *Leibniz's Philosophy*.

89. "Rationalize," as well, in the arithmetical sense of providing a common factor: see Leibniz's sketch "Veritas et proportio," *Opuscules et fragments inédits*, pp. 1–3.

90. Heidegger, "Das Wesen der Sprache," *Unterwegs zur Sprache*, pp. 161–62.

91. Leibniz, *Opuscules et fragments inédits*, p. 224.

92. "Among the infinite combinations of possibles and possible series, there is one by which the greatest quantity of essence or possibility can be brought into existence" (Leibniz, "De rerum origine radicali," *Philosophischen Schriften*, 7: 303). See also *Monadologie*, paras. 53–55 (*Philosophischen Schriften*, 6: 615–16).

93. On rhetoric as an inherently comparative discipline (one deriving its specific objects from an application of the form/content distinction to a plurality of possible utterances), see Dubois et al., *Rhétorique générale*, pp. 4–6.

94. The vocabulary comes from Kant's third *Critique*. See Introduc-

tion, *Kritik der Urteilskraft*, pt. II, *Werke*, 8: 245: "Concepts . . . have their fields, which are determined simply by the relation in which their object stands to our faculty of cognition in general. The part of this field in which knowledge is possible for us is a territory (*territorium*) for these concepts and the requisite cognitive faculty. That part of the territory over which they exercise legislative authority [*gesetzgebend sind*] is the realm (*ditio*) of these concepts, and of the appropriate cognitive faculty" (translation modified from Kant, *Critique of Aesthetic Judgement*, p. 12).

95. For the phrase "the space of representation," see Foucault, *Les Mots et les choses*, pp. 70–72, 92–95. And cf. Baumgarten, *Aesthetica* (1750), sect. 29, "Verisimilitudo aesthetica" (paras. 478–504, pp. 306–26).

96. The phrase is Walter Benjamin's; see "Die Aufgabe des Über-setzers," *Gesammelte Schriften*, 4.1: 21.

Chapter 2

EPIGRAPH: Kant, *Kritik der Urteilskraft*, para. 17, last footnote, *Werke*, 8: 319.

1. Literally "lodged words" (i.e., words temporarily dwelling away from home: cf. Quintilian as cited in note 69 to Chapter 1), *yü-yen* as a critical term is most common in discussions of fiction. Its early currency and connotations of implausibility derive from fabulous and satirical works such as the *Chuang-tzu*. See ch. 33, "T'ien-hsia": *i yü-yen wei kuang*, "[Chuang Chou] lodged his words [sc. in the mouths of historical or fantastic personages] to give them breadth" (*Chuang-tzu chi-shih*, p. 1098). Some writers call any story or legend that cannot be verified or attached to a definite person a *yü-yen*: see, e.g., Kung Mu-lan, *Yüeh-fu shih hsüan-chu*, p. 16. Another term often rendered as "allegory," *chi-t'o*—the "entrusting" or "projection" of human feelings in an object—hardly surfaces in work on the *Odes*, except as an occasional gloss on the trope known in *Odes* studies as *hsing*, "stimulus" or "evocation." The seventh-century poet Ch'en Tzu-ang went so far as to fuse the two in a new term, *hsing-chi* (see Owen, *Poetry of the Early T'ang*, pp. 169 and 133, on the T'ang understanding of *hsing*). But *chi-t'o* has less to do with com-mentary than with poetic devices such as those found in the later lyric genre of *yung-wu* poems ("poems in praise of objects," comparable to Swift's "Meditation upon a Broom-Stick"). See, however, the "Hsieh-yin" ("Riddle and Enigma") chapter of Liu Hsieh's *Wen-hsin tiao-lung*. If

yü-yen refers to the wrong genre and *chi-t'o* to a poetic, but not a critical, stance, neither term applies directly to the problems that concern us here.

2. See Chapter 1. We can dispense with detail in recalling the drop in the fortunes of allegory from the eighteenth century on, a development presupposed by Legge, Giles, and the other early translators of Chinese poetry.

3. For Chu Hsi's study of the *Odes*, see his *"Shih" chi chuan* (SPTK) and *Chu-tzu yü-lei*, ch. 80–81 (6: 2065–140; for passage quoted here, see p. 2085). On Chu Hsi's hermeneutics generally, see Chu Hsi, *Learning to Be a Sage*, pp. 128–62; and Van Zoeren, *Poetry and Personality*, pp. 218–49. For Wang Po, see Chi et al., *Ssu-k'u ch'üan-shu tsung-mu t'i-yao*, 17.3b–6b. See also Ku Chieh-kang, "Ch'ung-k'an *Shih i* hsü" [Preface to a reprinting of Wang Po's *Doubts About the Odes*], in Ku et al., *Ku shih pien*, 3: 406–19.

4. Cheng Chen-to, "Tu *Mao Shih hsü*," pp. 388, 400.

5. Pauline Yu, *Reading of Imagery*, pp. 33, 36, 60, 116.

6. For instance, Karlgren ("Early History") uses citations of and in the *Odes* commentary to authenticate writings supposedly forged in the middle Han period.

7. See Spitzer, "Marvell's 'Nymph Complaining for the Death of Her Faun': Sources Versus Meaning," *Essays*, pp. 98–115; Hartman, " 'The Nymph Complaining for the Death of Her Faun': A Brief Allegory," *Beyond Formalism*, pp. 173–92; and Zhang, "Letter or the Spirit."

8. *Lun yü* (Analects of Confucius) 8.8. Legge supplies "character" as the subject; Lau, on analogy with 7.6, makes the three verbs imperatives. The passage refers to three canonical works, of which the second has come down to us in much altered condition and the third is lost.

9. *Lun yü* 17.10.

10. For these and several dozen other fragments of "lost *Odes*" gleaned from classical texts, see Lu Ch'in-li, ed., *Hsien-Ch'in, Han, Wei, Chin, Nan-pei-ch'ao shih*, 1: 63–72. On the original corpus of "three thousand poems," see Confucius' biography in Ssu-ma Ch'ien, *Shih chi* ch. 47. Hsü Chung-shu ("Pin feng shuo," p. 432) dismisses the *Shih chi* story, partly from doubts that there could ever have been so many poems to choose among. The historian Ssu-ma Ch'ien's own *Odes* learning was drawn from the Lu school: see T'ang Yin, *Liang-Han, San-kuo hsüeh-an*, pp. 211–18.

11. *Shih*, 10:2.1a–1b. As the Mao Preface puts it, "the meaning [of these poems] remains, but their wording is lost." In the opinion of Cheng

Hsüan (seconded by K'ung Ying-ta and Chu Hsi), the titles of these six "lost odes" represent pieces of instrumental music (ibid., 9:4.10b–11b, 10:1.4b–5b; Chu Hsi, *"Shih" chi chuan*, p. 109; the external evidence is in "Hsiang yin," *I-li*, *SSCCS* ed., 9.11a–b). If this is true, the historical and moral interpretations appended to these titles seem rather detailed and rich in content for descriptions of wordless music. An example is: " 'Nan kai.' Filial sons admonish one another to care for [their parents]." Mao Heng may have created these prefaces on the speculation that a text should have existed for each of these Odes and that it would have been on such-and-such a theme. (The other three schools left neither texts nor interpretations of these songs: see Wang Hsien-ch'ien, *Shih san-chia i chishu*, pp. 592, 597.) In fairness to Mao Heng, it should be pointed out that the instrumental compositions of ancient China usually took their themes from songs and were referred to by the words of the songs; indeed, the transcription of lyrics seems to have been preferred to all other forms of musical notation. (Ceremonial dance music—e.g., the *shao* and *wu* dances—is the exception; but in their case memorized patterns of movement would have served the same transcribing function.) At some time in the missing songs' history, therefore, words would probably have been associated with their music, and the loss of those words is a part of the attrition of the *Odes* text prior to the Han.

12. See Dobson, "Linguistic Evidence"; and *Language of "The Book of Songs."*

13. On this prince's activities, see Pan Ku, "I-wen chih," "Ju-lin chuan," and "Ho-chien Hsien wang chuan," *Han shu*, 30.10a, 88.20b–21a, 53.1a–2b. For a selection of translated passages dealing with the origins of the Mao edition, see Karlgren, "Early History," pp. 13–14.

14. These are the schools of Lu, Ch'i, and Han, all extinct by the fifth century. The longest surviving document of *Odes* interpretation outside the Mao tradition is the *Han Shih wai chuan*, attributed to Han Ying. For other surviving fragments, see Wang Hsien-ch'ien, *Shih san-chia i chishu*. The *History of the Former Han Dynasty* credits Prince Yüan of Ch'u with an edition of the *Odes*, although it does not seem to have acquired a scholarly following. (It may have been an offshoot of the Lu school.) The *History of the Sui Dynasty* mentions another school whose teaching is lost, the "Yeh *Shih*." Archaeology is still adding to our knowledge of variant texts and interpretative traditions. (See Pan Ku, "Ch'u Yüan wang chuan," *Han shu*, 36.2b; Wei Cheng and Chang-sun Wu-chi, "Ching-chi chih," *Sui shu*, 32.15a.)

15. The *Kuo yü* is a chronicle showcasing pieces of epideictic rhetoric. Although it never attained classical status, it is most closely related to the *Tso Commentary* to the *Spring and Autumn Annals*.

16. For collections of remnants of these apocrypha, see Yasui and Nakamura, *Jūshū isho shūsei*, vol. 3. See also Dull, "Historical Introduction."

17. The Old Text–New Text controversy was most acute in reference to the *Book of Documents* and the *Spring and Autumn Annals*. The Old and New Text versions of the *Documents* clearly diverge; the *Annals* is a bare chronicle of events in the state of Lu, traditionally thought to have been written by Confucius in a designedly indirect and laconic style. Differing schools of commentary sprang up to fill out the *Annals'* understatements. For a recent examination of Han dynasty academic politics in light of a broad sampling of the evidence, see Huang, *Ching chin-ku wen-hsüeh wen-t'i*. See also Pelliot, "Le *Chou king*"; and Tjan, *Po Hu T'ung*.

18. Tjan, *Po Hu T'ung*, 1: 94; Dull, "Historical Introduction," pp. 114, 143. Dull, citing Dubs, hesitates to say whether the "Record of Music" mentioned in that passage of the *Han shu* is the same as that surviving today as a chapter of the *Li chi*, but the context (in which the "Record" is appealed to as an orthodox counterstroke to *yüeh-fu* music and the "licentious sounds of Cheng") by no means rules it out.

19. Huang, *Ching chin-ku wen-hsüeh wen-t'i*, pp. 87–127. The Duke of Chou had been regent for the child-king Ch'eng. The Old Text *Book of Documents* refers to the Duke of Chou as "king *pro tempore*" (*chia wang*): hence, according to New Text revivalists, Wang Mang's enthusiasm (oddly prescient) for Old Text learning. The Old Text passage in question may be supported by a bronze inscription mentioning the presence of the "king" on a battlefield some time during the first years of Ch'eng's reign (cited in Hsü and Linduff, *Western Chou Civilization*, p. 122). But since the "king" is not identified by name or reign title, it is unclear whether the Duke of Chou issued orders in the king's name or took the title himself. A similar problem attaches to the first words of the "Ta kao" chapter of the *Book of Documents*.

20. K'ang Yu-wei, *Hsin-hsüeh wei-ching k'ao* (1891); Ku Chieh-kang, *Han-tai hsüeh-shu shih lüeh* (1935) and contributions to *Ku shih pien* (1926–41).

21. "Thus the Old Texts may be regarded as having given a new and refreshing stimulus to classical studies . . . while at the same time they bear the stigma of having been faked in order to support the ambitions of a scheming mystic" (Tjan, *Po Hu T'ung*, 1: 145). Huang Chang-chien

points out that although Liu Hsin, chief of the Old Text school, was personally discredited by association with Wang Mang, his learning still commanded respect. First-century scholars continued discreetly to combine Old and New Texts in their researches (*Ching chin-ku wen-hsüeh wen-t'i*, p. 770).

22. Considering the way early thinkers taught—through memorization and exempla, before an audience of handpicked successors—there may not have been a *text* before the desire to have one supposed it to have existed. Tjan (*Po Hu T'ung*, 1: 141–45) asks whether the real difference between New and Old Text schools was not rather that between a faction in power and one out of it, a difference relevant to the middle Han but not to previous centuries.

23. *Tso*, Hsiang, 14th year (*Tso*, 31.18b–20a). This passage and another of comparable date in the *Kuo yü* ("Chou yü," pt. 1, pp. 9–10) follow one another so closely as to form virtually one document. See Diény, *Origines*, pp. 5–16, for several ancient testimonia on poetry collecting. The Mao Prefaces allude to folk songs in their discussion of the *shih* genre as a whole (preface to Ode 1, "Kuan chü"; see below). Occasionally they will ascribe the authorship of a poem not to an individual but to the people of one or another state.

24. Diény, *Origines*, p. 10. Diény is at pains to distinguish this collection network from the Han Yüeh-fu (Music Bureau), the existence of which is not in doubt.

25. Ku Chieh-kang, "Yeh yu ssu chün," in idem et al., *Ku shih pien*, 3: 440.

26. Granet, *Fêtes et chansons*, pp. 30, 31, 87–88, 152–53, 249–50, 255. It is an open question for Granet how far village customs were in fact altered by Chou rule. The *Book of Ritual* prescribes different customs for nobles and commoners ("Ch'ü li," *Li*, 3.6a; also cited by Granet, p. 87).

27. On this period generally, see Chow, *May Fourth Movement*; and Lee, *Romantic Generation*. Many historians of the 1920's and 1930's took inspiration from K'ang Yu-wei's polemic, in the name of the long-dormant New Text faction, against practically all of the received texts of the tradition. The scholarly correspondence of Hu Shih, Ku Chieh-kang, Cheng Chen-to, Ch'en P'an, Ho Ting-sheng, and others, reprinted in Ku Chieh-kang et al., *Ku shih pien*, vol. 3, stands for one type of *Odes* scholarship influenced by May Fourth theses. Cheng Chen-to's ideas had gained a broader circulation through publication in the periodical *Hsiao-shuo yüeh-k'an* (Fiction monthly) from the early 1920's onward. Fu Ssu-

nien, director of the newly founded Academia Sinica, lectured on the *Odes* from an archaeological perspective; Wen I-to's analyses of the poems (only partially represented in the posthumous collection of his writings, and now emerging from manuscript) uncover a fragmentary mythology where the Mao tradition had supplied only historical and moral anecdotes. See Fu, "*Shih-ching* chiang-i kao" (1928), *Fu Ssu-nien ch'üan-chi*, 1: 185–330; Wen, "*Shih-ching* hsin-i" and "*Shih-ching* t'ung-i," *Wen I-to ch'üan-chi*, 2: 67–101, 105–200; idem, "*Shih* 'Ko sheng'"; and Schneider, *Ku Chieh-kang*. For a modern folk literature movement, see Hung, *Going to the People*.

28. Ch'en P'an, "Chou, Shao erh-nan," p. 424. Ch'en P'an's objection to "those Han explainers" somewhat overstates the case. The *Odes* themselves, especially the temple and court songs of the "Elegantiae" and "Laudes" sections, are the main literary source for the Han-era Prefaces. The forced character so often attributed to the Prefaces in general is probably best described as a result of the prefacers' reading the "Airs of the States" as if they were "Elegantiae" and "Laudes"—and thus as an interpretative problem entirely native to the *Odes*.

29. On parallels between linguistic and political issues as they presented themselves to May Fourth writers, see M. Anderson, *Limits of Realism*.

30. Chen Shih-hsiang holds that "the 'Eulogiae' [*sung*] section was perhaps more instrumental than the popular 'Airs' [*feng*] in establishing firmly the genre concept of the *Songs*" ("The *Shih-ching*," p. 30). Ch'ü Wan-li finds an identical path of stylistic influence ("Lun *Kuo feng*," pp. 503–4). Chu Tzu-ch'ing, too, sees the collection as dominated by its ritual and dynastic elements. The "Airs of the States" section may be something of an accident. "That these pieces 'drawn from personal feeling' [in Lu Chi's phrase] were preserved at all had nothing to do with their intrinsic value; it was for other reasons. . . . Half of the *Book of Odes* consists of such 'poems of feeling'—recorded, however, by professional musicians on account of their melody alone, for use as musical accompaniment" (*Shih yen chih pien*, p. 202; see also p. 214).

31. See above for the first alternative. As to the second, Ku points out that as far back as Confucius' day the songs were being quoted all across China, irrespective of regional origin or differences in dialect; the only mark according to which a song might be classified by its origin among the airs of a particular state (as they are in the *Odes*' table of contents) would be according to the regional style of music used to perform it

("*Shih ching* tsai Ch'un-ch'iu Chan-kuo chien ti ti-wei," in Ku Chieh-kang et al., *Ku shih pien* 3: 344). This implies a guild of musicians able to perform in more than one regional style, and to know the difference: which is to locate the creative period of the *Odes* in a professional and courtly milieu. Hsü Chung-shu ("Pin feng shuo") suggests that the ancestor of the present text may have been a performance score from Lu.

32. Ku Chieh-kang, "*Shih ching* tsai Ch'un-ch'iu Chan-kuo chien ti ti-wei," in idem et al., *Ku shih pien* 3: 320. To the documents already cited may be added a much-quoted report from the Han. In year-end village meetings, "men and women who had grievances sang in turn. The hungry sang of their food; the exhausted sang of their work" (Ho Hsiu's note to *Kung-yang chuan*, Duke Hsüan, 15th year; *SSCCS* ed., 16.16a). Compare Granet's fourth interpretative principle (*Fêtes et chansons*, p. 27).

33. Holzman, "Confucius and Ancient Chinese Literary Criticism," pp. 33, 30. Similar concerns are voiced by Ch'ü Wan-li in "Hsien-Ch'in shuo *Shih*."

34. Zhang, "Letter or the Spirit," p. 205.

35. Pauline Yu, *Reading of Imagery*, p. 27.

36. Pers. comm., 1989.

37. Holzman, "Confucius and Ancient Literary Criticism," p. 34. See also Hightower's introduction to his translation of the *Han Shih Wai Chuan*. On the conventions of quotation, see Van Zoeren, *Poetry and Personality*, pp. 42–45, 64–67, 71.

38. Wang Chin-ling, *Chung-kuo wen-hsüeh li-lun shih*, p. 168. I use "metaphors and similes" as a convenient stand-in for Wang's *hsing* and *pi*.

39. Granet, *Fêtes et chansons*, pp. 13–15.

40. *Lun yü* 17.9; Legge's translation. Almost every word of this passage has been translated differently by one hand or another: *kuan*, "self-contemplation," most likely means "inspection of public morals by reviewing popular songs" (Hsün-tzu and the *Tso Commentary* use the word in senses approaching this); *hsing*, "stimulate the mind," becomes in Holzman's suggestive rendering "to make metaphorical allusions" (also called *hsing*); what one "learns" (a word not in the original) is more probably what one "does" with the *Odes*, and that is to quote it while on diplomatic missions "abroad" (better than "remoter duty" for *yüan*). What Legge translates is really Chu Hsi's influential commentary; see Chu Hsi, *Ssu-shu chi-chu*, *Lun yü*, 9.4b.

41. "Ta ssu-yüeh," *Chou li*, *SSCCS* ed., 22.7b–8a. The dating of the *Rituals* in relation to Confucius is uncertain.

42. Chu Tzu-ch'ing, *Shih yen chih pien*, p. 198.

43. Liu, *Chinese Theories of Literature*, pp. 106–16.

44. "Yao tien," *Shu*, 3.26a.

45. On quotation, see *Tso*, Hsiang, 27th year (the famous "interview" scene between Chao Meng and the advisors of Cheng), 38.12b–14a; see also Chu Tzu-ch'ing, *Shih yen chih pien*, pp. 205–7.

46. "Lu yü," ii, *Kuo yü*, p. 210. *Ho*, "suit, accompany, harmonize with" is glossed there as *ch'eng* ("complete").

47. Chow, "Early History," p. 207. For the source texts and a more detailed verdict see Chu Tzu-ch'ing, *Shih yen chih pien*, pp. 204–9.

48. *Tso*, Hsiang, 28th year, 38.25a–b.

49. "Project" is one name Steven Van Zoeren gives to the *chih*, the "intent" or "aim" that poetry "articulates" (*Poetry and Personality*, pp. 12, 56–57).

50. Stephen Owen has found a way of naming the particular kind of classical status the *Odes* enjoyed: in periods dominated by poems of circumstance "it was a *repeatable* literary experience" (*Great Age*, p. 94).

51. See Wittgenstein, *Philosophical Grammar*, p. 59. Deictics and pronouns are granted a nonce "meaning" only on the occasion of their "use," as Emile Benveniste observes ("La nature des pronoms," *Problèmes*, I, pp. 251–57).

52. *Shih*, 19:2.1a.

53. Ku Chieh-kang, "*Shih ching* tsai Ch'un-ch'iu Chan-kuo chien ti ti-wei," in idem et al., *Ku shih pien*, 3: 344 (speaking of the anthology as a whole).

54. Ode 297, *Shih*, 20:1.4b–10b. My translation, with debts to Karlgren (*Book of Odes*, pp. 253–54; "Glosses on the *Ta Ya* and *Sung* Odes," pp. 173–74). The Han historian Pan Ku tells us that "when Confucius edited the *Odes* . . . he included poems as ancient as the Yin [i.e., *Laudes of Shang*] and as recent as the [*Laudes of*] *Lu*" ("I-wen-chih," *Han shu*, 30.10a). Recent scholarship has questioned the early date assigned the *Shang sung*, but not the lateness of the *Lu sung*. On the dating problem, see Fu Ssu-nien, "*Lu sung, Shang sung* shu," *Fu Meng-chen hsien-sheng chi*, 6: 58–67; Ch'ü Wan-li, *Shih ching ch'üan-shih*, pp. 9–10, 600, 616; and C. H. Wang, *Bell and the Drum*, pp. 48–50.

55. *Shih*, 20. 4b–5a (Mao *chuan*). The Three Schools' interpretations did not differ significantly. The historian K'o was a contemporary of Duke Hsi's heir, Duke Wen (r. 626–608 B.C.).

56. K'ung Ying-ta in *Shih*, 20: 1.2b; referring to *Tso*, Hsi, 20th year, 14.24b–25a.

57. K'ung Ying-ta, *Shih*, 20:1.3b.

58. K'ung Ying-ta, *Shih*, 20:1.5b. The recurrence of "thought" (*ssu*) in this commentary alludes to Confucius' punning quotation of the poem's next-to-last line in *Lun yü* 2.2. "The Odes are three hundred in number, but one phrase sums them up: Thought without swerving." *Ssu*, an exclamation in each stanza of the poem, is here taken in its full sense as "thought" and replaces the chariot-teams as the subject of the sentence. Later readers have assumed Confucius was explicating the verse and extended the pun to the other occurrences of the word.

59. See also *Lun yü* 10.12: "The stables burned down. Confucius took leave and asked: 'Was anyone hurt?' He did not ask about the horses."

60. Plato, *Republic* 343b.1–4 (Thrasymachus speaking, in Shorey's translation). Horses are found buried with their masters in many Shang and Chou tombs, but horse bones never appear in kitchen middens (Kwang-chih Chang, *Shang Civilization*, p. 143).

61. Tuan Yü-ts'ai's notes to Hsü Shen, *Shuo wen chieh tzu*, p. 694, define *yeh* as: "The area of a hundred *li* surrounding the capital is called the *chiao* [suburbs]. . . . Outside the *chiao* is the *yeh*." For an analysis of Chou political and familial geography, see Vandermeersch, *Wangdao*, 1: 124–25.

62. Some editions and commentaries show a different *mu* in this place, "to herd, to pasture." Karlgren offers textual support for "stallion" as the oldest reading ("Glosses on the *Ta Ya* and *Sung* Odes," p. 172).

63. The domestication of horses came comparatively late to China. Horse trading was one of the constant economic relations between Chinese and nomadic peoples on their frontiers. Occasionally new breeds had to be fought for, as in a famous episode of Han Wu-ti's reign narrated by Herlee Creel ("The Horse in Chinese History," *What is Taoism?*, pp. 160–86).

64. Ssu-ma Ch'ien, "Chou pen chi," *Shih chi*, p. 73.

65. Reconstructed by Karlgren as *tsâng, dz'əg, tsâk, dz'o* (*Book of Odes*, pp. 253–54).

66. K'ung Ying-ta in *Shih*, 20:1.5b. Ode 163, "Huang-huang che hua," includes a similar horse catalogue, with its terms placed in the controlling rhyme position of each stanza.

67. Empson, *Some Versions of Pastoral*, p. 11. See also his *Structure of Complex Words*, p. 168, where one instance of "the pastoral idea" is said to suggest "that there is a *complete copy* of the human world among dogs, as among swains or clowns" (my italics). Perhaps Confucius' praise of the *Odes* as a handy reference for the "names of many birds, beasts, plants,

and trees" is a pastoral in the same spirit. Readers of the *Lun yü* will remember the old farmer who derided the Master's "inability to tell apart the five kinds of grain" (18.7; cf. 13.4).

68. As close kin to the Chou royal family, the dukes of Lu had special privileges. Noting that there are no "Airs of Lu"—either "correct" or "decadent"—in the "Airs of the States" section, K'ung Ying-ta supposes that Lu was exempt from the periodic tours of inspection to which the collecting of folk songs is traditionally tied (*Shih*, 20:1.4a–b).

69. Ibid., 5b.

70. Holzman's translation of the passage ("Confucius and Ancient Chinese Literary Criticism," p. 36).

71. "Yüeh chi," *Li*, 37.11b; paraphrased from "Yüeh lun" and "Cheng ming," in the *Hsün-tzu.* "To make intimate," *ch'in*, has the connotation of "making affines by marriage," a manner of relation whose importance to the Chou cannot be discounted. The Chou, few in number and widely dispersed over their newly acquired territory, won over many of the remaining Shang nobles through intermarriage. Political enfeoffment (the Chou contribution to Chinese political culture) was underpinned by a network of kinship status patterned on the Shang administration, which had been entirely organized by blood lineages. Thus the "re-articulation of power" indispensable to the stabilizing of the Chou polity "was based on the recognition of collateral kinship" (Vandermeersch, *Wangdao*, 1: 111). The "identification" made possible by songs in the folk mode then plays out in miniature the great issues of federation within, not just across, classes.

Chapter 3

EPIGRAPH: Butor, *Répertoire*, p. 64.

1. Hermann-Josef Röllicke expresses it well: "The *whole* poem is the history of its applications" ("Die Fährte des Herzens," p. 43). Jean-Pierre Diény, among others, remarks on the impersonality (which is the same thing as the applicability) of ancient lyric (see his *Les Dix-neuf poèmes anciens*).

2. Or, although the extra precision seems useless for the Chou period, "the general principles of the *Book of Poetry*" (K'ung Ying-ta, in *Shih*, 1.3b, echoing Cheng Hsüan, "*Shih p'u hsü*").

3. The translation given here is my own, with many debts to predecessors in the field. The paragraph numbers follow the divisions of the

SSCCS edition. For simplicity's sake I adopt the best-known form of a person's name throughout and silently correct the texts I am translating in keeping with this practice: thus Tzu-hsia instead of Pu-shang, Wei Hung instead of Wei Ching-chung, and so forth. For a list of translations and partial translations of this essential text, see Wixted, "*Kokinshū* Prefaces," pp. 217–18.

4. Chu Kuan-hua ("Kuan-yü '*Mao Shih* hsü'") tries to substantiate this tradition by distinguishing the part of the Prefaces that might have been written by Tzu-hsia. Röllicke ("Die Fährte des Herzens") argues that the essay we now call the Great Preface is derived from the lost *Book of Music* (*Yüeh-ching*), indeed authored by Tzu-hsia. For a remarkably clear and concise investigation of the Prefaces' sources, composition, and textual history, see Wang Chin-ling, "*Shih-hsü* tso-che chi ch'i shih-tai," *Chung-kuo wen-hsüeh li-lun shih*, 1: 295–326.

5. This theory of joint authorship is meant to account for allusions in the Little Prefaces that could not possibly have stemmed from Tzu-hsia. Tzu-hsia and the Elder Mao were separated by six or seven generations.

6. *Floruit* under the emperor Kuang-wu (r. A.D. 25–57) of the Eastern Han. The earliest authority for this opinion is Fan Yeh's biography of Wei Hung ("Ju-lin chuan," *Hou Han shu*, 79:2.5b–6b). It is unfortunate that so little is known about Wei Hung, a writer to whom so many crucial editions and stages in transmission have been assigned. He seems to have been a student of the *Odes* scholar Hsieh Man-ch'ing, whose place in the Mao text's history is well attested. See T'an Chia-ting, *Chung-kuo wen-hsüeh-chia*, p. 42. The editors of the *Imperial Epitome of the Complete Collection of Writings in Four Categories* list a dozen or so of the better-known hypotheses about the author(s) of this Preface: "a matter," they say, "as involved as a lawsuit" (Chi et al., *Ssu-k'u ch'üan-shu tsung-mu t'i-yao*, 15.1a–1b).

7. King Wen was the last pre-dynastic leader of the Chou. Ode 235, "Wen wang," names him as the "pattern" (*hsing*) of rulers to come. The Mao Preface to that poem states succinctly: "'King Wen': King Wen received the Mandate [of Heaven] and made the Chou [confederation]" (*Shih*, 16.1a).

8. The Mao Commentary to the first two lines of "Kuan chü" reads in part: "If husband and wife observe the separation of the sexes, fathers and sons will be close; if fathers and sons are close, then the relation of prince and subjects will be one of respect; if the relation of prince and subjects is one of respect, then all at court will be proper. If all at court is proper, then the kingly influence is brought to completion."

9. "All under heaven": the world, alternatively "the Chou empire." (Here and elsewhere I shall use "empire" more loosely than a historian can: strictly speaking, the Ch'in dynasty, founded in 221 B.C., was the first Chinese empire.)

10. *Lun yü* 12.19: "If you [addressed to the noble Chi K'ang-tzu] wish to be good, your people will be good. The ruler's virtue is the wind, the common man's is grass; when the wind comes to bear on it, the grass must bend" (paralleled in *Mencius* 3A, *SSCCS* ed., 5a.4b). "Influence" is, with its history, on many counts the best English near-equivalent.

11. Son of King Wen and author, according to the *Li chi*, of many standards of deportment. The Duke of Chou acted together with his brother, the Duke of Shao, as regents for their nephew, the child-king Ch'eng. *Hsün-tzu* (chap. 8, "Ju-hsiao") ascribes to the Duke of Chou the organization of the centralized feudal system of the Chou period.

12. The play on words here is not quite translatable. "Airs" and "wind" are represented by one character with the root meaning of "wind" and the acquired meaning of "songs, airs" as in the title *Kuo feng* ("Airs of the States"). The meaning of "transformation" ascribed to it here would seem to derive from the *Analects* quotation referred to in note 10 to this chapter and from association with another word, pronounced differently and written as a modification of the root word "wind"; this derived *feng* meant at first "to recite" and later "to admonish" or "to satirize" (see Karlgren, *Grammata Serica Recensa*, pp. 166–67; and Gibbs, "Notes on the Wind").

13. "Yao tien," *Shu*, 3.26a.

14. For the translation of *tung* as "is moved" rather than "moves," see the "Record of Music," *Li*, 37.1b: "The origin of all tone lies in the human heart. The movements of the human heart are caused by external objects. The heart is affected by objects and is moved. [This movement] takes shape in sound."

15. The "I-wen chih" follows the "Poetry tells of intent" formula of the *Shang shu* with: "Therefore to whatever feelings of joy and sorrow their hearts felt, the sound of their chants and songs gave expression. They intoned the words and called it poetry; they chanted the notes and called it song" (Pan Ku, "I-wen-chih," *Han shu*, 30.9b).

16. For the eight kinds of instrumental sound and the five notes of the movable scale, see DeWoskin, *Song for One or Two*, pp. 44–45, 52–53.

17. According to Kenneth Robinson and Joseph Needham, "clear" and "turbid" (*ch'ing, cho*) are to be taken as indicative of pitch, not timbre ("Sound [Acoustics]," p. 157). The sense of *ch'ing* and *cho* in old works on

music is unsure because the texts are not careful to separate pitch, volume, and timbre. See, e.g., the explanation of these terms in the *Huai-nan-tzu*: "The sound of clear water is small; that of turbulent water is big" (4.5b). From the Six Dynasties on, Chinese phoneticians use *ch'ing* and *cho* to distinguish "unvoiced" and "voiced" consonants. Poetic rule books of the T'ang make much of such classifications. K'ung is making this the occasion for a convergence of musical and linguistic frames of reference.

18. These stock examples of depravity in music and manners are alluded to in *Lun yü* 17.18; "Yüeh chi," *Li*, 38.29a–b; "Yüeh shu," *Shih chi*, p. 447.

19. *Hsiao ching*, chap. 12: "For changing customs and modifying habits, nothing surpasses music" (*SSCCS* ed., 6.4b). Compare "Yüeh lun," *Hsün-tzu*, pp. 253–54.

20. Compare "The *hsing* uses a good object to allude to a good deed" (Cheng Hsüan, note to "Ta ssu-yüeh," *Chou li*, *SSCCS* ed., 22.8b).

21. Pan Ku, "*Fu* on the Two Capitals," preface (Hsiao T'ung, *Wen hsüan*, 1.1b). Ch'eng and K'ang were the sagely inheritors of King Wu of the Chou. Pan Ku is trying to account for the several centuries' gap in Chinese poetic production that set in after the *Odes*. Both Pan Ku and the author of the Great Preface have in mind a passage of the *Mencius*: "When the traces of the [former] kings had been extinguished, poetry was no more; when poetry was no more, the *Spring and Autumn [Annals]* were composed" (*SSCCS* ed., 8a.12a). The *Spring and Autumn Annals* were always understood to contain an element of unspoken censure. By prolonging the effective period of the "grace of the former kings," the preface, Pan Ku, and K'ung Ying-ta extend the life of the *Odes* into the era, and also into the characteristic functions, of the *Annals*.

22. "Hsi tz'u," pt. 1, *I ching*, *SSCCS* ed., 7.16a. I have restored a phrase of the original, left out by K'ung. "Shape and form" may seem redundant. But *hsing* tends to imply solidity and *jung* concavity.

23. K'ung's reasoning (evidence, if any was needed, of the exegetical pressure his contemporaries expected the Mao Prefaces to withstand) is drawn from the distinction made earlier between "Airs" and "Elegantiae." The preface seems to refer to the Duke of Chou as a "ruler" and to the Duke of Shao as a "feudal lord," when, technically, we should expect a poem attached to a "ruler" to be classed with the "Elegantiae." The Duke of Chou acted as King Ch'eng's chief minister and could thus be styled a "ruler" (in all but name); his younger brother the Duke of Shao,

put in charge of one of the great southern fiefdoms, is invoked here as the ideal feudal lord.

24. Chou-nan and Shao-nan are recorded as geographical names prior to any association with the Dukes of Chou and Shao. Shao (or Shao-fang) was the name of a tribe allied with the pre-dynastic Chou (Hsü and Linduff, *Western Chou Civilization*, p. 92).

25. The preface here elaborates, with a story, on Confucius' judgment that "in the 'Kuan chü' there is joy without abandon and grief without self-injury" (*Lun yü* 3.20; following D. C. Lau's translation of *shang*).

26. *Shu* ("self-effacement," "reciprocity") is elevated to the status of a virtue for all seasons in *Lun yü* 15.23. It is not clear from the last sentence of Cheng's commentary whether he takes *chün-tzu hao-ch'iu* to mean "the superior man is eager [to meet with] companions" or "[for] the superior man [she] eagerly [seeks out] companions." The line as translated by readers untrammeled by the Mao story runs simply: "A good [marriage] companion for the lord."

27. *Shih*, 1.1a–20a.

28. Wixted, "The *Kokinshū* Prefaces," pp. 221, 222. The *Kokinshū* anthology was composed between A.D. 905 and 917.

29. Liu Hsieh, *Wen-hsin tiao-lung*, pp. 31, 83. The editors (p. 87) correlate "unfolding" with "prolonging the words" and "sending forth in words" and "a record of authenticity" with "expresses intent" and "it is intent." The whole paragraph is thus an "unfolding" of the Great Preface's citation of the *Documents*. The inclination to stress the *Odes'* authenticity sometimes takes unusual forms. In one venerable Han text, the *Odes* are even said to be "dominated by substance" (*chih*), and it falls to the *Ritual* to embody "art" (*wen*) (Tung Chung-shu, "Yü-pei," *Ch'un-ch'iu fan-lu*, 1.10a; see also Shih, *The Literary Mind*, pp. 33, 61).

30. Owen, *Traditional Chinese Poetry*, p. 58; Pauline Yu, *Reading of Imagery*, p. 32.

31. Fu-tan ta-hsüeh, *Chung-kuo wen-hsüeh p'i-p'ing shih*, p. 51.

32. Chow Tse-tsung ("The Chinese Word *Shih*," *Wen-lin*, p. 164) points out a long-forgotten reason for *yen*'s failure to capture attention: *chih* is the main etymon of *shih*. *Yen*, also an element of the character *shih*, plays there the lesser role of classifier. So *shih yen chih* could be read as a nominal, not real, definition, with its emphases distributed as "*shih* = *yen* (adjunct) + *chih* (root)." However, the word *chih*—the root of the whole phrase—drops out of the *Shih chi* paraphrase of the *Book of Documents*, proving that the etymological interest of the passage had

already been superseded by its poetological message before 75 B.C. There it reads *shih yen i*: "poetry expresses thoughts" ("Wu ti pen chi," *Shih chi*, p. 37).

33. The Great Preface has "and" (*erh*). The "Record" refers to an earlier paragraph establishing the doctrine in nearly the same words.

34. "Yüeh chi," *Li*, 37.4a–b.

35. The absence in the Preface of "for this reason" before "the tone of a well-governed era" is simply enough accounted for. The paragraph in the "Record of Music" had the form of a definition and an application, which is no longer the case in the Preface.

36. *Li*, 39.33a–b.

37. Van Zoeren, *Poetry and Personality*, pp. 97–98; cf. p. 133.

38. *Li*, 37.1b. Juan Yüan's note to *fang* makes it identical with *wen* (pattern). "Pattern" is good, but the leading sense of *fang* in classical times is more narrowly technical, as in "carpenter's square, standard, method, norm." I choose "mode" because a mode is "more than merely a scale" yet "never just a fixed melody," rather "always at least a melody type or melody model" (Stanley Sadie, ed., *The New Grove Dictionary of Music and Musicians*, s.v. "mode"). Without a hint as to how many "tones" (*yin*) are intended, it is impossible to know for certain whether to translate the word as "instrumental timbres" (of which there are eight) or "notes" (of the pentatonic scale). The sense of *pi* as "order" (for which reading see also *Chou li*, *SSCCS* ed., 3.14b, text and note) seems to require the latter. The whole passage is a puzzle; for alternative translations, see Couvreur, *Li Ki*, 2: 45–46; and DeWoskin, *Song for One or Two*, pp. 45–54.

39. *Li*, 37.7b–8a.

40. *Lü-shih ch'un-ch'iu*, 5.5b. The third occurrence of "music" (*yüeh*) can of course be read as "joyful" (*le*), but the sentence then contributes nothing to the passage in which it occurs. See also the "Chih yüeh" and "Shih yüeh" sections (5.8b–10a).

41. *Li*, 37.5a–7a (compare Aristotle, *Politics*, 8 1339b20–1340a11). The nonce-equivalents for the notes are drawn from Chavannes, *Les Mémoires historiques*, 3: 636. But the positions should be understood as relative: the five-note scale could start at any of twelve positions (*lü*).

42. Since the differences among the five notes in any "key" or *lü* are their only constant definition, the pentatonic system as set forth in the ancient writers on music is a semiotic "form" to which the scales of the twelve *lü* are as a "substance," in Louis Hjelmslev's sense (see, e.g., "La stratification du langage," *Essais linguistiques*, esp. pp. 56–57).

43. It might be a piece of Chinese "correlative thinking" (cf. Needham and Robinson, "Sound [Acoustics]," pp. 182, 205). But in and of itself "correlative thought" is unable to answer questions about the grounds for correlation. And to claim that such questions never arose leaves later interpreters equally stymied. See Lloyd, *Polarity and Analogy*, p. 65, for the shortcomings of pure categorical parallelism and its consequent need to go beyond its own devices.

44. None of the older Chinese music texts appears to represent the scale as a "row" or "line" of ascending pitches; rather, they prefer to speak of the fundamental note of a scale as inhabiting the "middle" of an acoustic space. See Needham and Robinson, "Sound (Acoustics)," pp. 157–59. The old texts give the term *kung* a double gloss, by sound and by meaning: "*Kung* [etymologically, 'palace'] is *chung* ['center']. It is the prince [*chün*]. It acts as the plumb line [*kang*] for the four [other] notes" (Liu Hsin, cited in *Erh ya*, 7.1a). "[The tone] *kung* set to [the pitch] *huang-chung*: this is the root of all the standard pitches" ("Shih yin," *Lü-shih ch'un-ch'iu*, 5.11b).

45. See, e.g., "Ti-yüan p'ien," *Kuan-tzu*, 19.2a; and "Yin lü" (where the names given are those of the corresponding *lü* or standard pitches), *Lü-shih ch'un-ch'iu*, 6.5a.

46. The vocabularies of music theory and poetics developed unequally. The oldest discussions of poetry have more to say about the music that accompanied it than about its meaning, yet the use of music in society was to communicate in *yüeh-yü*, a language, as Chu Tzu-ch'ing supposes, "emphasizing the song lyrics" (*Shih yen chih pien*, p. 198).

47. See *Li*, 37.7b–8a and elsewhere; "Yüeh lun," *Hsün-tzu*, opening paragraph (p. 252) and elsewhere.

48. Readers skeptical of the validity, in any possible world, of such a formulation may consult Geertz, *Negara*, for a fuller picture.

49. The word *tz'u* as used in Ode 264, "Chan yang," means something rather less gentle—"chastise" would be better (*Shih*, 18:5.11b).

50. *Shih*, 1:5.8a. Compare K'ung Ying-ta on Paragraph 12 of the Great Preface: "Because the grace of the former kings had not yet been exhausted, the people still knew [the importance of] ritual and were able to use ritual to save the world" (ibid., 1:1.13a).

51. K'ung Ying-ta, in *Shih*, 1:1.12a.

52. I must once again warn the reader not to take "high" and "low" in their English musical sense, irrelevant here.

53. K'ung Ying-ta in *Shih*, 1:1.12a; italicized phrase in imitation of *Lun yü* 12.19.

54. *Pien* ("altered") could also be rendered as "chromatic," to give the word its musical sense. Chromaticism is often spoken of as a symptom of dissoluteness, and the music of Cheng and Wei as being overcharged with superfluous harmonies: see DeWoskin, *Song for One or Two*, pp. 92–94.

55. Isidore of Seville, *Etymologiae*: "Irony . . . occurs when we praise a man whom we wish to blame or blame a man whom we wish to praise" (Halm, *Rhetores latini minores*, p. 521; the definition has classical precedent behind it).

56. *Shih*, 3:1.9b–10b. On the decision to see in a poem the expression, not of its author, but of a "persona" chosen by that author, see Van Zoeren, *Poetry and Personality*, pp. 169–72, 227–29.

57. Quintilian, *Institutio* IX.2.58.

58. The Fu-tan University group summons the theory of "praise and blame" as its first witness to the Prefaces' "demand that poetry put itself directly at the service of feudal government" (*Chung-kuo wen-hsüeh p'i-p'ing shih*, p. 48). Chu Tzu-ch'ing notes that in the ritually defined context of "offering" (*hsien*) poems to a superior, "praise" and "blame" could indeed jointly exhaust the field of poetic meaning (*Shih yen chih pien*, p. 197). The topic of "praise and blame" therefore seems rooted in structures of behavior characteristic of courtly life and thus makes obvious, for many modern *Shih* specialists, its secondary character. Comparative evidence from unrelated languages may only blur the issue, but see, for a discussion of the poet in his quasi-priestly role as distributor of praise and blame in early Greece, Nagy, *Best of the Achaeans*, pp. 222–42; and Detienne, *Les Maîtres de vérité*, pp. 18–27, 60–62. For the Indo-European background, see Dumézil on "censor" and "census," *Idées romaines*, pp. 103–24.

59. Liu Hsieh (expanding on this paragraph of the Preface in "Ming-shih," *Wen-hsin tiao-lung*, p. 83) puts satire and rebuke in the orbit of the southern *sao* (lamentation) genre represented by Ch'ü Yüan.

60. See K'ung Ying-ta, comment to Paragraph 1 of the Great Preface: the poem does not need to call the queen's virtue by name, it simply "responds" to it (*Shih*, 1:1.4a).

61. Indeed K'ung Ying-ta resorts to medical vocabulary in his discussion of poetic satire and decadence (*Shih*, 1:1.14b).

62. Since instances of *yüeh-yü* can involve taking song lyrics, or even the associative connotations of instrumental music, ironically, what is said here of theory need not hold for practice: see, e.g., the story about

the dinner given for the old-fashioned *Book of Odes* scholar Wang Shih in Pan Ku, "Ju-lin chuan," *Han shu*, 88.17b–18a. For a detailed investigation of the musical codes of association, see Allanbrook, *Rhythmic Gesture in Mozart.*

63. See *Tristram Shandy*, Book 8, chap. 25. On the "extraneous principle" that orients the interpretation of ironies and allegories, and of figurative language generally, see de Man, "The Rhetoric of Temporality," *Blindness and Insight*, p. 209.

64. Ode 112, "Fa t'an," termed by the Mao Preface "a satire on the greedy," contains the line: "That gentleman does not eat the bread of idleness!" (*Shih*, 5: 3.9b). Mencius sees no satire: "A true gentleman inhabits that state, his lord employs him, and peace, plenty, honors, and glory appear. . . . As for 'not eating the bread of idleness,' who has done more?" ("Chin hsin," *Mencius*, *SSCCS* ed., 13B.5b–6a).

65. *Shih*, 1:1.20a. See the discussion of this and subsequent commentaries in Pauline Yu, *Reading of Imagery*, pp. 49–53.

66. See Wang Hsien-ch'ien, *Shih san-chia i chi-shu*, pp. 1–16.

67. Chu Hsi, *Chu-tzu yü-lei*, p. 2085.

68. See K'ung Ying-ta, *Shih*, 1:1.10a: "praise" and "blame" use the same tropes and can occur indifferently in the "Airs" and "Elegantiae" (the "Laudes," by definition poems of praise, are a generic exception). Formally, nothing distinguishes them. On the relationship—historical, but also, as I would argue, semiological—of moralizing commentary to the loss of the *Odes'* music, see Van Zoeren, *Poetry and Personality*, pp. 28–34, 48–49, and 226.

69. The description of the historians' "perceptions" and "regrets" (Preface, para. 13) constructs a model for the doubled or ironic reading the decadent Odes require. See K'ung's comments on Paragraph 12 of the Preface, where the memory or hope of historical change is said to trigger composition.

70. Aristotle, *De motu animalium* 699a6–11; trans. Nussbaum, p. 28.

71. Compare Wilson, *Axel's Castle*, p. 163. A longer excerpt from DeWoskin's survey of early music theory may be helpful here. "The twelve pitches did not make a scale on which music could be played. Rather, each of the twelve provided a pitch level at which one of the five tones could be set for the establishment of a mode-key and the performance of music. The twelve pitches were merely initializing sounds, used only to begin a performance and fix the position of the movable pentatonic relata. . . . Control over the moment and pitch at which the music

began was control over the entire performance" (*Song for One or Two*, p. 48).

72. DeWoskin, *Song for One or Two*, p. 64. See also Needham and Robinson, "Sound (Acoustics)," pp. 179, 200–201.

73. On Master Mao's direct borrowings from Hsün-tzu and an attempt at establishing his scholarly pedigree, see Karlgren, "Early History," pp. 18–33. Shen P'ei studied with Fou-ch'iu Po, a student of Hsün-tzu's. On Hsün-tzu and the Han school, I follow Hightower, *Han Shih Wai Chuan*, p. 3. The *Yen-t'ieh lun* of Huan K'uan, which draws heavily on Hsün-tzu and is laced with Ch'i interpretations of the *Odes*, provides a parallel case to the *Ta Tai* and *Hsiao Tai* versions of the *Li chi*. For the history of the various schools, see T'ang Yin, *Liang-Han, San-kuo hsüeh-an*, pp. 211–321, 340. See also Wang Hsien-ch'ien, *Shih san-chia i chi-shu*, Preface, pp. 7–9; and Knoblock, *Xunzi*, 1: 36–44.

74. On Hsün-tzu's rise and fall, see Karlgren, "Early History," pp. 19–20; and Hsiao, *Chinese Political Thought*, p. 192.

75. "Hsing o," *Hsün-tzu*, beginning (p. 289).

76. "Li lun," "Wang chih," *Hsün-tzu*, pp. 231, 103–4.

77. Quoted in Wang Ch'ung, "Pen hsing p'ien," *Lun heng*, p. 65. Full quotation gives a better idea of the nature of Liu's disbelief: "If this is so, then there is no *ch'i* [operative force] in Heaven, and good and evil are no longer each other's match. Where then would man ever get an opportunity of doing good?"

78. Quoted terms from Needham et al., *Science and Civilisation*, 2: 279–303, 582–83; see also Mote, "Cosmological Gulf."

79. "Li lun," "Yüeh lun" (same wording), *Hsün-tzu*, pp. 231, 252.

80. "Ch'üan hsüeh," ibid., pp. 7–9. For Yang Hung-ming, that also comes close to exhausting the topic of Hsün-tzu's literary interests (*Hsün-tzu wen-i yen-chiu*).

81. "Yüeh lun," *Hsün-tzu*, p. 256; for a list of things the eye does see and the ear hear, see chap. 22, "Cheng ming," pp. 276–79. The difference between perception and interpretation is carried on into the broadest implications of the "Record of Music." Music, it may be remembered, unites, while ritual differentiates. (Ontology, insofar as the catalogue of the "Cheng ming" chapter stands for a table of categories, belongs to ritual.) Yet the contrast does not run very deep, because all forms of music are judged by their adherence to ritual codes. Music, too, is a "loyal opposition."

82. "Ch'üan hsüeh," *Hsün-tzu*, p. 10.

83. Compare Hegel, *Aesthetik* II.3.b 2: "And so it is rightly said of allegory, that it is cold and bald and . . . more a creature of rationality than of concrete intuition or of fantasy with its depth of feeling" (*W*, 13: 512–13).

84. *Han Shih wai chuan*, 5.1a–b; trans. Hightower, pp. 159–60. The internal quotation is from Ode 244, "Wen wang yu sheng," and in that context would have to read: "From the east to the west, from the south to the north, there was not a one but thought of submitting [to the newly victorious Chou ruler] [*wu ssu pu fu*]." But it also rewrites a line from the "Kuan chü" ode: the prince who is to be married "sought her and could not find her; waking and sleeping he was vanquished by her in his thought [*wu-mei ssu fu*]." The quick course in *Odes* interpretation offered by the *Wai chuan* passage is typical of all four Han era schools.

85. Compare the sages' sudden creation of culture. One does not discover a standard pitch or a moral canon; these things have to be instituted, which requires speech acts. An episode from the *Han shu* turns on the question of the linguistic mode inherent to making the *Odes* exhibits in a course on general ethics. "Wang Shih was tutor to the Prince of Ch'ang-i. Upon the death of the emperor Chao [in 73 B.C.] the Prince of Ch'ang-i was elevated in rank, but his behavior proved lewd and wasteful. [Subsequently] all his officials were imprisoned and sentenced to death. Only Wang Chi and Kung Sui were excused, on the grounds that they had frequently remonstrated with the prince. Shih was jailed with the rest and slated for death. The official in charge asked him why he, as teacher, had not presented any remonstrances to his pupil. Shih said: 'Day and night your humble servant taught the prince the 305 odes. When we came to a poem about loyal officials and dutiful children, I never failed to make the prince recite it repeatedly. When we came to a poem about reckless and undisciplined rulers, I never failed to shed tears and expound the poem in its utmost details for the prince's benefit. Your humble servant remonstrated by means of the 305 odes. That is why I submitted no [other] criticisms.' On hearing him out, the official commuted his sentence" (Pan Ku, *Han shu*, 88.17b–18a). For a discussion of Confucius' teachings on ritual in comparison to Austin's treatment of performative utterances, see Fingarette, *Confucius*, pp. 11–17, 76–77.

Chapter 4

1. See Chapter 3 for K'ung Ying-ta's notes to Paras. 12–16 of the Great Preface. Antiquity's most complete representation of this "field" is found

in the well-known episode "Prince Chi Cha of Wu Inspects the Music of Chou," *Tso*, Hsiang, 29th year; Watson, trans., *The "Tso Chuan,"* pp. 149–53. For a description of a similar process in another society—the formation of a pan-Hellenic culture through rituals, festivals, and epic poetry—see Nagy, *Greek Mythology and Poetics*, pp. 43–47. Martin J. Powers finds in Han stone engravings effects comparable to what I am calling the "field" of the *Odes* aesthetic. According to Powers, this art's "emphasis on symmetry and its thin registers allow an artist to display as in a diagram the basic social relations illustrated. . . . By creating a simple visual standard (a thin register), comparisons can be made" between the figures depicted. "The ability to make comparisons was an intrinsically critical feature of the classical tradition" (*Art and Political Expression in Early China*, pp. 369–70).

2. See Chapter 1.

3. Hsiao Kung-ch'üan, *Chung-kuo cheng-chih ssu-hsiang shih*, p. 109.

4. Granet, *Fêtes et chansons*, p. 15. "Private" reading of the *Book of Odes* did, of course, take place, but records of it are to be found in poetic allusions and other contexts far from the official genre of Classics exposition.

5. As the "Record of Music" puts it (*Li*, 37.8a); see Chapter 3.

6. Karlgren, *Book of Odes*, pp. 4–5.

7. Granet, *Fêtes et chansons*, p. 20.

8. Yeh, "Metaphor and *Bi*," p. 251.

9. Chu Hsi, *Shih hsü pien-shuo*, p. 7. Fang Yü-jun (1811–83) notes that "this young lady" is no way to speak of a royal spouse (*"Shih-ching" yüan-shih*, 1: 82).

10. See also *Tso*, Hsiang, 7th, 27th, 28th years. These examples follow *i* with a verb, which is what Granet makes of *shih-chia*, although others take it as a noun. In the *Shih ching*, see Ode 196, "Hsiao yüan" (and Karlgren's helpful notes, "Glosses on the *Siao Ya* Odes," p. 106); Ode 214, "Shang shang che hua" (where *i* is again a verb: "to do properly"); and the commentary on lines 1 and 2 of Ode 84, "Shan yu fu-su": "High and low, great and small, each gets what is suited to it." For *i* used, somewhat ambiguously, as a transitive verb in a context of praise, see also the text and Little Preface of Ode 75, "Tzu i." The *Li chi* passage depends entirely on the "T'ao yao" line (see note 12 to this chapter). Arthur Waley has "Our lady going home / Brings good to family and house," which is just possible (*Book of Songs*, p. 106).

11. Granet, *Fêtes et chansons*, p. 29.

12. Granet merely cites the encyclopedic collection *Imperial Ch'ing Explications of the Classics* (*Huang-Ch'ing ching-chieh*) as the source for this gloss. His reference is probably Li Fu-p'ing (1770–1832), *Mao Shih ch'ou-i*, 1331.5b, where the "she will order" reading is merely mentioned. Ch'en Huan makes much more of it in his *Shih Mao shih chuan shu* (1847; reprinted in Wang Hsien-ch'ien's unofficial continuation of the Imperial Explications, *Huang-Ch'ing ching-chieh hsü-pien*, 1888). The "Great Learning" passage is the one exceptional case of "*i ch'i . . .*" mentioned above. "The gentleman must have [goodness] in himself before he can seek it in others. . . . Thus the administration of a kingdom depends on the ordering of a single household. The Ode says: 'How delicately beautiful is the peach tree, its leaves are luxuriant; this young lady goes to her new home, she will order well her house-people.' When one has 'ordered well one's house-people,' then one can teach the people of one's country" ("Ta hsüeh," *Li*, 60.8b–9a). The passage testifies to a pre-Han reading of "T'ao-yao" in the sense adopted by Ch'en Huan and Karlgren. This reading may depend in turn on a textual parallel in Ode 164, "Ch'ang ti" (one of the "Lesser Elegantiae"). There the line is evidently an imperative: "Order well your chamber and house, / Take joy in your wife and children."

13. Here a point of method. The earliest commentaries on the *Odes* are already eclectic to the point of tolerating a great deal of contradiction. They consolidate centuries of study and may as well be read as being of one class with those who follow and add to them. Since the discussion below points toward a typology, rather than a history, of readers and reading methods, it dispenses with most of the niceties of influence, period, and school.

14. A. N. Prior's example of such "is-ought" statements: "He is a sea-captain" and ought to do whatever a sea-captain ought to do (quoted in MacIntyre, *After Virtue*, p. 57). Confucius argues from the rightness of words at *Lun yü* 6.23 and 11.12. For a splendid example of the flexibility of *i*, see Ode 249, "Chia le," lines 3 ("he orders the people," strong sense) and 10 ("he is fit to be a king," weak sense).

15. In "T'ao-yao" "there is no contrast, conceptual or imagistic, concomitant with the comparison" (Yeh, "Metaphor and *Bi*," p. 251).

16. *Shih*, 1:2.15a–b.

17. *SMSCS*, p. 30, comment to first stanza. Ch'en refers to the *Chou li* ("Mei shih," *SSCCS* ed., 14.15a–16a) and to Ode 20, "Piao yu mei." See also Bodde, *Festivals in Classical China*, pp. 243–61. Another Ch'ing

commentator suggests that "T'ao-yao" praises a late marriage, only not quite so late a one as is described in "Piao yu mei." "The Way of husband and wife is to bear children, as it is that of plants and trees to bear fruit. The peach tree flowers after the plum, but bears fruit before the plum does; so the Ode says: 'well-set are its fruits.' . . . But when the fruits are being 'scooped up in slanting baskets' [as in Ode 20], it is already too late" (Hui Chou-t'i, *Shih shuo*, in Juan Yüan, *Huang-Ch'ing ching-chieh*, 191.2a–b).

18. The "leaves" of stanza 3 make a graphic, and in ancient times a phonetic, pun with the word for "generations." That basis for praise needs to be put in the future too. For a comparable case, see Spitzer, "*Explication de Texte* Applied to Three Great Middle English Poems," *Essays*, pp. 193–247.

19. "Kao-tzu," pt. 1, *Mencius*, SSCCS ed., 11A.7b–8a. The Ode is number 260, "Cheng min."

20. "Wan chang," pt. 1, *Mencius*, SSCCS ed., 9A.10a.

21. "Hsi-tz'u," *I ching*, SSCCS ed., 8.6b; "Wu ch'eng," *Shu*, 11.26a.

22. SMSCS, pp. 35–37. Shirakawa Shizuka observes that the opening parallels that of the sacrificial song "Nan yu chia yü" (Ode 171). For his analysis, which relies mostly on the *Han Shih wai chuan*'s notes to the poem, see "*Shikyō*," pp. 47–51.

23. *Shih*, 1:3.5b–6a.

24. Karlgren, *Book of Odes*, p. 6.

25. *Shih*, 1:3.6a.

26. SMSCS, pp. 37–38.

27. Cheng Hsüan, in *Shih*, 1:3.6b.

28. Confucius (apocryphal, of course) in *Han Shih wai chuan*, 5:1, cited above; Ode 205, "Pei shan." "Empire" is used here as a rough synonym for the cumbersome *t'ien-hsia*, *oikoumenē* or "inhabited world." Although the Chinese empire properly speaking was founded on the ruins of the Chou polity by the First Emperor of Ch'in, the theory of the Chou monarch's universal dominion held for early ritualists and classicists the same attraction as did the idea of a revived Rome for medievals such as Dante.

29. *Shih*, 17:3.5b, 13b; as translated by Karlgren, *Book of Odes*, pp. 207–8. The reader may wish to compare my reading of the poems on kingly "work" with C. H. Wang's proposal to see in five poems of the "Greater Elegantiae" elements of a Chou "epic" (*From Ritual to Allegory*, pp. 73–114).

30. Thus poetry "unites what is different" and interpretation "distinguishes between things that are similar": for the formula, see Chapter 2.

31. *Shih*, 8:3.1a. For the translation of the first two lines, I could not improve on Waley (*Book of Songs*, p. 236).

32. *Shih*, 8:3b.

33. Ibid., p. 4b.

34. Compare Ode 101, "Nan shan"; Ode 59, "Chu kan" ("Long and tapering are the bamboo poles for fishing in the Ch'i"; commentary: "A hook is for catching fish, a wife requires ritual to confirm her position"); and Ode 24, "Ho pi nung i" (with its pun on *hun*, "fishing line" and "marriage": but the fishing line is there meant to catch the husband's family a set of powerful relations). *Shih*, 5:2.1a; 3:3.7a; 1:5.10b.

35. Granet, *Catégories matrimoniales et relations de proximité en Chine ancienne* (Paris: Alcan, 1939), p. 97.

36. The application to literary criticism is made by Lu Chi, "Wen fu," in Hsiao T'ung, *Wen-hsüan*, 17.2a.

37. *Shih*, 1:3.4b–5a. Wang Hsiao (cited at ibid.) thought the offering vessels were supposed to have been laid out by the Duke of Chou, evidence of his attention to ritual. Compare Waley: "This song represents, I think, the popular view that marriage was a very simple matter, and a match-maker by no means necessary" (*Book of Songs*, p. 68).

38. "Performance" in the sense of John Austin's "speech act" or "performative" (*How to Do Things with Words*, p. 6). Despite the habitual disclaimer regarding frivolous and theatrical repetitions, repetition (and thus mimesis) is what gives the performative its "force." Compare Derrida, "Signature événement contexte," in *Marges*, esp. pp. 388–89.

39. Wallace Stevens, "Anecdote of the Jar," *Collected Poems* (New York: Vintage, 1982), p. 76.

40. *Shih*, 17:3.8b. See also Karlgren, "Glosses on the *Ta Ya* and *Sung* Odes," p. 7.

41. Wang Ching-chih, *"Shih-ching" t'ung-shih*, p. 549.

42. Whether noble "work" counts as work is the issue on which Mencius's reading of an ode as "praise" or "blame" turns (see Chapter 3). Jean Lévi comments on the role of inventor-kings such as Shen Nung and Fu Hsi: "In the manner of a decree, invention manifests the ruler's organizing power. . . . In this sense, there is nothing to distinguish the sovereign's technical activity from his ability to issue laws" ("Mythe de l'âge d'or," p. 82).

43. The elaboration on "Fa k'o" attributed to Confucius in the "Doc-

trine of the Mean" has always been understood to refer to law. "The way is not far from people, yet to take a way that departs from the people— that cannot be considered a way. The Ode says: 'In hewing an axe haft, the pattern is not far-off.' One axe hews another; [only] someone who looks on them slightingly will see them as far apart" ("Chung yung," *Li,* 52.9a).

44. So the *Chou li* text that prescribes the right length and breadth for axe handles is itself an "axe."

45. "Yüeh chi," *Li,* 39.9b.

46. The word "figure" is used here in preference to a host of narrower rhetorical terms. Its Latin connotations—etymologically a "made thing," it can mean "shape" or "portrait"—makes it an apt equivalent of the *Odes'* axe. "Figurative language" is usually understood as a matter of likenesses, i.e., tropes, a sense that can only be secondary here. Or as Quintilian puts it: trope occurs when a word is "transferred [*translatus*] from its natural and principal sense to another," while what distinguishes figure from non-figure, or discriminates among the kinds of figure, is the shape or organization (*conformatio*) of the utterance (*Institutio,* IX.1.4).

47. *Shih,* 2:3.16a–b.

48. Wen, "*Shih-ching* t'ung-i," *Wen I-to ch'üan-chi,* 2: 199–200; Karl-gren, "Glosses on the *Kuo Feng* Odes," p. 132.

49. *Shih,* 2:3.16b–17a.

50. "A shadow never moves of itself": axiom of the Mohist school, cited in Needham et al., *Science and Civilisation,* 4.1, p. 81; text in Liang Ch'i-ch'ao, *Mo ching chiao shih,* p. 112. For a valuable discussion of shadow examples, see Graham, *Later Mohist Logic,* pp. 372–74. I am indebted to Qian Nanxiu for referring me to the *Mo-tzu.* An examination of the vocabulary of waves, shadows and echoes may offer the best chances for bridging the opposition suggested by some recent critics between a Chinese "expressive" view of art and a "mimetic" tradition deriving from the Greeks.

51. "Shuo fu," *Lieh-tzu chu,* p. 89.

52. See Karlgren, *Grammata Serica Recensa,* pp. 166–67 (etyma 625, 626). *Fan* may be an alternative for a rare musical term *feng* ("easy flowing"). See also Chou, *Ku wu-i,* pp. 198–99.

53. The Lu and Han schools seem to have held that the song was composed by the mother of the "two gentlemen" as they boarded the fatal boat (Wang Hsien-ch'ien, *Shih san-chia i chi-shu,* p. 213). Cheng Hsüan does not discuss the story about the two princes' mother, but paraphrases

lines 7 and 8, "I think of you two gentlemen, may you not come to harm!" as a statement about the historical past: "I remember and think of those two gentlemen: although their conduct was without fault, could they avoid going [to their deaths]?" (*Shih*, 2:3.17a). The reading is by no means inevitable, but shows how, for Cheng, the "two gentlemen" have become legends worth "spreading everywhere."

54. For gnomons, see Needham et al., *Science and Civilisation*, 3: 284–302, 569–79. For an extended discussion of surveying practices in the time of the *Odes* and their commentators, see "Ti kuan," *Chou li, SSCCS* ed., 10.9a–13a. The vocabulary there is strongly reminiscent of the descriptions of exemplary kingship. Surveying may therefore be in the *Chou li* what it was in parts of the *Book of Documents*: the first and greatest artifice of the ancient kings.

55. See, e.g., Chen, "The *Shih-ching*," pp. 16–26; Chao, *"Shih ching" fu pi hsing*; Wang Chin-ling, *Chung-kuo wen-hsüeh li-lun shih*, pp. 167–74; Levy, "Constructing Sequences"; and Pauline Yu, *Reading of Imagery*, pp. 57–60.

56. Liu Hsieh, chap. 36, "Pi hsing," *Wen-hsin-tiao-lung*, p. 677; Chu Hsi, *"Shih" chi chuan*, commentary on "Kuan chü." Likewise Waley: *hsing* are "formulae . . . in which a series of statements concerning natural phenomena, trees, birds, etc., are correlated to a series of statements concerning a human situation" (*"Book of Changes,"* p. 128).

57. *SMSCS*, p. 13. "Entrust, rely on, consign, commission, ask a favor, make a pretext of": the meanings of *t'o* resemble those of the *chi* and *yü* ("to lodge temporarily," or "to attribute [words to another]") that so often surface in Chinese rhetorical terminology.

58. *Shih*, 1:1.10a.

59. Texts collected in *SMSCS*, p. 13; for a slightly different version, see Chapter 3.

60. *SMSCS*, p. 13. Compare Cheng Hsüan's explanation of the *Chou li* passage listing *hsing* among the devices of "musical language": "A *hsing* uses a good object to allude to a good deed" (cited in *Chou li, SSCCS* ed., 22.8b).

61. *Shih*, 11:1.6b.

62. Just this way of asserting identity on the basis of shared qualities is put on stage in the courtroom rhetoric of Ode 17, "Hsing lu."

63. Wen, *"Shih-ching* t'ung i," *Wen I-to ch'üan-chi*, 2: 161. Another *ju* word, meaning "disgrace," may be relevant (cf. Karlgren, *Grammata Serica Recensa*, pp. 43, 314; etyma 94, 1223). Liu Hsiang tells a story about

this poem: it was composed by the widow of a marquis of Wei to protest her family's desire that she remarry (*Lieh nü chuan*, 4.5a–b). But the Mao Prefaces apply the same story to another poem, also entitled "Po chou" (Ode 45), in the "Airs of Yung" section. In the Han dynasty, apparently, the Prefaces still circulated in a separate volume from the text of the *Odes*; the difference between Liu and Mao may stem from this arrangement. See also Ch'ien Chung-shu, *Kuan-chui pien*, 1: 76–78.

64. Cheng Hsüan, in *Shih*, 2:1.6a.

65. Tung Chung-shu, "Yü pei," *Ch'un-ch'iu fan-lu*, 1.10a.

66. K'ung Ying-ta, expounding Cheng, *Shih*, 2:1.6a.

67. "Wei cheng," *Lun yü*, SSCCS ed., 2.5a. Wang Yü-lin suggested the parallel.

68. SMSCS, p. 78.

69. "Ching-chieh," *Li*, 50.3b–4b.

70. To put it somewhat summarily, Cheng reads an allegory as a metaphor. Aristotle opens the way to identifying allegory and pun in *Rhetoric* 1412a26–b1, where puns are described, in language that looks forward to future definitions of allegory, as a device for making words "say what they do not say," or as Aristotle puts it in reference to an example: *exapatāi, allo gar legei*, "it astonishes, for it says something other [than what it seemed to say]." The rest of the passage draws distinctions between metaphors, grounded in conceptual identity, and puns, grounded in homonymy or the play of letters (*ta para gramma skōmmata*). For the structural resemblances between allegory and punning, see Quilligan, *Language of Allegory*.

71. Shirakawa Shizuka's chapter "The *Odes* and Narrative" glides smoothly from the narrative poems to the narratives told about the poems in sources like *Mencius* and *Tso chuan*; see *Shikyō*, pp. 242–49.

72. The best reference is Chu Tzu-ch'ing, *Shih yen chih pien*. The *Han Shih wai chuan* contains dozens of anecdotes, mostly apocryphal, involving quotations of Odes. For several poetry-quoting jousts from the *Tso chuan*, see Röllicke, "Die Fährte des Herzens," pp. 26–30, 34–57. For a treatment of parts of the *Lun yü* as expanded quotations from the Odes, see Riegel, "Poetry."

73. "Chin t'eng," *Shu*, 13.11a. Tuan Yü-ts'ai (1735–1815) advanced paleographic reasons for reading *hsin* in place of *chiao*, thus making the last sentence: "The king did not yet dare to *trust* the Duke of Chou" (cited in Chu T'ing-hsien, *"Shang-shu" yen-chiu*, p. 509).

74. "Ch'ih-hsiao," *Shih*, 8:2.1a. I should emphasize once more that the

Shang shu passage represents not history, nor even the history of the "Ch'ih-hsiao" ode, but the view (or myth) of history adopted by the early commentators on the *Odes.*

75. Chu Tzu-ch'ing, *Shih yen chih pien*, pp. 207–8.

76. *Shu*, 13.11a. For the archaeological evidence for the rebellion, see Shirakawa, *Kimbun no sekai*, pp. 41–47.

77. First stanza, "Ch'ih-hsiao," *Shih*, 8:2.1b–2a. Compare Karlgren, *Book of Odes*, pp. 99–100.

78. Cheng Hsüan's reading seems to start from the position that the person to whom the *poem* is addressed (King Ch'eng) must be identical to the owl addressed *in* the poem. The results depart so widely from the tale told in the *Documents* that I am inclined to see Cheng Hsüan as trusting in the poem (and in his own rather cut-and-dried style of topical interpretation) to the utter neglect of the prose source. But the *Documents* has never received a clean bill of health from classical scholars. Perhaps King Ch'eng's reluctance to "blame the duke," which many commentators take as evidence of his fear of the duke, indicates that Ch'eng at first *misunderstands* the poem in a sense close to Cheng Hsüan's.

79. I owe this idea to a conversation with Tu Kuo-ch'ing.

80. Fang Yü-jun, *"Shih-ching" yüan-shih*, 1: 316. For a survey of skeptical opinions by Yüan Mei and others on the "Chin t'eng" story, see ibid., pp. 317–18.

81. *Shih*, 11:1.8b.

82. See "Ch'ü li," *Li*, 1.18b–23a, for examples of the son's self-effacing conduct. What is said toward the end of the same chapter about the proper way of addressing sovereigns (5.14b) is qualified by Confucius' advice ("T'an Kung," *Li*, 6.2b).

83. "Chi t'ung," *Li*, 49.12a: "The Way of sacrifices is this: a grandson is the 'corpse' of his departed grandfather. The one who acts the role of 'corpse' has the position of a son relative to the person doing the sacrifice. The father faces north and serves [the son], thereby illuminating the Way of sons' service to fathers. This is the relation [*lun*] of fathers and sons."

84. Compare Shirakawa, *Kimbun no sekai*, pp. 41–42. The Duke of Chou prefigured the "king without a crown" that Han Confucians wished to make of the historical Confucius: see Fung, *History of Chinese Philosophy*, 2: 71–77. On the Duke of Chou as substitute, see also Allan, "Drought, Human Sacrifice, and the Mandate," pp. 523–24.

85. "Ju hsiao," *Hsün-tzu*, p. 81. The chapter begins with a disquisition

on the Duke of Chou's regency, the concluding words of which furnish the chapter's title: "And so [the duke] is called the Model of the Great Confucian." Hsün-tzu's phrase about "demurring and yielding, yet conquering," may have inspired Cheng Hsüan's reading of "Ch'ih-hsiao," so often seen as bizarre: Cheng may have felt he had to give the Duke of Chou something to be yielding about.

86. For many readers of the *Odes* and *Documents*, history is identical to that interpretation of historical events: K'ung Ying-ta does not seem to be ironizing when he states that the Duke of Chou composed his poem in order to "explain" (*chieh*) his reasons for pursuing the rebels (*Shu*, 13.12a).

87. *Shu*, 13.12b; wording echoed by the commentary of the Ch'i school (Wang Hsien-ch'ien, *Shih san-chia i chi-shu*, p. 526).

88. *Lun yü* 17.19: "Does heaven speak? The four seasons continue in their courses, the hundred things are generated, and does heaven speak?"

89. *Shih*, 18:1.7a. The Shang had overthrown the Hsia, and King Wen at the time of speaking was about to overthrow the Shang. Karlgren explains the proverb: "So the 'root' of the state, the royal house, is disposed of, without the branches and leaves, *i.e.* the people, coming to any harm" (*Book of Odes*, p. 216). Another influence on Heaven's spectacle may be the "Hung fan" chapter of the *Documents*.

90. The play on Confucius' words is just one of many reminders that the *Book of Documents*, for all its purported antiquity, is a compilation from many sources, some of them predated by the early versions of the *Odes*. It may be significant that the *Shih chi* omits the events of the "Chin-t'eng" chapter from its account of the early Chou dynasty, deeming them relevant to the Duke of Chou's personal history and lineage instead (Ssu-ma Ch'ien, "Lu Chou Kung shih-chia," *Shih chi*, pp. 566–67).

91. This is an interpretative conclusion, but it may have some philological substance as well. The moralizing legends about Chinese history are part of the stock in trade of the same thinkers who indelibly moralized the message of the *Odes*. Beyond this, it can be argued that those legends' currency helped to stabilize the anthology (including its interpretative annexes) as we now have it. Although there is little to distinguish the Mao, Ch'i, Lu, and Han interpretations of the ritual hymns of the *Odes* (the "Laudes" and many "Elegantiae"), they often disagree about the targets and import of the songs in the "Airs of the States." The exception to the second half of this pattern is the "Airs of Pin" cycle of

poems dealing with events surrounding the Duke of Chou's regency: their teaching on these seven songs is, once again, strongly similar. Even when they disagree on a nuance (for example, the Ch'i school's explanation of "Ch'ih-hsiao"), they do so in a way that shows their dependence on common sources such as the *Book of Documents*. If there was an Urtext and if the variations in *Odes* teaching can be described as a pattern of dispersal from that common source, then the "Airs of Pin" and the ritual songs would seem to have strayed the least. Perhaps the earliest versions of the anthology gave commentaries only for the ritual poems and the cycle of songs relating to the Chou dynasty's formation. The reason the commentaries on the "Airs of the States" diverge so widely may be that their authors simply had no prior (pre-Han) tradition to base themselves on and were trying to extend the pattern of the existing comments on the "Airs of Pin" and the "Laudes" to cover the whole of the *Odes*—even to those songs recorded, if Chu Tzu-ch'ing is right, solely in order to preserve their music. See Chapter 2 for Chu Tzu-ch'ing's hypothesis. Wang Chin-ling observes the relative unanimity of commentators on the "Laudes" and "Elegantiae" but makes no distinction between the "Airs of Pin" and the airs of the other states (*Chung-kuo wen-hsüeh li-lun shih*, 1: 324).

92. Franz Kafka, "Von den Gleichnissen" (On parables), *Sämtliche Erzählungen* (Frankfurt am Main: Fischer, 1981), p. 359.

Chapter 5

EPIGRAPHS: "NOTHING / WILL HAVE TAKEN PLACE / BUT PLACE." Mallarmé, "Un coup de dès," *Oeuvres complètes*, pp. 474–75; Eduard Gans, "Vorrede" to Hegel's *Philosophie der Geschichte*.

1. For some reasons why this conclusion is embarrassing, see Benjamin, "Das Kunstwerk im Zeitalter seiner technischen Reproduzierbarkeit," epilogue, *Gesammelte Schriften*, I.2: 506–8; trans. in idem, *Illuminations*, pp. 241–42. For historical reinforcements of Benjamin's topical equation—"fascism is the aestheticization of politics"—see Elizabeth M. Wilkinson and L. A. Willoughby, Introduction, in Schiller, *On the Aesthetic Education of Man*, pp. cxli–iv; and de Man, "Kant and Schiller," conclusion.

2. Eduard Gans, "Vorrede," to Hegel, *Vorlesungen über die Philosophie der Geschichte*, in *Werke, vollständige Ausgabe durch einen Verein von Freunden des Verewigten*, 9: xvi, xix; also quoted in "Anmerkung der

Redaktion zu Band 12," *W*, 12: 564. Hegel's *Philosophy of History* is a synthetic text made out of incomplete manuscript drafts and several sets of student notes. In the absence of an adequate critical text of the lectures, we are forced to work with several parallel editions: the *Werke* edition, based on Karl Hegel's 1840 revision of Gans's 1837 text; Georg Lasson's edition of 1917–23 (cited here under the names of its sections: *Die orientalische Welt, Die griechische und römische Welt, Die germanische Welt*); and Johannes Hoffmeister's enlarged 1955 edition of Lasson's text of the Introduction (*Die Vernunft in der Geschichte*).

3. Hegel, *Philosophie der Natur*, pt. II of the *Enzyklopädie der philosophischen Wissenschaften*, *W*, 9: 437. Henceforth references to the *Encyclopedia* cite the paragraph numbers given in the *Werke* edition. The work is subdivided into "The Science of Logic" (or "Little Logic"), paras. 19–244; "The Philosophy of Nature," paras. 245–376; and "The Philosophy of Spirit," paras. 377–577; below I make occasional reference to these part titles.

4. Hegel, *Enzyklopädie*, para. 353 (*W*, 9: 436–38). In the "Supplement" (*Zusatz*) compiled from students' notes, Hegel is quoted as saying: "The simple identity-with-itself of the concept's general subjectivity, that which feels, that which in the [realm of] spirit we call the 'Ego,' is [here called] 'sensibility.' Touched by any other thing, it immediately refers [*verkehrt*] that thing back to itself." On Albrecht von Haller's physiology, the immediate source of Hegel's "system of sensibility," see Hegel, *Philosophy of Nature*, 3: 302–5. Michael John Petry, the translator of this work, notes the passage's Fichtean overtones (p. 301). The technical term "irritability" is used to mean "the capacity of being excited to vital action by the application of an external stimulus" (*OED*, s.v., citing use from 1751).

5. Hegel, *Enzyklopädie*, para. 354 (*W*, 9: 439). For an examination of similar transitions from utter particularity to utter generality, see de Man, "Sign and Symbol"; and Warminski, *Readings in Interpretation*, pp. 163–79.

6. Hegel, "Beobachtung der Natur," *Phänomenologie des Geistes* (*W*, 3: 190). "Distinguishing/distance" attempts to translate the pun on "unterscheiden/scheiden." Compare ibid., pp. 85–86, 97; *Grundlinien der Philosophie des Rechts*, para. 6 (*W*, 7: 82); *Enzyklopädie*, para. 20 (*W*, 8: 74); and "Bestimmung, Beschaffenheit und Grenze," *Wissenschaft der Logik* (*W*, 5: 131–39). The 1805–6 Jena writings show Hegel undecided whether to put claws and horns under the heading "skin" or "bone" and

appealing along the way to the schemata of classical logic: see Hegel, *Jenaer Systementwürfe III*, pp. 142–43, 152–53, 158.

7. Hegel, *Enzyklopädie*, para. 351, *Zusatz*: "Dieses Punktuelle . . . [ist] das Subjekt als Selbst-Selbst, als Selbstgefühl." ("This point-like thing [i.e., animal consciousness; Petry translates the epithet as 'punctiform'] is the subject as self-itself, as feeling of self.") On the model of the "point," see below.

8. Hegel, *Enzyklopädie*, para. 354 (*W*, 9: 439).

9. Hegel, *Jenaer Systementwürfe III*, pp. 138–41.

10. Hegel, *Enzyklopädie*, para. 354, *Zusatz* (*W*, 9: 440–41). On "Voraussetzen" ("presupposition"), see Derrida, *Glas*, p. 110.

11. Hegel, *Enzyklopädie*, para. 354, *Zusatz* (*W*, 9: 442). The earth is a bone too (para. 337, *Zusatz*, *W*, 9: 340). The bone is the body's equivalent of what the later syntheses of practical spirit and social organization will know as the tool and the slave. Through their mediation, "I have inserted cunning between myself and external thinghood" (Hegel, *Jenaer Systementwürfe III*, p. 189; see also pp. 204 [marginal sketch in note], 206–7). For Hegel's thinking on tools and work, see Lukács, *Young Hegel*, pp. 174, 325–29, 343–44. At the beginning of the introduction to the *Phenomenology*, Hegel rejects the idea that cognition is a tool for attaining the absolute (*W*, 3: 68).

12. See Hegel, *Philosophie des Rechts*, para. 355 (*W*, 7: 509–10); *Philosophie der Geschichte*, *W*, 12: 96–101, 147, 178–79. "Translation" in its legal sense is the orderly transfer of a right or possession; the "translation of rule" is the right to govern supposedly conveyed by Providence from the defunct Roman emperors to Charlemagne. On the popular life of the concept, see Hulin, *Hegel et l'Orient*, pp. 59–61, 140; and Kiesewetter, *Von Hegel zu Hitler*, pp. 142–44. When exception is taken to a linear, unifying model of historical time, Hegel is usually cited as the prime culprit. (For a particularly detailed indictment, where only the name "Habermas" updates the topic, see Sakai, "Modernity and Its Critique," pp. 475–78.) See Althusser and Balibar, *Lire "Le Capital,"* 1: 51–53, 116–23, for Althusser's advocacy, against linearity, of historical "complexity"; cf. the rejection of linear strains of Marxism in Godelier, "La Notion," p. 2020.

13. "[The plant] knows no other way to save itself from its becoming-another than to let it [that 'alienated' or dead part of the self, e.g., wood and rind] lie indifferently where it falls" (Hegel, *Enzyklopädie*, para. 353, *Zusatz*; *W*, 9: 437, see also p. 436).

14. Hegel, *Enzyklopädie*, para. 344 and *Zusatz* (*W*, 9: 373–75).

15. Hegel, *Philosophie des Rechts*, para. 346 (*W*, 7: 505); see also *Philosophie der Geschichte, W*, 12: p. 72. Compare the translation by T. M. Knox, in Hegel, *Philosophy of Right*, p. 217. On "Außereinanderheit" as spatial "Vielheit," see Hegel, *Enzyklopädie*, para. 254 (*W*, 9: 41–43); and Heidegger, *Sein und Zeit*, pp. 428–36 (*Being and Time*, pp. 480–86).

16. Compare Hegel, *Philosophie des Rechts*, para. 323 (*W*, 7: 491); *Enzyklopädie*, paras. 125, 126, and *Zusätze* (*W*, 8: 256–57).

17. As does international law; see Hegel, *Philosophie des Rechts*, paras. 333, 340 (*W*, 7: 499–500, 503).

18. Hegel, *Vernunft in der Geschichte*, p. 180. This passage does not appear in the Suhrkamp *Werke*, which was based on the 1840 edition by Eduard Gans and Karl Hegel; but for a rough equivalent, see *W*, 12: 104–5.

19. Hegel, *Philosophie der Geschichte, W*, 12: 103.

20. Hulin, *Hegel et l'Orient*, pp. 49, 55.

21. Hegel, *W*, 12: 145, 147.

22. Hegel, *Die orientalische Welt*, pp. 454–55, 512. On Phoenicia (accounts of which Hegel had read in Constantin de Volney) see d'Hondt, *Hegel secret*, pp. 101–6.

23. Hegel, *Die orientalische Welt*, p. 446; idem, "Der Geist des Christentums und sein Schicksal," *W*, 1: 277. With Egypt, the case is somewhat different. The Egyptians express themselves in a monstrous semiology of riddles, figures the Greeks must invert in order to read.

24. Hegel, *Die orientalische Welt*, pp. 509–11. Oedipus's answer to the Sphinx takes on emblematic importance here and in the *Aesthetics*: see *W*, 12: 272; 13: 246, 271, 279, 287; 15: 545, 551.

25. Hulin signals the consequences of this framework for Hegel's characterization of India: "India is the knot of the contradictions with which [Hegel's] Orient is beset. . . . [Its] history is made of pendulum swings. The whole question is whether this singular construction, summarizing as it does the whole Orient, really forms a channel of communication between [Asia's] two extremes." India, the mediator, dissolves on closer inspection into the features of the moments it should connect; the three-part system is no different from the old two-part system (*Hegel et l'Orient*, pp. 68–69).

26. Or of "logistics." The approach taken here must therefore differ from that of referential studies such as Edward Said's *Orientalism*. The whole question of the logical and other forces affecting Hegel's history writing awaits a better edition of Hegel's lectures. All the available texts,

though some may be fuller than others, present the lectures "as if Hegel had pronounced once and for all and all at the same time what he said over a period of years and under perpetually changing hermeneutical conditions" (Kurt Rainer Meist of the Hegel-Archiv, Bochum, pers. comm.).

27. Hegel, *Philosophie der Geschichte, W,* 12: 90; see also idem, *Geschichte der Philosophie, W,* 18: 146.

28. Hegel, *Philosophie der Geschichte, W,* 12: 141. Presenting the Chinese as Wolffians or Wolff as Chinese had been done before, and Hegel, by alluding to the topos, does not put himself in good company. See Lovejoy, "The Chinese Origin of a Romanticism," *Essays,* pp. 107–8.

29. Formalism and changelessness are exactly what Hegel reproaches Leibniz with. "Leibniz let his reason deceive him into thinking a wholly written language constructed in a hieroglyphic manner most desirable. . . . The hieroglyphic written language of the Chinese is suited only to the static character of that people's spiritual formation" (*Enzyklopädie,* para. 459; *W,* 10: 273–74).

30. Hegel, *Die orientalische Welt,* pp. 453–55.

31. "In China and India [Hegel] wished, as he himself put it, to demonstrate in a *merely exemplary* way how a national character ought to be conceived of philosophically. The stagnant nations of the Orient lent themselves more easily to this aim than would those peoples who have a real history and whose character has undergone historical development" (Karl Hegel, "Vorrede," to *Philosophie der Geschichte,* in Hegel, *Werke, vollständige Ausgabe,* 9: xxi; my italics).

32. Hegel, *Enzyklopädie,* para. 18 (*W,* 8: 63–64). But "the representation of a *division* has the incorrectness of setting the different departments or sciences [of philosophy] *next to one another,* as if these were simply inert and substantial in their [mutual] difference, like *kinds.*" The representation of division, because it spatializes, is itself a translation of "Spirit" into "Nature."

33. Hegel, *Enzyklopädie,* paras. 247, 248 (*W,* 9: 24–28). The Introduction to the *Encyclopedia* distinguishes philosophy from "mere aggregates of data," such as philology, and from "sciences that have pure arbitrariness as their ground, e.g., Heraldry: sciences of this second type are *positive* from beginning to end" (para. 16; *W,* 8: 61). "Positedness" is thus a near-synonym for "arbitrary." In the eyes of spirit, both nature and such institutions as the sign are alike "positive." (I thank Roger Blood for calling this passage to my attention.)

34. Hegel, *Enzyklopädie,* para. 248 (*W,* 9: 27).

35. Aristotle, *Poetics* 1452a30: "a change from ignorance to knowledge." The compressed Adamic fable that leads into the *Philosophy of Nature* (*Enzyklopädie*, para. 246, *Zusatz*; *W*, 9: 23) is Hegel's *Anti-Oedipe*.

36. "La première en date, la nature" (Mallarmé, "Bucolique," *Oeuvres complètes*, p. 402); "Nature comes first in time, but the absolute starting point is the Idea" (Hegel, *W*, 9: 30). The transition from Nature to Spirit is accomplished when "Spirit, having comprehended itself, goes on to recognize itself in Nature too" (*Enzyklopädie*, para. 376; *W*, 9: 539).

37. Hegel suggests both readings. Jacques Derrida develops the "orientalizing" treatment of Leibniz (see "Le Puits et la pyramide: introduction à la sémiologie de Hegel" and "La Mythologie blanche," both in *Marges*, esp. pp. 123, 321), Pierre Macherey that of Spinoza (*Hegel ou Spinoza*, pp. 24–28, 254). On Fichte as oriental thinker, see Hegel, *Geschichte der Philosophie*, *W*, 18: 122. Hegel's student Bruno Bauer, for his part, saw the oriental episode as emblematic of the whole of history, and the "world-spirit" as slaughtering its way like Tamerlane from one continent to another (*Die Posaune des jüngsten Gerichts über Hegel den Atheisten und Antichristen*, reprinted in Löwith, *Die Hegelsche Linke*, pp. 158–65; cf. Bloch, *Subjekt-Objekt*, p. 215).

38. Hegel, *Enzyklopädie*, para. 339, *Zusatz* (*W*, 9: 345, 348).

39. On the family as "ethical substance," "immediate or *natural* ethical spirit," see Hegel, *Philosophie des Rechts*, paras. 156–58 (*W*, 7: 305–7). Contrast the Abraham of Hegel's early theological writings, who founds a new nation on a total break with the old. That the separation is not simply from a family but (oddly for a "forefather") from the family as such and that the break forms the transition into politics and history proper emerge from the later text. Every full (male) participant in civil society is severed from the family too (*Philosophie des Rechts*, para. 238; *W*, 7: 386). "Thus does the individual become a *son of civil society*," a change in status and in the modalities of status that goes a long way toward explaining the place of China in that "society"—surely not "family"—"of nations" constituted, after the fact, in world history.

40. Hegel, *Philosophie der Geschichte*, *W*, 12: 153, 142, 147, 174. It especially annoys Hegel that in China ancestors may posthumously be given titles because of their descendants' actions, thereby obliterating the distinction between father and son (see pp. 154–55).

41. Ibid., pp. 152–53. "The substance [of the Chinese state] is immediately one subject, the emperor, whose law forms the opinions [of all]." For an earlier view of the Chinese emperor, free only to "offer a good

example" and praised or blamed with no reference to his actual deeds, see Herder, *Ideen*, Book 11, *Sämtliche Werke*, 14: 12.

42. Montesquieu, *De l'esprit des lois*, in *Oeuvres complètes*, pp. 536, 539, 630–32, 644–46, and elsewhere.

43. Justice cannot be done to this complex question here. See Karl Marx, Preface to *Contribution to the Critique of Political Economy*, in *Early Writings*, pp. 424–28; *Pre-Capitalist Economic Formations*; and three articles published in 1853 in the *New York Daily Tribune*: "Revolution in China and Europe" (May 20), "The British Rule in India" (June 25), and "The Future Results of the British Rule in India" (August 8); for these articles, see *MEGA*, pt. I, vol. 12. For the history of the concept and the debates surrounding it, see Wittfogel, *Oriental Despotism*, pp. 369–412; Centre d'Etudes et de Recherches Marxistes, *Sur le "Mode de production asiatique"*; Tökei, *Essays on the Asiatic Mode of Production*; and Hindess and Hirst, *Pre-Capitalist Modes of Production*.

44. Hegel, *Enzyklopädie*, para. 339, *Zusatz* (*W*, 9: 348).

45. Hegel, *Die orientalische Welt*, p. 453.

46. The time specific to such a figure is that of delay, of delayed recognition. Redefining Hegelian historical time as delay would mark it off from the Aristotelian time to which Derrida seems to assimilate it, e.g., in "Ousia et grammé" (*Marges*, pp. 59–61).

47. Hegel, *Geschichte der Philosophie*, *W*, 18: 146. *Kasus* taken etymologically translates as *Geschichte*.

48. Kant, *Kritik der reinen Vernunft* A 32, B 48–49 (Kant, *Werke*, 3: 80); cf. Aristotle, *de Interpretatione* 24b9.

49. Goethe's correspondence with Schiller, as quoted in Harald Weinrich, *Tempus* (Stuttgart: Kohlhammer, 1964), pp. 21–22.

50. Hegel, *W*, 12: 136. "The static" (*das Dauernde*) is defined in the Jena manuscripts as "a self-sameness into which time has receded: space" (*Jenaer Systementwürfe III*, p. 14).

51. Marx, *Capital*, pp. 99–101; *MEGA*, pt. II, 5: 54–55. See also Marx, *Pre-Capitalist Economic Formations*, pp. 69–71.

52. In *Pre-Capitalist Economic Formations*, Marx invokes warfare and urban life as influences in the transition from tribal to personal property (pp. 68–95). *Capital* adheres more closely to the Hegelian and Asiatic pattern, even when the Asiatic model is taken to other continents: see *MEGA*, pt. II, 5: 88, on the features of the pre-conquest Peruvian economy.

53. Hegel, *Enzyklopädie*, para. 257, *Zusatz* (*W*, 9: 48). The German text

reads: "In der Vorstellung ist Raum und Zeit weit auseinander, da haben wir Raum und dann _auch_ Zeit; dieses 'Auch' bekämpft die Philosophie."

54. Ibid. "Die Wahrheit des Raumes ist die Zeit, so wird der Raum zur Zeit; wir gehen nicht so subjektiv zur Zeit über, sondern der Raum selbst geht über." In the 1804 _Naturphilosophie_ it was a matter of indifference whether space is derived from time or time from space, since both of them are only moments of the all-encompassing "Aether" (_Jenaer Systementwürfe II_, p. 206). And in the manuscripts from 1805–6, stasis (_die Dauer_) is the "ground" or substance in which alone space and time can exist. By 1817 (date of the first _Encyclopedia_) Hegel had clearly chosen to take time's side.

55. Heidegger, _Sein und Zeit_, p. 429; following Macquarrie and Robinson's translation, _Being and Time_, p. 481.

56. Hegel, _Enzyklopädie_, para. 257 (_W_, 9: 47–48).

57. Heidegger, _Being and Time_, p. 481; trans. modified.

58. Ibid., trans. modified. Derrida discusses this family of passages from Aristotle, Hegel, and Heidegger in "Ousia et grammé," _Marges_, pp. 33–78.

59. By leaving "the indifference of subsisting" behind, the point anticipates the animal's "annihilation" of the spatial character of plant life (connection made explicit in Hegel, _Enzyklopädie_, para. 344; _W_, 9: 375–76). The Jena _Naturphilosophie_ calls time a "leaping point, richer than fire" (_Jenaer Systementwürfe III_, p. 10 _m_). Like the "starting note" of Chinese musicology, the point replaces a continuous, undifferentiated realm with a new realm composed of nothing but differentiations. The stories told about the point by Hegel and Heidegger are thus allegories, representing in narrative form a qualitative difference to which representation is itself a party.

60. Kant, _Kritik der Urteilskraft_ A 78–101 / B 79–102 (Kant, _Werke_, 8: 333–48). Thomas Weiskel divides the sublime into "three phases or economic states": the state of normal perception, that of surprise or astonishment, and finally a defensive or reactive phase in which "the very indeterminacy which erupted in phase two is taken as symbolizing the mind's relation to a transcendent order" (_Romantic Sublime_, pp. 22–26).

61. Kant, _Kritik der Urteilskraft_ A 98–99 / B 99–100 (Kant, _Werke_, 8: 346); trans. Meredith, slightly modified, _Critique of Aesthetic Judgement_, pp. 107–8. In the _Critique of Pure Reason_ B 39–40 (Kant, _Werke_, 3: 73), Kant expressly makes the representation of an infinitely divisible space an "intuition" and not a "concept."

62. The violence is necessary, the result of an incompatibility between the object of knowledge and the means used to attain it. Here is another form of that violence: when Aristotle engages the same problem, the measurement of space—a necessary preliminary to constructing the concepts of movement and time—proves to have finalities of its own. Measurement may be the bond between space and time (if time is a "number of movement"; *Physics* 219b2), but the act of measuring introduces a set of differences independent of those belonging to unmeasured space and time. Between considering a point (*stigmē*) as the end of one segment of a line and as the beginning of another, *anangkē histasthai*, "we are forced to stop," although—or rather because—the point is one and the same throughout our measurement. The "stop" is, moreover, exactly what is not given in time (220a13).

63. Weiskel, *Romantic Sublime*, p. 4.

64. Hegel, *Enzyklopädie*, para. 448 (*W*, 10: 249). The immediate topic is the relations of Intelligence, Memory (*Erinnerung*), and perception, but the side-reference to the philosophy of time and space (in paras. 247, 254) is made by Hegel himself.

65. Hegel, *W*, 13: 288.

66. Hegel, *Vorlesungen über die Ästhetik*, I (*W*, 13: 491). For philosophy, cf. *Geschichte der Philosophie*, *W*, 18: 138.

67. Hegel does, however, and in a way that marvelously demonstrates the reciprocal positions of aesthetics and history in his work, discuss the absence from China of certain kinds of artworks—epic poems (see *W*, 15: 396). As an *Ersatz* for epic, Hegel mentions the Chinese novel, "those extended . . . and astonishingly self-contained works." But the Chinese novel is doubly an *Ersatz*: not only is it, by its genre, no match for the epic, but it comes "too late," that is, long after the historical period that, in the linear scheme of world history, should have belonged to China. For Hegel's notes on the novel *Yü Chiao Li* (which he knew through Rémusat's translation and which he briefly mentioned in the *Philosophy of History*, *W*, 12: 158), see H. Schneider, "Unveröffentlichte Vorlesungs-manuskripte Hegels," pp. 46–48. The fuller version of the *Philosophy of History* edited by Georg Lasson contains a few notes on Chinese poetry and painting, and the summary: "Their art is, like their constitution, devoid of spirit" (*Die orientalische Welt*, pp. 319, 390).

68. Hegel, *Philosophie der Geschichte*, *W*, 12: 136, 156, 174, 207–8.

69. Hegel, *Ästhetik*, III (*W*, 15: 396).

70. Already in 1822 Hegel characterized the Chinese mentality as lead-

ing to a "phantasielosen Verstand, prosaisches Leben" ("rationality without imagination, a prosaic life") and described Chinese history as a "ganz prosaische Erzählung" ("a wholly prosaic recital") of outward events. See Hegel, "Philosophie der allgemeinen Weltgeschichte," pp. 185, 187.

71. For a summary of the evolution of this part of the doctrine of Absolute Spirit, see Harris, *Hegel's Development*, 2: 65–66, 155, 500–501.

72. Hegel, *Ästhetik*, I (*W*, 13: 454–66); *Philosophie der Geschichte*, *W*, 12: 245–71.

73. Hegel, *Ästhetik*, II (*W*, 14: 13).

74. Coleridge, *Table Talk*, p. 238.

75. Hegel, *Die orientalische Welt*, p. 455; cf. *Ästhetik*, I (*W*, 13: 482).

76. On sublimity (*Erhabenheit*) as the vanishing point of the "specifically symbolic character of art," see Hegel, *Ästhetik*, I (*W*, 13: 468), and de Man's commentary in "Kant's Materialism," pp. 4–5. I have also found useful de Man's 1982 lectures "Aesthetic Theory from Kant to Hegel," as presented in course notes put at my disposal by Roger Blood, Cathy Caruth, and Suzanne Roos.

77. Hegel, *Ästhetik*, I (*W*, 13: 497). Compare Walter Benjamin's drafts for a new version of his "Theses on the Philosophy of History" (*Gesammelte Schriften*, 1: 1234–35): "Not every universal history has to be reactionary. . . . The idea of prose goes together with the messianic idea." Paul de Man sets out to disengage prose and the lesser genres from their "enslaved place" and put them on a footing with the noble prose that follows after the sublime (see "Hegel on the Sublime," pp. 152–53; and "Sign and Symbol," pp. 774–75). Ferenc Tökei reads Hegel on the lesser genres quite literally, seeing them, moreover, as steps in a literary-historical dialectic (*Naissance de l'élégie chinoise*, pp. 35, 55, 61, 66–67).

78. Hegel, *Ästhetik*, I (*W*, 13: 491). The "searching after" true art is most often put in the form of a chronology (see, e.g., ibid., pp. 390–92). Prose in its "Greek" variant is frequently associated with personification-allegory or prosopopoeia, the anthropomorphic turning of a mere predicate into a subject. (On prosopopoeia, see de Man, "Sign and Symbol," pp. 774–75; and "Hegel on the Sublime," pp. 146–49.)

79. Hegel, *Ästhetik*, II (*W*, 14: 109). The early writings make Aesop, as slave, embody the inequalities of wealth to which the withering away of the old cults is linked, a theme succinctly brought out in Lukács, *Young Hegel*, pp. 45–48, 58–61. In the *Aesthetics* no such economic explanation is offered: Aesop's shallowness and the failure of Greek religion occur separately and side by side. For a glimpse of a more rigorous organization

of Hegel's aesthetic terminology into periods and peoples, see Rose, *Hegel Contra Sociology,* pp. 135–42: Roman prose there presupposes Greek poetry. On the clash of systematic (generic) and historical (evolutionary) modes of presentation in the *Aesthetics,* see Bungay, *Beauty and Truth,* p. 59.

80. Hegel, *Ästhetik,* I (*W,* 13: 390–92).

81. On this topos, and the related one of "outdoing," see Curtius, *European Literature,* pp. 159–65.

82. See e.g., Hindess and Hirst, *Pre-Capitalist Modes of Production,* pp. 275–78, 312, 335–36.

83. Hegel, *Ästhetik,* I (*W,* 13: 482); cf. *Die griechische und römische Welt,* pp. 726–27.

84. Hegel, *Phänomenologie die Geistes, W,* 3: 152–53.

85. Gregory Nagy finds in the ancient *Life of Aesop* reasons for believing Aesop is the slave or ritual antagonist of Apollo, who makes him his scapegoat (*Best of the Achaeans,* pp. 279–92).

86. For Vico the basis and singularity of Jewish religion is its prohibition against divination (*La scienza nuova,* Book I, para. 24, p. 187).

87. Rosenkranz, *Ästhetik des Häßlichen.*

88. Hegel, *Ästhetik,* I (*W,* 13: 485); see de Man, "Hegel on the Sublime," p. 149.

89. For this description of personification-allegory, see Hegel, *Ästhetik,* I (*W,* 13: 511–17).

90. On these passages, cf. Derrida, "Le Puits et la pyramide" (*Marges,* pp. 81–127, esp. pp. 118–23).

91. Hegel, *Enzyklopädie,* para. 457, *Zusatz;* para. 458 (*W,* 10: 269, 270).

92. Hegel, *Ästhetik,* I (*W,* 13: 480).

93. Ibid., pp. 497, 105. The reference there is to Aesop and the animal-fable genre. A parallel passage is *Enzyklopädie,* para. 451, where the faculty of "representation," as a stage on the way to thinking, "begins from perception and its *found materials*" (*W,* 10: 257).

94. Hegel, *Enzyklopädie,* para. 451, *Zusatz,* 457, 548 (*W,* 10: 258, 269–71); *Vorlesungen über die Philosophie der Religion,* pt. II, *Die bestimmte Religion,* 4a: 533–34, 549, 569–70 (hereafter cited as *Die bestimmte Religion*).

95. For a knotting together of these three themes, see *Ästhetik,* I (*W,* 13: 410), on art as the "translator" of religious forms.

96. Walter Jaeschke's edition of the lectures gives Hegel's manuscript outline of 1821, the 1824 and 1827 courses as distilled from students' notes, a short version of the 1831 lectures by David Friedrich Strauss, and a

comparison with the first printed editions of 1831 and 1840. I have somewhat overstated the harmony between versions. In 1824, for example, Hegel experiments with making Egyptian belief a "religion of the riddle" that would furnish a "transition"—always that missing link!—"between the natural religions [of China, India, and Persia] and the spiritual religions [of Israel and Greece]" (*Die bestimmte Religion*, 4a: 259–81). In 1827 and 1831, Egyptian religion shares this function with a growing set of "transitional religions" (ibid., pp. 518–32, 629–31). But the endpoints of the transition—"nature religions" on one side, and the "religions of beauty and sublimity" on the other—retain the same shape and examples from one year to the next (e.g., the very same Psalms cited as model statements of the sublime in *Die bestimmte Religion*, pp. 42, 333, 569–70, and in the *Aesthetics* [*W*, 13: 483–84]).

97. Hegel, *Die bestimmte Religion*, 4a: 95–137, 579–91, 640–42. For the manuscript sheet (beginning: "Prosa—Negative Zustände—für uns . . ."), see ibid., p. 648; the version given by Helmut Schneider ("Unveröffentlichte Vorlesungsmanuskripte Hegels," pp. 41–42) is preferable, however.

98. Hegel, *Die bestimmte Religion*, p. 176.

99. Hulin, *Hegel et l'Orient*, p. 88.

100. Hegel, *Die bestimmte Religion*, p. 445. The section "Religion of Measure" appears in Strauss's version and the 1840 edition edited by Bruno Bauer. Reinhard Leuze sees the theory of "measure" gradually taking over from the theory of Chinese religion as a form of magic, an evolution in Hegel's thinking still under way in 1831 (*Die außerchristlichen Religionen*, pp. 15, 59).

101. Hegel, *Die bestimmte Religion*, 4a: 447–49. I follow the text of the second edition of the *Lectures*.

102. Hegel, *Wissenschaft der Logik*, I (*W*, 5: 395–96). Trans. A. V. Miller, modified, Hegel, *Science of Logic*, p. 334.

103. On the ineffability of measures, see also Leibniz, *Nouveaux essais*, II.xiii. "It is impossible to have the idea of a specific and precise measure. No one can say or understand mentally what an inch is, or a foot. Nor can anyone preserve the meaning of those names through some actually existing and supposedly unchanging measurements to which one could always refer" (*Philosophischen Schriften*, 5: 134).

104. Hegel, *Ästhetik* I (*W*, 13: 107–9).

105. See Chapter 3. Hegel's sources on China included Amiot's "Sur la musique des Chinois"; plate 8 of this monograph depicts a "musical foot-measure" derived from the *huang-chung* pitch.

106. Hegel, *Philosophie der Geschichte*, W, 12: 134.

107. Hegel, *Die bestimmte Religion*, 4a: 449 (text of the first edition). The second edition reads here: "his subjects show him the same honor that he shows to the laws."

108. Locus classicus: Kojève, *Introduction*, pp. 288–91, 383–95, 436–37. See Auffret, *Alexandre Kojève*, pp. 331–56, for Kojève's last thoughts on the subject; and Fukuyama, "End of History?," for a contemporary application.

109. Hegel alludes to the play frequently in his early writings: see, e.g., "Die Positivität der christlichen Religion," *W*, 1: 131.

110. Compare notes 50 and 59 above; see also Hegel, *Enzyklopädie*, para. 260 (*W*, 9: 55). If history has to learn to coexist with what was always already the "post-historical," it can do so only in space (as opposed to the more familiar coexistence of contradictory statements in time). Absolute knowledge can have it both ways: the ending of the *Phenomenology* proposes to translate the "depth" of the concept into its "extension" (*Ausdehnung*), an "internalization" that is also a "dilation." Another name for this change is universal history (*W*, 3: 591). See also, on the same passage, Hartman, "Elation in Hegel and Wordsworth," *Unremarkable Wordsworth*, pp. 182–93.

111. "*Prorsus* (collat. form *prōsus*) . . . adj. [for *pro-versus*]. I. Straightforwards, right onwards, straight, direct: . . . *prorsi limites appellantur in agrorum mensuris, qui ad orientem directi sunt* (Festus) . . . II. Trop., of style, straightforwards, i.e. prosaic, in prose, opp. to verse . . . *prorsum est porro versum, id est ante versum. Hinc et prorsa oratio, quam non inflexit cantilena* (Aelius Donatus)." Lewis and Short, *New Latin Dictionary* (Oxford: Oxford University Press, 1972), *s.v. prorsus.*

112. Thus the Chinese aesthetic is the symmetrical counterpart of that "identity of identity and non-identity" which was Fichte's formula for the Absolute (see Hegel, "Differenz des Fichteschen und Schellingschen Systems der Philosophie," *W*, 2: 96).

113. See Shklovsky, *Theory of Prose*, esp. chap. 7. A more faithful translation would be "the laying bare (root: *nag-*) of the device," which pairs off nicely with "sinnliche *Erscheinung* der Idee."

Chapter 6

EPIGRAPHS: Victor Segalen, letter to Henri Manceron, Sept. 23, 1911 (describing his own book *Stèles*), *Trahison fidèle*, p. 108; Marcel Proust, *Le côté de Guermantes*, II, *À la recherche du temps perdu* (Paris: Gallimard, 1988), 2: 587.

Bibliography

For the abbreviations used here, see the list on pp. xv–xvi.

Works in Western Languages

Abel, Carl. *Sprachwissenschaftliche Abhandlungen*. Leipzig: Friedrich, 1885.

Adorno, Theodor. *Ästhetische Theorie. Gesammelte Schriften*, vol. 7. Frankfurt am Main: Suhrkamp, 1970.

Allan, Sarah. "Drought, Human Sacrifice and the Mandate of Heaven in a Lost Text from the *Shang shu*." *Bulletin of the School of Oriental and African Studies* 47 (1984): 523–29.

Allanbrook, Wye Jamison. *Rhythmic Gesture in Mozart*. Chicago: University of Chicago Press, 1980.

Althusser, Louis. "Sur le rapport de Marx à Hegel." In Jacques d'Hondt, ed., *Hegel et la pensée moderne*. Paris: Presses Universitaires de France, 1970, pp. 85–111.

Althusser, Louis, and Etienne Balibar. *Lire "Le Capital."* 2d ed. 2 vols. Paris: Maspero, 1970.

Amiot, Jean-Joseph-Marie. "Sur la musique des Chinois, tant anciens que modernes." In *Mémoires concernant l'histoire, les sciences, les arts, les mœurs et les usages des Chinois. Par les missionaires de Pékin*. Paris, 1780, 6: 1–254.

Anderson, Benedict. *Imagined Communities: Reflections on the Origins and Spread of Nationalism*. London: Verso, 1983.

Anderson, Marston. *The Limits of Realism: Chinese Fiction in the Revolutionary Period*. Berkeley: University of California Press, 1990.

249

Anderson, Perry. *Lineages of the Absolutist State*. London: New Left Books, 1974.

Anderson, Warren D. *Ethos and Education in Greek Music*. Cambridge, Mass.: Harvard University Press, 1966.

Aristotle. *De motu animalium*. Trans. and comm. Martha Craven Nussbaum. Princeton: Princeton University Press, 1985.

Auffret, Dominique. *Alexandre Kojève: la philosophie, l'état, la fin de l'histoire*. Paris: Grasset, 1990.

Austin, John. *How to Do Things with Words*. Cambridge, Mass.: Harvard University Press, 1962.

Barker, Andrew, ed. *Greek Musical Writings*, Vol. 1, *The Musician and His Art*. Cambridge, Eng.: Cambridge University Press, 1984.

Barthes, Roland. *L'Empire des signes*. Paris: Skira/Flammarion, 1980.

Baudelaire, Charles. *Oeuvres complètes*. 2 vols. Ed. Claude Pichois. Paris: Gallimard, 1975.

Baumgarten, Alexander Gottlieb. *Aesthetica* (1750). Reprinted—Hildesheim: Olms, 1986.

Behn, Aphra. *The Emperor of the Moon: A Farce, as it is acted by their Majesties Servants at the Queen's Theatre*. London, 1687.

Benjamin, Walter. *Gesammelte Schriften*. 4 vols. Ed. Rolf Tiedemann and Hermann Schweppenhäuser. Frankfurt am Main: Suhrkamp, 1980.

———. *Illuminations*. Trans. Harry Zohn. New York: Schocken Books, 1969.

Benveniste, Emile. *Problèmes de linguistique générale* [I]. Paris: Gallimard, 1966.

———. *Problèmes de linguistique générale, II*. Paris: Gallimard, 1974.

Bettray, Johannes, S.J. *Die Akkomodationsmethode des P. Matteo Ricci S.J. in China*. Rome: Gregorian University, 1955.

Bielenstein, Hans. *The Restoration of the Han Dynasty*, Part IV, *The Government*. BMFEA, 51. Stockholm: Museum of Far Eastern Antiquities, 1979.

Birch, Cyril, ed. *Studies in Chinese Literary Genres*. Berkeley: University of California Press, 1974.

Black, Max. "Metaphor." *Proceedings of the Aristotelian Society* n.s. 55 (1955): 273–94.

Bloch, Ernst. *Subjekt-Objekt: Erläuterungen zu Hegel*. Berlin: Aufbau, 1951.

Bloch, Marc. *Les Rois thaumaturges: étude sur le caractère surnaturel attribué à la puissance royale*. Strasbourg: Istra, 1924.

Bodde, Derk. *Festivals in Classical China*. Princeton: Princeton University Press, 1975.

Bodemann, Eduard, comp. *Der Briefwechsel des Gottfried Wilhelm Leibniz*. Hildesheim: Olms, 1966.

―――. *Die Leibniz-Handscriften der königlichen öffentlichen Bibliothek zu Hannover*. Hildesheim: Olms, 1966.

Brailou, Constantin. *Problems of Ethnomusicology*. Cambridge, Eng.: Cambridge University Press, 1984.

Brooks, E. Bruce. "A Geometry of the *Shr pin*." In Chow Tse-tsung, ed., *Wen-lin: Studies in the Chinese Humanities*. Madison: University of Wisconsin Press, 1968, pp. 121–50.

Buffière, Félix. *Les Mythes d'Homère et la pensée grecque*. Paris: Les Belles Lettres, 1956.

Bungay, Stephen. *Beauty and Truth: A Study of Hegel's Aesthetics*. Oxford: Clarendon Press, 1984.

Bush, Susan, and Christian Murck, eds. *Theories of the Arts in Ancient China*. Princeton: Princeton University Press, 1983.

Butor, Michel. *Répertoire, I*. Paris: Minuit, 1960.

Caruth, Cathy. *Empirical Truths and Critical Fictions: Locke, Wordsworth, Kant, Freud*. Baltimore: Johns Hopkins University Press, 1991.

Centre d'Etudes et de Recherches Marxistes [Jean Chesnaux et al.]. *Sur le "Mode de production asiatique."* Paris: Editions Sociales, 1969.

Chang, Kang-i Sun. "Chinese 'Lyric Criticism' in the Six Dynasties." In Susan Bush and Christian Murck, eds., *Theories of the Arts in Ancient China*. Princeton: Princeton University Press, 1983, pp. 215–24.

―――. "The Concept of Time in the *Shih-ching*." *Ts'ing-hua Journal of Chinese Studies* n.s. 12.1 (1979): 73–85.

―――. *The Evolution of Chinese Tz'u Poetry from Late T'ang to Northern Sung*. Princeton: Princeton University Press, 1980.

―――. *Six Dynasties Poetry*. Princeton: Princeton University Press, 1986.

―――. "Symbolic and Allegorical Meanings in the *Yüeh-fu pu-t'i* Poem Series." *HJAS* 46 (1986): 353–85.

Chang, Kwang-chih. *The Archaeology of Ancient China*. 4th ed. New Haven: Yale University Press, 1987.

―――. *Art, Myth and Ritual: The Path to Political Authority in Ancient China*. Cambridge, Mass.: Harvard University Press, 1983.

―――. *Shang Civilization*. New Haven: Yale University Press, 1980.

————, ed. *Early Chinese Civilization: Anthropological Perspectives.* Cambridge, Mass.: Harvard University Press, 1976.

Chao, Chia-ying Yeh. "The Ch'ang-Chou School of *Tz'u* Criticism." In Adele Austin Rickett, ed., *Chinese Approaches to Literature from Confucius to Liang Ch'i-ch'ao.* Princeton: Princeton University Press, 1978, pp. 151–88.

Charles, Michel. *Rhétorique de la lecture.* Paris: Seuil, 1977.

Chase, Cynthia. *Decomposing Figures: Rhetorical Readings in the Romantic Tradition.* Baltimore: Johns Hopkins University Press, 1986.

Chavannes, Edouard. "Des rapports de la musique grecque avec la musique chinoise." In idem, trans., *Les Mémoires historiques de Se-ma Ts'ien,* vol. 3, part I. Paris: Leroux, 1898, App. II, pp. 630–45.

Chen Shih-hsiang. "The Genesis of Poetic Time: The Greatness of Ch'ü Yüan, Studied with a New Critical Approach." *Ts'ing Hua Journal of Chinese Studies* n.s. 10 (1973): 1–43.

————. "In Search of the Beginnings of Chinese Literary Criticism." *Semitic and Oriental Studies* 11 (1951): 45–64.

————. "The *Shih-ching*: Its Generic Significance in Chinese Literary History and Poetics." In Cyril Birch, ed., *Studies in Chinese Literary Genres.* Berkeley: University of California Press, 1974, pp. 8–41.

Cheng, François. *L'Ecriture poétique chinoise.* Paris: Seuil, 1977.

Chou Fa-kao. "Reduplicatives in the *Book of Odes.*" *BIHP* 34 (1963): 661–98.

Chow Tse-tsung. "The Early History of the Chinese Word *Shih* (Poetry)." In Chow Tse-tsung, ed., *Wen-lin: Studies in the Chinese Humanities.* Madison: University of Wisconsin Press, 1968, pp. 151–209.

————. *The May Fourth Movement.* Cambridge, Mass.: Harvard University Press, 1960.

————, ed. *Wen-lin: Studies in the Chinese Humanities.* Madison: University of Wisconsin Press, 1968.

Chu Hsi. *Learning to Be a Sage: Selections from the "Conversations of Master Chu, Arranged Topically."* Trans. and annot. Daniel K. Gardner. Berkeley: University of California Press, 1990.

Cicero. *M. Tulli Ciceronis Rhetorica.* Ed. A. S. Wilkins. Oxford: Oxford University Press, 1978.

Cigliano, Maria, ed. *Atti del Convegno Internazionale di Studi Ricciani.* Macerata: Centro di Studi Ricciani, 1984.

Clifford, James, and George F. Marcus, eds. *Writing Culture: The Poetics and Politics of Ethnography.* Berkeley: University of California Press, 1986.

Coleridge, Samuel Taylor. *The Table Talk and Omniana of Samuel Taylor Coleridge.* Ed. T. Ashe. London: George Bell, 1909.

Collani, Claudia von. *Eine wissenschaftliche Akademie für China. Studia Leibnitiana*, Special issue 18. Stuttgart: Steiner, 1989.

Colloque International de Sinologie. *La Mission française de Pékin aux XVIIe et XVIIIe siècles.* Paris: Les Belles Lettres and Cathasia, 1976.

Comotti, Giovanni. *Music in Greek and Roman Culture.* Trans. Rosaria Munson. Baltimore: Johns Hopkins University Press, 1989.

Cordier, Henri. *Essai d'une bibliographie des ouvrages publiés en Chine par les Européens aux XVIIe et XVIIIe siècles.* Paris: Leroux, 1883.

————, comp. *Bibliotheca Sinica.* 4 vols. 2d ed. Paris: Guilmoto, 1904–8.

Couvreur, Séraphin, S.J., trans. *Chou King, texte chinois avec traduction.* 2d ed. Hsien-hsien, Hopei: Imprimerie de la Mission Catholique, 1916.

————. *I Li: Cérémonial, texte chinois avec traduction.* Hsien-hsien, Hopei: Imprimerie de la Mission Catholique, 1916.

————. *Li Ki, ou Mémoires sur les bienséances et les cérémonies.* 2 vols. 2d ed. Ho-chien, Hopei: Imprimerie de la Mission Catholique, 1913.

Creel, Herlee Glessner. *The Origins of Statecraft in China*, vol. 1. Chicago: University of Chicago Press, 1970.

————. *Sinism: A Study of the Evolution of the Chinese World-view.* Chicago: Open Court, 1929.

————. *What Is Taoism? and Other Essays in Chinese Cultural History.* Chicago: University of Chicago Press, 1982.

Crump, James I. *Intrigues: Studies of the "Chan-kuo-ts'e."* Ann Arbor: University of Michigan Press, 1964.

Cua, A. S. "Dimensions of *Li* (Propriety): Reflections on an Aspect of Hsün-tzu's Ethics." *Philosophy East and West* 29 (1979): 373–94.

————. "*Li* and Moral Justification: A Study in the *Li Chi.*" *Philosophy East and West* 33 (1983): 1–16.

Curtius, Ernst Robert. *European Literature and the Latin Middle Ages.* Trans. Willard B. Trask. Princeton: Princeton University Press, 1953.

Cyrano de Bergerac, Savinien. *L'Autre Monde, ou les états et empires de la lune et du soleil.* 1657, 1662. Montreal: Le Cercle du Livre de France, 1960.

Dante Alighieri. *Tutte le Opere.* Ed. Luigi Blasucci. Florence: Sansoni, 1965.

Davidson, Donald. "On the Very Idea of a Conceptual Scheme." In John Rajchman and Cornel West, eds., *Post-Analytic Philosophy.* New York: Columbia University Press, 1985, pp. 129–144.

d'Elia, Pasquale M., S.J., ed. *Fonti Ricciane.* 4 vols. Rome: Libreria dello Stato, 1942–49.

de Man, Paul. *Allegories of Reading.* New Haven: Yale University Press, 1979.

———. *Blindness and Insight.* 2d ed. Minneapolis: University of Minnesota Press, 1983.

———. "Hegel on the Sublime." Typescript, 1983. Also published in Mark Krupnik, ed., *Displacement: Derrida and After.* Bloomington: Indiana University Press, 1983, pp. 139–53.

———. "Kant and Schiller." Typescript, 1983; revised typescript incorporating taped variants, 1988.

———. "Kant's Materialism." Typescript, 1983.

———. "Phenomenality and Materiality in Kant." Typescript, 1983.

———. "Sign and Symbol in Hegel's *Aesthetics.*" *Critical Inquiry* 8 (1982): 761–75.

Dembo, L. S. *The Confucian Odes of Ezra Pound: A Critical Appraisal.* Berkeley: University of California Press, 1963.

Derrida, Jacques. *De la grammatologie.* Paris: Minuit, 1967.

———. *La Dissémination.* Paris: Seuil, 1972.

———. *Glas.* Paris: Galilée, 1974.

———. *Marges de la philosophie.* Paris: Minuit, 1972.

———. *Psyché: inventions de l'autre.* Paris: Galilée, 1987.

Descartes, René. *Oeuvres.* Ed. Charles Adam and Paul Tannery. Paris: Vrin, 1964.

Detienne, Marcel. *Les Maîtres de vérité dans la Grèce archaïque.* Paris: Maspero, 1967.

DeWoskin, Kenneth. "Early Chinese Music and the Origins of Aesthetic Terminology." In Susan Bush and Christian Murck, eds., *Theories of the Arts in Ancient China.* Princeton: Princeton University Press, 1983, pp. 187–214.

————. *A Song for One or Two: Music and the Concept of Art in Early China*. Michigan Papers in Chinese Studies, 42. Ann Arbor: University of Michigan, Center for Chinese Studies, 1982.

Diény, Jean-Pierre. *Aux origines de la poésie classique en Chine: étude sur la poésie lyrique à l'époque des Han*. Leiden: Brill, 1968.

————. *Les Dix-neuf poèmes anciens*. Tokyo: Association Franco-Japonaise and Presses Universitaires de France, 1964.

————. *Pastourelles et magnanarelles: essai sur un thème littéraire chinois*. Geneva: Droz, 1977.

Dobson, W. A. C. H. *The Language of the "Book of Songs."* Toronto: University of Toronto Press, 1968.

————. "Linguistic Evidence and the Dating of the *Book of Songs*." *T'oung Pao* 51 (1964): 322–34.

————. "The Origin and Development of Prosody in Early Chinese Poetry." *T'oung Pao* 54 (1968): 231–50.

Doz, André, trans. and comm. *Hegel: la théorie de la mesure*. Paris: Presses Universitaires de France, 1970.

Dubois, Jacques, et al. *Rhétorique générale*. Paris: Larousse, 1970.

Dubs, Homer H. *Hsüntze, the Moulder of Ancient Confucianism*. London: Probsthain, 1927.

————, trans. *The Works of Hsüntze*. London: Probsthain, 1928.

Dull, Jack. "An Historical Introduction to the Apocryphal (*Ch'an-wei*) Texts of the Han Dynasty." Ph.D dissertation, University of Washington, 1966.

Dumézil, Georges. *Idées romaines*. Paris: Gallimard, 1969.

Durkheim, Emile. *Les Formes élémentaires de la vie religieuse*. Paris: Alcan, 1912.

Durkheim, Emile, and Marcel Mauss. "De quelques formes primitives de classification: contribution à l'étude des représentations collectives." *L'Année Sociologique* 6 (1901–2): 1–72.

Eberhard, Wolfram. *Lokalkulturen im alten China*, Part I, *Die Lokalkulturen des Nordens und Westens*. Supplement to *T'oung Pao*, vol. 37. Leiden: Brill, 1942. Part II, *Die Lokalkulturen des Südens und Ostens*. *Monumenta Serica*, monograph 3. Peking: Catholic University Press, 1942.

Egan, Ronald C. "Narratives in *Tso Chuan*." *HJAS* 37 (1977): 323–52.

Eliséeff-Poisle, Danielle. *Nicolas Fréret (1688–1749): réflexions d'un* *humaniste du XVIIIe siècle sur la Chine.* Paris: Collège de France, Institut des Hautes Etudes Chinoises, 1976.

Elman, Benjamin A. *From Philosophy to Philology.* Cambridge, Mass.: Harvard University, Council on East Asian Studies, 1984.

Elvin, Mark. *The Pattern of the Chinese Past.* Stanford: Stanford University Press, 1973.

Empson, William. *Argufying.* Ed. John Haffenden. Iowa City: University of Iowa Press, 1987.

————. *Some Versions of Pastoral.* New York: New Directions, 1974.

————. *The Structure of Complex Words.* London: Chatto & Windus, 1951.

Engels, Friedrich. *Anti-Dühring: Herr Eugen Dühring's Revolution in Science.* Peking: Foreign Languages Press, 1976.

Etiemble. *L'Europe chinoise,* Vol. 1, *De l'empire romain à Leibniz*; Vol. 2, *De la sinophilie à la sinophobie.* Paris: Gallimard, 1988, 1989.

————. *Les Jésuites en Chine.* Paris: Julliard, 1966.

Falkenhausen, Lothar von. *Suspended Music: The Chime-Bells of the Chinese Bronze Age.* Berkeley: University of California Press, 1993.

Felber, Roland. "Neue Möglichkeiten und Kriterien für die Bestimmung der Authentizität des *Zuo-Zhuan.*" *Archiv Orientální* 34 (1966): 80–91.

Fenves, Peter D. *A Peculiar Fate: Metaphysics and World-History in Kant.* Ithaca: Cornell University Press, 1991.

Feuerbach, Ludwig. *Gesammelte Werke.* Ed. Werner Schuffenhauer. Berlin: Akademie-Verlag, 1970.

Fingarette, Herbert. *Confucius: The Secular as Sacred.* New York: Harper & Row, 1972.

Firth, J. R. *Selected Papers of J. R. Firth, 1952–1959.* Ed. F. R. Palmer. Bloomington: Indiana University Press, 1968.

Fletcher, Angus. *Allegory: The Theory of a Symbolic Mode.* Ithaca: Cornell University Press, 1964.

Foucault, Michel. *Les Mots et les choses.* Paris: Gallimard, 1966.

Frankel, Hans H. *The Flowering Plum and the Palace Lady: Interpretations of Chinese Poetry.* New Haven: Yale University Press, 1976.

Frege, Gottlob. *Collected Papers on Mathematics, Logic, and Philosophy.* Ed. Brian McGuinness. Oxford: Blackwell, 1984.

Freud, Sigmund. "The Antithetical Meaning of Primal Words." In *Standard Edition of the Complete Psychological Works of Sigmund Freud.*

Trans. and ed. James Strachey. London: Hogarth Press, 1957, 11: 153–62.

Fukuyama, Francis. "The End of History?" *The National Interest* 16 (1989): 3–18.

Fung Yu-lan. *A History of Chinese Philosophy.* 2 vols. Trans. Derk Bodde. Princeton: Princeton University Press, 1953.

Gadamer, Hans-Georg. *Hegel's Dialectic: Five Hermeneutical Studies.* Trans. P. Christopher Smith. New Haven: Yale University Press, 1976.

———. *Truth and Method.* Trans. Garrett Barden and John Cumming. London: Sheed & Ward, 1975.

Gärtner, Helga, Waltraut Hekye, and Viktor Pöschl, eds. *Bibliographie zur antiken Bildersprache.* Heidelberg: Winter-Universitätsverlag, 1964.

Gasché, Rodolphe. "Hegel's Orient or the End of Romanticism." In Irving J. Massey and Sung-won Lee, eds., *History and Mimesis.* Buffalo: State University of New York, Department of English, 1983, pp. 17–29.

Geertz, Clifford. "Anti Anti-Relativism." *American Anthropologist* 86 (1984): 263–78.

———. *The Interpretation of Cultures.* New York: Basic Books, 1983.

———. *Local Knowledge: Further Essays in Interpretive Anthropology.* New York: Basic Books, 1983.

———. *Negara: The Theatre-State in Nineteenth-Century Bali.* Princeton: Princeton University Press, 1980.

Gentili, Bruno. *Poetry and Its Public in Ancient Greece.* Trans. A. Thomas Cole. Baltimore: Johns Hopkins University Press, 1989.

Gernet, Jacques. *Chine et christianisme: action et réaction.* Paris: Gallimard, 1982.

Gibbs, Donald A. "Notes on the Wind: The Term 'Feng' in Chinese Literary Criticism." In David C. Buxbaum and Frederick W. Mote, eds., *Transition and Permanence: Chinese History and Culture, a Festschrift in Honor of Dr. Hsiao Kung-ch'üan.* Hong Kong: Cathay Press, 1972, pp. 285–94.

Giles, Herbert A. *A History of Chinese Literature.* New York: Appleton-Century, 1928.

Glockner, Hermann. *Beiträge zum Verständnis und zur Kritik Hegels.* Bonn: Bouvier, 1965.

Godelier, Maurice. "La Notion de 'Mode de production asiatique.'"
Les Temps Modernes 228 (1965): 2002–27.

Goethe, Johann Wolfgang von. *West-Östlicher Divan*. 1819. Frankfurt
am Main: Insel, 1951.

Grafton, Anthony. "Renaissance Readers and Ancient Texts: Comments on Some Commentaries." *Renaissance Quarterly* 38 (1985):
615–49.

Graham, A. C. "'Being' in Classical Chinese." In John W. M. Verhaar,
ed., *The Verb "Be" and Its Synonyms*. Foundations of Language,
supplementary series, 1. Dordrecht: Reidel, 1967, 1: 1–39.

————. "'Being' in Linguistics and Philosophy." In John W. M.
Verhaar, ed., *The Verb "Be" and Its Synonyms*. Foundations of Language, supplementary series, 14. Dordrecht: Reidel, 1972, 5: 225–
33.

————. "'Being' in Western Philosophy Compared with *Shih/Fei*
and *Yu/Wu* in Chinese Philosophy." *Asia Major* n.s. 7 (1959): 79–
112.

————. *Disputers of the Tao: Philosophical Argument in Ancient China*.
La Salle, Ill.: Open Court, 1989.

————. *Later Mohist Logic, Ethics and Science*. Hong Kong: Chinese
University Press; London: School of Oriental and African Studies,
1978.

————. *Studies in Chinese Philosophy and Philosophical Literature*. Albany: State University of New York Press, 1990.

Granet, Marcel. *Catégories matrimoniales et relations de proximité dans la
Chine ancienne*. Paris: Alcan, 1939.

————. *Fêtes et chansons anciennes de la Chine*. 2d ed. Paris: Leroux,
1929.

Greenblatt, Stephen. *Renaissance Self-fashioning*. Chicago: University
of Chicago Press, 1980.

Hackenesch, Charles. *Die Logik der Andersheit: Eine Untersuchung zu
Hegel's Begriff der Reflexion*. Frankfurt am Main: Athenäum, 1987.

Halliwell, Stephen. *Aristotle's Poetics*. London: Duckworth, 1986.

Halm, Carolus, ed. *Rhetores Latini minores*. Leipzig: Teubner, 1863.

Hamacher, Werner. "*pleroma*: zu Genesis und Struktur einer dialekt-
ischen Hermeneutik bei Hegel." Introduction to Hegel, *Der Geist
des Christentums: Schriften, 1796–1800*. Berlin: Ullstein, 1978.

Hansen, Chad. *Language and Logic in Ancient China*. Ann Arbor: University of Michigan Press, 1983.

Harris, H. S. *Hegel's Development*, Vol. 1, *Toward the Sunlight (1770–1801)*; Vol. 2, *Night Thoughts (Jena, 1801–1806)*. Oxford: Clarendon Press, 1972, 1983.

Hartman, Geoffrey H. *Beyond Formalism: Literary Essays, 1958–1970*. New Haven: Yale University Press, 1970.

————. *Saving the Text*. Baltimore: Johns Hopkins University Press, 1981.

————. *The Unremarkable Wordsworth*. Minneapolis: University of Minnesota Press, 1987.

Hart Nibbrig, Christiaan L. *Ästhetik: Materialien zu ihrer Geschichte. Ein Lesebuch*. Frankfurt am Main: Suhrkamp, 1978.

Hawkes, David, trans. and annot. *The Songs of the South*. Harmondsworth, Eng.: Penguin, 1985.

Hegel, Georg Wilhelm Friedrich. *Jenaer Systementwürfe I: Das System der spekulativen Philosophie*. Ed. Klaus Düsing and Heinz Kimmerle. Hamburg: Meiner, 1986.

————. *Jenaer Systementwürfe II: Logik, Metaphysik, Naturphilosophie*. Ed. Rolf-Peter Horstmann. Hamburg: Meiner, 1982.

————. *Jenaer Systementwürfe III: Naturphilosophie und Philosophie des Geistes*. Ed. Rolf-Peter Horstmann. Hamburg: Meiner, 1987.

————. "Philosophie der allgemeinen Weltgeschichte, vorgetragen von Hegel im Winterhalbenjahre 1822–23." Lectures transcribed by Karl Gustav Julius von Griesheim. Berlin Staatsbibliothek, Preussischer Kulturbesitz, ms. germ. qu. 550, 551.

————. *Philosophy of Nature*. Trans. and annot. A. V. Miller. Oxford: Clarendon Press, 1970.

————. *Philosophy of Nature*. 3 vols. Trans and annot. M. J. Petry. London: Allen & Unwin, 1970.

————. *Philosophy of Right*. Trans. and annot. T. M. Knox. Oxford: Oxford University Press, 1958.

————. *Philosophy of Subjective Spirit*. Trans. and annot. M. J. Petry. Dordrecht: Reidel, 1979.

————. *Science of Logic*. Trans. and annot. A. V. Miller. London: Allen & Unwin, 1969.

————. *Die Vernunft in der Geschichte*. Ed. Johannes Hoffmeister. *Vorlesungen über die Philosophie der Weltgeschichte*, vol. I. Hamburg: Meiner, 1955.

————. *Vorlesungen über die Philosophie der Religion*. Ed. Walter Jaeschke. Volumes 3, 4a, and 4b of Hegel, *Vorlesungen: Ausgewählte Nachschriften und Manuskripte*. Hamburg: Meiner, 1983–85.

————. *Vorlesungen über die Philosophie der Weltgeschichte.* Three parts: *Die orientalische Welt, Die griechische und römische Welt, Die germanische Welt.* Ed. Georg Lasson. Hamburg: Meiner, 1919–23.

————. *Werke in zwanzig Bänden.* Theorie-Werkausgabe. Frankfurt am Main: Suhrkamp, 1969–71.

————. *Werke, vollständige Ausgabe durch einen Verein von Freunden des Verewigten.* 2d ed. Berlin: Duncker und Humblot, 1840.

Heidegger, Martin. *Being and Time.* Trans. John Macquarrie and Edward Robinson. New York: Harper & Row, 1962.

————. *Der Satz vom Grund.* Pfullingen: Neske, 1957.

————. *Sein und Zeit.* 15th ed. Tübingen: Niemeyer, 1986.

————. *Unterwegs zur Sprache.* Pfullingen: Neske, 1959.

Henderson, John B. *The Development and Decline of Chinese Cosmology.* New York: Columbia University Press, 1984.

————. *Scripture, Canon and Commentary: A Comparison of Confucian and Western Exegesis.* Princeton: Princeton University Press, 1991.

Heraclitus [Ponticus]. *Allégories d'Homère [Homērika problēmata].* Ed. Félix Buffière. Paris: Les Belles Lettres, 1962.

Herder, Johann Gottfried. *Ideen zur Philosophie der Geschichte der Menschheit.* In *Herders sämmtliche Werke,* ed. Bernhard Suphan, vols. 13–14. Belin: Weidmannsche, 1908.

Hightower, James Robert. "The *Han-shih Wai-chuan* and the *San Chia Shih.*" *HJAS* 11 (1948): 241–310.

————. *Topics in Chinese Literature: Outlines and Bibliographies.* Rev. ed. Cambridge, Mass.: Harvard University Press, 1971.

————. "The *Wen Hsüan* and Genre Theory." In John L. Bishop, ed., *Studies in Chinese Literature.* Cambridge, Mass.: Harvard University Press, 1966, pp. 142–63.

————, trans. and annot. *Han Shih Wai Chuan: Han Ying's Illustrations of the Didactic Application of the "Classic of Songs."* Harvard-Yenching Institute Monograph Series, vol. 11. Cambridge, Mass.: Harvard University Press, 1952.

Hindess, Barry, and Paul Q. Hirst. *Pre-Capitalist Modes of Production.* London: Routledge & Kegan Paul, 1975.

Hjelmslev, Louis. *Essais linguistiques.* Paris: Minuit, 1971.

Holoch, Donald. "*The Travels of Laocan*: Allegorical Narrative." In Milena Doleželová-Velingerová, ed., *The Chinese Novel at the Turn of the Century.* Toronto: University of Toronto Press, 1980, pp. 129–49.

Holzman, Donald. "Confucius and Ancient Chinese Literary Criticism." In Adele Austin Rickett, ed., *Chinese Approaches to Literature from Confucius to Liang Ch'i-ch'ao*. Princeton: Princeton University Press, 1978, pp. 21–41.

———. "Literary Criticism in China in the Early Third Century A.D." *Asiatische Studien* 28.2 (1974): 113–49.

Hondt, Jacques d'. *Hegel secret*. Paris: Presses Universitaires de France, 1968.

———, ed. *Hegel et la pensée moderne*. Paris: Presses Universitaires de France, 1970.

Hsiao Kung-ch'üan. *A History of Chinese Political Thought*. Trans. Frederick W. Mote. Princeton: Princeton University Press, 1979.

Hsu, Cho-yun. *Ancient China in Transition*. Stanford: Stanford University Press, 1965.

Hsu, Cho-yun, and Katheryn M. Linduff. *Western Chou Civilization*. New Haven: Yale University Press, 1988.

Hu, Chi-hsi. "Mao Tsé-toung, la révolution et la question sexuelle." *Tel Quel* 59 (1974): 49–70.

Hulin, Michel. *Hegel et l'Orient*. Paris: Vrin, 1979.

Hung, Chang-tai. *Going to the People: Chinese Intellectuals and Folk Literature, 1918–1937*. Cambridge, Mass.: Harvard University Press, 1985.

Husserl, Edmund. *The Crisis of European Sciences and Transcendental Phenomenology*. Trans. David Carr. Evanston, Ill.: Northwestern University Press, 1970.

Imber, Alan. "*Kuo yü: An Early Chinese Text and Its Relations with the Tso chuan.*" Ph.D. dissertation, University of Stockholm, 1975.

Intorcetta, Prosper, Christian Herdtrich, François Rougemont, and Philippe Couplet. *Confucius Sinarum philosophus, sive scientia Sinensis latine exposita*. Paris, 1687.

Ishiguro, Hidé. *Leibniz's Philosophy of Logic and Language*. London: Duckworth, 1972.

Jakobson, Roman. "Closing Statement: Linguistics and Poetics." In Thomas A. Sebeok, ed., *Style in Language*. Cambridge, Mass.: MIT Press, 1960, pp. 350–77.

———. "Two Aspects of Language and Two Types of Aphasic Disturbances." In idem and Morris Halle, *Fundamentals of Language*. The Hague: Mouton, 1956, pp. 55–82.

Jakobson, Roman, and Linda Waugh. *The Sound Shape of Language.* Bloomington: Indiana University Press, 1979.

Jambet, Christian. *La Logique des Orientaux: Henry Corbin et la science des formes.* Paris: Seuil, 1983.

Jameson, Fredric. "Third-World Literature in the Era of Multinational Capitalism." *Social Text* 15 (1986): 65–88.

Jullien, François. *Encre de Chine: la révolution et sa lettre.* Lausanne: Alfred Eibel, 1978.

———. " 'Fonder' la morale, ou comment légitimer la transcendance de la moralité sans le support du dogme ou de la foi (au travers du *Mencius*)." *Extrême-Orient Extrême-Occident* 6 (1985): 23–81.

———. "Ni Ecriture sainte ni œuvre classique: du statut du Texte confucéen comme texte fondateur vis-à-vis de la civilisation chinoise." *Extrême-Orient Extrême-Occident* 5 (1984): 75–127.

———. *La Valeur allusive: des catégories originales de l'interprétation poétique dans la tradition chinoise.* Paris: Ecole Française d'Extrême-Orient, 1985.

Kant, Immanuel. *Kant's Critique of Aesthetic Judgement.* Trans. James Creed Meredith. Oxford: Clarendon Press, 1911.

———. *Werke in zehn Bänden.* Ed. Wilhelm Weischedel. Darmstadt: Wissenschaftliche Buchgesellschaft, 1983.

Kantorowicz, Ernst H. *The King's Two Bodies: A Study in Mediaeval Political Theology.* Princeton: Princeton University Press, 1957.

———. *Laudes Regiae: A Study in Liturgical Acclamations and Mediaeval Ruler Worship.* University of California Publications in History, vol. 33. Berkeley: University of California Press, 1946.

Kao, Karl S. Y. "Rhetoric." In William H. Nienhauser, Jr., ed., *The Indiana Companion to Traditional Chinese Literature.* Bloomington: Indiana University Press, 1986, pp. 121–37.

Karlgren, Bernhard. "Cognate Words in the Chinese Phonetic Series." *BMFEA* 28 (1956): 1–18.

———. "The Early History of the *Chou Li* and *Tso Chuan* Texts." *BMFEA* 3 (1931): 1–58.

———. "Glosses on the *Book of Documents*." *BMFEA* 20 (1948): 39–315; *BMFEA* 21 (1949): 163–206.

———. "Glosses on the *Kuo Feng* Odes." *BMFEA* 14 (1942): 71–247.

———. "Glosses on the *Li Ki*." *BMFEA* 43 (1971): 1–65.

———. "Glosses on the *Siao Ya* Odes." *BMFEA* 16 (1944): 25–169.

———. "Glosses on the *Ta Ya* and *Sung* Odes." *BMFEA* 18 (1946): 1–198.

———. *Grammata Serica*. *BMFEA* 12 (1940): 1–471. Reprinted—Taipei: Ch'eng-wen, 1978.

———. *Grammata Serica Recensa*. *BMFEA* 29 (1957). Reprinted—Stockholm: Museum of Far Eastern Antiquities, 1972.

———. "Legends and Cults in Ancient China." *BMFEA* 18 (1946): 199–365.

———. "Loan Characters in Pre-Han Texts." *BMFEA* 35 (1963): 1–128; *BMFEA* 36 (1964): 1–105; *BMFEA* 37 (1965): 1–136; *BMFEA* 38 (1966): 1–82; *BMFEA* 39 (1967): 1–51.

———, trans. *The Book of Documents*. *BMFEA* 22 (1950): 1–81.

———, trans. *The Book of Odes*. Stockholm: Museum of Far Eastern Antiquities, 1950.

Kauppi, Raili. *Über die Leibnizsche Logik*. Helsinki: Societas Philosophica, 1960.

Keightley, David N. "The Religious Commitment: Shang Theology and the Genesis of Chinese Political Culture." *History of Religions* 17 (1978): 211–25.

———, ed. *The Origins of Chinese Civilization*. Berkeley: University of California Press, 1983.

Kiesewetter, Hubert. *Von Hegel zu Hitler*. Hamburg: Hoffman & Campe, 1974.

Knoblock, John, trans. *Xunzi: A Translation and Study of the Complete Works*, Vol. 1, *Books 1–6*. Stanford: Stanford University Press, 1988.

Kojève, Alexandre. *Introduction à la lecture de Hegel*. Ed. Raymond Queneau. Paris: Gallimard, 1968.

Köster, Hermann, trans. *Hsün-tzu*. Kaldenkirchen: Steyler, 1967.

Kuttner, Fritz A. "A Musicological Interpretation of the Twelve *Lü* in China's Traditional Tone System." *Ethnomusicology* 6.1 (1965): 22–38.

Lach, Donald F. "Leibniz and China." *Journal of the History of Ideas* 6 (1945): 436–55.

———, ed. and annot. *The Preface to Leibniz' "Novissima Sinica."* Honolulu: University of Hawaii Press, 1957.

Lacoue-Labarthe, Philippe. *La Fiction du politique*. Paris: Bourgois, 1987.

Lamberton, Robert. *Homer the Theologian.* Berkeley: University of California Press, 1986.

Lee, Leo Ou-fan. *The Romantic Generation of Modern Chinese Writers.* Cambridge, Mass.: Harvard University Press, 1973.

Legge, James, trans. *The Chinese Classics.* 5 vols. Reprinted—Hong Kong: University of Hong Kong Press, 1960.

Leibniz, Gottfried Wilhelm. *Discourse on the Natural Theology of the Chinese.* Trans., with commentary, Henry Rosemont, Jr., and Daniel J. Cook. Honolulu: University of Hawaii Press, 1977.

———. *Discours sur la théologie naturelle des Chinois.* Ed. Christiane Frémont. Paris: Editions de l'Herne, 1987.

———. *Die Hauptschriften zur Dyadik von Leibniz.* Ed. Hans Joachim Zacher. Frankfurt am Main: Klostermann, 1973.

———. Manuscripts and letters deposited in the Leibniz-Archiv, Niedersächsische Landesbibliothek, Hannover. Cited according to Bodemann's catalogue numbers, preceded by LH (*Leibniz-Handschriften*) or LBr (*Leibniz-Briefe*).

———. *Novissima Sinica historiam nostri temporis illustratura.* Hannover, 1697.

———. *Opera omnia.* Ed. Ludovicus Dutens. Geneva, 1768.

———. *Opuscules et fragments inédits.* Ed. Louis Couturat. Paris: Alcan, 1903.

———. *Die philosophischen Schriften von G. W. Leibnitz.* Ed. G. I. Gerhardt. 1890. Reprinted—Hildesheim: Olms, 1965.

———. *Sämtliche Schriften und Briefe.* Ed. Preussischen Akademie der Wissenschaften, Berlin. Darmstadt: Akademie-Verlag, 1923–38; Leipzig: Akademie-Verlag, 1938; Berlin: Akademie-Verlag, 1950– .

———. *Zwei Briefe über das binäre Zahlensystem und die chinesische Philosophie.* Ed. Renate Loosen and Franz Vonessen. Stuttgart: Belser, 1968.

Leslie, Donald D., Colin Mackerras, and Wang Gungwu, eds., *Essays on the Sources for Chinese History.* Canberra: Australian National University Press, 1973.

Leuze, Reinhard. *Die außerchristlichen Religionen bei Hegel.* Göttingen: Vandenhoeck und Ruprecht, 1975.

Lévi, Jean. "Le Mythe de l'âge d'or et les théories de l'évolution en Chine ancienne." *L'Homme* 17 (1977): 73–103.

———. "Solidarité de l'ordre de la nature et de l'ordre de la société:

'loi' naturelle et 'loi' sociale dans la pensée légiste de la Chine ancienne." *Extrême-Orient Extrême-Occident* 3 (1983): 23–36.

Levy, Dore J. *Chinese Narrative Poetry.* Durham, N.C.: Duke University Press, 1988.

———. "Constructing Sequences: Another Look at the Principle of *Fu* 'Enumeration.'" *HJAS* 46 (1986): 471–93.

Li Xueqin. *Eastern Zhou and Qin Civilizations.* Trans. K. C. Chang. New Haven: Yale University Press, 1986.

Lin, Shuen-fu, and Stephen Owen, eds. *The Vitality of the Lyric Voice.* Princeton: Princeton University Press, 1986.

Liu, James J. Y. *Chinese Theories of Literature.* Chicago: University of Chicago Press, 1975.

Lloyd, G. E. R. *Polarity and Analogy.* Cambridge, Eng.: Cambridge University Press, 1966.

Longobardi, Nicolas, S.J. *Traité sur quelques points de la religion des Chinois.* Paris, 1701. Reprinted in Leibniz, *Opera omnia.* Ed. Ludovicus Dutens. Geneva, 1768, 4: 89–144.

Louie, Kam. *Inheriting Tradition: Interpretations of the Classical Philosophers in Communist China, 1949–1966.* New York: Oxford University Press, 1986.

Lovejoy, Arthur O. *Essays in the History of Ideas.* Baltimore: Johns Hopkins University Press, 1948.

Löwith, Karl, ed. *Die Hegelsche Linke.* Stuttgart and Bad Cannstatt: Frommann, 1962.

Lübbe, Hermann, ed. *Die Hegelsche Rechte.* Stuttgart and Bad Cannstatt: Frommann, 1962.

Lukács, Georg. *The Young Hegel.* Trans. Rodney Livingstone. Cambridge, Mass.: MIT Press, 1976.

Lyotard, Jean-François. *La Condition post-moderne.* Paris: Minuit, 1979.

Macherey, Pierre. *Hegel ou Spinoza.* Paris: Maspero, 1979.

MacIntyre, Alasdair. *After Virtue.* Notre Dame, Ind.: University of Notre Dame Press, 1984.

———. "Hegel on Faces and Skulls." In idem, ed., *Hegel: A Collection of Critical Essays.* New York: Anchor Books, 1972, pp. 219–36.

Malebranche, Nicolas. *Entretien d'un philosophe chrétien et d'un philosophe chinois sur l'existence et la nature de Dieu.* Ed. André Robinet. *Oeuvres complètes de Malebranche,* vol. 15. Paris: Vrin, 1958.

Mallarmé, Stéphane. *Oeuvres complètes*. Ed. Henri Mondor. Paris: Gallimard, 1945.

March, Andrew L. *The Idea of China: Myth and Theory in Geographic Thought*. New York: Praeger, 1974.

Marcus, George E., and Michael M. J. Fischer. *Anthropology as Cultural Critique: An Experimental Moment in the Human Sciences*. Chicago: University of Chicago Press, 1986.

Marx, Karl. *Capital*, vol. 1. Trans. Samuel Moore and Edward Aveling. New York: Modern Library, n.d.

————. *Early Writings*. Trans. Rodney Livingstone and Gregor Benton. New York: Vintage, 1975.

————. *Pre-Capitalist Economic Formations*. Trans. Jack Cohen. Ed. Eric J. Hobsbawm. New York: International Publishers, 1965.

Marx, Karl, and Friedrich Engels. *Marx-Engels Gesamtausgabe* [*MEGA*]. Berlin: Dietz, 1984.

Maverick, Lewis A. "A Possible Chinese Source of Spinoza's Doctrine." *Revue de Littérature Comparée* 19 (1939): 417–28.

Medhurst, W. H. *An Inquiry into the Proper Mode of Rendering the Word God in Translating the Sacred Scriptures into the Chinese Language*. Shanghai: Mission Press, 1848.

Merleau-Ponty, Maurice. *Signes*. Paris: Gallimard, 1960.

Miner, Earl. *Comparative Poetics: An Intercultural Essay on Theories of Literature*. Princeton: Princeton University Press, 1990.

Miyoshi, Masao. "Against the Native Grain: The Japanese Novel and the 'Postmodern' West." *South Atlantic Quarterly* 87 (1988): 525–50.

Montesquieu, Charles-Louis de. *Oeuvres complètes*. Paris: Seuil, 1964.

Mote, Frederick W. "The Arts and the 'Theorizing Mode' of the Civilization." In Christian Murck, ed., *Arts and Traditions: Uses of the Past in Chinese Culture*. Princeton: Princeton University Press, 1976, pp. 3–8.

————. "The Cosmological Gulf Between China and the West." In David C. Buxbaum and Frederick W. Mote, eds., *Transition and Permanence: Chinese History and Culture, a Festschrift in Honor of Dr. Hsiao Kung-ch'üan*. Hong Kong: Cathay Press, 1972, pp. 3–21.

Mounin, Georges. *Les Problèmes théoriques de la traduction*. Paris: Gallimard, 1963.

Mungello, David E. *Curious Land: Jesuit Accommodation and the Origins of Sinology*. Honolulu: University of Hawaii Press, 1989.

————. *Leibniz and Confucianism: The Search for Accord.* Honolulu: University of Hawaii Press, 1977.

Munro, Donald J. *The Concept of Man in Early China.* Stanford: Stanford University Press, 1969.

Murck, Christian, ed. *Arts and Traditions: Uses of the Past in Chinese Culture.* Princeton: Princeton University Press, 1976.

Nagy, Gregory. *The Best of the Achaeans.* Baltimore: Johns Hopkins University Press, 1979.

————. *Greek Mythology and Poetics.* Ithaca: Cornell University Press, 1990.

Nakaseko, Kazu. "Symbolism in Ancient Chinese Music Theory." *Journal of Music Theory* 1.2 (1957): 147–80.

Needham, Joseph. *The Grand Titration: Science and Society in East and West.* London: Allen & Unwin, 1969.

Needham, Joseph, et al. *Science and Civilisation in China.* 6 vols. Cambridge, Eng.: Cambridge University Press, 1954–71.

Needham, Joseph, and Ho Ping-yü. "Theories of Categories in Early Medieval Chinese Alchemy." *Journal of the Warburg and Courtauld Institutes* 22 (1959): 173–210.

Needham, Joseph, and Kenneth Robinson. "Sound (Acoustics)." In J. Needham et al., *Science and Civilisation in China,* vol. 4, pt. I. Cambridge, Eng.: Cambridge University Press, 1962, pp. 126–228.

Nienhauser, William H., Jr. "An Allegorical Reading of Han Yü's 'Mao Ying chuan' (Biography of Fur Point)." *Oriens Extremus* 23 (1976): 153–74.

————, ed. *The Indiana Companion to Traditional Chinese Literature.* Bloomington: Indiana University Press, 1986.

Nietzsche, Friedrich. *Sämtliche Werke.* Ed. Giorgio Colli and Mazzino Montinari. Munich: DTV; Berlin: de Gruyter, 1988.

Northrop, F. S. C. *The Meeting of East and West.* New York: Macmillan, 1946.

Owen, Stephen. *The Great Age of Chinese Poetry: The High T'ang.* New Haven: Yale University Press, 1981.

————. *Mi-Lou: Poetry and the Labyrinth of Desire.* Cambridge, Mass.: Harvard University Press, 1989.

————. *The Poetry of the Early T'ang.* New Haven: Yale University Press, 1977.

————. *Remembrances: The Experience of the Past in Classical Chinese Literature.* Cambridge, Mass.: Harvard University Press, 1986.

————. *Traditional Chinese Poetry and Poetics: Omen of the World*. Madison: University of Wisconsin Press, 1985.

Pang, Ching-jen. *L'Idée de Dieu chez Malebranche et l'idée de "li" chez Tchou Hi*. Paris: Vrin, 1942.

Parry, Milman. *The Making of Homeric Verse*. Ed. Adam Parry. Oxford: Oxford University Press, 1971.

Pechmann, Alexander von. *Die Kategorie des Maßes in Hegels "Wissenschaft der Logik": Einführung und Kommentar*. Cologne: Pahl-Rugenstein, 1980.

Pelliot, Paul. "Le *Chou king* en caractères anciens et le *Chang chou che wen*." *Mémoires Concernant l'Asie Orientale* 2 (1916): 123–84.

Percy, Walker. *The Message in the Bottle*. New York: Farrar, Strauss & Giroux, 1975.

Petry, Michael John, ed. *Hegel und die Naturwissenschaften*. Stuttgart and Bad Cannstatt: Frommann-Holzboog, 1987.

Pfister, Louis, S.J. *Notices biographiques et bibliographiques sur les jésuites de l'ancienne mission de Chine (1552–1773)*. 2 vols. Shanghai: Imprimerie de la Mission Catholique, 1932–34.

Philastre, P.-L.-F., trans. *Le "Yi: King" ou Livre des Changements de la dynastie des Tsheou*. *Annales du Musée Guimet*, vols. 8, 23 (1885, 1893). Reprinted—Paris: Maisonneuve, 1982.

Picken, Laurence E. R. "The Shapes of the *Shi Jing* Song-Texts and Their Musical Implications." *Musica Asiatica* 1 (1977): 85–109.

Pinot, Virgile. *La Chine et la formation de l'esprit philosophique en France*. Paris: Geuthner, 1932.

————, ed. *Documents inédits relatifs à la connaissance de la Chine en France de 1685 à 1740*. Paris: Geuthner, 1932.

Pippin, Robert B. *Hegel's Idealism: The Satisfactions of Self-Consciousness*. Cambridge, Eng.: Cambridge University Press, 1989.

Plaks, Andrew. *Archetype and Allegory in "Dream of the Red Chamber."* Princeton: Princeton University Press, 1976.

————, ed. *Chinese Narrative: Critical and Theoretical Essays*. Princeton: Princeton University Press, 1977.

Powers, Martin J. *Art and Political Expression in Early China*. New Haven: Yale University Press, 1991.

Quilligan, Maureen. *The Language of Allegory: Defining the Genre*. Ithaca: Cornell University Press, 1979.

Quine, W. V. *From a Logical Point of View*. Cambridge, Mass.: Harvard University Press, 1961.

————. "Meaning and Translation." In Reuben A. Brower, ed., *On Translation*. Cambridge, Mass.: Harvard University Press, 1959, pp. 148–72.

————. *Ontological Relativity and Other Essays*. New York: Columbia University Press, 1969.

————. *Theories and Things*. Cambridge, Mass.: Harvard University Press, 1981.

————. *Word and Object*. Cambridge, Mass.: MIT Press, 1960.

Quintilian. *Institutionis oratoriae libri duodecim*. Ed. M. Winterbottom. Oxford: Oxford University Press, 1970.

Reding, Jean-Paul. *Les Fondements philosophiques de la rhétorique chez les sophistes grecs et chez les sophistes chinois*. Bern: Peter Lang, 1985.

Régis, Jean-Baptiste, S.J., et al., trans. and annots. *Y-king, antiquissimus Sinarum liber*. Ed. Julius Mohl. Stuttgart and Tübingen: Cotta, 1839.

Rémusat, Abel. *Mélanges asiatiques*. Paris: Dondey-Dupré (*Journal Asiatique*), 1825.

————. *Nouveaux mélanges asiatiques*. Paris: Schubart et Heideloff (*Journal Asiatique*), 1829.

————, trans. *Iu-kiao-li, ou les deux cousines: Roman chinois*. Paris: Moutardier, 1826.

Richards, I. A. *Mencius on the Mind*. London: Routledge & Kegan Paul, 1964.

Rickett, Adele Austin, ed. *Chinese Approaches to Literature from Confucius to Liang Ch'i-ch'ao*. Princeton: Princeton University Press, 1978.

Rickett, W. Allyn. *Guanzi: Political, Economic and Philosophical Essays from Early China*, vol. 1. Princeton: Princeton University Press, 1985.

Riegel, Jeffrey K. "Poetry and the Legend of Confucius' Exile." *Journal of the American Oriental Society* 106 (1986): 13–22.

Riffaterre, Michael. *Semiotics of Poetry*. Bloomington: Indiana University Press, 1978.

Robinet, André. *Malebranche et Leibniz: relations personnelles*. Paris: Vrin, 1955.

Röllicke, Hermann-Josef. "Die Fährte des Herzens: Die Lehre vom Herzensbestreben (*zhi*) im grossen Vorwort zum *Shijing*." M.A. thesis, University of Tübingen, 1989.

Rorty, Richard. *Consequences of Pragmatism: Essays, 1972–1980.* Minneapolis: University of Minnesota Press, 1982.

Rose, Gillian. *Hegel Contra Sociology.* London: Athlone, 1981.

Rosenkranz, Karl. *Ästhetik des Häßlichen.* 1853. Reprinted— Darmstadt: Wissenschaftliche Buchgesellschaft, 1979.

———. *Georg Wilhelm Friedrich Hegels Leben.* 1844. Reprinted—Darmstadt: Wissenschaftliche Buchgesellschaft, 1977.

Russell, Bertrand. *A Critical Exposition of the Philosophy of Leibniz.* London: Allen & Unwin, 1937.

Said, Edward. *Orientalism.* New York: Pantheon, 1978.

Sakai, Naoki. "Modernity and Its Critique: The Problem of Universalism and Particularism." *South Atlantic Quarterly* 87 (1988): 475–504.

Saussure, Ferdinand de. *Cours de linguistique générale.* Paris: Payot, 1970.

———. *Cours de linguistique générale: édition critique.* Ed. Rudolf Engler. 2 vols. Wiesbaden: Harrassowitz, 1967.

Schiller, Friedrich. *On the Aesthetic Education of Man.* Trans. and ed. Elizabeth M. Wilkinson and L. A. Willoughby. Oxford: Clarendon Press, 1985.

———. *Schriften zur Ästhetik, Literatur und Geschichte.* Munich: Goldmann, n.d.

Schleiermacher, Friedrich Daniel Ernst. *Ästhetik [1819/25]; Über den Begriff der Kunst [1831/32].* Ed. Thomas Lehnerer. Hamburg: Meiner, 1984.

Schneider, Helmut, ed. and comm. "Unveröffentlichte Vorlesungsmanuskripte Hegels." *Hegel-Studien* 7 (1972): 9–59.

Schneider, Laurence A. *Ku Chieh-kang and China's New History.* Berkeley: University of California Press, 1971.

———. *A Madman of Ch'u: The Chinese Myth of Loyalty and Dissent.* Berkeley: University of California Press, 1980.

Schoeps, Hans Joachim. "Die außerchristlichen Religionen bei Hegel." *Zeitschrift für Religions- und Geistesgeschichte* 7 (1955): 1–34.

Schwab, Raymond. *The Oriental Renaissance.* New York: Columbia University Press, 1988.

Segalen, Victor. *Essai sur l'exotisme.* Paris: Librairie Générale Française, 1986.

———. *Lettres de Chine.* Ed. Jean-Louis Bedouin. Paris: Plon, 1967.

———. *Stèles.* Ed. Henry Bouillier. Paris: Mercure de France, 1982.

Segalen, Victor, and Henry Manceron. *Trahison fidèle: correspondance, 1907–1918.* Ed. Gilles Manceron. Paris: Seuil, 1985.

Semedo, Alvaro. *Histoire universelle de la Chine ... avec l'histoire de la guerre des Tartares ... par le P. Martin Martini.* Lyon, 1667.

Serres, Michel. *Le Système de Leibniz et ses modèles mathématiques.* 2 vols. Paris: Presses Universitaires de France, 1968.

Seznec, Jean. *The Survival of the Pagan Gods.* Trans. Barbara P. Sessions. New York: Pantheon, 1953.

Shen, Sinyan. "Acoustics of Ancient Chinese Bells." *Scientific American* 256.4 (April 1987): 104–10.

Shih, Vincent Yu-chung, trans. and annot. [Liu Hsieh,] *The Literary Mind and the Carving of Dragons.* Hong Kong: University Press of Hong Kong, 1983.

Shklovsky, Viktor. *Theory of Prose.* Trans. Benjamin Sher. Elmwood Park, Ill.: Dalkey Archive, 1990.

Smith, John H. *The Spirit and Its Letter: Traces of Rhetoric in Hegel's Philosophy of Bildung.* Ithaca: Cornell University Press, 1988.

Souche-Dagues, Denise. *Logique et politique hégéliennes.* Paris: Vrin, 1983.

Spitzer, Leo. *Essays in English and American Literature.* Princeton: Princeton University Press, 1962.

Spivak, Gayatri Chakravorty. "Translator's Preface." In Jacques Derrida, *Of Grammatology.* Baltimore: Johns Hopkins University Press, 1976, pp. ix–lxxxv.

Stumpfeldt, Hans. *Staatsverfassung und Territorium im antiken China.* Düsseldorf: Bertelsmann, 1970.

Suidas. *Lexicon.* Ed. Immanuel Bekker. Berlin: Reimer, 1854.

Szondi, Peter. *On Textual Understanding.* Trans. Harvey Mendelsohn. Minneapolis: University of Minnesota Press, 1986.

Tarski, Alfred. "The Semantic Conception of Truth." *Philosophy and Phenomenological Research* 4 (1944): 341–75.

Tchang, Mathias, S.J. *Synchronismes chinois.* Shanghai: Imprimerie de la Mission Catholique, 1905.

Texier, Jacques. "Le Concept de *Naturwüchsigkeit* dans *L'Idéologie allemande.*" *Hegel-Jahrbuch* 27 (1990): 339–55.

Theunissen, Michael. *Hegels Lehre vom absoluten Geist als theologisch-politischer Traktat.* Berlin: de Gruyter, 1970.

———. *Sein und Schein: Die kritische Funktion der Hegelschen Logik.* Frankfurt am Main: Suhrkamp, 1978.

Tjan Tjoe Som, trans. and annot. *Po Hu T'ung: The Comprehensive Discussions in the White Tiger Hall.* 2 vols. Sinica Leidensia, no. 6. Leiden: Brill, 1949, 1952.

Todorov, Tzvetan. "Comprendre une culture: du dedans/du dehors." *Extrême-Orient Extrême-Occident* 1 (1982): 9–15.

Tökei, Ferenc. *Essays on the Asiatic Mode of Production.* Budapest: Akadémiai Kiadó, 1979.

————. *Naissance de l'élégie chinoise.* Paris: Gallimard, 1967.

————. "Sur le rythme du *Chou king.*" *Acta Orientalia Academiae Scientiarum Hungaricae* 7 (1957): 77–104.

Tu Wei-ming. *Centrality and Commonality: An Essay on "Chung-yung."* Honolulu: University of Hawaii Press, 1976.

Turbayne, Colin Murray. *The Myth of Metaphor.* New Haven: Yale University Press, 1962.

Tuve, Rosemond. *Allegorical Imagery: Some Mediaeval Books and Their Posterity.* Princeton: Princeton University Press, 1966.

Vandermeersch, Léon. *La Formation du légisme: recherche sur la constitution d'une philosophie politique caractéristique de la Chine ancienne.* Paris: Ecole Française d'Extrême-Orient, 1965.

————. *Wangdao ou la voie royale: recherches sur l'esprit des institutions de la Chine archaïque,* Vol. 1, *Structures cultuelles et structures familiales;* Vol. 2, *Structures politiques, les rites.* Paris: Ecole Française d'Extrême-Orient, 1977, 1980.

Van Dyke, Carolynn. *The Fiction of Truth: Structures of Meaning in Narrative and Dramatic Allegory.* Ithaca: Cornell University Press, 1985.

Van Zoeren, Steven Jay. *Poetry and Personality: Reading, Exegesis and Hermeneutics in Traditional China.* Stanford: Stanford University Press, 1991.

Vernant, Jean-Pierre, and Jacques Gernet. "Histoire sociale et évolution des idées en Chine et en Grèce du VIᵉ au IIᵉ siècle avant notre ère." In J.-P. Vernant, *Mythe et société en Grèce ancienne.* Paris: Maspero, 1974, pp. 83–102.

Vernière, Paul. *Spinoza et la pensée française avant la Révolution.* Paris: Presses Universitaires de France, 1954.

Vico, Giambattista. *La Scienza nuova.* Milan: Rizzoli, 1977.

Vissière, Isabelle, and Jean-Louis Vissière, eds. *Lettres édifiantes et curieuses de Chine par des missionaires jésuites, 1702–1776.* Paris: Garnier-Flammarion, 1976.

Waley, Arthur. "The *Book of Changes*." *BMFEA* 5 (1933): 121–42.
———, trans. *The Book of Songs*. New York: Grove Press, 1974.
Wandschneider, Dieter. *Raum, Zeit, Relativität: Grundbestimmungen der Physik in der Perspektive der Hegelschen Naturphilosophie*. Frankfurt am Main: Klostermann, 1982.
Wang, C. H. *The Bell and the Drum: "Shih Ching" as Formulaic Poetry in an Oral Tradition*. Berkeley: University of California Press, 1974.
———. *From Ritual to Allegory: Seven Essays in Early Chinese Poetry*. Hong Kong: Chinese University Press, 1988.
Wang Zhongshu. *Han Civilization*. New Haven: Yale University Press, 1982.
Warminski, Andrzej. *Readings in Interpretation: Hölderlin, Hegel, Heidegger*. Minneapolis: University of Minnesota Press, 1987.
Watson, Burton, trans. *The "Tso Chuan": Selections from China's Oldest Narrative History*. New York: Columbia University Press, 1989.
Weber, Max. *The Rational and Social Foundations of Music*. Trans. and ed. Don Martindale, Johannes Riedel, and Gertrude Neuwirth. Carbondale: Southern Illinois University Press, 1958.
———. *The Religion of China: Confucianism and Taoism*. Trans. and ed. Hans H. Gerth. Glencoe, Ill.: Free Press, 1951.
Weinrich, Uriel. *Languages in Contact: Findings and Problems*. The Hague: Mouton, 1968.
Weiskel, Thomas. *The Romantic Sublime: Studies in the Structure and Psychology of Transcendence*. Baltimore: Johns Hopkins University Press, 1976.
Wells, Rulon S. "Metonymy and Misunderstanding: An Aspect of Language Change." In Roger W. Cole, ed., *Current Issues in Linguistic Theory*. Bloomington: Indiana University Press, 1977, pp. 195–214.
Wheatley, Paul. *The Pivot of the Four Quarters*. Chicago: Aldine, 1972.
Whitman, Jon. *Allegory: The Dynamics of an Ancient and Modern Technique*. Oxford: Clarendon Press, 1987.
Whitney, William Dwight. *Language and the Study of Language*. New York: Charles Scribner, 1868.
Widmaier, Rita. *Die Rolle der chinesischen Schrift in Leibniz' Zeichentheorie*. Studia Leibnitiana Supplementa, vol. 24. Stuttgart: Steiner, 1983.
———, ed. *Leibniz korrespondiert mit China*. Frankfurt am Main: Klostermann, 1990.

Wilson, Edmund. *Axel's Castle*. New York: Scribner's, 1931.

Wittfogel, Karl A. *Oriental Despotism*. New Haven: Yale University Press, 1957.

Wittgenstein, Ludwig. *Philosophical Grammar*. Berkeley: University of California Press, 1978.

Wixted, John Timothy. "The *Kokinshū* Prefaces: Another Perspective." *HJAS* 43.1 (1983): 215–38.

———. *Poems on Poetry: Literary Criticism by Yüan Hao-wen*. Wiesbaden: Steiner, 1982.

Wohlfart, Günter. *Der spekulative Satz*. Berlin: de Gruyter, 1981.

Wolf, Eric R. *Europe and the People Without History*. Berkeley: University of California Press, 1982.

Wu Hung. *The Wu Liang Shrine: The Ideology of Early Chinese Pictorial Art*. Stanford: Stanford University Press, 1989.

Xue Hua. "Weltgeist und Chinageist." *Hegel-Jahrbuch* 20 (1981–82): 203–13.

Yandell, Cathy. "A la recherche du corps perdu: A Capstone of the Renaissance *Blasons anatomiques*." *Romance Notes* 26 (1985): 135–42.

Yeh, Michelle. "Metaphor and *Bi*: Western and Chinese Poetics." *Comparative Literature* 39 (1987): 237–54.

Yu, Anthony C., trans. *The Journey to the West*. 4 vols. Chicago: University of Chicago Press, 1976–83.

Yu, Pauline R. "Allegory, Allegoresis, and the *Classic of Poetry*." *HJAS* 43.2 (1983): 377–412.

———. "Metaphor in Chinese Poetry." *CLEAR* 3 (1981): 27–53.

———. "Poems in Their Place: Collections and Canons in Early Chinese Literature." *HJAS* 50.1 (1990): 163–96.

———. *The Reading of Imagery in the Chinese Poetic Tradition*. Princeton: Princeton University Press, 1987.

Zhang Longxi. "The Letter or the Spirit: The *Song of Songs*, Allegoresis, and the *Book of Poetry*." *Comparative Literature* 39 (1987): 193–217.

———. "The Myth of the Other: China in the Eyes of the West." *Critical Inquiry* 15 (1988): 108–31.

———. *The Tao and the Logos*. Durham, N.C.: Duke University Press, 1992.

Zottoli, Angelo, S.J. *Cursus litteraturae sinicae*. 5 vols. Shanghai: Typographia Missionis Catholicae, 1879–82.

Züfle, Manfred. *Prosa der Welt: Die Sprache Hegels*. Einsiedeln: Johannes-Verlag, 1968.

Works in Chinese and Japanese

Chang Han-liang 張漢良. "Te-hsi-ta, shu-hsieh yü Chung-wen" 德希達, 書寫與中文. *Tang-tai* 4 (1986): 30–33.

Chao Chih-yang 趙制陽. *"Shih-ching" fu pi hsing tsung-lun* 詩經賦比興綜論. Hsin-chu, Taiwan: Feng-ch'eng, 1974.

Ch'en Fei-lung 陳飛龍. *Hsün-tzu li-hsüeh chih yen-chiu* 荀子禮學之研究. Taipei: Wen-shih-che, 1979.

Ch'en Huan 陳奐, ed. *Shih Mao shih chuan shu* 詩毛氏傳疏. 1847. Reprinted—Taipei: Hsüeh-sheng, 1986.

Ch'en Kuo-ch'ing 陳國慶, ed. *I-wen-chih chu-shu hui-pien* 藝文志注疏彙編. Peking: Chung-hua, 1983.

Ch'en P'an 陳槃. "Chou, Shao erh-nan yü Wen wang chih hua" 周召二南與文王之化. 1928. In Ku Chieh-kang et al., eds., *Ku shih pien*. Hong Kong: T'ai-p'ing, 1962, 3: 424–39.

———. "Shih san-pai-p'ien chih ts'ai-chi yü shan-ting wen-t'i" 詩三百篇之采集與刪定問題. In Lo Lien-t'ien, ed., *Chung-kuo wen-hsüeh-shih lun-wen hsüan-chi*. Taipei: Hsüeh-sheng, 1978, 1: 33–48.

Ch'en Wang-tao 陳王道. *Hsiu-tz'u-hsüeh fa-fan* 修辭學發凡. Hong Kong: Ta-kuang, 1981.

Cheng Chen-to 鄭振鐸. "Tu '*Mao Shih* hsü'" 讀毛詩序. 1924. In Ku Chieh-kang et al., eds., *Ku shih pien*. Hong Kong: T'ai-p'ing, 1962, 3: 382–401.

Cheng Ch'iao 鄭樵. *T'ung-chih lüeh* 通志略. SPPY. Shanghai: Chung-hua, 1946.

Cheng Hsüan 鄭玄. *Mao Shih Cheng chien* 毛詩鄭箋. Taipei: Hsin-hsing, 1980.

Chi Yün 紀昀, ed. *Ssu-k'u ch'üan-shu tsung-mu t'i-yao* 四庫全書總目提要. Taipei: Shang-wu, 1983.

Chien Po-hsien 簡博賢. *Chin-ts'un San-kuo liang-Chin ching-hsüeh i-chi k'ao* 今存三國兩晉經學遺籍考. Taipei: San-min, 1986.

Ch'ien Chung-shu 錢鍾書. *Kuan-chui pien* 管錐編. Peking: Chung-hua, 1979.

Ch'ien Mu 錢穆. *Hsien-Ch'in chu-tzu hsi-nien* 先秦諸子繫年. 2d ed. Hong Kong: Hong Kong University Press, 1956.

———. *Liang-Han ching-hsüeh chin ku wen p'ing-i* 兩漢經學今古文評義. Hong Kong: Hsin-ya yen-chiu-so, 1958.

Chou Ts'e-tsung (Chow Tse-tsung) 周策縱. "'Chüan-o' k'ao" 「卷阿」考. *Ch'ing-hua hsüeh-pao* n.s. 7.2 (1969): 176–205.

———. *Ku wu-i yü "liu-shih" k'ao* 古巫醫與「六詩」考. Taipei: Lien-ching, 1986.

———. *"P'o-fu" hsin-ku* 「破斧」新詁. Singapore: Island Society, 1969.

Chu Ch'ien-chih 朱謙之. *Chung-kuo yin-yüeh wen-hsüeh-shih* 中國音樂文學史. Shanghai: Shang-wu, 1935.

Chu Hsi 朱熹. *Chu-tzu yü-lei* 朱子語類. Ed. Li Ching-te 黎靖德. 8 vols. Peking: Chung-hua, 1986.

———. *"Shih" chi chuan* 詩集傳. Taipei: Cheng-hua, 1975.

———. *"Shih hsü" pien-shuo* 詩序辨說. SKCS, 69: 3–42.

———. *Ssu-shu chi-chu* 四書集注. SPPY. Shanghai: Chung-hua, 1930.

Chu Kuan-hua 朱冠華. "Kuan-yü '*Mao Shih* hsü' ti tso-che wen-t'i" 關於毛詩序的作者問題. *Wen-shih* 16 (1982): 177–87.

Chu T'ing-hsien 朱廷獻. *"Shang-shu" yen-chiu* 尚書研究. Taipei: Shang-wu, 1987.

Chu Tung-jun 朱東潤. *Shih san-pai-p'ien t'an-ku* 詩三百篇探故. Shanghai: Ku-chi, 1981.

Chu Tzu-ch'ing 朱自清. *Shih yen chih pien* 詩言志辨. 1945. In *Chu Tzu-ch'ing ku-tien wen-hsüeh lun-wen chi* 朱自清古典文學論文集. Shanghai: Ku-chi, 1981, pp. 185–355.

Ch'ü Wan-li 屈萬里. "Hsien-Ch'in shuo *Shih* ti feng-hsiang ho Han-ju i *Shih* chiao shuo *Shih* ti yü-ch'ü" 先秦說詩的風象和漢儒以詩教說詩的迂曲. *Nan-yang hsüeh-pao* 5 (1971): 1–10.

———. "Lun 'Ch'u-chü' chih shih chu-ch'eng ti shih-tai" 論「出車」之詩著成的時代. *Ch'ing-hua hsüeh-pao* n.s. 1.2 (1957): 102–10.

———. "Lun *Kuo Feng* fei min-chien ko-yao ti pen-lai mien-mu" 論國風非民間歌謠的本來面目. *BIHP* 34.2 (1963): 477–504.

———. *Shih ching ch'üan-shih* 詩經詮釋. *Ch'ü Wan-li ch'üan-chi* 屈萬里全集, vol. 5. Taipei: Lien-ching, 1983.

Chuang-tzu chi-shih 莊子集釋. Ed. Kuo Ch'ing-fan 郭慶藩. Taipei: Han-ching, 1983.

Erh ya 爾雅. Ed. Hao I-hsing 郝懿行. Taipei: Han-ching, 1985.

Fan Yeh 范曄. *Hou Han shu* 後漢書. Ed. Wang Hsien-ch'ien 王先謙. Peking: Chung-hua, 1981.

Fang Yü-jun 方玉潤. *"Shih-ching" yüan-shih* 詩經原始. 1871. Reprinted—2 vols. Peking: Chung-hua, 1986.

Fu Ssu-nien 傅斯年. *Fu Meng-chen hsien-sheng chi* 傅孟真先生集. 7 vols. Taipei: Lien-ching, 1980.

———. "Sung Chu Hsi ti *Shih-ching chi-chuan ho Shih-hsü pien*" 宋朱熹的詩經集傳和詩序辨. *Hsin ch'ao* 1.4 (1919): 693–701.

Fu-tan ta-hsüeh. Chung-wen-hsi. Ku-tien wen-hsüeh chiao-yen-tsu 復旦大學中文系古典文學教研組. *Chung-kuo wen-hsüeh p'i-p'ing shih* 中國文學批評史. Shanghai: Ku-chi, 1979.

Han Ying 韓嬰. *Han Shih wai chuan* 韓詩外傳. SPTK. Shanghai: Shang-wu, 1929.

Hsiao Kung-ch'üan 蕭公權. *Chung-kuo cheng-chih ssu-hsiang shih* 中國政治思想史. *Hsiao Kung-ch'üan hsien-sheng chi* 蕭公權先生集, vol. 4. Taipei: Lien-ching, 1982.

Hsiao T'ung 蕭統, ed.; Li Shan 李善, annot. *Wen hsüan* 文選. Taipei: Lien-ching, 1983.

Hsiung Kung-che 熊公哲 et al. *"Shih-ching" lun-wen-chi* 詩經論文集. Taipei: Yung-yü, 1980.

Hsü Chung-shu 徐中舒. "Pin-feng shuo" 豳風說. *BIHP* 6 (1936): 431–52.

Hsü Shen 許慎. *Shuo-wen chieh-tzu* 說文解字. Ed. Tuan Yü-ts'ai 段玉裁. Taipei: Han-ching, 1983.

Hsü Wen-shan 徐文珊. *Hsien-Ch'in chu-tzu tao-tu* 先秦諸子導讀. Taipei: Yu-shih, 1964.

Hsün-tzu chi-chieh 荀子集解. Ed. Wang Hsien-ch'ien 王先謙. Taipei: Shih-chieh, 1983.

Hu P'ing-sheng 胡平生 and Han Tzu-ch'iang 韓自強. *Fu-yang Han-chien "Shih-ching" yen-chiu* 阜陽漢簡詩經研究 Shanghai: Ku-chi, 1988.

Huai-nan-tzu 淮南子. Annot. Kao Yu 高誘. SPPY. Taipei: Chung-hua, 1970.

Huang Chang-chien 黃彰健. *Ching chin-ku wen-hsüeh wen-t'i hsin-lun* 經今古文學問題新論. Taipei: Chung-yang yen-chiu-yüan, Li-shih yü-yen yen-chiu so, 1982.

Hui Chou-t'i 惠周惕. *"Shih" shuo* 詩說. In Juan Yüan, ed., *Huang-Ch'ing ching-chieh*. Canton: Hsüeh-hai-t'ang, 1860, ch. 190–93.

Hung Yeh 洪業. "P'o-fu" 「破斧」. *Ch'ing-hua hsüeh-pao* n.s. 1.1 (1956): 21–60.

Hung Yeh et al. *Ch'un-ch'iu ching-chuan yin-te* 春秋經傳引得. Harvard-Yenching Sinological Index Series, vol. 11. Peking: Harvard-Yenching Institute, 1937.

————. *Mao Shih yin-te* 毛詩引得. Harvard-Yenching Sinological Index Series, vol. 9. Peiping: Harvard-Yenching Institute, 1934.

Jao Tsung-i 饒宗頤. "Lu Chi *Wen-fu* li-lun yü yin-yüeh chih kuan-hsi" 陸機文賦理論與音樂之關係. *Chūgoku Bungakuhō* 14 (1961): 22–37.

Juan Yüan 阮元, ed. *Huang-Ch'ing ching-chieh* 皇清經解. Canton: Hsüeh-hai-t'ang, 1860.

————. *Shih-san ching chu-shu* 十三經注疏 (*SSCCS*). 1815. Reprinted —Taipei: Ta-hua, 1987.

K'ang Hsiao-ch'eng 康曉城. *Hsien-Ch'in ju-chia shih-chiao ssu-hsiang yen-chiu* 先秦儒家詩教思想研究. Taipei: Wen-shih-che, 1988.

K'ang Yu-wei 康有為. *Hsin-hsüeh wei-ching k'ao* 新學偽經考. Canton: Wan-mu-ts'ao-t'ang, 1891.

Kao Heng 高亨. *Chu-tzu hsin-chien* 諸子新箋. Chi-nan, Shantung: Ch'i-lu, 1980.

K'o Ch'ing-ming 柯慶明 and Lin Ming-te 林明德, eds. *Chung-kuo ku-tien wen-hsüeh yen-chiu ts'ung-k'an: Shih-ko chih pu* 中國古典文學研究叢刊:詩歌之部. Taipei: Chü-liu, 1977.

K'o Ch'ing-ming and Tseng Yung-i 曾永義, eds. *Chung-kuo wen-hsüeh p'i-p'ing tzu-liao hui-pien*, Vol. 1, *Liang-Han, Wei, Chin, Nan-pei-ch'ao* 中國文學批評資料彙編:兩漢, 魏, 晉, 南北朝. Taipei: Ch'eng-wen, 1978.

Ku Chieh-kang 顧頡剛. *Han-tai hsüeh-shu shih lüeh* 漢代學術史略. 1935. Reprinted—Taipei: T'ien-shan, 1985. Revised and reissued as *Ch'in-Han ti fang-shih yü ju-sheng* 秦漢的方士與儒生. Shanghai: Ch'ün-lien, 1955.

Ku Chieh-kang et al., eds. *Ku shih pien* 古史辨. 7 vols., 1926–41. Reprinted—Hong Kong: T'ai-p'ing, 1962.

Ku Yen-wu 顧炎武. *Jih chih lu* 日知錄. In Juan Yüan, ed., *Huang-Ch'ing ching-chieh*. Canton: Hsüeh-hai-t'ang, 1860, ch. 18–19.

Kuan-tzu 管子. Annot. Fang Hsüan-ling 房玄齡. SPPY. Shanghai: Chung-hua, 1930.

Kung Mu-lan 龔慕蘭, ed. *Yüeh-fu shih hsüan-chu* 樂府詩選註. Taipei: Kuang-wen, 1971.

K'ung Ying-ta 孔穎達. *Mao Shih cheng-i* 毛詩正義. *SSCCS*.

Kuo Shao-yü 郭紹虞 and Wang Wen-sheng 王文生, eds. *Chung-kuo li-tai wen-lun hsüan* 中國歷代文論選. Shanghai: Ku-chi, 1979.

Kuo yü 國語. Shanghai: Ku-chi, 1978.

Li Chih-tsao 李之藻, ed. *T'ien-hsüeh ch'u-han* 天學初函. 1628. Reprinted—Taipei: Hsüeh-sheng, 1965.

Li Fu-p'ing 李黼平. *Mao Shih ch'ou i* 毛詩紬義. In Juan Yüan, ed., *Huang-Ch'ing ching-chieh*. Canton: Hsüeh-hai-t'ang, 1860, ch. 1331–54.

Li Ma-tou 利馬竇 (Matteo Ricci) et al. *T'ien-chu-chiao tung-ch'uan wen-hsien* 天主教東傳文獻. Taipei: Hsüeh-sheng shu-chü, 1982.

Li Nai-yang 李迺楊 and Nakatsuhama Wataru 中津濱涉, eds. *Shih-san ching chu-shu ching-wen so-yin* 十三經注疏經文索引. Taipei: Ta-hua, 1987.

Li Tse-hou 李澤厚. *Chung-kuo ku-tai ssu-hsiang shih lun* 中國古代思想史論. Peking: Jen-min, 1986.

Li Tse-hou and Liu Kang-chi 劉綱紀. *Chung-kuo mei-hsüeh-shih* 中國美學史. 2 vols. Peking: Hsin-hua, 1984, 1987.

Liang Ch'i-ch'ao 梁啟超. *Mo ching chiao shih* 墨經校釋. Taipei: Hsin-wen-feng, 1975.

Lieh-tzu 列子. Ed. Chang Chan 張湛. Taipei: Shih-chieh, 1983.

Lin Ch'ing-chang 林慶彰, ed. *"Shih-ching" yen-chiu lun-chi* 詩經研究論集. Taipei: Hsüeh-sheng, 1983.

Liu Hsiang 劉向. *Lieh nü chuan* 列女傳. SPTK. Shanghai: Shang-wu, 1929.

Liu Hsieh 劉勰. *Wen-hsin tiao-lung* 文心雕龍. Ed. Chou Chen-fu 周振甫. Taipei: Li-jen, 1983.

Liu Kuang-i 劉光義. *Han Wu-ti chih yung-ju chi Han-ju chih shuo "Shih"* 漢武帝之用儒及漢儒之說詩. Taipei: Shang-wu, 1969.

Lo Cho-han 羅倬漢. *Shih yüeh lun* 詩樂論. Taipei: Cheng-chung, 1954.

Lo Lien-t'ien 羅聯添, ed. *Chung-kuo wen-hsüeh-shih lun-wen hsüan-chi* 中國文學史論文選集. Taipei: Hsüeh-sheng, 1978.

Lu Chi 陸機. *"Mao Shih" ts'ao mu niao shou ch'ung yü shu* 毛詩草木鳥獸蟲魚疏. SKCS.

Lu Ch'in-li 逯欽立, ed. *Hsien-Ch'in, Han, Wei, Chin, Nan-pei-ch'ao shih* 先秦漢魏晉南北朝詩. 3 vols. Peking: Chung-hua, 1983.

Lü-shih ch'un-ch'iu 呂氏春秋. Ed. Hsü Wei-yü 許維遹. Peking: Chung-kuo shu-tien, 1985.

Ma Jui-ch'en 馬瑞辰. *Mao Shih chuan chien t'ung shih* 毛詩傳箋通釋. SPPY. Shanghai: Chung-hua, 1930.

Nieh Ch'ung-i 聶崇義. *San li t'u* 三禮圖. SPTK. Shanghai: Shang-wu, 1936.

Pan Ku 班固. *Han shu* 漢書. Ed. Wang Hsien-ch'ien 王先謙. Peking: Chung-hua, 1983.

Pao Shih-jung 包世榮. *"Mao Shih" li cheng* 毛詩禮徵. Reprinted—Taipei: Ta-t'ung, n.d.

P'ei P'u-hsien 裴普賢. *"Shih-ching" yen-tu chih-tao* 詩經研讀指導. Taipei: Tung-ta, 1977.

P'i Hsi-jui 皮錫瑞. *Ching-hsüeh li-shih* 經學歷史. Taipei: I-wen, 1974.

Shirakawa Shizuka 白川靜. *Kimbun no sekai* 金文の世界. Tokyo: Heibonsha, 1971.

———. *"Shikyō": Chūgoku no kodai kayō* 詩經：中國の古代歌謠. Tokyo: Chūō kōronsha, 1970.

Ssu-ma Ch'ien 司馬遷. *Shih chi [hui-chu k'ao-cheng]/Shiki kaichū kōshō* 史記會注考證. Ed. Takigawa Kametarō 瀧川龜太郎. 1932–34. Reprinted—Taipei: Hung-shih, 1982, 1 vol.

T'an Chia-ting 譚嘉定, ed. *Chung-kuo wen-hsüeh-chia ta-tz'u-tien* 中國文學家大辭典. Taipei: Shih-chieh, 1967.

T'ang Yen 唐晏. *Liang-Han, San-kuo hsüeh-an* 兩漢，三國學案. Reprinted—Taipei: Hua-shih, 1987.

Tung Chung-shu 董仲舒. *Ch'un-ch'iu fan-lu* 春秋繁露. SPPY. Shanghai: Chung-hua, 1930.

Tung Wan-hua 董挽華. *"Shih ta hsü yü Shih p'in hsü ti pi-chiao kuan"* 詩大序與詩品序的比較觀. In Yeh Ch'ing-ping 葉慶炳, Wu Hung-i 吳宏一, et al., *Chung-kuo ku-tien wen-hsüeh p'i-p'ing lun-chi* 中國古典文學批評論集. Taipei: Yu-shih, 1985, pp. 127–42.

Wang Chin-ling 王金凌. *Chung-kuo wen-hsüeh li-lun shih*, Vol. 1, *Shang-ku p'ien* 中國文學理論史：上古篇. Taipei: Hua-cheng, 1987.

Wang Ching-chih 王靜芝, ed. *"Shih-ching" t'ung-shih* 詩經通釋. Taipei: Fu-jen ta-hsüeh, Wen-hsüeh yüan, 1985.

Wang Ch'ung 王充. *Lun heng chi-chieh* 論衡集解. Ed. Liu P'an-sui 劉盼遂. Peking: Ku-chi, 1957.

Wang Fu-chih 王夫之. *Shih kuang chuan* 詩廣傳. Shanghai: Chung-hua shu-chü, 1965.

Wang Hsien-ch'ien 王先謙, ed. *Huang-Ch'ing ching-chieh hsü-pien* 皇清集解續編. Chiang-yin: Nan-ch'ing shu-yüan, 1888.

———. *Shih san-chia i chi-shu* 詩三家義集疏. Reprinted—Peking: Chung-hua, 1987.

Wang Kuo-wei 王國維. *Wang Kuo-wei i-shu* 王國維遺書. Shanghai: Ku-chi, 1983.

Wei Cheng 魏微 and Chang-sun Wu-chi 長孫無忌, eds. *Sui shu* 隋書. Shanghai: T'ung-wen, 1884.

Wen I-to 聞一多. "*Shih* 'Ko sheng,' 'Ts'ai wei' hsin-i" 詩「葛生」,「采薇」新義. Ed. Fei Chen-kang 費振剛. *Wen-shih* 13 (1982): 159–66.

———. *Wen I-to ch'üan-chi* 聞一多全集. 4 vols. Shanghai: K'ai-ming, 1948.

Yang Hung-ming 楊鴻銘. *Hsün-tzu wen-i yen-chiu* 荀子文藝研究. Taipei: Wen-shih-che, 1980.

Yang Sung-nien 楊松年. "Yen-chiu Chung-kuo wen-hsüeh p'i-p'ing tso-p'in so hui mien-tui ti wen-t'i: i *Mao Shih* 'Kuan-chü hsü' wei li ti shuo-ming" 研究中國文學批評作品所會面對的問題:以毛詩關睢序為例的説明. *Chung-wai wen-hsüeh* 20 (1991): 187–206.

Yao Chi-heng 姚際恆. "*Shih-ching*" *t'ung-lun* 詩經通論. Hong Kong: Chung-hua, 1963.

Yasui Kōzan 安居香山 and Nakamura Shōhachi 中村璋八, eds. *Jūshū isho shūsei* 重修緯書集成. Tokyo: Meitoku, 1971.

Yeh Shan 葉珊. "*Shih ching* kuo-feng ti ts'ao-mu ho shih ti piao-hsien chi-ch'iao" 詩經國風的草木和詩的表現技巧. In K'o Ch'ing-ming and Lin Ming-te, eds., *Chung-kuo ku-tien wen-hsüeh yen-chiu ts'ung-k'an: Shih-ko chih pu*. Taipei: Chü-liu, 1977, pp. 11–45.

Yü Hsing-wu 于省吾. "*Shih-ching* chung 'chih' tzu ti pien-shih" 詩經中「止」字的辨釋. *Chung-hua wen-shih lun-tsung* 3 (1963): 121–32.

Yü Ying-shih 余英時. *Chung-kuo chih-shih chieh-ts'eng shih-lun: ku-tai p'ien* 中國知識階層史論:古代篇. Taipei: Lien-ching, 1980.

Yü Yüan 郁沅. "Lun 'Yüeh chi' mei-hsüeh ssu-hsiang ti liang p'ai" 論樂記美學思想的兩派. In *Chung-kuo wen-i ssu-hsiang-shih lun-ts'ung* 中國文藝思想史論叢. Peking: Pei-ching ta-hsüeh, 1984, 1: 44–78.

Chinese Character List

The entries are ordered syllable by syllable; aspirated and unaspirated initial consonant pairs are treated as separate letters, with the aspirated forms following the unaspirated forms. Individual Odes are cited by their *Mao Shih* title, followed by their number in the Harvard-Yenching *Concordance to Shih Ching*. Authors and titles listed in the Bibliography are not included here.

ai 哀

"Chan yang" (Ode 264) 瞻仰
chang-chü 章句
cheng ("correct") 正
Cheng (state) 鄭
cheng-chiao 政教
"Cheng min" (Ode 260) 烝民
cheng-shih chih tao 正始之道
chi 寄
chi-chi 几几
chi-t'o 寄託
Chia K'uei 賈逵
"Chia le" (Ode 249) 假樂
chia wang 假王
chiao ("blame") 誚
chiao ("instruct") 教
chiao ("suburbs") 郊

chiao-hua 教化
chieh 解
chih ("be hindered") 寁
chih (musical note) 徵
chih ("project," "aim") 志
chih ("substance") 質
chih tzu 之子
"Chin t'eng" 金縢
ching ("capital") 京
ching ("classic") 經
ching ("scene," "great") 景
ching-shih 京師
chiung ("far away") 迥
"Chiung" (Ode 297) 駉
cho 濁
Chou, Duke of 周公

Chou Li 周禮
"Chou-nan" 周南
"Chou sung" 周頌
chu 注
"Chu kan" (Ode 59) 竹竿
chuan 傳
chüeh 角
chung ("center") 中
chung ("sincere") 衷
chü 屨
"Chü-hsia" (Ode 218) 車舝
chün 君
chün-tzu 君子
chün-tzu hao-ch'iu 君子好逑

"Ch'ang ti" (Ode 164) 常棣
ch'ao-tsung 朝宗
ch'eng 成
Ch'eng, King of the Chou
  周成王
ch'i 氣
ch'i-ch'ing 起情
ch'iao-ch'iao 翹翹
"Ch'iao yen" (Ode 198) 巧言
"Ch'ih-hsiao" (Ode 155) 鴟鴞
ch'in 親
ch'ing ("feeling") 情
ch'ing ("pure," "clear") 清
Ch'ü Yüan 屈原
"Ch'üeh-ch'ao" (Ode 12) 鵲巢

erh 而
erh i 而已
"Erh tzu ch'eng chou" (Ode 44)
  二子乘舟

"Fa k'o" (Ode 158) 伐柯
fan 汎

fan-fan ch'i ching 汎汎其景
fan-feng 反風
fang 方
feng ("admonish") 諷
feng ("easy-flowing") 渢
feng ("wind," "Airs," "customs," "transformation") 風
feng-hua 風化
feng-tz'u 諷刺
Fou-ch'iu Po 浮丘(邱)伯
fu ("axe") 斧
fu ("beautiful") 膚
fu ("father") 父
fu ("present," "expound") 賦
Fu Hsi 伏羲
fu-hui 附會
fu Shih 賦詩
"Fu yu" (Ode 150) 蜉蝣

"Han kuang" (Ode 9) 漢廣
"Hao t'ien yu ch'eng ming"
  (Ode 271) 昊天有成命
ho 合
"Ho ming" (Ode 184) 鶴鳴
"Ho pi nung i" (Ode 24) 何彼
  穠矣
Hou Ts'ang 后倉
hsi 鳥
Hsi, Duke of Lu 魯僖公
hsiang 象
hsiang ch'eng che 象成者
"Hsiang shu" (Ode 52) 相鼠
Hsiao ching 孝經
Hsiao ya 小雅
"Hsiao yüan" (Ode 196) 小宛
Hsieh Man-ch'ing 謝曼卿
hsien ("manifest") 顯
hsien ("offer") 獻

Hsien, Prince of Ho-ch'ien
　河間獻王
hsin 信
hsing ("shape," "pattern") 形
hsing ("stimulus," "allusion")
　興
hsing-chi 興寄
hsing-jung 形容
"Hsing lu" (Ode 17) 行露
hsün 巽
hua 化
huang-chung 黃鐘
"Huang huang che hua" (Ode
　163) 皇皇者華
hun 縉/婚

i ("present") 貽
i ("suitable") 宜
i chih 異志
i ch'i shih-chia 宜其室家
I ching 易經
I li 儀禮
i yü-yen wei kuang 以寓言為廣

jen shih 人事
ju ("assimilate") 茹
ju ("like," "as") 如
jung 容

kan 感
kang 綱
ku ("gloss") 詁
ku ("past") 古
ku ("therefore") 故
Ku-liang chuan 穀梁傳
kuan 觀
"Kuan chü" (Ode 1) 關雎
kuan-kuan 關關

kuei 規
kung (musical note) 宮
"Kung Liu" (Ode 250) 公劉
Kung-sun Lung 公孫龍
Kung-yang chuan 公羊傳
Kuo feng 國風

"Lang pa" (Ode 160) 狼跋
lei 類
li (distance measure) 里
li ("reason," "pattern") 理
li ("ritual") 禮
Li chi 禮記
Li sao 離騷
liang-ma i-mao 良馬異貌
"Lin-chih" (Ode 11) 麟趾
liu-i 六義
"Liu yüeh" (Ode 177) 六月
Lu-p'u Kuei 盧蒲癸
"Lu sung" 魯頌
Lu Te-ming 陸德明
lun 倫
Lun yü 倫語
lü 律

Mao Ch'ang 毛萇
Mao Heng 毛亨
Mao Shih 毛詩
mei, so-i yung li yeh 媒，
　所以用禮也
"Mien shui" (Ode 183) 沔水
min 民
mu ("herd") 牧
mu ("stallion") 牡

nai 乃
"Nan kai" (unnumbered Ode)
　南陔

"Nan shan" (Ode 101) 南山
"Nan yu chia yü" (Ode 171)
　南有嘉魚

pa 跋
Pao Hsien 包咸
"Pei shan" (Ode 205) 北山
pi ("compare," "order") 比
pi ("must") 必
"Pi kung" (Ode 300) 閟宮
pi-yü 比喻
"Piao yu mei" (Ode 20) 標有梅
pien 變
Pin 豳
"Po chou" (Ode 26, Ode 45)
　柏舟
po-shih 博士
pu k'o chuan yeh 不可轉也
pu k'o chüan yeh 不可捲也
pu k'o i ju 不可以茹

"P'an shui" (Ode 299) 泮水
"P'o fu" (Ode 157) 破斧
p'u 鋪

"Sang chung" (Ode 48) 桑中
sao 騷
"Shan yu fu-su" (Ode 84) 山有
　扶蘇
shang ("injury") 傷
shang (musical note) 商
"Shang shang che hua" (Ode
　214) 裳裳者華
Shang shu 尚書
shao 韶
shao-chuang 少壯
"Shao-nan" 召南
Shen Chung 沈重
Shen P'ei 申培

sheng 聲
shih 詩
shih-chia 室家
shih chih ta-kang 詩之大綱
Shih ching 詩經
shih i yen chih 詩以言志
shih so i ho i 詩所以合意
shih yen chih 詩言志
shih yen i 詩言意
shu ("annotation") 疏
shu ("reciprocity") 恕
shu-yuan 書院
shuo 碩
ssu 思
sung 頌

"Ta hsüeh" 大學
Ta Tai Li chi 大戴禮記
Ta ya 大雅
tao ("exposition") 道
tao ("to lead") 導
te 德
te-yin 德音
"Ting chih fang chung" (Ode
　50) 定之方中
tsai chiung chih yeh 在迥之野
tso 作
Tso chuan 左傳
"Tsou-yü" (Ode 25) 騶虞
tung 動
"Tzu i" (Ode 75) 緇衣
tzu-jan 自然

t'a-wu 它物
"T'ang" (Ode 255) 蕩
"T'ao-yao" (Ode 6) 桃夭
t'ien 天
t'ien-hsia 天下
t'o 託

"T'ung-lei hsiang-tung" 同類
　相動
tz'u 刺

wang-hua 王化
Wang I 王逸
Wang Mang 王莽
Wang Po 王柏
Wang Shih 王式
Wei (state) 衛
Wei Hung 衛宏
wei shih i i wang 為詩以貽王
wei-shu 緯書
wen 文
Wen, King of the Chou 周文王
"Wen wang" (Ode 235) 文王
"Wen wang yu sheng" (Ode
　244) 文王有聲
wen i tsai-tao 文以載道
wu 武
Wu, King of the Chou 周武王
wu-mei ssu-fu 寤寐思服
wu ssu pu fu 無思不服

ya 雅
ya-hua 雅化
yao 夭

yeh 野
Yeh *Shih* 業詩
"Yeh yu ssu chün" (Ode 23)
　野有死麕
yen ("bend") 偃
yen ("speech") 言
yin ("hidden") 隱
yin ("tone") 音
ying 影
"Yu pi" (Ode 298) 有駜
yü ("language") 語
yü ("lodge") 寓
yü (musical note) 羽
Yü Chiao Li 玉嬌梨
yü-hou 于後
yü-shih ch'u-ch'u 于時處處
yü-yen 寓言
yüan 怨
Yüan, Prince of Ch'u 楚元王
Yüan Mei 袁枚
yüeh 樂
"Yüeh chi" 樂記
yüeh-fu 樂府
yüeh-te 樂德
yüeh-yü 樂語
yung 詠
yung-wu 詠物

Index

In this index an "f" after a number indicates a separate reference on the next page, and an "ff" indicates separate references on the next two pages. A continuous discussion over two or more pages is indicated by a span of page numbers, e.g., "57–59." *Passim* is used for a cluster of references in close but not consecutive sequence.

aesthetics, 2, 8f, 44, 85, 91, 94, 103, 108f, 150, 151f, 174ff, 179, 184, 186ff, 199; of music, 86–94, 107f; and history, 173–77. *See also* poetics

"Airs of the States" (*Kuo feng*) section of the *Odes, see Odes, Book of*

allegoresis, 59f, 65, 73f, 105, 195

allegory, 2, 13, 17–20, 24–47 *passim*, 50, 74f, 84, 96, 99, 103, 105, 118, 119–22, 128, 147ff, 183, 188, 193, 195, 207, 232, 242; Quintilian's definition of, 13, 27f, 103, 105, 196f; Western, 17, 19, 24f, 27, 200; and Chinese literature, 17f, 24–27, 30, 33, 36, 39, 42, 47, 59, 74f, 194; of the theologians and of the grammarians, 27f, 46, 197, 201; vs. allegoresis, 60, 105, 195; vs. example, 147–50. *See also chi-t'o*; fable; *fu-hui*; *Mao Shih*; met-

aphor; *Odes, Book of*; parable; personification; *yü-yen*

Althusser, Louis, 237

Analects, *see* Confucius

anthropology, 6, 10, 41f

antiphrasis, 41

arbitrariness as semiotic principle, 100, 180ff

Aristotle, 100, 107, 175, 194, 199, 202, 232, 240, 243

Artemidoros, 194

Austin, John, 200, 229

Balibar, Etienne, 237

Barthes, Roland, 8, 182, 184

Bauer, Bruno, 240, 246

being, 7ff, 26, 35, 40–43, 45, 185, 204f

Benjamin, Walter, 235, 244

Blason, 198. *See also* emblem; rebus

boundedness, 9ff, 187

289

Library of Congress
Cataloging-in-Publication Data

Saussy, Haun, 1960–
The problem of a Chinese aesthetic / Haun Saussy.
p. cm.
Includes bibliographical references and index.
ISBN 0-8047-2074-6 :
1. Chinese literature—History and criticism.
2. Literature—Aesthetics. I. Title.
PL2264.S28   1993
895.1'09—dc20
92-22582   CIP

⊗ This book is printed on acid-free paper.
It has been typeset in Adobe Garamond and Lithos
by Keystone Typesetting, Inc.